ORIGINS OF PAPAL INFALLIBILITY
1150-1350

STUDIES IN THE HISTORY
OF
CHRISTIAN THOUGHT

EDITED BY

HEIKO A. OBERMAN, Tübingen

IN COOPERATION WITH

HENRY CHADWICK, Oxford
EDWARD A. DOWEY, Princeton, N.J.
JAROSLAV PELIKAN, New Haven, Conn.
BRIAN TIERNEY, Ithaca, N.Y.

VOLUME VI

BRIAN TIERNEY

ORIGINS OF PAPAL INFALLIBILITY
1150-1350

LEIDEN
E. J. BRILL
1972

ORIGINS OF
PAPAL INFALLIBILITY
1150-1350

A STUDY ON THE
CONCEPTS OF INFALLIBILITY, SOVEREIGNTY
AND TRADITION IN THE MIDDLE AGES

BY

BRIAN TIERNEY

LEIDEN
E. J. BRILL
1972

72—188202

PRINTED IN THE NETHERLANDS

TO
THERESA

TABLE OF CONTENTS

PREFACE

At the time when I was completing the final draft of this book a major dispute broke out among Catholic scholars concerning the theology of papal infallibility. It was occasioned principally by Hans Küng's study, *Unfehlbar? Eine Anfrage*, and it is still continuing. My book was not provoked by the current controversy and it is not addressed directly to the theological issues that are now being debated —though it may prove to have some relevance for them. The present work deals with the history of papal infallibility. But its aim is not to demonstrate by ingenious historical arguments—in the manner of some older polemical works on this theme—either that the popes have sometimes contradicted one another in the course of the centuries or, alternatively, that the papal magisterium has never erred "from the path of apostolic tradition" in its more solemn pronouncements. My purpose has not been to retrace the paths of old controversies. Instead I have tried to do something new—to provide for the first time an adequate historical account of how the doctrine of papal infallibility originally grew into existence.

Much of the research for this book was carried out in Munich during the academic year 1966-1967. I would like to express my gratitude to the authorities of the Bayerische Staatsbibliothek and of the Monumenta Germaniae Historica for permission to work in their rich collections. Through the kind hospitality of Professor Dr. Hermann Tüchle I was also able to use the resources of the Seminar für Kirchengeschichte of the Ludwig-Maximilians-Universität.

I am indebted to the American Council of Learned Societies and to the Society for Religion in Higher Education for research stipends. Cornell University has been generous in making available time for research and writing.

The book includes some paragraphs from two previously published articles. These are "'Sola Scriptura' and the Canonists" in *Studia Gratiana*, 11 (1967) and "From Thomas of York to William of Ockham" in the Proceedings of the *Congressus De Historia Sollicitudinis Omnium Ecclesiarum* held at Rome in 1967. I am grateful for permission to use this material in the present work.

My wife helped with the index and the typing; but that is not why this book is dedicated to her.

Ithaca, N.Y.   B.T.

ABBREVIATIONS

AFH   *Archivum Franciscanum Historicum.*

AHDL   *Archives d'histoire doctrinale et littéraire du moyen âge.*

ALKG   *Archiv für Literatur- und Kirchengeschichte des Mittelalters.*

Baluze, Misc.   E. Baluze and J. D. Mansi, *Miscellanea* (Lucca, 1761-1764).

Clem.   *Clementis Papae V Constitutiones* in E. Friedberg (ed.), *Corpus Iuris Canonici* (Leipzig, 1879).

Extrav. Ioann. XXII   *Extravagantes D. Ioannis XXII* in E. Friedberg (ed.), *Corpus Iuris Canonici* (Leipzig, 1879).

Foundations   B. Tierney, *Foundations of the Conciliar Theory* (Cambridge, 1955).

"Pope and Council"   B. Tierney, "Pope and Council: Some New Decretist Texts," *Mediaeval Studies*, 19 (1957), pp. 197-218.

PL   *Patrologia Latina.*

RTAM   *Recherches de théologie ancienne et médiévale.*

Sext.   *Liber Sextus Decretalium* in E. Friedberg (ed.), *Corpus Iuris Canonici* (Leipzig, 1879).

X (Liber Extra)   *Decretalium D. Gregorii Papae IX Compilatio* in E. Friedberg (ed.), *Corpus Iuris Canonici* (Leipzig, 1879).

Abbreviations not listed are considered self-explanatory.
Full titles of all works cited are given in the Bibliography.

INTRODUCTION

THEOLOGY AND HISTORY

> Therefore faithfully adhering to the tradition received from the beginning of the Christian faith, ... We teach and define that it is a dogma divinely revealed: that the Roman Pontiff, when he speaks *ex cathedra*, that is, when in discharge of the office of Pastor and Doctor of all Christians, by virtue of his supreme Apostolic authority he defines a doctrine regarding faith or morals to be held by the Universal Church, by the divine assistance promised to him in blessed Peter, is possessed of that infallibility with which the divine Redeemer willed that His Church should be endowed for defining doctrine regarding faith or morals: and that therefore such definitions of the Roman Pontiff are irreformable of themselves, and not from the consent of the Church. (Vatican Council I, July 18, 1870)[1]

"*Infallibility* in the spiritual order and *sovereignty* in the temporal order are two perfectly synonymous words."[2] This view of Joseph de Maistre was widely accepted as a self-evident truth—almost a platitude—by the various parties in the nineteenth century debates over papal infallibility. The most ardent Ultramontanes, the most reluctant inopportunists, and the most stalwart opponents of the dogma of 1870 were all agreed on this one point, that to declare the pope infallible would be to enhance his sovereign power as head of the Church. Louis Veuillot wrote, "We must affirm squarely the authority and omnipotence of the pope as the source of all authority, spiritual and temporal. The proclamation of the dogma of the infallibility of the pope has no other objective."[3] At the other end of the spectrum, Döllinger called an early draft of the infallibility decree a "Magna Carta of ecclesiastical absolutism" and complained that the doctrine finally promulgated had reinforced the "sovereign caprice" of the

---

[1] This translation is taken from C. Butler, *The Vatican Council*, II (London, 1930), p. 295. Butler also gives the Latin original (p. 294).

[2] J. de Maistre, *Du pape* (Geneva, 1966), p. 27, "*L'infaillibilité* dans l'ordre spirituel et la *souveraineté* dans l'ordre temporel, sont deux mots parfaitement synonymes." (First published in 1817).

[3] Cited in Butler, *op. cit.*, I, p. 76.

pope.[1] The dogmatic decree itself proclaimed the infallibility of the pope and his supreme jurisdiction over the church as two inter-related aspects of a single coherent doctrine.

Yet de Maistre's dictum is not really a platitude. It is more of a paradox. The words "infallibility" and "sovereignty" do not have the same meaning. It would be more true to suggest that the ideas they express are intrinsically incompatible with one another. It is of the essence of sovereignty (as the concept was understood both in the nineteenth century and in the Middle Ages) that a sovereign ruler cannot be bound by the acts of his predecessors. It is of the essence of infallibility (as the doctrine was formulated at Vatican Council I) that the infallible decrees of one pope are binding on all his successors since they are, by definition, irreformable.

This point is not presented as a mere verbal equivocation. Real issues of ecclesiastical power are involved. If the popes have always been infallible in any meaningful sense of the word—if their official pronouncements as heads of the church on matters of faith and morals have always been unerring and so irreformable—then all kinds of dubious consequences ensue. Most obviously, twentieth century popes would be bound by a whole array of past papal decrees reflecting the responses of the Roman church to the religious and moral problems of former ages. As Acton put it, "The responsibility for the acts of the buried and repented past would come back at once and for ever." To defend religious liberty would be "insane" and to persecute heretics commendable. Judicial torture would be licit and the taking of interest on loans a mortal sin. The pope would rule by divine right "not only the universal church but the whole world." Unbaptized babies would be punished in Hell for all eternity. Maybe the sun would still be going round the earth.

All this is impossible of course. No one understands the fact better than modern theologians of infallibility. If past popes have always been infallible—again, we must add, in any meaningful sense of the word—then present popes are hopelessly circumscribed in their approaches to all the really urgent moral problems of the twentieth century, problems involving war, sex, scientific progress, state power, social obligations, and individual liberties. The ex-istence of this dilemma helps to explain the rather eccentric develop-

---

[1] Quirinus, *Letters From Rome On the Council* (London, 1870), p. 207; J. J. I. von Döllinger, *A Letter Addressed To the Archbishop of Munich* (London, 1871), pp. 22-23.

ment of the doctrine of infallibility during the past century.[1] Since
Vatican Council I, Catholic theologians have felt obliged to defend
some form of papal infallibility. Real infallibility has regrettable
implications. In the years since 1870, therefore, theologians have
devoted much ingenuity to devising a sort of pseudo-infallibility for
the pope, a kind of Pickwickian infallibility.

Their usual technique has been to raise endless, teasing, really
unanswerable questions about the meaning of the term *ex cathedra* as
used in the decree of Vatican Council I and about the phrases "ordinary magisterium" and "extraordinary magisterium" that came to be
associated with it in discussions on papal infallibility. Already in 1874
Gladstone could write, "... There is no established or accepted
definition of the phrase *ex cathedra* and (the Catholic) has no power
to obtain one, and no guide to direct him in his choice among some
twelve theories on the subject, which, it is said, are bandied to and fro
among Roman theologians, except the despised and discarded agency
of his private judgment."[2]

Things have not improved since. To be sure, modern apologists
often insist that the conditions needed to guarantee the infallibility
of a papal pronouncement were set out, once and for all, simply
and clearly, in the decree of Vatican Council I. But then they find it
impossible to agree as to which particular papal pronouncements
actually satisfy these supposedly simple and clear requirements.
There is no authoritative or agreed list of the infallible pronouncements made before 1870. The uncertainty as to what is and what is not
infallible extends to papal declarations touching the most fundamental
issues of public and private morality. Concerning the Syllabus of
Pope Pius IX, for instance, the *Catholic Encyclopedia* declared in 1912,
"Many theologians are of the opinion that to the Syllabus as such an
infallible teaching authority must be ascribed... Others question
this."[3] *The New Catholic Encyclopedia*, recording the theological progress

---

[1] A good survey of developments since 1870, with substantial bibliographical
notes is provided by G. Thils, *L'infaillibilité pontificale* (Gembloux, 1969).

[2] W. E. Gladstone, *The Vatican Decrees in Their Bearing on Civil Allegiance* (New
York, 1875), p. 26.

[3] *Catholic Encyclopedia*, XIV (New York, 1912), p. 368. Cf. *New Catholic Encyclopedia*, XIII (New York, 1967), p. 855, "Many theologians attribute infallible
teaching authority to the syllabus itself, while others deny this." On the other hand,
according to the *Dictionnaire de théologie catholique* belief in the infallibility of the
Syllabus was "à peu près abandonnée" in 1922 (Vol. VII, col. 1704).

of half a century, tells us that things remained exactly the same in 1967.

The one papal definition made since 1870 which has been commonly accepted as infallible is Pope Pius XII's proclamation of the dogma of the Assumption. But if, in due course, Catholic theologians find it desirable to retreat from the view that this late-blooming dogma forms an intrinsic part of the Christian faith, there will be no lack of theological argumentation devoted to proving that Pius XII (in spite of his best efforts) did not succeed in making an infallible pronouncement after all. The one consistent rule of interpretation we can be sure of encountering is this: whenever a theologian disagrees with some old teaching or new ruling of a pope he will find good theological grounds for deciding that the papal pronouncement was "not infallible." The whole modern doctrine of infallibility in its Pickwickian form might be summed up in the general principle, "All infallible decrees are certainly true but no decrees are certainly infallible."

To be sure this is not the only position open to a contemporary Catholic theologian. During the 1950s Pope Pius XII's encyclical *Humani generis* stirred a strange eddy of controversy in academic theological circles. In this document the pope declared, "It is not to be thought that matters proposed in Encyclical Letters do not in themselves command assent because (in Encyclicals) the pontiffs do not exercise the supreme power of their magisterium. For these things are taught by the ordinary magisterium, to which also the words apply, 'He who hears you, hears me'."[1] Pope Pius' reference to the authority of the "ordinary magisterium" led some theologians to insist once again that the decree of Vatican Council I actually meant what it said—that the pope was infallible whenever he pronounced on matters of faith and morals "in discharge of the office of pastor and doctor of all Christians."[2] The difficulty in this position is that the pronouncements of popes, even of modern popes, sometimes contradict one another (notably, for example, in the matter of religious toleration). Some theologians therefore have upheld the infallibility of contemporary decrees without giving serious consideration to the possibility of their conflicting with preceding ones.

---

[1] *Acta Apostolicae Sedis*, 42 (1950), p. 568.

[2] This controversy concerning the infallibility of the pope's ordinary magisterium is described in G. Thils, *op. cit.*, pp. 181-185 and, more fully, in P. B. Bilaniuk, *De magisterio ordinario summi pontificis* (Toronto, 1966).

In effect, they are content to pretend that the past did not happen. There is at least a beguiling innocence in this approach. Other theologians, more reprehensibly (from a historian's point of view), have devised hermeneutical principles so ingenious that the documents of the past can never embarrass them. By applying such principles, they can re-interpret any doctrinal pronouncement, regardless of its actual content, to mean whatever the modern theologian thinks that its framers ought to have meant.[1] The infallible doctrine of the past remains infallible but it is deprived of all objective content. This procedure seems based on a kind of Alice-in-Wonderland logic. One is reminded of the Cheshire Cat—the body of a past pronouncement disappears but its grin of infallibility persists. The general principle underlying this second major approach to the problem of infallibility might be summarized in the formula, "All infallible pronouncements are irreformable—until it becomes convenient to change them." It seems only fair to add that most Catholic theologians have continued to opt for some version of the relatively simple and straightforward Pickwickian position.

By the time of Vatican Council II the Catholic theology of infallibility had become a tangle of paradoxes and evasions. The theologians had worked themselves into a complicated cul-de-sac. But the council refrained from any thorough-going reconsideration of this question and merely repeated with minor variations the doctrine of 1870. In the years since Vatican Council II, however, a new development of thought has occurred. Very recently—while this book was being written—a few Catholic scholars have begun overtly to challenge the validity of the doctrine that was defined at Vatican Council I and re-affirmed at Vatican Council II.[2] It remains to be seen whether their point of view will establish itself as a viable position that can be held within the Roman Catholic church.

Fortunately, for the purposes of the present work we shall not need to pursue in more detail the intricacies of contemporary apologetics and hermeneutics. A historian cannot do the theologians'

---

[1] A good introduction to the hermeneutical problems that arise when theologians try to reconcile doctrinal statements from different ages of the church's past that are really irreconcilable with each other is provided by H. Riedlinger, "Hermeneutische Ueberlegungen zu den Konstanzer Dekreten" in *Das Konzil von Konstanz*, ed. A. Franzen and W. Müller (Freiburg, 1964), pp. 214-238.

[2] F. Simons, *Infallibility and the Evidence* (Springfield, Ill., 1968); F. Oakley, *Council Over Pope?* (New York, 1969); H. Küng, *Unfehlbar? Eine Anfrage* (Zurich, 1970).

work for them; he cannot show them how to get out of their cul-de-sac; it is enough, perhaps, if he can show them how they got into it in the first place. In this book, therefore, we shall be concerned with the historical origins of the doctrine of infallibility. We have begun by emphasizing the paradoxes of modern theology because it is impossible to understand the history of infallibility without some awareness of those paradoxes. The central point is that to attribute infallibility to a whole line of rulers is to curtail radically the sovereign power of each individual monarch (since each monarch is bound by the infallible decrees of his predecessors). Yet, perversely it may seem, modern partisans of the doctrine of papal infallibility have always wanted to increase the power of the reigning pope—hence their paradoxes and evasions. Historians of infallibility have started out from the same mistaken assumptions as the theologians. They have always assumed that the first advocates of a doctrine of papal infallibility must necessarily have been ardent defenders of absolute papal power. They are sometimes a little puzzled that they do not find infallibility proclaimed in the writings of the extreme papalists of the high Middle Ages—men like Giles of Rome, James of Viterbo, Henry of Cremona, Augustinus Triumphus. In fact the pre-suppositions that historians have commonly brought to the consideration of this question render the whole early history of papal infallibility unintelligible. The truth is that the earliest defenders of the doctrine were much more interested in limiting the power of the pope than in enhancing it.

Our central theme will be the emergence of the doctrine of papal infallibility in the years around 1300. It is impossible, however, to pursue the history of infallibility as an isolated concept. Both in its medieval development and in its modern expression the idea of infallibility is so interwoven with the ideas of sovereignty and of ecclesiastical Tradition that we have had to pay some attention to those subjects also. We have already mentioned one relevant aspect of the concept of sovereignty—the doctrine that a sovereign ruler is not bound by his predecessors. The other aspect which is important for our theme relates to the location of ultimate authority in the church as between pope and general council. The partisans of papal infallibility at Vatican Council I were anxious to demolish once and for all the doctrine that a general council was greater than a pope in matters of faith. Accordingly, the decree on papal infallibility enacted in 1870 contained a clause explicitly denying that a Catholic could appeal from a pope to a general council as to a superior authority. This problem has its roots in twelfth century canon law and we shall need to give some consideration to it.

The concept of Tradition is at least as complex as the concept of sovereignty. Nowadays Catholic theologians agree that revealed truth is known to us through Scripture and Tradition. There are, however, various ways of understanding this duality. It is possible to assert that all the essential truths of faith are contained in the Old and New Testaments and that Tradition is, so to speak, a perpetual meditation of the church on Scripture, a continuing activity that makes ever more explicit the implicit truths of Holy Writ. Since the Council of Trent, Catholic theologians have more commonly maintained that truths of faith exist which are not to be found in Scripture at all, but which were transmitted orally by Christ to the Apostles and by the Apostles to the church. In either case there is an ambiguity inherent in the word Tradition itself. Normally, if we wished to determine whether a given doctrine or practice was "traditional" we should enquire whether it did actually exist in earlier times. But this normal usage by no means exhausts the theological implications of the word Tradition. Theologians like to speak of "living Tradition." They point out that, in handing down a Tradition from age to age, the church constantly enriches that Tradition. They insist that Tradition is a principle of growth, not of stagnation. Some theologians, when they refer to "living Tradition," mean to assert essentially the same principle that Newman discussed when he wrote of "development of doctrine." Others go much further. They see no need to trace out any processes of historical development in defining the Tradition of the church. The faith of the church, they hold, is unchanging; therefore any doctrine currently taught by the church is necessarily a part of the church's perennial Tradition. The point was put crisply by Deneffe in the phrase "Tradition is the church teaching."[1] In its most extreme form this doctrine identifies Tradition solely and simply with the teaching of the church's official magisterium—or even of the pope alone—at any given moment. Critics of the doctrine suggest that it opens the way to unbridled innovation in the sphere of church doctrine for each new declaration can be presented, without reference to Scripture, as an implicit, even if hitherto unheard-of

---

[1] A. Deneffe, *Der Traditionsbegriffe* (Münster i. W., 1931), p. 96. Modern developments in the theology of Tradition are conveniently summarized in J. P. Mackey, *The Modern Theology of Tradition* (New York, 1962).

part of the undefined doctrine enshrined in the Tradition of the
church. (The teaching that infallible pronouncements can apply only
to an initial "deposit of divine revelation" is no obstacle to innovation
when the act of definition itself is sufficient to establish that a given
doctrine was indeed a part of the "deposit.") Whether or not Pio
Nono actually said, "La tradizione son'io", such ideas played a
significant part in the movement of thought leading up to the dogmatic decree of 1870. The modern ideas of Tradition have medieval
antecedents. We shall need to explore them in some detail if we are to
understand the thirteenth century origins of the doctrine of papal
infallibility.

The history of infallibility—as distinct from its theology—has
attracted little attention among modern scholars. In most standard
treatments of the theme one encounters only long lists of texts from
Scripture, patristic writings, medieval and modern theologians, all
presented in chronological order but without any meaningful historical context. (This is true even of the best modern account of medieval
ideas on infallibility, that of Paul de Vooght.[1]) According to the
defenders of papal infallibility the texts cited show that the doctrine
has been held since the very beginning of the church—at least im-
plicity. (Everyone agrees that papal infallibility was not explicitly
asserted in the age of the Fathers.) According to opponents of the
doctrine, the texts in question—or at any rate the earlier ones—have
no such implication.

To trace connections between pure ideas in a historical vacuum is
an interesting pursuit and it can be rewarding for philosophers and
theologians. But a historian ignores a whole dimension of existence
if he forgets that ideas are rooted in real life. We have tried therefore
to bear in mind the admonition of Hubert Jedin: to understand ecclesiology we must orient ourselves primarily to the facts of church
history. The doctrine of papal infallibility was not overtly proclaimed by the early councils and Fathers of the church. It did not
emerge imperceptibly, as if out of nowhere, in the long centuries of
the Middle Ages. The doctrine was created at a particular point in

---

[1] "Esquisse d'une enquête sur le mot 'infaillibilité' durant la période scolastique," in *L'infaillibilité de l'église*, ed. O. Rousseau etc. (Chevetogne, 1962), pp. 99-
146. The same is true of the best historical work stimulated by the disputes of 1870,
J. Langen, *Das Vatikanische Dogma von dem Universal-Episcopat und der Unfehlbarkeit
des Papstes*, 4 vols. (Bonn, 1871-1874). Another example is the long article, "Infaillibilité du pape" in *Dictionnaire de théologie catholique*, VII (Paris, 1923), cols. 1638-1717
(E. Dublanchy).

time to meet the needs of particular persons and groups in the church. Franciscan theologians, we shall find, played a major role in the interplay of ideas and events that we shall try to explain. Hence, in order to understand their positions, we shall need to discuss some of the special problems that faced the Franciscan Order from the mid-thirteenth century onward.

Although the history of the doctrine of infallibility has been rather neglected by recent scholars, the subject received its fair share of attention in the controversies of 1870. Then two general lines of argument emerged which we can illustrate in their more extreme forms from the polemical writings of Manning and Döllinger. Manning maintained that the doctrine of papal infallibility had been held by the church from its first foundation. Among Scriptual texts he emphasized especially Luke 22.32. "I have prayed for you Peter that your faith shall not fail." According to Manning, the stability of the faith of the Roman see was acknowledged by the Fathers from the time of Irenaeus onward. He insisted particularly on the formula of Pope Hormisdas (514-523), "In the apostolic see religion has always been preserved without stain," and on the similar formula of Pope Agatho (678-681), "This apostolic see... will never be convicted of erring from the path of apostolic tradition." Naturally, Manning did not neglect to point out that this second formula was accepted by the Sixth General Council of the church.[1]

Manning conceded that none of the texts that he produced from the first fifteen centuries of the church's history actually asserted that the pope was infallible. What they proved, he maintained, was that the church had constantly acted on the assumption that this was the case. The doctrine of papal infallibility was "in possession" down to the time of the Council of Constance. It was never challenged before the fifteenth century. That is the reason, according to Manning, why we find the doctrine overtly stated and defended only from the fifteenth century onward. Manning was really relying on an argument from silence (though he sharply attacked Döllinger for using the same kind of argument in a contrary sense). "The thought that either the See or the Successor of Peter could fail in faith is not to be found in those thousand years (from the fifth century to the fifteenth century)," he wrote.[2] For Manning, the fact that the doctrine of

---

[1] H. E. Manning, *The Oecumenical Council and the Infallibility of the Roman Pontiff: A Pastoral Letter to the Clergy* (London, 1869), p. 84.

[2] *Op. cit.*, p. 91.

infallibility was not denied in the early church proved that it was universally accepted.

For Döllinger, on the other hand, the silence of the early Fathers and councils concerning papal infallibility established beyond doubt that the doctrine was utterly alien to the primitive church. "Up to the time of the Isidorian forgeries no serious attempt was made anywhere to introduce the neo-Roman theory of Infallibility. The popes did not dream of laying claim to such a privilege."[1] Döllinger attributed the subsequent growth of the doctrine to "forgeries and fictions." He emphasized especially a text of the pseudo-Isidorian forgeries of the mid-ninth century, "The Roman church remains to the end free from the stain of heresy." Misled by such forgeries, later popes and canonists propounded wildly exaggerated theories of papal power. Pope Gregory VII in particular "must have held the prerogative of Infallibility the most precious jewel of his crown."[2] Döllinger traced the influence of the Pseudo-Isidorian forgeries through the canonistic collections of Deusdedit, Anselm of Lucca and Burchard of Worms to the Decretum of Gratian (c. 1140). Gratian's book was a massive work of synthesis whose appearance marked the beginning of a new era in the history of church law. Döllinger correctly observed that it "displaced all the older collections of canon law and became the manual and repertory, not for canonists only, but for the scholastic theologians."[3] He seems to have regarded its influence as wholly baneful.

According to Döllinger, the doctrine of papal infallibility was firmly established in the canonical literature of the church by the mid-twelfth century. Down to the thirteenth century, however, dogmatic theology remained unaffected by the canonists' theory, for the theologians hardly ever wrote on problems of papal power in their technical treatises. It was Thomas Aquinas, according to Döllinger, who "made the doctrine of the pope a formal part of dogmatic theology." Seeking for arguments against the Greeks he turned to the forged texts of Gratian and to other, more recent forgeries. The effect of his work was to introduce "the doctrine of the Pope and his infallibility... into the dogmatic system of the Schola."[4]

---

[1] Janus, *The Pope and the Council* (Boston, 1870), p. 62.

[2] *Op. cit.*, p. 90.

[3] *Op. cit.*, p. 116.

[4] *Op. cit.*, p. 215. Langen presented a similar argument in *Das Vatikanische Dogma*, III (Bonn, 1873). He too regarded Thomas Aquinas as the first major theologian to propound a theory of papal infallibility and held that Thomas was

There would be little point in our retracing step by step all the weary arguments of the nineteenth century polemicists about the significance of the texts referring to papal authority in the early church. But it is necessary to note at the outset that neither of the two sharply opposed positions that we have presented—nor any subsequent variation of them—provides an acceptable account of the historical origins of papal infallibility. Manning's version of the argument from silence may seem as irrefutable as it is unconvincing. But, after all, the silence of the early church was not altogether unbroken. The scriptural text most commonly cited in favor of papal infallibility is Luke 22.32. There is no lack of patristic commentary on the text. None of the Fathers interpreted it as meaning that Peter's successors were infallible. No convincing argument has ever been put forward explaining why they should not have stated that the text implied a doctrine of papal infallibility if that is what they understood it to mean. Again, it is difficult for us to know exactly what men of the sixth and seventh centuries understood by formulas like those of Hormisdas and Agatho. But we do know that the general council which accepted Agatho's formula also anathematized Agatho's predecessor, Pope Honorius, on the ground that he "followed the views of the heretic Sergius and confirmed his impious dogmas." Agatho's successor, Pope Leo II, in confirming the decrees of the council, added that Honorius "did not illuminate the apostolic see by teaching the apostolic tradition but, by an act of treachery strove to subvert its immaculate faith."[1] Whatever the council fathers may have meant by the formula they accepted concerning the unfailing faith of the apostolic see, their meaning can have had little connection with the modern doctrine of papal infallibility. We shall see that, in the twelfth and thirteenth centuries also, the ecclesiological doctrines derived from such formulas were quite different from those of the nineteenth century Ultramontanes.[2]

---

misled by the pseudo-Isidorian texts incorporated in Gratian's Decretum. Langen argued that, down to the early thirteenth century, all theological writing on the nature of the church was biblically oriented. Later it became dominated by juridicism and speculative philosophy. This development in turn led on to the formulation of the doctrine of papal infallibility.

[1] C.-J. Hefele and H. Le Clercq, *Histoire des Conciles*, III, Pt. 1 (Paris, 1909), pp. 502, 519.

[2] No doubt Congar was right when he observed in this connection, "Au fond, le vrai magistère était moins celui d'une autorité liée à une supériorité, que celui de la Tradition dont les évêques avaient la garde et que l'Église de Rome avait eut la grâce de bien conserver." *L'ecclésiologie du haut moyen âge* (Paris, 1968), p. 160.

Döllinger's argument is no more convincing than Manning's. The fundamental objection to his account is that it is based on a radical misunderstanding of the canonical tradition of the medieval church. Döllinger was anxious to prove that the doctrine of papal infallibility originated in ninth century forgeries. But this led him to apply a kind of double standard in his interpretation of canonical texts. When dealing with genuine patristic writings Döllinger always used the argument from silence in a negative sense. Since the doctrine of papal infallibility was not explicitly affirmed it was taken to be implicitly denied. But, when he dealt with forged texts, Döllinger was quite willing to see papal infallibility implied even though it was not explicitly asserted. And, in this interpretation, he was very probably wrong. It is by no means clear that any of the forgers, or the popes and canonists who accepted their texts, the men whom Döllinger regarded as the originators of the doctrine of papal infallibility, actually embraced any such doctrine.

A modern historian cannot exclude the possibility that some eccentric or prescient pope or canonist in the ninth, tenth or eleventh century may have secretly cherished in his heart the dogma of 1870.[1] The point cannot be proved one way or the other. What can be proved is that no public teaching affirming the infallibility of the pope was transmitted to the canonists of the twelfth and thirteenth centuries in whose works, for the first time, abundant texts for the investigation of this whole question become available. The commentators on Gratian's Decretum knew all the most important texts—genuine and forged—relating to the authority of the pope and the indefectibility of the Roman church. They did not associate those texts with any doctrine of papal infallibility. They showed no awareness that any of their predecessors had ever associated them

---

The fullest recent treatment of these questions is provided by K. F. Morrison, *Tradition and Authority in the Western Church, 300-1140* (Princeton, 1969).

[1] Pope Gregory VII would be a strong candidate in that he applied the text at Luke 22.32 to Peter's successors and included in his *Dictatus Papae* the pseudo-Isidorian formula, "The Roman church has never erred; nor will it err to all eternity, as Scripture bears witness." But such language was inherently ambiguous. Contemporaries were quite capable of distinguishing between the pope and the Roman church. It seems unlikely on the whole that Gregory was intending to assert a new doctrine of personal infallibility. On his views see most recently L. F. J. Meulenberg, *Der Primat der römischen Kirche im Denken und Handeln Gregors VII* ('s Gravenhage, 1965) and the comments on Meulenberg of J. Gilchrist, "Gregory VII and the Primacy of the Roman Church," *Tijdschrift voor Rechtsgeschiedenis*, 36 (1968), pp. 123-135. Also K. Morrison, op. cit., pp. 269-291.

with such a doctrine. We shall argue that the theologians of the thirteenth century could not possibly have taken the doctrine of papal infallibility from the canonical tradition of the church because the doctrine simply did not exist in the writings of the canonists.

An investigation of the thought of the medieval canonists provides the necessary starting-point for a work on the origins of papal infallibility and the ideas associated with it. Döllinger thought that the canonists were primarily responsible for creating the doctrine of infallibility itself. Other, more recent scholars have seen the canonists as the originators of various modern ideas concerning ecclesiastical Tradition. And certainly the canonists' works influenced all subsequent writings on papal sovereignty. Moreover, on one important point Döllinger was entirely correct. Early scholastic theologians offered almost no discussions on the structure of the church.[1] In the twelfth century the whole field of study that we call ecclesiology was regarded as a province of ecclesiastical jurisprudence. If, then, we are to understand the medieval church's conception of its own nature and structure in the century before the emergence of the doctrine of papal infallibility we must turn first to the writings of the Decretists and the Decretalists.

---

[1] After a lifetime of research on the manuscripts of early scholastic theology A. M. Landgraf presented his findings on papal infallibility in a brief article entitled "Scattered Remarks on the Development of Dogma and on Papal Infallibility in Early Scholastic Writings," *Theological Studies*, 7 (1946), pp. 577-582. The material was reprinted in *Dogmengeschichte der Fruhscholastik*, I. i (Regensburg, 1952), pp. 30-36. Landgraf observed that "problems in ecclesiology were rarely discussed by the early Scholastics." None of the few "scattered texts" that he presented actually asserted a doctrine of papal infallibility.

CHAPTER ONE

THE CANONISTS

The dogmatic constitution on the church promulgated at Vatican Council I included several inter-related doctrines whose origins we intend to explore. We shall consider first the attitude of the medieval canonists during the period 1150-1250 to a group of five propositions that were of central importance for the teaching of the Council.[1] In the order in which we shall consider them these are (1) The sphere of revealed truth within which the pope's supreme teaching authority can be exercised is comprised of "sacred Scripture and apostolic Tradition." (2) *Ex cathedra* definitions of the pope on faith and morals are infallible. (3) The infallible magisterium of the pope, his teaching authority, was included in the primacy bestowed on Peter with the power of the keys. (4) To appeal from the pope to a general Council as to a higher authority is unlawful. (5) *Ex cathedra* decrees are irreformable *ex sese*.[2] In summarizing the canonistic positions on

---

[1] The following discussion of the canonists' views is based in part on texts originally published in my *Foundations of the Conciliar Theory* (Cambridge, 1955) and "Pope and Council: Some New Decretist Texts," *Mediaeval Studies*, 19 (1957), pp. 197-218. These works will be cited subsequently as *Foundations* and "Pope and Council." The best guides to modern literature on the canonists are S. Kuttner, *Repertorium der Kanonistik* (Vatican City, 1937); A. Van Hove, *Prolegomena* (Commentarium Lovaniense in Codicem Iuris Canonici, I, i) (Malines-Rome, 1945); A. Stickler, *Historia iuris canonici latini* (Turin, 1950); H. E. Feine, *Kirchliche Rechtsgeschichte*, I, *Die katholische Kirche* (Weimar, 1955); G. Le Bras etc., *Histoire du droit et des institutions de l'église en Occident*, Vol. VII, *L'âge classique 1140-1378* (Paris, 1965). Since 1956 the *Bulletin* of the Institute of Medieval Canon Law has presented annual bibliographies in the journal *Traditio*. Good general accounts of the canonists and their activities in our period are provided by W. Ullmann, *Medieval Papalism* (London, 1949), pp. 1-37; S. Mochi Onory, *Fonti canonistiche dell'idea moderna dello stato* (Milan, 1951), pp. 3-76; R. L. Benson, *The Bishop-Elect* (Princeton, 1968), pp. 10-20.

[2] C. Butler, *The Vatican Council*, II (London, 1930), (1) p. 293, "And the Roman pontiffs ... defined as to be held those things which with the help of God they had recognized as conformable with the Sacred Scriptures and Apostolic Traditions." (2) p. 295, "We teach and define that ... the Roman pontiff, when he speaks ex cathedra ... is possessed of that infallibility with which the divine Redeemer willed that his church should be endowed ...." (3) pp. 281-283, 289, "For none can doubt ... that the holy and Blessed Peter ... received the keys of the kingdom from our Lord Jesus Christ .... Whence, whosoever succeeds to Peter in this See, does by the institution of Christ Himself obtain the Primacy of Peter over the whole

these questions we shall emphasize especially the views of the two most outstanding and influential of the Decretists who were writing in the years around 1200, Huguccio and Johannes Teutonicus. Huguccio's great *Summa* (c. 1190) was an impressive work of synthesis based on the preceding fifty years of Decretist scholarship. The commentary of Johannes Teutonicus (c. 1216) was a less coherent, more eclectic work but it acquired great influence since it was accepted as the *glossa ordinaria* to the Decretum and so was studied in the law schools of Europe throughout the Middle Ages.[1]

1. Scripture and Tradition

(i) *The Concept of Tradition*

The authority of Tradition—in some sense of the term—has been acknowledged since the first centuries of the Christian era.[2] The early Fathers could not fail to be aware that many approved practices of the church found their source in ancient custom rather than in scriptural teaching. Augustine held indeed that the fact of a usage being universally observed in the church was evidence of its apostolic origin. This principle was applied to liturgical rites and customs rather than to the divinely revealed truths of faith. But, in the sphere

---

church .... Moreover, that the supreme power of teaching (*magisterii potestatem*) is also included in the Apostolic primacy, which the Roman Pontiff, as the successor of Peter, Prince of the Apostles, possesses over the whole Church, this Holy See has always held ...." (4) pp. 287-289, "Wherefore they err from the right path of truth who assert that it is lawful to appeal from the judgements of the Roman Pontiffs to an Oecumenical Council, as to an authority higher than that of the Roman Pontiff." (5) p. 295, "... such definitions of the Roman Pontiff are irreformable of themselves, and not from the consent of the Church."

[1] The most detailed treatment of Huguccio's thought on the papacy is that of M. Ríos Fernández, "El primado del Romano pontífice nel pensamiento de Huguccio de Pisa decretista," *Compostellanum*, 6 (1961), pp. 44-97; 7 (1962), pp. 97-149; 8 (1963), pp. 65-99; 11 (1966), pp. 29-67. The views of Johannes Teutonicus are mentioned in every extensive treatment of thirteenth-century canonistic ideas but there is no work of synthesis on his ecclesiology. The best guide to his thought in this area is the Cornell Ph.D. dissertation of K. Pennington, *Johannes Teutonicus: A Thirteenth Century Lawyer.*

[2] A substantial body of new work on Scripture and Tradition was stimulated by the debates preceding and accompanying Vatican Council II. A good introduction to this work is C. Balić (ed.), *De Scriptura et Traditione* (Rome, 1963) which presents essays on both historical and theological aspects of the question. (It includes an extensive bibliography of earlier work at pp. 85-112). Yves Congar has provided a major work of synthesis in *Tradition and Traditions*, transl. M. Naseby and T. Rainborough (New York, 1967) (translation of *La Tradition et les traditions* [Paris, 1960-1963]).

of revealed truth itself, the Fathers never hesitated to appeal to the authority of the universal church in settling disputed points of interpretation. The fifth century St. Vincent of Lérins declared, in a famous formula, that Catholic truth could be ascertained by determining what had been believed "everywhere, always, by everyone." A few patristic texts, it has been maintained, suggested that certain specific truths of faith were known to the church solely from Tradition. The interpretation of such texts remains a matter of controversy. But there was at any rate general agreement that the truths of Scripture themselves were to be understood in the light of the church's Tradition.[1] St. Augustine even declared, "I would not believe the truth of the Gospel unless the authority of the Catholic church moved me to do so."[2]

Such texts were often quoted and discussed by medieval theologians. But, before the thirteenth century, there is little trace in their works of the view that Tradition constituted a source of divine revelation separate from Scripture and little inclination to set up a distinction—still less an opposition—between Scriptural revelation and church doctrine. One modern author has observed that, for twelfth century theologians (as for the Fathers themselves), church and Scripture "co-inhered."[3] This seems true in the sense that the teaching of the church and the teaching of Scripture were conceived of as essentially one. "The men of the Middle Ages lived in the Bible and by the Bible."[4] When twelfth century theologians observed—as they sometimes did—that many things were held by the church that were not to be found in Scripture they seem to have had in mind only liturgical customs or pious practices. An extra-Scriptural source of faith like the Apostles' Creed (which was commonly regarded as a work of the apostles themselves) was held to define various tenets of Christian doctrine with absolute fidelity; but it was not considered to be a body of revealed truth supplementary to sacred Scripture. Rather the Creed could be called in the twelfth century a "summary" of the contents of Scripture.[5] In this view Scripture recorded divine truth once and for all and the living voice of the church, guided by

---

[1] For a selection of patristic texts see Congar, *op. cit.*, pp. 42-55.

[2] *Contra epistolam Manichaei quam vocant Fundamenti*, Migne *PL*, 42, col. 176, "Ego vero Evangelio non crederem, nisi me catholicae Ecclesiae commoveret auctoritas."

[3] G. H. Tavard, *Holy Writ or Holy Church* (London, 1959), p. 22.

[4] Congar, *op. cit.*, p. 86.

[5] Rupert of Deutz, cited by Tavard, *op. cit.*, pp. 15-16.

the Holy Spirit, interpreted that truth and proclaimed it anew to each succeeding generation. The question—widely debated from the late thirteenth century onward—whether, in case of conflict, a man ought to follow the teaching of Scripture or the teaching of the church, was never raised in earlier periods. The dilemma posed by the question was indeed hardly imaginable.

A vast new literature on the history and theology of Tradition has appeared during the past two decades. Our own aim here is a limited one. Out of all the current argumentation we wish to isolate and criticize only one particular strand of thought. This is the assertion, made in several recent works, that, from the time of Gratian's Decretum onward, the medieval canonists were responsible for the launching of new doctrines which presented ecclesiastical Tradition as a fount of divine revelation separate from Scripture and which held that the decrees of the pope (as supreme exponent of the church's Tradition) possessed an authority equal to or greater than that of Scripture in matters of faith. We can illustrate these views from two recent books on medieval and early modern ecclesiology.

Heiko Oberman, in his brilliant and perceptive work on medieval nominalism, was interested in exploring the doctrine of a primitive "constitutive Tradition" in the church; i.e., the doctrine maintaining that the apostles transmitted orally to the first Christian community a body of revealed truths apart from those recorded in Scripture. He suggested that the Decretum of Gratian gave a major impetus to the development of this doctrine in the later Middle Ages since Gratian included in his collection a text of St. Basil which declared "We accept some ecclesiastical institutions from the Scriptures, some from apostolic tradition..." On this Oberman commented, "For the canon lawyer, then, the two-sources theory has been established: canon law stands on the two pillars of Scripture and Tradition." He added that, in the fourteenth century, when the canonists stood at the height of their prestige, "the canon-law tradition started to feed into the major theological stream..."[1]

G. H. Tavard in his study entitled *Holy Writ or Holy Church* was more interested in canonistic influence on the modern doctrine of "living Tradition." In Tavard's view the medieval canonists so grossly exaggerated the authority of the popes that they came to

---

[1] H. A. Oberman, *The Harvest of Medieval Theology* (Cambridge, Mass., 1963), pp. 369, 372.

regard contemporary papal pronouncements as providing a more certain guide to the permanent truths of faith than any ancient authority. (This view, moreover, seems to find some support in the magisterial work of Yves Congar, *La Tradition et les traditions*.) According to Tavard, the canonists' way of thinking, pressed to its logical conclusion, could lead to the view that "Living authority replaces both Scripture and its traditional interpretation." He quoted canonistic authors who asserted that "The pope is wonderful for he holds the power of God on earth" and that, "The pope may do whatever God may do."[1]

If these views of Oberman and Tavard could be fully substantiated we should perhaps need to enquire no further into the origins of papal infallibility. It would seem then that the earlier accounts, which saw the medieval canonists as the principal authors of the modern doctrine, were substantially correct. But the arguments of our two authors are hardly compatible with each other. One asserts that the canonists favored a "two-sources theory" of divine revelation because of their excessive regard for ancient tradition, the other that they favored this same theory because of an excessive regard for the innovative powers of the pope. In fact neither assertion is correct. Canonistic teaching throughout the twelfth and thirteenth centuries was entirely consistent with the doctrines commonly taught by the theologians of that age—that sacred Scripture contained implicitly or explicitly all the revealed truths of Christian faith and that papal power was wholly subordinate to Scriptural revelation where matters of faith were concerned. We use the words "consistent with" because the precise issue of the relationship between Scripture and Tradition was not extensively discussed by the earlier canonists. But, when the problem did arise as a matter of overt controversy at the beginning of the fourteenth century, the definitive canonical solution of it took the form of a strong re-affirmation of the "single-source theory," if we may adopt Oberman's terminology. (We shall use the term "single-source theory" to describe the view that all the revealed truths of Christian faith are contained, at least implicitly, in sacred Scripture and the term "two-sources theory" to describe the opposing view that the Tradition of the church reveals truths of faith that cannot be known from Holy Writ.)

We can best show how the texts cited by Oberman and Tavard fit

---

[1] Tavard, *op. cit.*, p. 48.

into the real canonical tradition of the Middle Ages by analyzing the *Tractatus de legibus*, the first twenty *distinctiones* of Gratian's Decretum, for here we find a discussion of both ancient tradition and innovative papal decrees embedded in a systematic exposition of the sources of law which provided a foundation for all subsequent medieval canonistic jurisprudence. Let us begin with the more moderate arguments advanced by Oberman.

Oberman was entirely correct when he wrote that "canon law stands on the two pillars of Scripture and Tradition." But this does not in the least imply that the canonists believed in two sources of divine revelation. The essential point is that the great bulk of medieval canon law was not, and did not purport to be, divinely revealed truth. On the contrary, the task of distinguishing what was divine and permanent in the life of the church from what was human and transitory lay at the very heart of the whole medieval enterprise of constructing a science of canon law separate from the science of theology. We should not be misled by the canonists' frequent assertions that the whole of their jurisprudence constituted a sacred science. Canon law was sacred in that it regulated the life of holy church. It was sacred again in that the popes and bishops who administered it held divinely ordained offices. Moreover, every kind of law, including secular human law, was conceived of as divine in the sense that "the powers that be are ordained of God." In such a climate of thought it was easy for the canonists to call their laws "sacred" while maintaining a sharp and clear distinction between those that were of merely human origin, and so subject to change, and those that were truly divine, and hence immutable.[1]

---

[1] On the "divinity" of human law see *Dist.* 8 c. 1, "... iura humana per imperatores et reges saeculi Deus distribuit generi humano" and *Dig.* 1.2.2, "... omnis lex inventum et munus deorum est ..." Similarly Hostiensis, *Lectura in quinque Decretalium Gregorianarum libros* (Paris, 1512), ad X. 1. 14.4, "... ars artium est divina lex a qua non est excludenda canonica nec humana ...." On the high claims of Hostiensis and other canonists for their own science see especially S. Kuttner, *Harmony from Dissonance* (Latrobe, 1960), pp. 48-50, 62-64. The distinction between canon law which could be called divine because founded by God and canon law which could be called divine because founded by men for God was brought out clearly in an anonymous gloss of the twelfth century cited by W. Ullmann, *Medieval Papalism* (London, 1949), p. 42, "(Jus divinum est) a Deo insitum menti, ut lex naturalis; a Deo traditum: lex Mosaica; a Deo editum: evangelicum; pro Deo conditum: canones." Similarly Guido de Baysio, *Rosarium Decretorum* (Strasbourg, 1473), ad *Dist.* 1 c. 1, "Divine (leges), i.e. a Deo per ministros suos late vel de divinis rebus late."

This was made clear in the very first words of Gratian's Decretum:

> The human race is ruled by two (laws), namely by natural law and cus-
> toms. Natural law is what is contained in the Law and Gospels whereby
> each man is commanded to do to others what he wishes to be done to
> himself ....[1]

The word "customs" (*moribus*) could be taken to mean human law
in general according to the *glossa ordinaria*.[2] Thus there were two
sources, natural law (here identified with the scriptural "golden
rule") and human law. Later on Gratian explained (and his commentators would explain more clearly) that Scripture contained both natural
law, which could be known to all men, and truths of faith which were
revealed only to Christians. The point is that, neither here at the
outset nor in subsequent discussions, did Gratian (or his commentators) envisage a further source of law for the church constituted by
supernatural, extra-Scriptural revelations of truths of faith.

The first six *Distinctiones* of the Decretum defined the various types
of human law and explained that the term "natural law" was being
used to mean, not the whole content of Scripture in general, but the
permanent principles of morality revealed in it. Having made this
clear, Gratian could next describe the degree of authority of the
various kinds of law he had mentioned. In *Distinctio* 9 he explained
that human statutes were not only a part of the whole complex of
laws governing the human race but also that they constituted a part of
canon law in particular. In case of conflict, however, they always had
to give way to natural law:

> If statutes, whether ecclesiastical or secular, are shown to be con-
> trary to natural law, they are to be altogether excluded.[3]

---

[1] *Dist.* 1 *ante* c. 1, "Humanum genus duobus regitur naturali videlicet iure et
moribus. Ius naturale est, quod in lege et evangelio continetur, quo quisque iube-
tur alii facere quod sibi vult fieri ...."

[2] Johannes Teutonicus, *Glossa ordinaria* in *Decretum Gratiani* (Venice, 1600), *gl.
ad Dist.* 1 *ante* c. 1, "*Moribus*, i.e. consuetudinario iure vel etiam iure humano sive
scripto sive non scripto."

[3] *Dist.* 9, *post.* c. 11. Some confusion has arisen because the term "natural law"
had many other connotations in medieval jurisprudence. When the words referred
merely to a supposed primitive condition of mankind then papal legislation could
over-ride "natural law." But no legislation could over-ride "natural law" as Gratian himself understood the term at this point of the Decretum. On natural law as
divine see Guido Fasso, "Dio e la natura presso i Decretisti ed i Glossatori," *Il
diritto ecclesiastico*, 67 (1956), pp. 3-10 and my "*Natura id est deus*; A Case of Juristic
Pantheism?" *Journal of the History of Ideas*, 24 (1963), pp. 307-322. For a general
review of the whole question see R. Weigand, *Die Naturrechtslehre der Legisten und
Dekretisten* (Munich, 1967).

Distinctio 10 stated that canon law was of higher authority than civil and *Distinctio* 11 that statute law was superior to custom. Gratian next wished to point out that custom was not altogether lacking in authority even though it stood below statute law and, *a fortiori*, below natural law and Scripture. It was to make this point that he introduced the crucial text of St. Basil with its assertion that some established liturgical practices were based on Scripture and some on apostolic tradition. The text was cited in support of the proposition that, "When a custom is not opposed to sacred canons or human law it is to be kept unchanged."[1] Gratian was quite prepared to admit that certain ecclesiastical practices were deserving of respect simply because they could be traced back to the time of the apostles but, far from regarding such traditions as a second source of divine revelation, he presented them as merely a sub-division of the least authoritative branch of the man-made law that constituted one province of ecclesiastical jurisprudence. For Gratian ecclesiastical Tradition was essentially human custom, not divine revelation. The Decretist commentators on Basil's text, following Gratian's lead, never sought to extend the scope of Tradition to include extra-Scriptural revelations of truths of faith. On the contrary they were inclined to argue that a scriptural basis could be found even for those liturgical practices which Basil mentioned as deriving solely from Tradition.[2]

Distinctio 15 and *Distinctio* 16 discussed the authority of general councils. We shall consider the canonists' treatment of this question in a later section.

Distinctio 17 dealt with the origins of papal power and the Decretists' comments on it provide an excellent illustration of their attitude to Scripture and Tradition. One of Gratian's texts suggested that the authority of the Holy See might be based in part on the decrees of church councils and some of the canonists, fascinated as always by a possible analogy with Roman law, played with the idea that, just as

---

[1] *Dist.* 11, *post* c. 4. St. Basil's text follows at *Dist.* 11, c. 5, "Ecclesiasticarum institutionum quasdam scripturis, quasdam vero apostolica traditione per successiones in ministerio confirmatas accepimus, quasdam vero consuetudine roboratas approbavit usus, quibus par ritus et idem utrisque pietatis debetur affectus." It seems most improbable that Basil intended to propound a theory of the sources of divine revelation in this text, for he put post-Apostolic custom on the same level as Scripture and Apostolic tradition.

[2] See e.g. *gl. ord. ad Dist.* 11 c. 5 s.v. *Scriptura* and s.v. *Quae orientem*. On the whole question of the authority of custom in canonical jurisprudence see R. Wehrlé, *De la coutume dans le droit canonique* (Paris, 1928).

the *populus* had conferred authority on the emperor so too councils might have conferred authority on the pope. They always pointed out, however, that such a theory could not be accepted without major qualifications. Papal primacy, they acknowledged, was established in the first place by Christ himself so that subsequent councils could only have conferred authority "secondarily" or made manifest an authority that already existed.[1] There could hardly be a better example of the "single-source theory" of divine revelation than the canonists' treatment of the origins of papal power. They regarded the primacy as a doctrine divinely revealed in the New Testament which was affirmed and interpreted by subsequent ecclesiastical Tradition. The first medieval thinker of major importance who suggested that the pope's power was based only on Tradition, considered as a source separate from Scripture, was Marsilius of Padua. The popes did not like the idea at all. In considering the argument that papal claims tended to detract from the unique authority of Scripture, it is important always to bear in mind the scriptural basis of those claims themselves.

Gratian's *Dist.* 17 introduced a series of *distinctiones* (*Dist.* 17-*Dist.* 20) dealing mainly with the authority of papal decretals. In commenting on *Dist.* 19 and *Dist.* 20 the canonists commonly put forward high claims for the pope as a legislator and judge set over the whole church. Hence we can appropriately turn at this point to the problems of papal power raised by Tavard.

(ii) *Scripture, Tradition, and Papal Power*

Tavard, we have seen, maintained not only that the canonists regarded ecclesiastical Tradition as a source of revealed truth separate from Scripture but also that they grossly exaggerated the pope's authority as an exponent of this Tradition. Tavard's characteristic argument was that the canonists' magnification of papal authority tended to "devalue" Scripture. "The most extreme instances of devaluation of Scripture are culled from the writings of canon-lawyers," he observed, and added, "We can hardly imagine nowadays to what an extent this could reach."

The most substantial text that Tavard quoted in support of these assertions was the following passage from an anonymous writer of the fourteenth century:

---

[1] *Gl. ord. ad Dist.* 17 *post* c. 6, s.v. *Iussione*, "Habet ergo Romana ecclesia auctoritatem a conciliis sed imperator a populo .... Sed dic principaliter habuit a Domino, secundario a conciliis." See *Foundations*, pp. 55-56.

He, the Pope, is above all Council and all statute; he it is who has no superior on earth; he, the Pope gives dispensations from every Law. ... He it is who holds the plenitude of power on earth and takes the place and seat of the Most High ... He it is who changes the substance of a thing, making legitimate what was illegitimate ... and making a monk into a canon regular. ... He it is who absolves in heaven when he absolves on earth ... over whose binding nobody trespasses, for it is not a man, but God, who binds by giving that power to a man .... He it is who in his absolute knowledge strengthens and heals what is sick, who supplies what is defective .... To him nobody may say: why do you do that? ... He it is in whom the will is sufficient reason, for what pleases him has the strength of Law ... he is not bound by laws. ... He, the Pope is the Law itself and the living rule, opposition to which is illegitimate.[1]

We shall return to this passage, but we may note at the outset that, for all its extravagant language, it does not say anything specifically about the authority of Scripture or about the pope as a source of new revelation. The canonists certainly taught that the pope was the legitimate judge of cases involving disputed questions of faith;[2] but this does not necessarily mean that they held him to be a fount of extra-Scriptural doctrine. There seems to be only one Decretist comment which, even on the surface, might appear to support the view that they interpreted his role as supreme judge in such a fashion. This is to be found in a gloss of the English canonist Alanus, who raised the delicate question whether a pope could create new articles of faith by his decisions. His answer, however, was so cautious and nuanced that it provides no real support for the view that the pope could promulgate non-Scriptural doctrines as truths of faith.

In posing his question Alanus had in mind the decretal, *Cum Christus*, promulgated by Pope Alexander III in 1177. This decree was

---

[1] G. H. Tavard, *op. cit.*, p. 39, citing R. Scholz, *Unbekannte kirchenpolitische Streitschriften aus der Zeit Ludwigs der Bayern*, II (Rome, 1914), p. 544.

[2] Huguccio included "questions of faith" in a long list of cases reserved to the Roman see. *Summa ad Dist.* 17 c. 3 (MS Pembroke College, Cambridge, 72, fol. 126va), "*Huic soli sedi concessa*, hec autem multa sunt scilicet episcoporum depositio, episcoporum abrenunciatio ... episcoporum mutacio ... episcoporum exemptio ... episcoporum restitutio ... *questio fidei* ... dispensatio in consanguinitate ... restitutio hereticorum ... cognitio eorum ...." Cf. Johannes Teutonicus, *gl. ord. ad* C. 24 q. 1 c. 12 s.v. *Quoties*, "Sed aliud est quaestionem de fide motam terminare quod nulli praeterquam Romanae sedi permittitur ... aliud est ipsum sine diffinitione ventilare." Bernardus Parmensis, *gl. ord. ad* X. 1.7.1. s.v. *Instituta*, "... quaestio religionis et fidei ad Petrum tantum referenda est ...." The phrase was repeated in many Decretalist commentaries. A good summary of canonistic doctrine on the pope as supreme judge is given by J. Watt, *The Theory of Papal Monarchy in the Thirteenth Century* (New York, 1965), pp. 75-105.

directed against a peculiar resurgence of the Adoptionist heresy among the theologians of Paris which led some of them to affirm the proposition *Christum non esse aliquid secundum quod homo*. Alexander condemned this view and against it quoted the old doctrine affirming that Christ was "perfect God and perfect man." Alanus' comment on the text was full of careful distinctions. He wrote that the pope's definition could be said to create an article of faith if the term *articulus fidei* were taken to mean "something we are required to believe which earlier we were not required to believe" (i.e., that the formula of the Paris masters was heretical). He added that if *articulus fidei* meant simply "what ought to be believed," then such articles were always true and immutable from the beginning; and that, strictly speaking, the term *articulus fidei* ought to be reserved for the doctrines of the Apostle's Creed.[1] Alanus was intending only to make the point that a new theological expression which had seemed permissible before the pope condemned it (because it was not clear whether the new formula actually contradicted ancient doctrine) could be regarded as heretical after a papal condemnation. This was not really an extreme position; and, in other contexts, Alanus introduced major reservations when considering the role of the pope as arbiter of the faith which make it quite plain that he did not regard the pope as a source of divine revelation, co-equal with Holy Writ. (He maintained for instance that if a pope disagreed with the bishops of the church or a majority of them on a matter of faith the decision of the bishops had to be accepted in preference to that of the pope.[2]) The main point for us to note here is that the Decretist arguments—however

---

[1] The Decretists often mentioned *Cum Christus* in their comments on Gratian's dictum at *Dist.* 20 *ante* c. 1. For references see "Pope and Council," p. 204 n. 28. Alanus' comment first appeared in his *gloss ad Comp.* I, 5.6.5 (MS Karlsruhe Aug. XL, fol. 68ra). It was incorporated into the collection of glosses on the *Decretum* compiled by Guido de Baysio (c. 1300) in his *Rosarium Decretorum* (Strasbourg, 1473) and was known to fourteenth century canonists through this source. The original form of the gloss as given in the Karlsruhe manuscript ran as follows, "Ante diffinitionem istam contrarium dicere licebat cum prohibitum non esset. Sed post nequaquam. Ergo quod prius non fuit fidei articulus per constitutionem factum est articulus, et ita papa potest facere novos articulos fidei, quod verum est in una acceptatione huius vocabuli 'fidei articulus', i.e. tali quod credi oportet cum prius non opporteret. Sed secundum quod dicitur 'articulus', i.e. tali quod credi debeat, quicquid semel fuit articulus semper fuit et semper erit articulus, et nota quod stricte hoc nomine appellantur illi soli qui in sinbolo apostolorum continentur et illos scire explicite est unicuique intellectu humani necessarium ad salutem."

[2] See below p. 52.

much authority they attributed to the pope—never presented his judgements as sources of faith divorced from Scripture. In *Cum Christus* Alexander III evidently was not acting as a source of new revelation. He was re-affirming the doctrine of the Council of Chalcedon which in turn was rooted in the scriptural accounts of the Incarnation.

The disinclination of the canonists to equate the pope's authority with that of Scripture was plainly evident in another series of comments on *Dist.* 20. This *Distinctio* brought to a conclusion Gratian's survey of the sources of ecclesiastical law and the canonists often took occasion to summarize his argument by setting out here a list of all those sources arranged in order of dignity. A typical example is this list from Huguccio.

> The writings of the Old and New Testaments hold first place; canons of the apostles and of councils second; decrees and decretal letters of the Roman pontiffs third; writings of the Greek fathers fourth; of the Latin fathers fifth; the examples of the saints sixth.[1]

The lists vary slightly from one to another but invariably the Scriptures were given first place. Usually the canons of General Councils came second. Never were papal decretals put on the same level as Scripture.

In such an approach there seems no hint of any disposition on the part of the canonists to "de-value" Scripture. How then are we to understand the extraordinary claims for the papacy that Tavard interpreted as having that implication? Here again it is all-important to remember the distinction between the human and divine elements in the life of the church that was always present in the minds of the canonists themselves. The letters of promulgation preceding the *Decretales* and the *Liber Sextus* stated explicitly that the main concern of the papal legislators was with the changing structure of human law needed to regulate the life of the church. Gregory IX referred to the *nova litigia* which necessitated new juridical rulings from the papacy and the *glossa ordinaria* quoted in explanation the famous words from Justinian's Proemium to the Code, *natura semper novas*

---

[1] *Summa ad Dist.* 20 c. 3, cited by C. Munier, *Les sources patristiques du droit de l'église* (Mulhouse, 1957), p. 200. Huguccio's comment was incorporated into the *glossa ordinaria ad Dist.* 20 c. 3. Munier gives examples of similar lists in works of the Bolognese and Anglo-Norman schools. Others can be found in works of the French school, e.g., *Summa Antiquitate et tempore* (See "Pope and Council," p. 201 n. 22) and Odo of Dover, MS London BM, Cotton, Vittel. A III. fol. 113r.

deproperat edere formas.[1] In the *Liber Sextus* these words of Roman law were incorporated into the papal letter of promulgation itself. But, in emphasizing the changing character of human affairs as the justification of their own legislative activity, the popes were by no means denying the existence of a sphere of divine revelation whose truths lay outside the scope of papal sovereignty. Innocent III insisted on his right to revoke the decrees of his predecessors in accordance with the Roman law theory of sovereignty and he once declared that he stood between man and God, "Higher than man but lower than God." But, in the same sermon in which he used those audacious words, Innocent declared, "For a sin against the faith I may be judged by the church."[2]

These considerations may help us to understand that fourteenth century litany of texts in praise of the pope that Tavard found so disconcerting. The anonymous author did not invent this list of papal prerogatives. He followed closely a similar list given by Gulielmus Durandus (the Speculator). Durandus apparently based himself on the *glossa ordinaria* of Bernardus Parmensis[3] and Bernardus in turn was amplifying a gloss of Tancred. The original form of the passage, as set down in Tancred's gloss on the *Comp. III*, written c. 1219, was as follows:

> *Vices.* In is gerit vicem dei quia sedet in loco Jesu Christi qui est verus deus et verus homo ut in constitutione *In nomine, Firmiter credimus.* Item de nichilo facit aliquid ut deus, arg. III q. vi, *Haec quippe* et *C. De rei uxo. art. 1. unico in prin.* Item in is gerit vicem dei quia plenitudinem potestatis habet in rebus ecclesiasticis ut II q. vii, *Decreto, De usu pallii,* c. ii. Item quia potest dispensare supra ius et contra ius ut infra, *De concessione preb. et ecc. non vac.,* c. 1. Item quia de iusticia potest facere iniusticiam, corrigendo ius et mutando ut in constitutione Innocentii III, *Ut debitus* et *extra III. De consang. et affin.,* c. *Non debet.* Nec est qui dicat ei: cur ita facies? ut *De pen., dist.* III *ex persona.* T.[4]

As Tavard observed, canon law could be cited to support every one of these "wondrous claims"—and sometimes Roman law too it will be

---

[1] *Glossa ordinaria* in *Decretales D. Gregorii IX cum glossis* (Lyons, 1624), *ad Proemium,* s.v. *Nova litigia,* "Hoc dicit quia humana natura prona est ad dissentiendum ... et semper novas deproperat edere formas. *C. de veter. iur. enuc. 1. secunda § sed quia divina.*"

[2] *Sermo II in consecratione pontificis maximi,* Migne *PL* 217, col. 656, "In tantum enim fides mihi necessaria est ut ... propter solum peccatum quod in fide committitur possem ab ecclesia judicari. Nam qui non credit jam judicatus est."

[3] *Gl. ad.* X. 1.7.3.

[4] MS Caius College, Cambridge 17, fol. 147va.

noticed. But that is the whole point. The claims were juridical ones. They referred to the legislative and dispensatory powers of the pope within the framework of positive ecclesiastical law. The whole passage was a sustained rhetorical analogy. Just as God exercised a creative power in the universe as a whole so too the pope could create and innovate in the sphere of positive canon law. This was admirably brought out by the sixteenth-century *correctores Romani* in a comment on the parallel passage in Bernardus Parmensis' *glossa ordinaria*. "This gloss expounds hardly anything in proper language, though if it is understood correctly it affirms things that are true. For to make something out of nothing is to establish a new law and to make justice out of injustice means through the constitution of law, and to change the substance of things has to be understood as referring to matters of positive law."[1] A check of Tancred's legal references makes it clear that this was indeed precisely what he meant.

Can we not say, even so, that the language that Tancred chose to use was highly misleading? The answer must be that it was not so to the professional canonists for whom the passage was written. The whole meaning of the text was conveyed by its citations of Roman and canon law and, in reading it, we must remember that medieval jurists knew by heart the content of the texts they cited by incipit in a way that no modern scholar does. In fact, the language was tiresome but the actual claims were ones that could readily be accepted by anyone who believed in the pope's primacy of jurisdiction. Let us add finally that Tancred, who in this passage so boldly compared the pope's power with God's maintained quite explicitly in other contexts that the pope could not go against articles of faith in his decisions nor act against "the general state of the church."[2]

The one widely-held doctrine of the canonists that might seem to justify Tavard's view that their writings implied a "devaluation of Scripture" was a persistent claim that the pope could, in certain circumstances, dispense against the words of the Bible—"against the words but not against the intention" as Innocent IV wrote.[3] But here again we must distinguish between eternal principles of faith and

---

[1] *Decretales D. Gregorii IX cum glossis* (ed. cit.), col. 217, "Tota haec glossa vix aliquid explicat propriis verbis; quod si bene intelligatur vera astruit. Nam de nihilo aliquid facere est ius novum condere et de iniustitia iustitiam intellige per constitutionem iuris et immutare substantiam rerum accipi debet in his quae sunt iuris positivi ...." On Tancred's text see also J. Watt, *op. cit.*, p. 81.

[2] MS Caius 17, fol. 147ra, fol. 197vb.

[3] *Foundations*, p. 89.

changing rules of church discipline. Not every precept of Holy Writ
was meant to be observed literally for ever. Medieval Christians
agreed, for instance,that the ceremonial precepts laid down for the
Jews in the Old Testament were not binding in the new dispensation
of the Gospels. Within the context of medieval Catholicism it was
natural that the authority of the Roman see should be invoked when a
question arose of deciding whether a given text was intended to
establish an absolute law binding for all time or merely to define for
the ancient Israelites or the church of the apostles a point of discipline
that was subject to change in the future.

When we turn to the actual contexts within which the canonists
discussed the pope's power to "dispense from Scripture" we find that
they were concerned with precisely this kind of question. The main issue
that arose was the extent of the pope's power to grant dispensations
from Scriptural impediments to the promotion of candidates for the
priesthood. One such dispute has been studied in illuminating detail
by Stephan Kuttner.[1] The question at issue was whether the pope
could permit a man who had been twice married and twice widowed
to be ordained as a bishop even though a text of Scripture stated that
a bishop be "a man of one wife." The canonists disagreed about this
but they all acknowledged that, if such an action were possible at all, it
lay at the extreme limit of the pope's dispensatory authority. And this
is hardly a fundamental issue of the Christian faith. To concede to the
pope such a power is not really to set him up as a second source of
divine revelation. The Decretists and Decretalists indeed had no such
intention. It would be hard to find in their works any evidence to
support the view that they regarded the pope as simply "above
Scripture."[2]

The issue of the "bigamous archbishop" is especially interesting
because the prohibition against a twice-married bishop occurs in a
letter of St. Paul. But, according to the canonists, Peter was head of
the church and so greater than Paul—and the pope inherited all the
powers of Peter. It might seem then that the pope could not be bound
by any Pauline text. In fact, however, whatever position the canonists

---

[1] S. Kuttner, "Pope Lucius III and the Bigamous Archbishop of Palermo" in
Medieval Studies Presented to Aubrey Gwynn S.J., ed. J. A. Watt, J. B. Morrall, F. X.
Martin (Dublin, 1961). This paper provides an abundance of canonistic texts on
the limits to the pope's dispensatory authority and references to modern literature
on the subject.

[2] As Congar suggested, *op. cit.*, p. 179.

adopted concerning fine points of church discipline, they all agreed that the pope's power to modify the precepts of "the Apostle" did not extend to matters of faith. This common teaching is found in the Ordinary Glosses to both the Decretum and the *Decretales*.[1] Where matters of faith were involved the teachings of the New Testament— whether proclaimed by Jesus himself or by Peter or Paul or any other author—were binding on the popes in all ages evidently because of the inherent authority of Scripture itself. The canonists never ceased to proclaim this principle that, where the eternal truths of Christian faith were concerned, papal power was limited by Scriptural revelation. One could construct an almost endless catena of texts to illustrate the point.[2]

It is clear then that the canonists' doctrine of papal sovereignty did not lead them to set up the pope as a second fount of divine revelation, the exponent of a Tradition of revealed truth as authoritative as or more authoritative than Scripture. We should finally note that the very reasons which led the canonists of Innocent III's day to extol papal power in the extravagant language that has misled some modern commentators actually discouraged them from developing any such theories. Ever since Gregory VII had revived the saying of Tertullian and declared, "Christ did not say 'I am custom' but 'I am truth'," a major task of ecclesiastical reformers had been to overcome the vast mass of worldly and often corrupt customs that dominated the life of the church. To clear away this debris of the centuries was a formidable undertaking. The rediscovery of the classical concept of legislative sovereignty provided for the first time a kind of authority proportionate to the magnitude of the task; for an essential element in the Roman law theory of sovereignty was the doctrine that the Prince was not bound by existing laws If such laws had been enacted by any inferior authority the Prince stood above them; if they had been enacted by the Prince's own predecessor then he was not bound

---

[1] *Gl. ord. ad* C. 25 q.1 c.6, "Papa contra apostolum dispensat: non tamen in his quae pertinent ad articulos fidei." Similarly, *Gl. ord. ad* X. 3.8.4, s.v. *Dispensare*. For the same doctrine in Innocent IV see Kuttner, art. cit., p. 426 n. 73.

[2] See e.g., Rufinus, Stephanus Tornacensis, Huguccio, *Summa Omnis qui iuste*, *Appar. Ecce vicit leo* in Kuttner, art. cit., pp. 416 n. 28, 417 n. 31, 425, 441, 444; *Summa Reginensis* in Congar, op. cit., p. 222; Innocent IV, Johannes Teutonicus in *Foundations*, pp. 89, 254; Simon de Bisignano, Ricardus Anglicus in "Pope and Council," pp. 210, 211. The same position was upheld by the later Decretalists. On the persistent tension in their works between the *plenitudo potestatis* of the pope and the inviolability of Christian doctrine see especially L. Buisson, *Potestas und Caritas* (Cologne-Graz, 1958).

by an equal—*par in parem non habet imperium*.[1] The Decretists and Decretalists enthusiastically accepted this argument.[2] It was of the essence of their doctrine that the pope could repeal old laws and make new ones. But it was also evident to the medieval canonists—if not to their modern critics—that a doctrine of sovereignty conceived in such terms could not possibly apply to the permanent truths of Scriptural revelation. By definition a permanent truth cannot be subject to repeal. Hence, the canonists were able to apply the Roman law doctrine of sovereignty to the pope only by carefully delimiting the sphere within which juridical sovereignty could be exercised. A pope could revoke the decisions of his predecessors; he could not revoke the revealed truths of Scripture.

The canonists of the early thirteenth century did not associate the idea of sovereignty with despotism but rather with reform and renewal in the life of the church. Hence some medieval canonists permitted themselves the same kind of rhetorical exaggeration in discussing the concept of sovereignty that some modern reformers have indulged in when discussing the concept of liberty. But, for the canonists, sovereignty in a real sense meant liberty—liberty from obsolete laws and bad customs. What it did not mean was liberty from Scriptural truth or liberty to set up new truths of faith co-equal with those of Scripture. Behind all their layers of accumulated glosses the canonists' teaching was rather simple and straightforward. In their view the pope was bound by Scripture in matters of faith; he was not bound by any Tradition conceived of as a source of revealed

---

[1] *Dig.* 1.3.31, "Princeps legibus solutus est." The Ordinary Gloss of Accursius commented, "*Princeps legibus*, ab alio conditis ut infra *de arb. 1. nam et magistratus* vel a seipso ut infra *de arb. 1. penultim.*" in *Corpus Iuris Civilis* (Lyons, 1627), I, col. 80. At *Dig.* 4.8.4, col. 626, Accursius cited the familiar maxim: *par parem cogere non potest.*"

[2] The Decretists referred to the Roman law maxim principally in three contexts (1) *Dist.* 34 c.18. This referred to the case of the 'bigamous archbishop' and the limits of the pope's dispensatory authority. Numerous texts citing the *par in parem* principle are given in Kuttner, art. cit. (2) *Dist.* 40 c.6, referring to the case of a heretical pope. Could he be bound by the sentence of a predecessor? For texts see "Pope and Council," pp. 214-218. (3) *Dist.* 63 c.22, which dealt with Pope Adrian's privilege permitting the emperor to designate future popes. The canonists pointed out that such an act could not bind the pope's successors. E.g. *Summa elegantius,* ed. G. Fransen and S. Kuttner (New York, 1969), p. 129, "... par pari non imperat nec in suis constitutionibus decessor successorem obligat ...." For the Decretalists the locus classicus was X. 1.6.20 where Innocent III, referring to the decrees of his predecessor Alexander III, wrote, "... successoribus suis nullum potuit in hac parte praeiudicium generare, pari post eum, immo eadem potestate functuris, quum non habeat imperium par in parem ...."

truth separate from Scripture. At no point did the canonists' treat-ment of papal power imply any "devaluation" of the Bible. For them the pope was a supreme ruler within the framework of divine revela-tion established by Scripture not an absolute monarch set above it. But, within that framework, they wanted the pope to be as free as possible; it was contrary to their whole climate of thought to invent an additional extra-scriptural Tradition that could also limit the pope's freedom of action. Hence, there is virtually no trace in their works of a "two-sources theory" of Scripture and Tradition.

2. Infallibility and Magisterium

(i) *Inerrancy and Indefectibility*

Although the canonists did not set up the pope as a second source of divine revelation they did attribute to him a pre-eminent role as head of the church. Their doctrine of papal primacy was based on the standard Petrine texts, especially Matt. 16.19. "I will give you the keys of the kingdom of Heaven and whatsoever you bind on earth it shall be bound in Heaven..." The canonists were naturally aware that Christ promised this same power of binding and loosing to all the apostles at Matt. 18.18. and Gratian noted that he actually conferred the authority to remit sins on them all with the words spoken at John 20.23 "Receive the Holy Spirit. Whose sins you shall forgive they shall be forgiven them."[1] In later times these texts led on to endless debates (some of which we shall have to examine) concerning the right relationship between the pope and his brother bishops. But to the Decretists their meaning seemed plain enough. Gratian ex-plained that Christ chose Peter to be head of the church when he promised to him the power of the keys "before all and on behalf of all."[2] Johannes Teutonicus added that the power of a supreme pastor was actually conferred on Peter with the words spoken at John 21.17 ("Feed my sheep...").[3] Following the terminology of St. Augustine the canonists often explained that Peter "signified" the church or

---

[1] C. 24 q.1 *post* c.4, "Apostolis enim dicturus 'Quorum remiseritis peccata etc.' premisit 'Accipite spiritum sanctum.'"

[2] *Dist.* 21 *ante* c. 1, "Petrum vero quasi in summum sacerdotem elegit, dum ei prae omnibus et pro omnibus claves regni coelorum tribuit ...." Gratian repeated the comment at C. 24 q. 1 *post* c. 4.

[3] *Gl. ord. ad Dist.* 21 c. 2, "(Petrus) fuit apostolus ante passionem, sed post pas-sionem fuit pastor creatus per illa verba, 'Si diligis me etc.' quod etiam hic innuitur cum dicit, 'Tibi dabo claves etc.' Hoc enim est promittere et non dare."

stood as a symbol of the church (*in figura ecclesiae*) when he received the promise of the keys.[1] In distinguishing between the authority conferred on Peter and that conferred on the other apostles the canonists commonly observed that all were equal in power of orders but that Peter excelled in "jurisdiction" or in "administration."[2] The Decretists' discussions on this question led to the first clear-cut definitions of the distinction between jurisdiction—the power to govern—and holy orders, the power to administer sacraments as a priest.[3] In their thought the apostles received both powers from Christ; the power of orders was equal in all of them; Peter, however, received a superior power of jurisdiction.

It is no part of our argument to minimize the claims that the canonists put forward on behalf of the pope in the sphere of ecclesiastical jurisdiction during the period 1150-1250. They certainly insisted that the jurisdiction of the Roman see included a right to decide disputed questions concerning matters of faith; and it is certainly true that this claim of the papacy provided an essential basis for later theories of papal infallibility. In Decretist writings, however, the idea of papal jurisdiction was sharply separated from the idea of papal infallibility. So far as the medieval canonists are concerned, there can be no question of maintaining that they took the doctrine of infallibility for granted but never saw any need to articulate it because it had never been disputed. There is no "argument from silence" involved here. The canonists were not silent on this matter. They discussed over and over again the problem of maintaining the unerring faith of the church and invariably came to the conclusion that the pope alone could not provide an adequate guarantee for the stability of that faith. "It would be too dangerous to entrust our faith to the judgement of a single man," one of them wrote.[4] The canonists did

---

[1] E.g., Rufinus *ad* C. 24 q. 1 c. 8, ed. H. Singer (Paderborn, 1902), "Petrus autem omnium sacerdotum figuram tenebat." For additional texts see *Foundations*, p. 35 n. 1. The marginal *glossa ordinaria* to the Bible has "Petrus dicitur in figura Christiani populi a petra Christo ... *super hanc petram*, i.e. super me non super te." See *Biblia sacra cum glossis* (Venice, 1588), gloss *ad* 1 Cor. 1.12.

[2] E.g., Huguccio ad *Dist.* 21 *ante* c. 1, MS Pembroke Coll. 72, fol. 129vb, "(apostoli) pares fuerunt quo ad ordinem, quia quecumque ordines habuit Petrus habuit quilibet aliorum sed Petrus prefuit illis in dignitate prelationis, in administratione, in iurisdictione ...." Additional texts in *Foundations*, p. 33 n. 3.

[3] On this development see M. Van de Kerckhove, "La notion de juridiction dans la doctrine des Décrétistes et des premiers Décrétalistes," *Études franciscaines*, 49 (1937), pp. 420-455.

[4] *Glossa Palatina ad Dist.* 19 c. 9, "... periculosum erat fidem nostram committere arbitrio unius hominis ...." (See *Foundations*, p. 50.)

not argue that an infallible head was necessary to sustain the faith of the church. Rather they maintained that, however much the head might err, divine providence would always prevent the whole church from being led astray.

The canonists were led to adopt this attitude in part by the nature of the source material that formed the foundation of their science. In Gratian's great compendium of canonical texts, drawn from every age of the church's past, they found no assertion that individual popes were infallible but they did find several cases of particular pontiffs who were alleged to have sinned and erred in matters of faith. Also Gratian included in the Decretum a text asserting that the pope's immunity from human judgment did not extend to cases in which he was found straying from the faith.[1] The particular case that attracted most attention from the Decretists concerned Pope Anastasius II (496-498). This Anastasius was a relatively blameless pontiff. He reigned at a time when the churches of Rome and Constantinople were divided by the Acacian schism, which had arisen out of a late variation of the monophysite heresy sponsored by the Greek patriarch, Acacius. Anastasius went so far in trying to reconcile the heretics that, according to his enemies, he became tainted with heresy himself. After the pope's death they recorded in the *Liber Pontificalis* that he had been "struck down by the divine will." Gratian incorporated this passage into the Decretum and it was widely accepted throughout the Middle Ages as historically accurate and canonically authoritative.[2] The medieval canonists knew nothing of Pope Honorius (625-638) who really did blunder in handling the recondite details of the monothelite controversy and whose case gave rise to interminable discussions in the nineteenth century controversies over papal infallibility. In medieval debate Anastasius served as a sort of substitute Honorius. (Dante duly found a place for him in the Inferno.)

Although the medieval Decretists knew of cases of erring popes they also had before them the whole body of texts (genuine and forged) from which the later theory of papal infallibility would be constructed. The decree *Pastor aeternus* of 1870 started out from the primacy promised to Peter at Matt. 16.19 ("I will give you the keys of the Kingdom of Heaven") and then went on to argue that this

---

[1] *Dist.* 40 c. 6.

[2] *Dist.* 19 c. 9. On Anastasius and his medieval reputation see J. J. I. von Döllinger, *Fables Respecting the Popes of the Middle Ages*, trans. A. Plummer (London, 1871).

primacy necessarily included an infallible magisterium by citing Luke 22.32 ("I have prayed for you Peter that your faith shall not fail"). Precisely the same juxtaposition of texts occurred in the Decretum at *Dist.* 21 *ante* c. 1.[1] *Pastor aeternus* presented the formula of Pope Hormisdas—"In the apostolic see the Catholic religion has always been kept undefiled" as evidence that papal infallibility had always been taught by the church. Gratian included the same formula in the Decretum along with other texts asserting that the Roman church had never erred "from the path of apostolic tradition."[2] To the Ultramontane theologians of the nineteenth century it seemed self-evident that a Catholic who accepted these scriptural and canonical texts must also accept the doctrine of papal infallibility. The medieval Decretists showed how a wholly different Catholic ecclesiology could be built on the foundation of these same passages.

The key to the understanding of this Decretist ecclesiology lies in the canonists' conservative, patristically-inspired exegesis of Luke 22.32.[3] Theorists of papal infallibility from the late Middle Ages onward generally assumed that Christ's prayer for Peter was intended to guarantee the unfailing faith of Peter's successors in the papacy. The Decretists knew of no such interpretation. A typical comment is this of Huguccio:

> *That your faith shall not fail* is understood to mean finally and irrecoverably for, although it failed for a time, afterward he was made more faithful. Or in the person of Peter the church is understood, in the faith of Peter the faith of the universal church which has never failed as a whole nor shall fail down to the day of judgement.[4]

For Huguccio and his contemporaries the words of Luke 22.32 did not confer any gift of infallibility on Peter himself, let alone on subsequent pontiffs. They often noted that Peter's faith had indeed "failed for a time," usually referring to his denial of Christ after the

---

[1] *Dist.* 21 *ante* c. 1, "Petrum vero quasi in summum sacerdotem elegit, dum ei prae omnibus et pro omnibus claves regni celorum tribuit et a se petra, Petri sibi nomen imposuit, atque pro eius fide specialiter rogasse testatus est, et ut ceteros confirmaret sibi iniunxit, dicens 'Ego rogavi pro te ....'"

[2] C. 24 q. 1 c. 11, "In sede apostolica extra maculam semper est catholica servata religio." See also c. 9, c. 10, c. 12, c. 14.

[3] On patristic exegesis of Luke 22.32 see J. Langen, *Das Vaticanische Dogma von dem Universal-Episcopat und der Unfehlbarkeit des Papstes*, I (Bonn, 1871), pp. 70-79.

[4] *Summa ad Dist.* 21 *ante* c. 1, MS Pembroke Coll. 72, fol. 129vb, "... intelligitur finaliter et irrecuperabiliter, licet enim ad tempora defecerit tamen factus est postea fidelior, vel tunc in persona petri intelligebatur ecclesia, in fide petri fides universalis ecclesie que numquam in totum deficit vel deficiet usque in diem iuditii ...."

Last Supper. They also sometimes recalled that Peter had erred in his judaizing policy and that Paul had had to rebuke him in this matter.[1] According to their interpretation, Christ did not promise to Peter immunity from error in his leadership of the church but rather the grace of final perseverance in the faith. Even if Luke 22.32 had been applied to Peter's successors in the papacy it could hardly have formed the basis of a theory of papal infallibility so long as it was understood in this sense.

But in fact Huguccio and his contemporaries did not apply the text to Peter's successors. They recognized that two interpretations were possible. Christ's words could be taken to refer to Peter alone or they could be given a wider interpretation. But in the latter case they referred, not to future popes, but to the faith of the universal church. This was the common doctrine of the Decretists. One encounters it over and over again in their works and it was included in the universally accepted *glossa ordinaria* of Johannes Teutonicus.[2]

Moreover, when the Decretists wrote that the universal church, or the faith of the church would not "fail" they were not thinking of "infallibility" in the modern sense but more strictly of indefectibility. Christ's promise to Peter was taken to mean simply that the church would always survive; it meant that the true faith would always live on, at least in some tiny remnant even in an age of mass apostasy. This is brought out more clearly in another comment of Huguccio (on Matt. 16.18):

> *The gates of Hell.* Vices and mortal sin ... shall never prevail so that there are no good persons in the church, whence Christ said to Peter as a symbol of the church "I have prayed for you Peter that your faith shall not fail ..." or "gates of hell" means heresies and schisms ... which likewise shall never prevail against the church so that they totally polute it.[3]

---

[1] Gratian discussed the incident at C. 2 q. 7 *post* c. 39. See G. H. M. Posthumus Meyjes, *De Controverse tussen Petrus en Paulus: Galaten 2:11 in de Historie* ('s-Gravenhage, 1967).

[2] *Gl. ord. ad Dist.* 19 c. 7, C. 24 q. 1 c. 9 (cited below). For texts of the *Glossa Palatina* and *Appar. Ecce vicit leo* see *Foundations*, p. 44, and for *Summa Omnis qui iuste* and *Summa Animal est substantia*, "Pope and Council," p. 206 n. 37.

[3] *Summa ad Dist.* 19 c. 7, MS Pembroke Coll. 72, fol. 128vb, "*Portae inferi*, vitia et peccata mortalia ... hec non prevalent contra ecclesiam sic quod non sint aliqui boni semper in ecclesia, unde in figura ecclesie dixit Christus petro, 'Ego rogavi pro te ...' vel porte inferi dicuntur hereses et schismata ... hec similiter nunquam contra ecclesiam prevalebunt sic ut eam totam polluant." For further texts on the *portae inferi* see F. Gillmann, "Zur scholastischen Auslegung von Mt. 16.18," *Archiv für katholisches Kirchenrecht*, 104 (1924), pp. 41-53.

Similarly Johannes Teutonicus wrote (*ad Dist.* 19 c. 7), "The church cannot be (reduced to) nothing for the Lord prayed for it that it should not fail." Sometimes, in Decretist writing, the doctrine of indefectibility based on Luke 22.32 was associated with the pious belief that the true faith had lived on in Mary alone at the time of the Crucifixion.

> *That your faith shall not fail*, that is the faith of the church which is your faith, for the church has never failed because it existed even at the Lord's death at least in the Blessed Virgin. The church can be small; it cannot be nothing.[1]

According to this interpretation of Luke 22.32 the unfailing faith promised to the church in Christ's words to Peter had survived in only one person at the time of the Passion—and that person was Mary, not Peter.

The canonists' understanding of Luke 22.32 was decisive for their interpretation of the phrase "The Roman church has never erred." Huguccio, we noted, observed that, when Christ prayed for Peter's faith, the apostle stood as a symbol of the church. This idea was inherently ambiguous. It could mean that all the authority Christ conferred on the church was epitomized in Peter and his successors. Some canonists were inclined to develop their thought in this direction when considering the extent of papal jurisdiction. But, in discussing the maintenance of the true faith in the church, the canonists invariably interpreted the idea that Peter "signified" the church in a

---

[1] *Summa Cantabrigiensis*, MS Trinity College, Cambridge 0.5.17, fol. 8va, *ad Dist.* 21 *ante* c. 1, "*Ut non deficiat fides tua*, i.e. ecclesie que est tua fides, enim ecclesia nunquam deficit quia etiam in morte domini fuit, saltem in beata virgine. Ecclesia enim parva esse potest, nulla esse non potest ut 24 q. 1 *pudenda*." For similar comments in the *Appar. Ecce vicit leo* and *Gloss Animal est substantia* see *Foundations*, p. 44 and "Pope and Council," p. 206 n. 37. On the origins of this Marian doctrine see Y. Congar, "Incidence ecclésiologique d'un thème de dévotion mariale," *Mélanges de science religieuse*, 8 (1951), pp. 277-292. Innocent III departed from the normal canonistic exegesis of his age in applying Luke 22.32 to contemporary pontiffs. In his *Sermo IV in consecratione pontificis* he repeated the doctrine that a pope could be deposed if he fell into heresy but said he would not easily believe that God would permit such a case to arise. "Propter causam vero fornicationis ecclesia Romana possit dimittere Romanum pontificem. Fornicationem non dico carnalem, sed spiritualem; quia non est carnale, sed spirituale conjugium, id est propter infidelitatis errorem .... Ego tamen facile non crediderim ut Deus permitteret Romanum pontificem contra fidem errare, pro quo spiritualiter oravit in Petro, 'Ego,' inquit, 'pro te rogavi Petre etc.'" (Migne, *PL* 217, col. 664-665). In *Sermo II* he more conventionally applied Luke 22.32 to the indefectible faith of the apostolic see, "... Domino protestante 'Ego, inquit, pro te rogavi Petre' ... et ideo fides apostolicae sedis in nulla nunquam perturbatione defecit." (*PL* 217, col. 656).

disjunctive sense, that is as implying a distinction between the whole
Christian community, whose faith could never fail, and the person of
an individual pope, who was a mere erring mortal after all and so only
an imperfect symbol of the church. Typically they explained that
phrases describing an unerring "apostolic see" or "Roman church"
could make sense only if they were taken to refer, not to the pope
alone, but to the whole congregation of the faithful. Huguccio
commented on such a text (attributed by Gratian to a pope Eusebius):

> (*The apostolic church*) *has never erred:* There is an objection concerning
> Anastasius. But perhaps this (pope) came earlier. Or perhaps, and this
> is better, he speaks of the faith of the universal church which has never
> erred. For although the Roman pope has sometimes erred this does not
> mean that the Roman church has, which is understood to be not he
> alone but all the faithful, for the church is the aggregate of the faithful;
> if it does not exist at Rome it exists in the regions of Gaul or wherever
> the faithful are. The church can indeed cease to be but this will never
> happen for it was said to Peter, and in the person of Peter to the uni-
> versal church, "that your faith shall not fail."[1]

Elsewhere Huguccio wrote "Wherever there are good faithful
Christians, there is the Roman church."[2] Such views were commonly
expressed by the Decretists. An anonymous French canonist observed
that the unerring "Roman church" was the "universal church" and
an anonymous English one that the church could not err simultaneously "in its whole body."[3] Laurentius wrote, "Although the pope,
who can be judged for heresy, has erred the Roman or Catholic
church which is understood as the congregation of Catholics has not
erred."[4] Similarly Alanus, "Even though the pope erred the faith
endured in the church which is the congregation of Catholics."[5] One

---

[1] *Summa ad* 24 q. 1 c. 9, MS Vat. lat. 2280, fol. 251vb, "*nunquam errasse.* Obicitur
de anastasio, sed forte iste precessit vel forte, quod melius est, loquitur de fide
universalis ecclesie que nunquam defecit licet forte possit deficere. (Licet) enim
papa romanus aliquando erraverit, non ideo ecclesia romana que non solus (papa)
intelligitur set universi fideles, nam ecclesia set aggregatio fidelium ut *de cons. dist.* 1
ecclesia, que (etsi) rome non sit, est tamen in partibus galiganis vel ubique fideles
existunt et ecclesia quidem potest desinere esse set nunquam contiget nam petro et
in persona petri universe ecclesie dictum est 'ut non deficiet fides tua.'" (This
reading is based on MS Vat. lat. 2280 with corrections from the text of MS Bam-
berg 61, printed by Landgraf, art. cit., p. 581.)
[2] For this and other similar expressions in Huguccio see *Foundations*, pp. 41-42.
[3] *Summa Animal est substantia ad* C. 24 q. 1 c. 9; *Summa Omnis qui iuste ad* C. 24 q. 1
c. 9 ("Pope and Council," pp. 214, 213).
[4] *Glossa Palatina ad* C. 24 q. 1 c. 9 (*Foundations*, pp. 43-44).
[5] *Appar. Ius naturale ad* C. 24 q. 1 c. 4, cited by J. A. Watt, "The Early Medieval
Canonists and the Formation of Conciliar Theory," *Irish Theological Quarterly*, 24

Decretist found the proposition that the Roman church could not err
so improbable that he suggested the relevant text might have been
written by an anti-pope. (He fell back, however, on the usual doctrine
that, in such a context the term 'Roman church' had to be taken to
mean the whole body of the faithful.)[1] Finally we may quote a text of
Johannes Teutonicus which brought together the two strands of
thought we have been pursuing, the distinction between the erring
pope and the unerring congregation of the faithful and the interpretation of Luke 22.32 as essentially a guarantee of the indefectibility
of the universal church.

> I ask of what church is it said here that it cannot err? ... It is certain
> that the pope can err as in *Dist*. 19 *Anastasius* and *Dist*. 40 *Si papa*. I
> answer: the congregation of the faithful itself is here called the church
> ... and such a church cannot not be ... for the Lord himself prayed for
> the church, Dist. 21 § 1 v. *"I have prayed for thee ...."*[2]

Evidently the medieval canonists were moving in a climate of thought
very different from that of the nineteenth century Ultramontane
theologians. The canonists believed that popes could err and could
err in their official capacity as supreme pontiffs (as in the case of
Anastasius). Of course modern theology does not deny that a pope
can err. But when Catholic theologians have to take note of errors
promulgated by popes as heads of the church they discriminate
between official infallible pronouncements and official non-infallible
pronouncements. The medieval canonists knew nothing of such
distinctions. They were content to distinguish between the pope
who could err—and err in any of his pronouncements so far as they
knew—and the universal church whose faith could never fail. Ideas

---

(1957), pp. 13-31 at p. 30, "Licet erraverit papa, tamen in fidem permansit ecclesia
que est catholica collectio."

[1] MS Wolfenbüttel, Helmst. 33, gloss *ad* C. 24 q. 1 c. 9, *"Errasse* ... auctor huius
capituli fuit antipapa anathasii (i.e. anastasii) vel apostolica ecclesia non dicitur
tantum papa sed papa et cardinales, vel dicitur ecclesia Christi congregatio fidelium ... quare ecclesia nunquam in universo corpore errat, licet quandoque in aliqua persona erret. Argumentum ut non dicitur ab ecclesia factum quod ab ipsa
universitate non fit ...." This text was reprinted in *Foundations*, p. 43 from the
original transcription by J. F. v. Schulte, "Die Glosse zur Dekret Gratians,"
Denkschriften der kaiserlichen Akademie der Wissenschaften (Phil.-Hist. Kl.), 21 (Wien,
1872), p. 11.

[2] *Gl. ord. ad* C. 24 q. 1 c. 9, "Quaero de qua ecclesia hic dicitur quod hic dicitur,
quod non possit errare ... certum est quod papa errare potest, 19 *dist. Anastasius*,
40 *dist. si papa*. Respondeo, ipsa congregatio fidelium hic dicitur ecclesia ut *de
consec. dist.* 1, *ecclesia* et talis ecclesia non potest non esse ... nam ipse dominus orat
pro ecclesia, 21 *dist.* § 1, *vers*. 'Ego pro te ....'"

akin to the modern doctrine of papal infallibility simply never occurred to them.

(ii) *Papal Magisterium and the "Key of Knowledge"*

In modern theology the idea of the pope's possessing a supreme magisterium, a supreme teaching authority, is sometimes associated with a doctrine asserting that one of the keys conferred on Peter was a "Key of knowledge." Thus Manning wrote, in his *Pastoral Letter* of 1869, "the supreme and ultimate power, both in jurisdiction and in faith, or the *clavis jurisdictionis* and the *clavis scientiae* was committed first and for ever to Peter, and in him... to his successors."[1] Similarly, Bishop Gasser, speaking on behalf of the deputation *De fide* at Vatican Council I, referred to "the supreme magisterium of the pontiff which is a part of his jurisdiction, for the jurisdiction of the pontiff is discharged with two keys, a key of knowledge and a key of power."[2] The idea that the keys received by Peter conferred on him a power to teach with certain truth as well as a power to rule with legitimate authority was indeed of the essence of the ecclesiology that dominated Vatican Council I. Much earlier, the doctrine that the pope possessed a key of knowledge had played a significant role in the development of the idea of papal infallibility during the late medieval period. The doctrine had no such connotation, however, in the earlier canonical tradition of the church. This is another case where the medieval Decretists started out from the same scriptural and patristic texts as later theologians but derived quite different conclusions from them. The terminology used by Gasser, "a key of knowledge and a key of power", is very ancient. But it was not until the fourteenth century that such language began to be associated with a doctrine of papal infallibility.

In canonistic works—and, indeed, in all medieval writing on the structure of the church—a persistent tension arose from the fact that the same term, "the keys of the kingdom of heaven," was used to designate both the supreme authority that inhered in the papacy and the general ability to remit sins that was diffused throughout the

---

[1] H. E. Manning, *The Oecumenical Council and the Infallibility of the Roman Pontiff* (London, 1869), p. 147. See also p. 90.

[2] J.-P. Torrell, *La théologie de l'épiscopat au premier concile du Vatican* (Paris, 1961), p. 176. The question whether "magisterium" is contained in "jurisdiction" or is a separate kind of authority has been discussed by modern theologians. Torrell *(loc. cit.)* gives references on this.

whole Catholic priesthood. So far as "power" was concerned the canonists insisted that the promise of the keys to Peter "before and on behalf of" the other apostles conferred on him a unique jurisdiction as head of the church. An obvious possibility existed of developing the idea of "knowledge" in the same way. It might have been claimed that just as the key of power conferred a supreme ruling authority on the pope so too the key of knowledge conferred a supreme teaching authority on him. In fact, however, the medieval canonists never propounded any such interpretation.

The phrase *clavis scientiae* is Scriptural. It occurs at Luke 11.52 where Christ said, "Woe to you lawyers... you have taken away the key of knowledge." Given their usual methods of biblical exegesis it was natural for medieval scholars to relate this application of the word "key" by Christ with his use of the same word in the promise to Peter. "I will give you the keys of the kingdom of Heaven." The association between the two passages was transmitted to theologians of the scholastic period by Bede, who wrote, in his commentary on St. Matthew, that the keys received by Peter consisted of a *clavis scientiae* and a *clavis potestatis*. Bede's terminology was repeated by Hrabanus Maurus and later incorporated into both Peter Lombard's *Sentences* and Gratian's *Decretum*. Thus, by the middle years of the twelfth century, the idea that Peter received from Christ two keys, one of knowledge, one of power, was firmly established in the mainstreams of medieval theology and of medieval canon law.[1]

Gratian introduced his discussion of the keys of knowledge and power at *Dist.* 20 of the Decretum. His argument here dealt with the relationship between patristic writings and papal legislation. The question under discussion was whether the theological expositions of revered church fathers like Jerome and Augustine possessed as much canonical authority as the decretals of a pope. Gratian replied:

---

[1] Bede, *In Matthaei evangelium expositio*, Migne *PL* 92, col. 79, "*Et tibi dabo claves regni coelorum*. id est discernendi scientiam potentiamque ...." The words were repeated in Bede's *Homilia in festo SS Petri et Pauli*, *PL* 94, col. 222. See also Hrabanus Maurus, *Commentariorum in Matthaeum libri octo*, *PL* 107, col. 992; Peter Lombard, *Sententiarum libri quatuor*, *PL* 192, col. 885; Gratian, *Dist.* 20 *ante* c. 1. The fourth century St. Maximus suggested that Peter received a key of power, Paul a key of knowledge (*PL* 57, col. 403-404). This interpretation seems to have been unknown in the Middle Ages. For the medieval doctrine of the power of the keys see M. Van de Kerckhove, art. cit.; P. Anciaux, *La théologie du sacrement de pénitence au XIIe siècle* (Louvain-Gembloux, 1949); L. Hödl, *Die Geschichte der scholastischen Literatur und der Theologie der Schlüsselgewalt*, I (Münster-in-Westf., 1960).

It is one thing to settle legal cases, another to expound the Scriptures diligently. In settling legal affairs not only knowledge is required but power also. Therefore, when Christ was about to say to Peter "Whatsoever you shall bind on earth it shall be bound in Heaven" he first gave to him the keys of the kingdom of Heaven, conferring in one the knowledge to discern between leper and leper (i.e. between sinner and sinner) and, in the other, power to expel some from the church and receive others....

It is clear that the expositors of divine Scripture, even if they excell the pontiffs in knowledge have not attained to the apex of their dignity. Therefore, in expositions of sacred Scripture they are to be preferred to the pontiffs; in deciding cases they deserve to be placed after them.[1]

Gratian's meaning seems reasonably straightforward. He was trying to discriminate between theological interpretations and judicial decisions. Thus an exegete, seeking to understand all the theological resonances of St. Paul's words, "The husband is the head of the wife as Christ is head of the church," would do well to turn to the writings of the Fathers. A judge, deciding a marriage case, would need to consult the appropriate decretals and canons.

However, as several of the Decretists realised, the distinction between theology and law could not be drawn so clearly as Gratian suggested in this text. Many of the pope's judicial decisions could have doctrinal implications, most obviously in cases of heresy. The canonists often pointed out that, where a definitive judgment concerning an article of faith was involved, the pope's decision took precedence over the opinion of a church Father. In this connection the canonists often distinguished between the pope's capacity as a private doctor and his official decisions as pope. As one of them explained, if the pope and St. Augustine separately wrote books of exposition, each in his own room, we should certainly prefer Augustine's; but if the pope pronounced definitively concerning a matter of faith the papal decision was binding.[2] Huguccio was of the same opinion but struck a note of caution by observing that a pope ought not to depart from the opinions of the Fathers in his judgments. He added an unusual variation on the old formula, *in partem sollici-*

---

[1] *Dist.* 20 *ante* c. 1.

[2] *The Summa Parisiensis on the Decretum Gratiani,* ed. T. P. McLaughlin (Toronto, 1952), p. 20, "Potest tamen dici quod in obscura et maxime circa articulos fidei quod in diffinitione dominus papa interpretaretur, maioris esset auctoritatis expositione Aug. Sed si alias in camera librum expositionis suae componat dominus papa, componat et Augustinus, praecellit et Augustini."

tudinis... in plenitudinem potestatis. Where matters of faith were concerned, he wrote, the popes were called to a "share of the solicitude"
not to a "plenitude of power."[1]

Gratian's *Dist.* 20—his text on the key of knowledge and the key of
power—became a *locus classicus* for the exposition of the common
doctrine that the pope's supreme jurisdiction included the right to
pronounce judgment in disputes concerning the faith.[2] But, since the
canonists all believed that a pope might err in his judgments, they
naturally did not derive from Peter's possession of a key of knowledge
any doctrine that an unerring teaching authority inhered in the
papacy. Gratian himself had indicated plainly enough that it was the
key of power, not the key of knowledge, that gave a special weight to
the pope's pronouncements. Hence the authority that the canonists
attributed to the pope in matters of faith was the authority of a supreme
judge, not that of an infallible teacher. Huguccio considered the case
of a pope who was a learned theologian. If he contradicted another
theologian his status as pope did not lend any additional weight to the
views he expressed as a teacher; but all were bound to hold what he
laid down as pope *in the decision of cases.*[3] If the pope erred in deciding a
case involving a matter of faith the canonists were confident that the
error would be corrected by the pope himself or by a successor (as in
the case of Anastasius) before the whole church had been led astray.

None of the Decretists based any theory of papal magisterium—let
alone an infallible magisterium—on Gratian's text concerning the key
of knowledge. Indeed they do not seem to have known of any
public magisterium conferred by Christ in the power of the keys.
The only magisterium the canonists recognized was the teaching of

---

[1] *Summa ad Dist.* 20 *ante* c. 1, MS Pembroke Coll. 72, fol. 129rb, "*Preponuntur,*
adeo etiam quod summis pontificibus non licet recedere ab eorum expositionibus
... sunt enim huiusmodi vocati in partem sollicitudinis, non in plenitudinem potestatis ...."

[2] We have already considered the comment of Alanus which was incorporated
into the *Rosarium* at this point (above, p. 24 n.1). Other works which discussed the
pope's role as judge in matters of faith at *Dist.* 20 were *Summa Prima primi, Summa
Antiquitate et tempore, Summa Et est sciendum, Summa Animal est substantia* ("Pope
and Council," pp. 199 n. 9, 204 n. 28). *Appar. Ecce vicit leo, Glossa Palatina* (Munier,
op. cit., pp. 190, 199).

[3] Huguccio, *Summa ad Dist.* 20, "Si dixerint autem adversa, utrique credendum
est. Si contraria, tenere iuberis quae ut papa dixit, sc. in decisione causarum. In his
vero quae ut expositor dixit videtur non magis esse credendum ei quia papa ...."
(Munier, *op. cit.,* p. 199). See also the anonymous gloss in MS Caius College,
Cambridge 676, fol. 10vb, "Unde peritissimi nisi habeant potestatem causas deci-
dere non possunt. Questio etiam fidei soli petro reservatur." (Watt, *art. cit.,* p. 28)

private doctors whose authority depended on the intrinsic value of their works. The author of the *Summa Elegantius* summed up the prevailing view thus, "There are three kinds of interpretation, princely, judicial and magisterial. The first is binding and universal, the second binding but not universal, the third neither."[1] When the canonists referred to a magisterial pronouncement of the pope they meant precisely that he was speaking as a private doctor, not as supreme pontiff.[2]

All this is not to say that the canonists never discussed the *clavis scientiae*. On the contrary, one finds many intricate arguments about this "key" in their glosses on *Dist.* 20. The point is that they never considered the key of knowledge in connection with the public authority of the papacy; their discussions concerning it always referred to the common, sacerdotal power of the keys, the power of all priests to bind and loose in the sacrament of penance. In this sphere a major difficulty had been posed by Peter Lombard. How could all priests possess a "key of knowledge," he asked, when many of them were shamefully ignorant before their ordination and remained so afterward. Peter concluded that not all priests, but only learned ones, were endowed with a *clavis scientiae*; and this solution was at first favored by theologians and canonists alike.[3] But it gave rise to a whole series of teasing problems. Did not every man possess some shred of *scientia* which could be turned into a key if he received ordination? And if an ignorant priest acquired *scientia* after his ordination did his new-found knowledge constitute a key? And how could *scientia* really be a "key" when some men possessed knowledge but no "keys" while others possessed the "keys" but no knowledge?

Peter Lombard's doctrine that a key of knowledge, conferred by Christ on the apostles, descended in a haphazard fashion to some priests but not to others, soon came to be regarded as unsatisfactory and, around 1200, the canonists and theologians began to shape alternative theories concerning the meaning of the word "keys" as used at Matt. 16.19. The canonists found it possible to dispense with the "key of knowledge" altogether. Gandulphus argued that the two

---

[1] *Summa Elegantius, ed. cit.,* p. 35, "Est enim interpretatio triplex: principalis, iudicialis, magistralis. Prima necessaria et universalis, secunda necessaria nec universalis, tertia neutra ...."

[2] See e.g., *Gl. ord. ad* C. 31 q. 3 c. 1 s.v. *Deprehensi*, "... non papaliter sed magistraliter ...."

[3] On Peter Lombard's doctrine and the problems arising out of it see Anciaux, *op. cit.,* pp. 328-335; Hödl, *op. cit.,* pp. 187-196.

keys were simply the power of binding and the power of loosing, while Huguccio asserted that there was only one key. "Truly there is only one sacerdotal key, the power of binding and loosing... but it is called two because of its two-fold effect, to bind and to loose." In the first years of the thirteenth century the author of the Apparatus, *Ecce vicit leo*, wrote that Huguccio's solution would be "beautiful if it were true" but himself felt bound to adhere to the doctrine of a plurality of keys. Later canonists evidently found Huguccio's argument too beautiful to resist. The author of the *Glossa Palatina* quoted his opinion and added, "I believe the key to be jurisdiction."[1] Johannes Teutonicus similarly concluded, "If you ask what the sacerdotal key really is, I say it is the sacerdotal power by which he binds and looses."[2] This doctrine of one key which was identified with the priestly jurisdiction exercised in the act of binding and loosing was adopted by Raymond de Pennaforte in his very influential *Summa de Penitentia* and, by the middle of the thirteenth century, it had come to be generally accepted among the canonists.[3]

Meanwhile theological speculation had taken a different path. The theologians were unwilling to abandon the text of Peter Lombard (together with the authority of Bede and Hrabanus Maurus that lay behind it) which asserted that a key of knowledge really existed. But they found unsatisfactory Peter Lombard's personal doctrine that only some priests possessed this key. Another solution was suggested by Radulphus Argentinus. He distinguished between the personal qualities of a priest and the office he held, arguing that all priests received the *clavis scientiae* and with it the "office of discerning" even though, regrettably, many of them were not discreet enough to discharge the office adequately. In the same way a man lacking in prudence could receive the office of kingship by accepting a scepter even though he was not really fit to be a king. This solution was repeated by Prevostinus who found it "probable enough." Stephen Langton rejected the argument and preferred another suggestion of Prevostinus, that a priest who possessed only scanty knowledge received just a little *clavis scientiae*, a *claviculam*.[4]

---

[1] For the views of Gandulphus, Huguccio, *Glossa Palatina* see Anciaux, *op. cit.*, pp. 544-549. For the *Appar. Ecce vicit leo* see *Foundations*, p. 32 n. 2.

[2] *Gl. ord. ad Dist.* 20 *ante* c. 1.

[3] *Summa de Penitentia*, 3.34 § 4, cited by Van de Kerckhove, *art. cit.*, p. 445, "... Alii autem dicunt et credo verius, quod non est nisi una clavis, que quidem est potestas seu iurisdictio ...."

[4] Anciaux, *op. cit.*, pp. 559, 562, 566. Hödl, *op. cit.*, pp. 208, 284, 351.

Although this view was quite widely accepted it was perhaps the most unsatisfactory of all the solutions put forward, and from the mid-thirteenth century onward the theologians came more and more to adopt the line of argument suggested by Radulphus. The doctrine most commonly accepted by the middle of the century was stated very clearly by St. Bonaventure in his commentary on the Sentences. The term *clavis scientiae*, he explained, did not refer to a *habitus*, a quality of mind, but to an office. Any act of judging involved two stages, first an enquiry into the merits of the case and then the promulgation of a decision. Hence two kinds of authority were required, an authority to investigate and an authority to pronounce sentence. These two authorities were conferred by the *clavis scientiae* and the *clavis potestatis* respectively. All priests received both keys regardless of their personal worthiness or unworthiness.[1] One finds essentially the same doctrine in Thomas Aquinas and in other contemporary theologians.

Thus, by the middle years of the thirteenth century, two dominant theories had emerged. Most canonists held that no *clavis scientiae* was included in the keys conferred by Christ on the church. Most theologians held that all priests received a *clavis scientiae* but that it did not confer any particular gifts of knowledge or insight on the recipients. No one had suggested that the term *clavis scientiae* could refer to a public power inhering in the papacy which conferred an unerring teaching authority on the popes.

3. INFALLIBILITY AND SOVEREIGNTY

(i) *Pope and General Council*

The relationship between pope and general council, considered in all its complexity, is a topic that belongs properly to a constitutional history of the church. In that connection, the canonists' views on the problem have received ample attention in modern scholarship. However, the Decretists' teachings concerning the authority of a general council in matters of faith also exercised some influence on the development of the doctrine of papal infallibility in the later Middle Ages. We shall present therefore a brief summary of their principal teachings in order to make the later developments of thought more intelligible.

---

[1] *In librum quartum sententiarum*, D. 18 p. 1 art. 3 q. 1 in *Opera omnia* (Quaracchi, 1882-1902), IV, p. 479, "... scientia non est clavis secundum quod dicit habitum, sed in quantum dicit auctoritatem sive officium discernendi ... et hanc tenent communiter doctores ...."

Decretist discussion centered principally around two texts of the Decretum. At *Dist.* 15 c. 2 a letter of Pope Gregory I proclaimed that the first four general councils were to be revered "like the four gospels" because they were "established by universal consent" (or "by a universal consensus" we might say). At C.25 q. 1 *post* c.16 Gratian expressed his own view that "The holy Roman church imparts authority to the sacred canons but is not bound by them."[1] As soon as extensive commentaries on the Decretum began to be written, around 1160, it became clear to the canonists that Gratian's remark was an oversimplification. Obviously the Trinitarian definitions of Nicea or the Christological definitions of Chalcedon could not be changed at the whim of a pope. We have observed that, in the eyes of the canonists, the pope was not bound by any non-Scriptural Tradition. But they did not conceive of the definitions of general councils as a source of revelation independent of Scripture. The dogmatic decrees of the councils were immutable because they were rooted in Scriptural truth. But the early general councils had also enacted many statutes concerning ecclesiastical discipline which had little relevance for the church of the twelfth century. The Decretists therefore very commonly argued that a pope could change the merely disciplinary decrees of general councils but was absolutely bound by their fundamental pronouncements concerning the truths of faith.[2] From this, several of them drew the explicit conclusion that, where matters of faith were concerned, a general council possessed an authority intrinsically superior to that of an individual pope. This view was transmitted to the later Middle Ages by Johannes Teutonicus in a very influential text of the *glossa ordinaria*.

---

[1] *Dist.* 15 c. 2, "Sicut sancti evangelii quatuor libros, sic quatuor concilia suscipere et venerari me fateor ... dum universali sunt consensu constituta se et non illa destruit, quisquis presumit aut absolvere quos religant, aut ligare quos absolvunt." C. 25 q. 1 *post* c. 16, "Sacrosancta romana ecclesia ius et auctoritatem sacris canonibus impertitur, sed non eis alligatur."

[2] The formula most widely adopted asserted that the pope was bound by statutes of general councils in matters concerning "articles of faith and the general state of the church." Numerous texts illustrating this common opinion of the canonists are presented in *Foundations*, pp. 49-53, "Pope and Council," pp. 210-212, and in S. Kuttner, *art. cit.* For further discussion see J. H. Hackett, "State of the Church: A Concept of the Medieval Canonists," *The Jurist*, 23 (1963), pp. 259-290 and, for a detailed examination of canonistic terminology, G. Post, "Copyists' Errors and the Problem of Papal Dispensations *contra statutum generale ecclesiae* or *contra statum generalem ecclesiae*," *Studia Gratiana*, 9 (1966), pp. 359-405.

It seems that the pope is bound to require a council of bishops, which is true where a matter of faith is concerned, and then a council is greater than a pope, 15 *dist. Sicut*.[1]

Johannes' concluding reference was to the text of Gregory I asserting that the four councils were to be revered "like the four Gospels." The canonists never deduced from Gregory's words *Sicut sancti Evangelii* that the councils were formally equal to the Gospels in authority. (In their lists of sources they always ranked general councils after sacred Scripture.) Nor did they ask explicitly whether general councils were "infallible." The word hardly existed in their technical vocabulary. But they never envisaged the possibility that the councils could have erred in faith and they certainly regarded the canons of a council, supported by the consensus of the church, as a more certain guide to the truths of faith than the pronouncements of an individual pope.

Such doctrines were eventually to prove important for conciliarist theories of church government. But, down to the end of the twelfth century, the Decretists' views concerning the nature and authority of a general council were significantly different from those held by late medieval conciliarists. For one thing the canonists assumed that any legitimate general council had to be summoned by the apostolic see and presided over by the pope or his legates.[2] Hence, when they used phrases like "A council is greater than a pope," they normally meant only that Pope-and-bishops together possessed a greater authority than the pope acting alone. Still more important, when they affirmed the "immutable" authority of general councils in matters of faith, they never seem to have had in mind the church assemblies of their own day or similar assemblies that might meet in the future. They were thinking rather of the ancient councils specifically mentioned in Gratian's texts as possessing pre-eminent authority. The canonists knew eight such general councils (which Gratian listed at *Dist*. 16 c.8). Among these they assigned a special eminence to the first four, those that Gregory the Great compared to the four Gospels—the councils of Nicea, Constantinople, Ephesus and Chalcedon.

---

[1] *Gl. ord. ad Dist*. 19 c. 9, s.v. *Concilio*, "Videtur ergo quod papa tenetur requirere concilium episcoporum, quod verum est ubi de fide agitur, et tunc synodus maior est Papa, 15 *dist. sicut* ...."

[2] *Dist*. 17 *ante* c. 1, "Auctoritas vero congregandorum conciliorum penes apostolicam sedem est."

> Among universal councils there are eight outstanding ones and, of
> these, four have superlative authority ... these the holy Roman church
> cannot change or mutilate by one iota.[1]

It simply never occurred to any of the Decretists to regard the two
twelfth century assemblies that are nowadays commonly called
general councils as equal in authority to the great synods of the past.
Some of them explicitly mentioned that it was the very antiquity of
the councils of the early church which gave them their special authority. For Rufinus the canons that had to be held inviolate were "statutes
of the ancient and venerable Fathers."[2] The author of the *Summa
Elegantius* taught that the authority of the first eight councils was
"more potent because more ancient."[3] In this way of thinking the
"universal consensus" that lent a special force to the definitions of the
early councils was not simply the consent of a specific group of
prelates at a particular time and place; it was rather the continuing
assent of the whole church over a long period of centuries.

In the years around 1200 this attitude began to change. The shift of
emphasis that is discernible in the Decretists' glosses at this time was
highly technical but also highly important for the future. The essential change was that the canonists began to apply specific principles of corporation law to the interpretation of the old texts on the
authority of general councils. They commonly cited the Roman law
dictum "What touches all is to be approved by all" in order to prove
that all faithful Christians were to be represented at Councils where
matters of faith would be discussed.[4] A few authors, commenting on

---

[1] *Summa Elegantius, ed. cit.*, p. 15, "Inter uniuersalia vero concilia viii. premi-
nentem et horum iiii. superlatiuam habent auctoritatem .... Sunt autem hec: Cal-
cedonense, Nicenum, Constantinopolitanum, Ephesinum primum. Que nullo dis-
pensationis colore uel mutare uel mutilare nec ad unum iota sancta Romana ecclesia
preualet."

[2] *Die Summa Decretorum des Magister Rufinus*, ed. H. Singer (Paderborn, 1902), p.
13.

[3] *Ed. cit.*, p. 40.

[4] *Dist.* 96 c. 4, "Ubinam legistis Imperatores ... synodalibus conuentibus inter-
fuisse, nisi forsitan in quibus de fide tractatum est, quae universalis est, quae omnium communis est ...." On this text Johannes Teutonicus commented, "Arg.
quod omnes tangit ab omnibus debere tractari et approbari, *Codex, De auctoritate
praestan* ...." The *Glossa Palatina* and Huguccio have the same comment. For medieval applications of the *quod omnes tangit* principle see O. Giacchio, "La Regola
'Quod omnes tangit' nel diritto canonico," *Jus. Rivista di scienze giuridiche*, New
Series, 3 (1952), pp. 77-100; Y. Congar, "Quod omnes tangit, ab omnibus tractari
et approbari debet," *Revue historique de droit français et étranger*, 36 (1958), pp. 210-
259; G. Post, "A Romano-canonical Maxim, *Quod omnes tangit* in Bracton," in
Studies in Medieval Legal Thought (Princeton, 1964), pp. 163-238.

the inerrancy which they attributed to the universal church, added to the usual doctrine of indefectibility a suggestion that this quality of inerrancy inhered in the decisions of the whole church acting as a corporate body.[1] Similarly, Huguccio and Alanus took the "universal consent" mentioned in Gregory the Great's text as being analogous to the consent of a corporation which was binding on all its members.[2] Such usages could (and would) lead to a new conception of the general council's authority. Implicitly, the canonists were substituting for the consensus of the ages the consent of a corporation, a consent expressed in a single definitive act that was at once binding on all the members.

None of the Decretists undertook a thorough exploration of all the implications of this position and certainly none of them constructed a systematic theory of conciliarism as an ideal system of church government. The texts of Gratian's Decretum reflected two traditions of Catholic ecclesiology, both far more ancient than the Decretum itself. One emphasized the unique authority of the head, the other the unfailing corporate life of the Christian community. The Decretists did not achieve a harmonious synthesis of the two traditions on the practical level of church government—perhaps the Catholic church has never succeeded in doing so—and in later centuries their texts were used to support both extreme papalist and extreme conciliarist positions.

So far as the authority of a general council was concerned, the Decretists, for the most part, left only hints for later conciliarist thinkers to follow up. But on one important point involving the pope, the council, and the defense of the true faith they wrote in intricate detail. This was the problem of deposing a heretical pope. Here the Decretists anticipated virtually every twist and turn of the later conciliarist (and anti-conciliarist) arguments. They all acknowledged that a pope could err in faith and they all agreed that a pope who became an obdurate heretic had to be somehow deposed from his

---

[1] *Glossa Palatina*, "Arg. ut non dicatur ab ecclesia factum quod ab ipsa universitate non factum, *ff de reg. iur., aliud* § 1 ... sed licet papa erraverit ... non tamen ecclesia romana sive apostolica erraverit quae collatio catholicorum intelligitur." (*Foundations*, p. 46). Similarly *Summa Omnis qui iuste*, "Nota hic arg. non intelligi fieri quod a tota universitate non fit." ("Pope and Council," p. 213).

[2] Huguccio, "*Universali consensu* ... arg. pro universitate et quod nulli a canonico et communi consensu sui capituli vel collegii vel civitatis recedere (licet) ...." (*Foundations*, p. 48 n. 2.) Similarly Alanus, "*Universali*, arg. non licere canonico suo dissentire capitulo ...." ("Pope and Council," p. 212.)

office. But no two of them seem to have agreed on precisely how the deposition was to be brought about. Among all their delicately nuanced positions we can discern three main lines of argument.[1] Some Decretists refused to admit that any juridical authority in the church could be superior to that of the Roman pontiff. Others found it necessary to admit that a council, understood as pope and bishops acting together in concert, wielded a jurisdiction superior to that of a pope acting alone. The third, most radical, point of view attributed a superior authority to the members of a council separated from the pope and acting against him. The outstanding exponent of the first point of view was Huguccio. The other two positions can both be illustrated from the work of his younger contemporary, Alanus. All three positions were presented in scattered contexts of Johannes Teutonicus' *glossa ordinaria*.

In spite of Huguccio's frequent assertions that individual popes could err and that only the universal church was unfailing in faith he never conceded that any organ of church government was competent to judge the Roman pontiff. His argument concerning a heretical pope was an elaborate development of one central thesis—that a pope who fell into heresy became "less than any Catholic." A man could not be at once a heretic and the head of the Christian church. If a pope fell into heresy therefore he ipso facto ceased to be pope. When such a man was removed from the papal throne there was no need to invoke a judicial authority superior to the papal authority since the person deposed was no longer a pope. Huguccio went on to specify the circumstances in which such automatic selfdegradation could be presumed. It was necessary that the pope publicly proclaim his heresy so that there was no need for a judge to determine the facts of the case. It was also necessary that the pope's heresy should violate some already defined article of faith so that there was no need for any tribunal to pronounce on the orthodoxy of the pope's teaching.[2] Huguccio even declared that, if a dispute arose over some novel theological issue, the opinion of the pope as supreme judge had to be accepted even if all the other prelates of the church stood opposed to it.[3]

---

[1] The various "nuanced positions" are explored in some detail in *Foundations*, pp. 57-67 and "Pope and Council," pp. 203-210, 214-218. For further discussion see H. Zimmermann, *Papstabsetzungen des Mittelalters* (Graz, 1968).

[2] Huguccio's lengthy gloss on *Dist.* 40 c. 6, setting out these arguments is printed in J. F. v. Schulte, *Die Stellung der Concilien, Päpste und Bischöfe* (Prague, 1871), pp. 262-264 and in *Foundations*, pp. 248-250.

[3] For Huguccio's teaching on this point see *Foundations*, p. 55; "Pope and Coun-

Huguccio's argument was internally consistent but it raised as many difficulties as it solved. Above all, it offered no solution to the important problem of who was legally empowered to take action against a heretical "pope." If such a man was really "less than any Catholic" it would seem that any Catholic prince could claim justification for deposing, without legal process, any pontiff whom he had decided to regard as a heretic. In the order of practical politics Huguccio's argument could lead on to anarchy. (William of Ockham would demonstrate this with enthusiasm in the controversies of the early fourteenth century.) Moreover, some canonists pointed out that a pope ought not to be presumed guilty of heresy until he had been formally convicted of the crime. And this implied the need for a superior authority that could pass judgment on a man presumed to be pope before his guilt was established.

The canonists commonly turned to the general council when seeking such a superior authority. In its more moderate form their argument asserted simply that a pope could be bound by decisions of past councils. Thus Alanus wrote:

> It is argued that in a matter of faith a council is greater than a pope ... and this is to be held firmly. It is for this reason that a council can judge and condemn him, and so it happens that he incurs the excommunication decreed for heresy in a council, which would not be the case if the pope was greater than the council in such a matter or equal to it.[1]

In this passage Alanus was still thinking of a council as pope and bishops together and was pointing out that such an assembly could enact judicial sentences that would be binding on future popes. But this still did not provide a completely satisfactory solution to the problem of a heretical pontiff. In real life it was most improbable that a pope would publicly renounce a dogmatic definition solemnly promulgated by a preceding general council. Any dispute involving

---

cil," p. 206; J. A. Watt, *art. cit.*, pp. 29-30. His position was not really contradictory to his clearly expressed view that a pope could err in his decisions. Even in modern theology one would not expect an infallible decision to emerge from a situation in which the pope was at loggerheads with the rest of the church.

[1] *Gloss ad Dist.* 19 c. 9, "Argumentum quod in questione fidei maior est sinodus quam papa, ar. supra di. xv *Sicut*, et di xvi *Sancta*, quod firmiter est tenendum. Unde accidit ex tali causa quod sinodus potest ipsum iudicare et dampnare, unde accidit quod incidit in excommunicationem latam super heresi in sinodo ut hic, quod non accideret si papa in hoc casu maior esset synodo vel equalis." (J. A. Watt, *art. cit.*, p. 30). On the canonical doctrine of excommunication *latae sententiae* see P. Huizing, "The Earliest Development of Excommunication *latae sententiae* by Gratian and the Earliest Decretists," *Studia Gratiana*, 3 (1955), pp. 278-320.

the pope's judgment on a matter of faith would almost certainly involve a point that had not previously been decided so authoritatively. In such a case—on the basis of the arguments that we have so far considered—the whole church might be bound to acknowledge as its head a man who was widely regarded as a heretic.

Alanus therefore carried his argument one step further. If a dispute arose between the pope and members of a council or between pope and cardinals on a matter of faith then, according to Alanus, the decision of the council fathers or the cardinals was to be preferred to that of the pope. He emphasized that this applied only to decisions concerning the faith. "In all other judicial controversies I prefer the sentence of the pope to the sentences of all others."[1] (It will be noted that, in typical canonistic fashion, Alanus regarded a dispute over the faith as a form of "judicial controversy" in which the pope pronounced sentence as a judge.) Given that cardinals or bishops possessed a superior jurisdiction to the pope's in this one sphere of church doctrine it was possible to argue that they could condemn a pope for any aberration from the true faith without the need to distinguish between a heresy previously condemned and a novel one. This was the conclusion that Alanus reached:

> It is true that for the one crime of heresy a pope can be judged even against his own will. It is so in this crime because, in matters that pertain to the faith, he is less than the college of cardinals or a general council of bishops.[2]

This argument of Alanus was rather radical for the early thirteenth century and it closely anticipates the more extreme conciliar theories of the later Middle Ages.

After the appearance of Johannes Teutonicus' *glossa ordinaria* the canonists concentrated their attention principally on interpreting the new collections of papal decretals promulgated in 1215 (*Compilatio quarta*), 1224 (*Compilatio quinta*) and 1234 (*Gregoriana*). These works

---

[1] *Gloss ad* C. 9 q. 3 c. 17, "Sed queritur, cum ipse concilio vel cardinalibus questionem fidei ventilat et contingit papam aliam habere sententiam, aliam cardinales, cuius sententia preualebit? Respondeo, concilii vel cardinalium si omnes in opinione concordent. Immo etiam si maior pars .... In aliis autem controversiis iudicialibus omnibus pape sententiam omnium aliorum sententiis prefero." (J. A. Watt, *art. cit.*, p. 31).

[2] *Gloss ad Dist.* 40 c. 6, "Est ergo verum quod de sola heresi invitus potest papa iudicari, ut hic dicitur, sed hoc ideo in hoc crimine, quia circa ea que ad fidem pertinent minor est collegio cardinalium, vel concilio generali episcoporum."

contained far fewer texts referring to the possible role of a general council in church government than the Decretum. Accordingly, the Decretalists on the whole presented a more simple, less qualified doctrine of papal sovereignty than the Decretists. But they never abandoned the view that a pope might err in faith and that an erring pope could be deposed. Later defenders of the doctrine of papal infallibility argued that God could not possibly impose on all Catholics an obligation to obey the pope and then permit the pope to err in faith. The canonists argued that, since self-evidently a pope could err, the obligation to obey could not be unconditional.

(ii) *Irreformable ex sese?*

Since the canonists did not adhere to a doctrine of papal infallibility one would expect the parallel doctrine of irreformability to be also lacking in their works. This is in fact the case. To have developed such a doctrine would have been contrary to their juridical theory of sovereignty with its central principle—*par in parem non habet imperium*. The canonists did of course believe that certain truths of faith were irreformable; but these were truths derived from Scripture and from the interpretations of Scripture presented in canons of general councils, not from the pronouncements of individual pontiffs.

On this whole question, however, the canonists expressed themselves with an ambiguity that gave rise to frequent misunderstandings in the later Middle Ages. The first systematic theories of papal infallibility propounded in the fourteenth century took as their starting point an assertion that the dogmatic decrees of one pope were binding on all his successors. The argument often moved from irreformability to infallibility rather than vice-versa. And the proponents of this argument claimed to prove its validity primarily from the texts of the Decretum and its *glossa ordinaria*. They relied principally on three sections of Gratian's work. C. 25 q.l presented a series of texts purporting to prove that the pope was bound by existing law. *Dist.* 19 mentioned the case of the erring pope Anastasius and here Gratian observed that this pope was culpable because he acted "against the decrees of his predecessors and successors." C. 24 q.l included texts that referred to the Roman church as unerring. (Later controversialists often used these texts without taking note of the canonists' careful distinction between the universal Roman church and the individual pope.)

If the fourteenth century controversialists had been experts in twelfth century canon law they would have been able to cite many more passages than those they actually knew, which, taken out of context, seem to assert that a pope was bound by the decisions of his predecessors. But, restored to their contexts and interpreted from within the framework of Decretist thought, none of these passages has precisely that significance. It would be tedious to explicate individually every such text. There are literally dozens of them. But they all fall into three main categories which we can illustrate from comments on each of the three main sections of the Decretum where the problem arose.

The texts of C. 25 q. 1 which were most often cited in fourteenth century controversies were c. 2: "Things generally established for perpetual utility are not to be changed" and c. 6: "Where the Lord or his apostles or, following them, the holy fathers have solemnly defined anything the Roman pontiff ought not to establish a new law." Also one finds references to c. 10, where Pope Pelagius declared his adherence to the faith professed by his predecessor; to c. 11 where Pope Hadrian laid down that no bishop or king was to violate the decrees of the Roman pontiffs; and to c. 12, where Pope Damasus commanded that all the decrees of all his predecessors were to be observed.

None of these texts established any principle of irreformability for Gratian himself. He cited them only to refute them. It was indeed in this context that Gratian laid down the principle we have already considered. "The holy Roman church imparts authority to the sacred canons but is not bound by them." These words led the canonists to discriminate between the areas of divine truth where the Roman church was indeed bound and the areas of human law where it was free to change and innovate. But, since the texts presented by Gratian mentioned as possible sources of inviolate law "Scripture," "apostles," "Councils," "holy fathers," "predecessors," all mixed together in rather indiscriminate fashion, the Decretist comments on them did sometimes seem to assert that the pope was bound by doctrinal decisions of his predecessors.

Such comments occur usually at C. 25 q.1 c.1. The author of the *Summa Parisiensis* remarked:

> Those decrees which say the supreme pontiff cannot change the statutes of his predecessors are to be understood especially of those that pertain to the faith ....[1]

---

[1] *Summa Parisiensis, ed. cit.*, p. 230, "Illa igitur decreta quae dicunt summum pontificem decessorum suorum statuta mutare non posse, intelligenda sunt de illis quae ad fidem specialiter pertinent."

The point is that C. 25 q.l c.l referred explicitly to decrees of earlier popes that had been promulgated in general councils. It declared, "No see ought to obey the decrees of a synod that the assent of the universal church has approved more than the first see which confirms each synod by its authority." Canonistic glosses cannot be understood if they are divorced from the text that the glossator was interpreting. When the Decretists commented on C. 25 q.l c.l their remarks would normally refer to conciliar decrees approved by the papacy. That the statutes of early councils could be referred to as statutes of a pope's "predecessors" was made plain in another passage of the *Summa Parisiensis*.

> The eight general councils ... are to be preserved inviolate. But, as regards other writings of his predecessors, the Lord pope can dispense, derogate, and abrogate ....[1]

Sometimes, then, a claim that the pope was bound by his "predecessors" meant that he was bound by doctrinal decisions of general councils approved by earlier popes.

This does not cover all the instances where a pope was said to be bound by the decrees of earlier pontiffs in matters of faith. Another kind of case arose at *Dist.* 19 where Gratian criticized Anastasius for going "against the decrees of his predecessors." Some canonists asserted that Gratian was simply wrong in making such a charge. "Cannot the pope abrogate decretals? Certainly he can, both his own and his predecessors'. Gratian therefore understands wrongly."[2] Other Decretists once again relied on a distinction between changing human law and unchanging divine law. The decrees of earlier popes were human statutes and so could normally be revoked by a successor. But such statutes might well incorporate in their texts truths of Scripture or universally accepted doctrinal definitions of councils (as the decrees of Anastasius' predecessors incorporated the teachings of Chalcedon). In these cases a subsequent pope was bound by the earlier decree not because of the authority of the pope who promulgated it but because of the intrinsic authority of the material it in-

---

[1] *Op. cit.*, p. 14, "Octo enim concilia ... immutilata servantur. Sed in aliis scripturis praedecessorum suorum dominus papa potest dispensare, derogare vel abrogare considerata ratione."

[2] Alanus *ad Dist.* 19 *post* c. 7, MS Paris BN 3909, fol. 3vb, "Nonne potest papa abrogare decreta? Potest quidem, tam sua quam predecessorum. Male ergo intelligit G."

corporated. This was what the Decretists most commonly meant
when they wrote that the pope was bound by existing law where
"matters of faith" or "articles of faith" were involved. Huguccio
explained the point with unusual clarity in commenting on the case of
Anastasius:

> It seems to say that the pope cannot ordain anything against the good
> statutes of his predecessors, which I do not believe to be true for he can
> revoke even good statutes for due cause—provided that he does not
> touch the precepts of the Old and New Testaments or the articles of
> faith or things necessary for salvation ....[1]

To take an example that we have already mentioned, when Alexander
III wrote in *Cum Christus, Christus perfectus Deus et perfectus sit homo,*
the proposition could be regarded as binding on his successors, not
because Alexander's decrees as such were irreformable but because he
had quoted here an ancient article of faith. Many such texts can be
found scattered through the Decretum and *Decretales.*

There is one further Decretist usage that requires explanation.
Johannes Teutonicus, once again discussing the case of Anastasius
and the Acacian schism, in a comment on C. 24 q.l, wrote:

> Here is a case where a pope can bind a pope, when a pope incurs a sen-
> tence already pronounced in a canon. The rule "an equal cannot bind
> or loose an equal" does not stand in the way because, if a pope is a
> heretic he is as such less than any Catholic.[2]

Here again the meaning was not that a doctrinal pronouncement of
one pope established a standard of orthodoxy such that any later pope
who departed from it became a heretic. The schismatic Acacius
(whom Anastasius was accused of favoring) had in fact offended
against the canons of a general council and the section of the Decretum on which Johannes was commenting was devoted to proving
precisely this point. Johannes Teutonicus was arguing that, if a pope
fell into a known, defined heresy, he could incur a canonical penalty

---

[1] *Summa ad Dist.* 19 *post* c. 7, MS Pembroke Coll. 72, vol. 128vb, "Videtur dicere
quod papa contra bona statuta suorum predecessorum non possit aliquid statuere,
quod non credo esse verum, nam etiam bona statuta potest revocare, inspecta
causa, dummodo non tangat precepta veteris vel novi testamenti vel articulos (fidei)
vel ea quae sunt necessaria ad salutem ...."

[2] *Gl. ord. ad* C. 24 q. 1 c. 1, s.v. *In heresim,* "Hic est casus in quo papa papam
potest ligare, in quo papa in canonem latae sententiae incidit, nec huic obviat regula illa quia par parem solvere vel ligare non potest ... quia si papa hereticus est,
in eo quod hereticus est minor quolibet catholico."

that had been decreed by a predecessor because, in the act of becoming a heretic, he had already ceased to be pope.

To sum up: Whenever a Decretist text seems to maintain that a pope was bound by decisions of his predecessors in matters of faith the author meant to assert either (1) The pope was bound by dogmatic decrees of general councils approved by his predecessors or (2) He was bound by any Scriptural teaching or accepted articles of faith that were incorporated in the decrees of his predecessors or (3) He could incur a canonical penalty decreed by a predecessor if, having fallen into heresy, he had ceased to be a true pope. There was no strict doctrine of irreformability—as later generations would understand the term—in Decretist writings. Since the canonists all believed that the doctrinal pronouncements of a pope might well be in error and so need to be corrected by a later pope they could not have developed such a doctrine without gross self-contradiction.

In every area of thought that we have considered there seems to be a gulf between the ecclesiology of the medieval canonists and the ecclesiology of Vatican Council I. The canonists did not present Tradition as a source of divine revelation separate from Scripture; they did not know of any magisterium conferred on Peter with the power of the keys; they believed that in matters of faith a general council was greater than a pope; they did not maintain that papal pronouncements were irreformable *ex sese*. Above all the canonists did not teach that the pope was infallible. The texts we have quoted contrasting the unfailing faith of the church with the fallibility of individual pontiffs seem to represent a position that was generally held. No canonist, so far as we know, taught a contrary doctrine. Nor did the theologians, in their much scantier comments on such questions, dissent from the doctrine of the canonists. The twelfth-century church simply did not believe that the pope was "possessed of that infallibility with which the divine Redeemer wished that his church should be endowed."

CHAPTER TWO

SAINT BONAVENTURE

So far we have emphasized that, down to the middle of the thirteenth century, the most searching enquiries into the structure of the church were conducted by canonists rather than theologians and we have seen that the canonistic discussions did not lead on to any doctrine of papal infallibility. After 1250 the situation changed rapidly. Eminent theologians began to concern themselves more and more with problems of ecclesiology and, by the end of the century, one of them at least had propounded and defended an explicit theory of papal inerrancy.

The decisive stimulus to these new ecclesiological speculations came from the complex struggle that broke out in 1254 between the Orders of mendicant friars and secular masters of the University of Paris (who were supported by influential French bishops).[1] As the struggle grew more embittered the seculars began to attack, not only alleged abuses in the conduct of the mendicants, but the very legitimacy of the new way of life that they had introduced into the church. The friars were wholly dependent on papal support. Hence their champions were soon led to undertake a searching re-examination of the nature of papal power. In the course of the ensuing disputes there emerged, not only a new doctrine of papal infallibility, but new appraisals of many theological problems which would become inextricably interwoven with the idea of infallibility in the course of its later development—e.g., problems concerning the authority of Scripture, the meaning of Tradition, the irreformable quality of dogmatic decrees, the nature of the power of the keys. Franciscans and Dominicans were equally involved in the disputes with the

---

[1] Another factor that stimulated fresh interest in ecclesiology among the theologians of this period was the attempted reconciliation with the Greek church leading to the abortive union of 1274. But the debates with the Greeks never came to focus precisely on the question of infallibility. Since the Latin doctors themselves did not believe in papal infallibility, the Greeks were naturally not required to subscribe to any such doctrine. The decree of union with the Greeks simply repeated the old canonical claim that the pope was supreme judge in matters of faith.

secular masters of Paris.[1] But the position of the Franciscans was complicated by their adherence to certain characteristic doctrines concerning the absolute poverty of Christ and the providential role of St Francis in the life of the church which their adversaries condemned as pernicious novelties. In defending such teachings, the Franciscans, far more than the Dominicans, became pre-occupied with the problems we have mentioned. A peculiar feature of their thought, one that we shall need to explore in some detail, was the way in which apocalyptic fantasies concerning the role of St Francis in sacred history influenced Franciscan theories of the papacy and eventually led on to the formulation of a novel doctrine of papal infallibility.

1. FROM FRANCIS TO BONAVENTURE

(i) *Franciscan Joachimism*

The problems of the Franciscans grew out of three major developments in the life and thought of the Order which took place between the death of St. Francis (1228) and that of St. Bonaventure (1274). (Bonaventure was minister-general of the Order in the period 1257-1274.) These three developments were: the widespread acceptance in the Order of various forms of Franciscan Joachimism; the acquisition by the Franciscans of numerous privileges from the papacy; and the growth within the Order of a new doctrine concerning the absolute poverty of Christ and the apostles.[2] In the following pages we have

---

[1] For an outline of the dispute within the university see D. Douie, *The Conflict Between the Seculars and the Mendicants at the University of Paris in the Thirteenth Century* (London, 1954). On the theological repercussions of the dispute the outstanding work is Y. Congar, "Aspects ecclésiologiques de la querelle entre mendiants et séculiers dans la seconde moitié du XIIIe siècle et le début du XIVe," *AHDL*, 36 (1961), pp. 35-151. This magisterial article provides a chronology of the disputes and information on editions and manuscripts of the medieval polemical writings, together with an ample bibliography of modern works. It provides an indispensable starting point for all subsequent work in the field.

[2] These developments are discussed in the various general histories of the Franciscan order, e.g., P. Gratien, *Histoire de la fondation et de l'évolution de l'ordre des Frères Mineurs au XIIIe siècle* (Paris, 1928); R. Huber, *A Documented History of the Franciscan Order* (Milwaukee, 1944); H. Holzapfel, *The History of the Franciscan Order*, transl. A. Tibesar and G. Brinkmann (Teutopolis, Ill., 1948); and, most recently, J. R. H. Moorman, *A History of the Franciscan Order* (Oxford, 1968). David Knowles, *The Religious Orders in England*, I (Cambridge, 1948) is especially perceptive on Franciscan problems. For a general bibliography see the "Research Bibliography" compiled by R. Brown in Omer Englebert, *Saint Francis of Assisi* (2nd English edition revised and augmented by I. Brady and R. Brown) (Chicago, 1965), pp. 493-607.

not tried to explore all the intricacies of these questions. Each one is a major subject in itself and each has attracted a formidable technical literature. Our purpose is only to provide enough background information to render intelligible the subsequent exposition of the growth of the idea of papal infallibility.

The doctrines that we have called Franciscan Joachimism were all variations on the thought of Joachim of Flora, the Calabrian abbot and mystic who lived in the generation before Saint Francis.[1] Joachim is most famous for his Trinitarian theory of history though this was in truth only one aspect of a most complex system of number symbolism that we have perhaps not yet fully understood. Joachim believed that, just as there were three persons in the Trinity, so there would be three epochs or "states" of human history—an age of the Father corresponding roughly to the era of the Old Testament (which had ended with Zachary, the father of John the Baptist), an age of the Son corresponding to the era of the New Testament (which had endured for some 1200 years at the time when Joachim was writing) and an age of the Holy Spirit (which was still to come). Each "state" had its own characteristics. The first was an era of servitude, the second of filial obedience, the third of liberty. The first was an era of knowledge, the second of partial wisdom, the third of full revelation. The first was an era of suffering, the second of action, the third of contemplation. The first era had married men as its leaders, the second clerics, the third monks. Each era had a precursor as well as an actual inaugurator. St. Benedict, the patron of western monasticism, was the precursor of the coming third "state" of monasticism and contemplation; Joachim also envisaged the emergence of a new Order—or two new Orders—of poor religious who would prepare the way for the final Order of perfect contemplatives.

---

[1] Two excellent guides to the intricacies of Joachim's thought and to the modern scholarship concerning it are M. W. Bloomfield, "Joachim of Flora: A Critical Survey of his Canon, Teaching, Sources, Bibliography, and Influence," *Traditio* (1957), pp. 249-311 and M. Reeves, *The Influence of Prophecy in the Later Middle Ages, A Study in Joachimism* (Oxford, 1969). The brief summary of Joachim's thought given above is indebted to these two works. Important among the earlier studies are G. Bondatti, *Gioacchinismo e Francescanismo nel dugento* (Assisi, 1924); H. Grundmann, *Studien über Joachim von Floris* (Leipzig, 1927) and *Neue Forschungen über Joachim von Fiore* (Marburg, 1950); E. Benz, *Ecclesia Spiritualis* (Stuttgart, 1934); E. Buonaiuti, *Gioacchino da Fiore* (Rome, 1931); L. Tondelli, *Il libro delle Figure dell' Abate Gioachino da Fiore*, I, 2nd ed. (Turin, 1953). As Reeves points out (p. 129), on the whole the German scholars tend to emphasize Joachim's radicalism; the Italians, to defend his orthodoxy.

In Joachim's time-scheme each "state" was divided into seven ages and, further, into forty-two generations, each of about thirty years. This pointed to 1260 as the date of the coming new era. The sixth and seventh ages of the second "state" were presented by Joachim as a time of confusion and transition. They would be "filled with the evil doings of the dragon of the Apocalypse." The church would suffer persecutions and tribulations culminating in the appearance of Antichrist. But these ages would also see the first revelation of the new spiritual understanding of the eternal gospel which would characterize the coming third "state." Joachim associated his seven ages both with the seven days of creation (an old parallel, familiar to medieval men especially from the works of Augustine) and with the seven angels of the Apocalypse. For Joachim the "angel of the sixth seal" had a special significance for he took the words of the Apocalypse concerning this angel as prophecies relating to the era of transition from the second to the third "states" of the church. The angel of the sixth seal would appear in the sixth age of the second "state" and, with the opening of the sixth seal of the scroll of the Lamb, the "veil of literal interpretation" would be drawn aside to make possible the spiritual understanding that would characterize the coming new era of the Holy Spirit.

Modern scholars have disagreed about the meaning that Joachim himself attached to his prophecy of a coming third "state." Sometimes he wrote as though the whole church founded on Peter was to be swept away to make place for a new "spiritual church" inspired by a new revelation. But the whole Trinitarian basis of his doctrine seems inconsistent with such interpretations. The procession of the Holy Spirit completes the Trinity; it does not destroy it. The problem is complicated by the fact that Joachim sometimes presented the whole of human history down to the end of the world in a two-fold rather than a three-fold pattern—the two ages corresponding roughly to the eras of the Old and New Testaments[1]—and in this time-scheme there is plainly no room for a new revelation superseding that of the Gospels. After reviewing the modern scholarship on the question Marjorie Reeves observed, "By a rather narrow margin we reach the conclusion that in intention and in the broad outline of his conception Joachim was faithful to the orthodoxy of the Latin church as he

---

[1] M. Reeves, *op. cit.*, pp. 16-27. Since the two ages overlapped, the first ran from Adam to Christ the second from King Osias to the Last Judgment.

understood it."[1] And yet Joachim's third "state" was clearly envisaged as being very different from the second one. One can best explain Joachim's understanding of the coming transition in his own words "The church of Peter shall not fail... but, having been transformed, it shall remain steadfast for ever in greater glory."[2]

Whatever Joachim's precise intentions may have been, his main influence was to give currency to the idea that an age of spiritual renewal, of radical innovation was impending in the life of the church. This idea dominated the first major work of Franciscan Joachimism, the startling and scandalous *Introductorius in Evangelium Eternum*, which was published at Paris in 1254 by the young Franciscan friar, Gerard of Borgo San Donnino.[3] The origin of the idea of an "eternal gospel" is to be found in the Apocalypse (14.6). The author tells how the angel of the sixth seal signed a hundred and forty-four thousand of the elect who gathered on Mount Sion and how there then appeared "an angel flying in midheaven, having an everlasting gospel to preach to those who dwell upon the earth." Joachim had associated the everlasting gospel with the angel of the sixth seal and with the sixth age of the church; but for him the everlasting gospel was essentially the old Gospel of Christ, revealed at last to men in its full "spiritual" significance. Gerard of Borgo San Donnino provided a much more eccentric interpretation. He declared that the "everlasting gospel" consisted of the major writings of Joachim himself and that, in the coming age of the Holy Spirit, they would replace the Gospel of Christ. Moreover, the age of the Holy Spirit was to begin in the near future, precisely in 1260 (Joachim was never so certain of the exact date). Finally, and most important for us, Gerard taught that St. Francis of Assisi was the angel of the sixth seal who proclaimed the new gospel and that the Franciscans were the order of spiritual men who were to inaugurate and then lead the new church of the third age.

---

[1] *Op. cit.*, p. 132.

[2] *Op. cit.*, p. 397, "Non igitur ... deficiet ecclesia Petri ... sed commutata in maiorem gloriam manebit stabilis in eternum."

[3] The work has not survived in full and its contents are known through the attacks of Gerard's opponents. See H. Denifle, "Das Evangelium aeternum und die Commission zu Anagni," *ALKG*, 1 (1885), pp. 49-124 and, for more recent work M. W. Bloomfield and M. Reeves, "The Penetration of Joachism into Northern Europe," *Speculum*, 29 (1954), pp. 772-793. B. Töpfer claims to have discovered a portion of Gerard's original work in a Dresden MS, "Eine Handschrift des Evangelium aeternum des Gerardino von Borgo San Donnino," *Zeitschrift für Geschichtswissenschaft*, 8 (1960), pp. 156-163. Cf. Reeves, *op. cit.*, pp. 60, 189.

These ideas were obviously heretical and Gerard's work was promptly condemned. But his judges did not single out for condemnation Gerard's identification of Francis with the angel of the sixth seal and this identification continued to fascinate many Franciscan teachers throughout the Middle Ages. The reasons are clear enough. The Angel of the sixth seal is described thus in the Apocalypse "I saw another angel ascending from the rising of the sun having the seal of the living God; and he cried with a loud voice to the four angels who had it in their power to harm the earth and the sea, saying 'Do not harm the earth or the sea or the trees, till we have sealed the servants of our God on their foreheads,'" (Apoc. 7:2-3). The sixth angel had "the seal of the living God" and Francis of Assisi bore on his body the marks of the Stigmata, nail marks on hands and feet and a wound in the side. Moreover the angel "sealed the servants of God on their foreheads." This was associated in medieval exegesis with Ezechiel 9.4 where those to be saved were likewise marked on the foreheads. But in Ezechiel the mark was specifically designated as the sign Tau. And Francis did actually sign his letters with the symbol Tau. The apparent coincidence of prophecies proved irresistible to many eminent Franciscan doctors and the identification of Francis with the angel of the sixth seal came to be widely accepted in the Order.

When Gerard's book appeared, the controversy between the secular masters of Paris and the friars had already broken out. The seculars were of course delighted at the publication of such a compromising book by one of their adversaries and they attacked it with zest and evident pleasure. The most vehement opponent of the mendicants at this stage of the controversy was William of St. Amour, who cast one of his major treatises, the *De periculis novissimorum temporum*,[1] in the form of an elaborate parody of the Joachimite expectations of the more extreme friars. He asserted that the appearance

---

[1] *Magistri Guillielmi de S. Amore opera omnia* (Constance, 1632), pp. 17-72. On William of St. Amour (besides Congar, art. cit.) see M. Bierbaum, *Bettelorden und Weltgeistlicheit an der Universität Paris* (Münster in Westf., 1920); E. Faral, "Les 'Responsiones' de Guillaume de Saint-Amour," *AHDL*, 25-26 (1950-1951), pp. 337-394; P. Glorieux, "Le conflit de 1252-57 à la lumière du Mémoire de Guillaume de Saint-Amour," *RTAM*, 24 (1957), pp. 364-372; M. Peuchmaurd, "Mission canonique et prédication," *RTAM*, 30 (1963), pp. 122-144, 251-276; P. R. McKeon, "The University of Paris as *Parens Scientiarum*," *Speculum*, 39 (1964), pp. 651-675; J. V. Fleming, "The 'Collations' of William of S. Amour Against S. Thomas," *RTAM*, 32 (1965), pp. 132-138.

of the new mendicant orders was indeed a sign of the coming last days of the church; but, he maintained, the friars were fore-runners of Antichrist, not heralds of a new age of the Holy Spirit.

It is not at all clear how seriously William took his own apocalyptic speculations. Perhaps he was merely indulging to the full a highly developed talent for sustained irony. Certainly the real ground of his opposition to the mendicant orders was not the indiscreet prophesying of one relatively unimportant Franciscan. Rather William believed that, in fulfilling their day-to-day tasks of preaching and administering sacraments by virtue of the papal licenses conferred on them, the friars were undermining the whole pastoral structure of the church which Christ himself had established. It was above all the papal privileges of the friars that aroused the hostility of the French bishops and of the secular masters who supported them.

(ii) *Papal Privileges*

Francis of Assisi, in his Testament, forbade the Franciscans to seek papal privileges and declared "If I were as wise as Solomon and met the poorest priests in the world, I would still refuse to preach against their will in the parishes in which they live."[1] Yet it is hard to see how the friars could ever have carried on their work of evangelical preaching throughout the church without specific papal authorizations—and Francis himself had turned willingly to the papacy when he needed approval for his new way of life[2]. Soon after Francis' death his followers took this problem to Pope Gregory IX. Gregory replied in the Bull *Quo elongati* (1230), a document of crucial importance in shaping the whole future life of the Franciscan Order. The pope ruled that the Testament was not juridically binding on the Franciscans. Citing the legal doctrine, "an equal has no power over an equal," he declared that the words of Francis could not oblige his successors in the office of minister-general.[3] Subsequent Bulls of Gregory IX and Innocent IV permitted the friars—without consent

---

[1] *Opuscula Sancti Patris Francisci Assisiensis* (Quaracchi, 1904), p. 78.

[2] This was emphasized by K. Esser, *Das Testament des heiligen Franziskus von Assisi* (Münster in Westf., 1949). After a century of controversies there is still disagreement among modern scholars about Francis' intentions and the extent to which his followers departed from them.

[3] *Bullarium Romanum*, III (Turin, 1858), p. 450, "... sine consensu fratrum, et maxime ministrorum quos universos tangebat, obligare nequivit, nec successorem suum quomodolibet obligavit, cum non habeat imperium par imperare (*corr.* in parem)."

of the local parish priests—to build churches, preach, hear confessions and even bury lay-folk in their churchyards. (This last privilege was particularly resented by the parish clergy since the right of burial was a source of fees and, often, of legacies.) In the last days of his life Innocent IV severely curtailed these privileges, but his successor Alexander IV promptly renewed them in the Bull *Nec insolitum* (1254). During the ensuing disputes the popes consistently supported the friars and, in 1281, Pope Martin IV promulgated the most all-embracing privilege of the whole series in the Bull, *Ad fructus uberes*. This Bull exempted the friars from virtually all control by the local episcopate. It gave rise to a new round of controversies in which Henry of Ghent and Godfrey of Fontaines were the principal spokesmen for the secular clergy while Pietro Olivi and Richard of Middletown defended the Franciscans. A crisis came in 1290 when Pope Nicholas IV (a Franciscan himself) sent two cardinal-legates to preside over a council of French bishops. One of them was Benedict Gaetani, the future Pope Boniface VIII. The legates made no concessions at all to the French prelates. They insisted that the privileges of the friars be fully maintained and they suspended Henry of Ghent from teaching. According to one account Benedict Gaetani declared that he would rather dissolve the University of Paris than revoke the privileges of the friars.[1] When he became pope, however, Benedict found it convenient to adopt a more conciliatory position and, in 1300, he promulgated a compromise settlement that came to be accepted as a practical solution to the problem of privileges.[2] The theoretical issue concerning the extent of the pope's right to grant exemptions from episcopal authority continued to be debated throughout the Middle Ages.

The main lines that this whole theoretical controversy followed were determined by the first exchange of polemical treatises at Paris

---

[1] On this phase of the dispute see especially K. Schleyer, *Anfange des Gallikanismus im 13. Jahrhundert* (Berlin, 1937) and P. Glorieux, "Prélats français contre religieux mendiants (1281-1290)," *Revue d'histoire de l'église de France*, 11 (1925), pp. 309-331; G. de Lagarde, *La naissance de l'esprit laique*, II (2nd ed., Louvain-Paris, 1958).

[2] Boniface's bull *Super cathedram* was revoked by his successor Benedict XI (a Dominican) but re-enacted by Clement V in the Council of Vienne. The text is in *Clem*. 3.7.2. The principal provisions of the Bull were: Friars could preach in their own churches but not at times that conflicted with parochial services; they required permission of the local bishop to hear confessions but each bishop was required to accept a quota of friars; a quarter of all mortuary fees received by the friars was to be handed over to the parish priest.

in the years 1255-1256. The position of the secular masters was based on the old belief that Christ had established three classes of prelates to govern the church who were typified in Peter, the apostles, and the disciples. The pope succeeded to Peter, bishops to the apostles, and parish priests to the disciples.[1] According to the seculars the popes were destroying the whole divinely established structure of the church by assigning the pastoral work of the secular clergy to new orders of friars. The most obvious line of reply for the friars was to assert that they were not destroying any established institutions but were simply providing a useful supplement to the pastoral activities of the local clergy and that the pope, by virtue of the powers entrusted to him as head of the church, was entirely qualified to authorize their activities. Such arguments were indeed presented by the Franciscan, Thomas of York, in his treatise, *Manus quae contra omnipotentem* (1256).[2] But Thomas went a step further. In any case, he argued, no action of the pope could be considered prejudicial to the rights of other prelates since all their authority was derived from him. "An inferior prelate has nothing except what he has from a superior, namely the supreme pontiff..."[3] The secular masters replied that, according to the plain words of the New Testament, Christ himself—not Peter— conferred authority on the apostles and disciples. Hence their successors also derived their power from Christ.[4] The friars responded

---

[1] William of St. Amour based this argument on the *Decretum* (*Dist*. 21 c. 2) and on the *Ordinary Gloss* to the *Bible* (*Luke* 10, 1). See e.g., his *De periculis* in *Opera*, p. 24. The doctrine that priests succeeded to the seventy-two disciples just as bishops succeeded to the twelve apostles goes back to Bede (see Congar, *art. cit.*, p. 61). Since the rights of parish priests seemed especially threatened by the mendicants this doctrine received great emphasis in the thirteenth-century controversies. However, for the future development of ecclesiology, the really important issue was the relationship between the pope as successor of Peter and the bishops as successors of the apostles.

[2] Ed. M. Bierbaum, *Bettelorden*, pp. 37-168. Thomas argued that the apostolic see could change or establish anything in the church provided that its commands were not contrary to justice or equity or the truths of Holy Scripture (p. 140). The friars' privileges were justified by the needs of the people and the inadequacy of many of the priests (p. 148).

[3] *Op. cit.*, p. 154, "Ita nichil habet prelatus inferior nisi a superiori, uidelicet summo pontifice ... et ideo quicquid faciat superior circa actionem inferioris ex ratione, non est in eius preiudicium ..."; p. 155, "Et insuper non est in preiudicium inferioris concessio superioris, ubi et iurisdictio inferioris totaliter pendet ex ordinatione superioris."

[4] E.g., Gerard of Abbeville, *Exceptiones contra ... Manus quae omnipotentem*, ed. Bierbaum, *op. cit.*, pp. 200-201, "... statum videtur totius ecclesie in prelatis maioribus et minoribus enervare, qui hanc potestatem non ab homine, sed a Christo Domino acceperunt ... Unde non solo Petro vocato, sed *convocatis 12 apostolis*,

with counter arguments of their own based on fresh interpretations of the disputed texts of Scripture.[1] Thus a great deal of intellectual energy, that might profitably have been devoted to the urgent practical problem of determining how the pastoral work of the church could best be carried on, was diverted into a theological dispute about the meaning of the New Testament texts relating to the foundation of the apostolic hierarchy. Since the question of papal privileges was of crucial importance for all the mendicant orders, Dominicans were as active as Franciscans in this particular dispute.

(iii) *Apostolic Poverty*

For the Franciscans in particular there was another issue, at least as important as that of papal privileges, in shaping their attitudes to the authority of pope, church and Scripture. This was the doctrine of the absolute poverty of Christ and the apostles that grew up in the Order. If the Franciscans had been content to assert that their way of practicing poverty was a new form of ascetic discipline, well suited to the needs of a preaching order in the thirteenth century, their position would hardly have been controversial. But in fact the friars maintained that renunciation of property "singly and in common" was an essential element in the perfect way of life that Christ had taught to his apostles. Since earlier scriptural exegesis had not pointed to any such conclusion, the Franciscan claim necessitated a radical reinterpretation of many passages of the New Testament. Here again, an issue that might have been considered essentially as a problem of church discipline became inflated into a major theological dispute.

Although they seldom put their position so bluntly, the more pugnacious Franciscan apologists came to assert, in effect, that, since the days of the first apostles, no one had understood Scripture correctly before St. Francis. This implied further that no members of the church were leading lives of evangelical perfection except the Franciscans. These were controversial propositions—and all the more so since the doctrine of poverty, which the Franciscan polemicists used to establish the superior perfection of their own Order,

---

dedit eis *potestatem spirituum immundorum* etc. Matth. 10, (1), Luc. 9, (1), ... quorum statum tenent episcopi. Idem etiam dixit 72 discipulis ... quorum statum tenent sacerdotes secundi ordinis ..." The problem of whether a bishop's jurisdiction was transmitted through inferiors (in the act of election) or through a superior (in the act of confirmation) had arisen in twelfth-century canon law. For a full treatment of the question see R. L. Benson, *The Bishop-Elect* (Princeton, 1968).

[1] See below pp. 160-164.

bore only a tenuous relationship to the reality of poverty that St. Francis had exemplified in all his activities.

For Francis, voluntary poverty was a virtue to be practiced in day to day living not a concept to be theorized about in fine-spun arguments. He was inspired above all by the text of Matthew, "Freely you have received; freely give. Do not keep gold or silver in your girdles, nor wallet for your journey, nor two tunics nor sandals nor staffs..." There is a familiar story in Celano's *Vita Prima* telling how, while Francis was still seeking for his true vocation, he heard these words read by a priest at mass. At once he exclaimed "This is it! This I will do with all my heart."[1] Poverty meant for Francis a total absence of solicitude for material possessions. He would accept only enough food and clothes barely to sustain life. He forbade his friars to store up wealth. They were not to accept the ownership of land or buildings or to touch money at all. They were to beg only the food they needed for a single day, taking "no thought for the morrow" in the most literal sense. In the final version of Francis' Rule, the *Regula Bullata* approved by the papacy in 1223, the obligation of poverty was expressed in the phrase "The friars are to appropriate nothing for themselves neither a house, nor a place, nor anything else." But the Rule also declared that "The friars may have one tunic with a hood" and that "The clerics may have breviaries."[2] These apparently simple provisions—that the friars could "appropriate" nothing but could "have" certain necessities—gave rise to interminable debates after Francis' death.[3]

Gregory IX provided a clarification of decisive importance in the Bull, *Quo elongati* that we have already mentioned. In this decree, Gregory introduced the phrase "neither singly nor in common" to explain the mode of renunciation that Francis had wanted his followers to practice. Still more important, he explained that the basis of Franciscan poverty lay in a technical distinction between ownership and use. The friars were to hold nothing as their own property but they were to have the use of such books, utensils and other movable

---

[1] *Vita prima S. Francisci Assisiensis* (Quaracchi, 1926), p. 25.

[2] *Regula II* in *Opuscula* (Quaracchi, 1904), pp. 68, 65-66, "Fratres nihil sibi approprient, nec domum nec locum nec aliquam rem." "Et illi ... habeant unam tunicam cum caputio." "Clerici ... habere poterunt breviaria."

[3] The arguments continue among modern scholars. A convenient introduction to the poverty-disputes of the Middle Ages is M. D. Lambert, *Franciscan Poverty* (London, 1961).

goods as were permitted to them.[1] They could not alienate such things without the permission of the cardinal-protector of the Order. Ownership of land or buildings used by the Franciscans remained with the donor of the property who had made it available to them. The friars were permitted to appoint an *amicus spiritualis* who could accept gifts of alms for them and to whom they could apply for necessities. In 1245 Innocent IV modified these arrangements in the Bull *Ordinem vestrum*. He decreed that, henceforth, the ownership of all property held by the Franciscans should inhere in the Roman church. Innocent also provided that the friars could ask their "spiritual friend" to make purchases on their behalf for reasons of convenience as well as necessity. This was a radical departure from Francis' own ideal. Indeed from this time onward, Franciscan poverty was essentially a legal fiction. An individual friar might choose to practice voluntary asceticisms and many did so; but it was also open to a Franciscan to live in modest comfort and complete security without violating the precepts of the Rule as interpreted by the papacy.

In the controversies of the 1250's the opponents of the friars attacked their doctrine of poverty on two main grounds. It was, they argued, both non-Scriptural and nonsensical. In the first place, many texts of Scripture stated or implied that Christ and the Apostles did in fact own property.[2] In the second place, the distinction between ownership and use on which the whole Franciscan doctrine was founded could not possibly apply to consumable articles. In what conceivable sense could a friar be said not to possess an apple as his own when he was in the process of eating it? This was the state of the argument when Bonaventure emerged as the leading champion of the Franciscans, first as an academic controversialist, then as Minister-General of the Order. In reply to his adversaries' Scriptural arguments Bonaventure developed a theory of "condescension." Christ practised absolute poverty, Bonaventure insisted, when he was showing the

---

[1] *Bullarium Romanum*, III (Turin, 1858), p. 451, "Dicimus itaque, quod nec in communi, nec in speciali debent proprietatem habere, sed utensilium, et librorum, et eorum mobilium, quae licet habere, Ordo usum habeat." On the Bulls of Gregory IX and Innocent IV see especially F. Elizondo, *"Bullae* 'Quo elongati' Gregorii IX et 'Ordinem vestrum' Innocentii IV,"* Laurentianum, 3 (1962), pp. 349-394.

[2] See e.g., William of St. Amour, *De periculis, Opera*, pp. 49-51; *Collationes Scripturae Sacrae, Opera*, pp. 360-365. For Scriptural support William emphasized especially John 13.29 which referred to a common purse of Christ and the apostles and Acts 4.32, "... they had all things in common." The Franciscans referred most frequently to Matt. 8.20, Matt. 19.21, Matt. 19.27, Mark 6,8, Luke 9.3.

way of perfection. When Christ assumed the ownership of any goods he was "condescending to the weak," that is graciously intimating to the frailer spirits among his followers, those who could not sustain the rigors of a life of perfection, that ownership of property was not actually sinful.[1] In responding to the argument about goods consumable in use Bonaventure drew a series of legalistic distinctions. Gregory IX had been content to distinguish between ownership and use. Bonaventure wrote, "Concerning temporal goods four things are to be considered, property, possession, usufruct, and simple use," and he sought to prove by juridical arguments that the last (simple use) could be exercised without any of the other three.[2] Pope Nicholas III in turn adopted Bonaventure's terminology with some further refinements. In his bull *Exiit qui seminat* (1279) he gave papal sanction to Bonaventure's doctrine of condescension and declared that Franciscan poverty consisted in the exercise of a "simple use of fact" divorced from property, possession, usufruct, and right of using. Pope Nicholas also repeated that this Franciscan way of life did indeed correspond to the way of perfection that Christ had taught to the Apostles.[3]

Bonaventure has often been called the "second founder" of the Franciscan Order, sometimes approvingly, sometimes with the pejorative implication that he founded a new institution alien to the ideals of Francis himself.[4] It is certain that the Order Bonaventure

---

[1] On Bonaventure's doctrine of poverty see S. Clasen, *Der hl. Bonaventura und das Mendikantentum* (Werl-in-Westf., 1940). The doctrine of condescension is developed at length in the *Apologia pauperum, S. Bonaventurae ... opera omnia* (Quaracchi, 1882-1902), VIII, pp. 233-330. See especially 7.35, p. 284, "Unde et huiusmodi actus, scilicet habere loculos, in Christo respectu *infirmorum* fuit *condescensivus*, ad consolandum scilicet eos qui propriis loculis carere non volunt."

[2] *Apologia*, 11.5, p. 312, "... intelligendum est, quod cum circa res temporales quatuor sit considerare, scilicet *proprietatem, possessionem, usumfructum* et *simplicem usum*; et primis quidem tribus vita mortalium possit carere, ultimo vero tanquam necessario egeat ..." He went on to argue that in Roman law a *filiusfamilias* used his *peculium* without owning it. Other friars quoted the example of a slave who used his master's goods without ever acquiring a legal right to them, even in the case of consumables.

[3] *Sext.* 5.12.3. The crucial passages of Nicholas' decree are quoted below p. 98. On their relationship to Bonaventure's doctrine see V. Maggiani, "De relatione scriptorum quorundam S. Bonaventurae ad Bullam 'Exiit' Nicolai III (1279)," *AFH*, 5 (1912), pp. 3-21.

[4] Bonaventure's role in shaping the government of the Order is discussed by R. B. Brooke, *Early Franciscan Government* (Cambridge, 1959). For literature on Bonaventure as "second founder" see H. Roggen, "Saint Bonaventure second fondateur de l'Ordre des Frères Mineurs?" *Études franciscaines*, 17 (1967), pp. 67-79 at p. 69 n. 2.

shaped as Minister-general was different from anything that Francis had envisaged. Bonaventure was true to the original Franciscan ideal in that he wanted the friars to be effective evangelical preachers, converting infidels and rekindling a love of Christ among luke-warm Christians. He differed from Francis principally in insisting that intensive theological training was essential for the fulfillment of such a vocation. This necessitated the establishment of permanent endowments (held by the papacy of course), and abandonment of both mendicancy and manual labor as the normal ways of providing for the upkeep of the friars. (Bonaventure insisted on the continued practice of mendicancy but more and more it became merely a picturesque penitential practice.)

Recently Ratzinger and, following him, Roggen have argued that Bonaventure believed Francis' ideal could be realized in all its purity only in a later age of the church after a new "break-through" of divine grace and that, accordingly, he deliberately set himself to shape an institution which he knew was not wholly in keeping with Francis' ideals but which was well-adapted to serve the imperfect men of his own generation.[1] This seems a complete misreading of Bonaventure's intentions. There is no evidence that he was ever conscious of departing from the ideals of St. Francis (though he did depart from them of course) and it is abundantly clear that he did not regard the way of life he proposed for the friars as in any way a concession to human frailty. On the contrary he regarded theological study as a higher, more arduous vocation than manual labor;[2] and he never doubted that Franciscan poverty was preserved in all its pristine purity by the arrangement which existed between the Order

---

[1] J. Ratzinger, *Die Geschichtstheologie des hl. Bonaventura* (Munich, 1959), p. 52; Roggen, art. cit., pp. 76-77. Ratzinger pointed out that Bonaventure looked forward to the emergence of a "seraphic" order in the last days of the church and that he regarded Francis as an exemplar of this order. Yet he referred to the Franciscan Order of his own day as existing on a lower "cherubic" level. (*Collationes in Hexaemeron*, XXII; *Opera* V, p. 440). This seems readily explicable without Ratzinger's hypothesis. Bonaventure did not believe that the ideals he proposed for the Order were different from those of St. Francis, but he was well aware that many of the friars in the existing Order were failing to realize those ideals in their day-to-day lives. It was the evident gap between ideal and reality, not any sense of having compromised the ideal itself, which made him distinguish between the actual Order and the coming perfected one.

[2] *Epistola de tribus quaestionibus* in *Opera* VIII, p. 334, "Ego autem dico, non intendere beatum Franciscum manualem laborem nec praecipere nec consulere nec monere ..." *Expositio super Regulam* in *Opera* VIII, p. 420, "Praeterea, labor sapientiae simpliciter melior est corporeo labore ..."

and the papacy. Bonaventure was vehemently convinced that the
Franciscan life of his own day was a faithful re-enactment of the life of
evangelical perfection that Christ had taught to the apostles. That
conviction shines through every page of his writings on behalf of
the Order. And it provided the basis for his whole structure of ecclesiology to which we can now turn.

2. The "New Tradition" of St. Francis

(i) *Development of Doctrine*

The leading adversary of the Franciscans in the controversy of the
1250's, William of St. Amour, was such an obdurate conservative
that, for him, novelty was almost a sin in itself. One of his most
sustained and biting passages of invective was directed against the
"new traditions" that he attributed to the friars:

> They practice certain new, unheard of and superstitious traditions con-
> trary to divine Scripture and canonical institutes and the custom of the
> church ....[1]

The principal "new tradition" that William attacked was the
Franciscan doctrine of "absolute poverty," their claim that renunciation of dominion "singly and in common" was essential to the
highest form of Christian perfection. After presenting all the standard
Scriptural arguments against the Franciscan position he concluded:

> It is evident that such traditions can be called "superstition" from this,
> that they were not handed down to us by the Lord Jesus Christ nor by
> his Apostles nor by the Holy Councils nor by the canonical writings of
> the holy doctors but were introduced by certain newcomers of their
> own will ....[2]

This is a very clear statement of a prevailing way of thought. Valid
tradition was teaching handed down in Scripture or in the canons of
councils or the writings of the Fathers. Antiquity was an essential
criterion of valid Tradition. Novelty was its antithesis. Moreover

---

[1] *Collationes Sacrae Scripturae* in *Opera*, p. 345, "... quasdam traditiones novas, et
insuetas, ac superstitiosas faciunt, contra Divinas Scripturas, et contra canonica
instituta, et contra morem Ecclesie ..."

[2] *Op. cit.*, pp. 389-390, "Quod autem tales traditiones *Superstitio* dici possunt, ex
eo videtur; quod nec a Domino Iesu Christo, nec ab eius Apostolis, nec a Sanctis
Conciliis, nec ab Antiquis Sanctis, nec a Scripturis Sanctorum Doctorum Canonicis
sunt nobis relictae; sed a Quibusdam Recentioribus ex eorum arbitrio, praeter vel
contra Sanctorum authoritates canonicas, ut preostensum est, sunt inductae."

this ancient Tradition constituted a standard by which the orthodoxy of new doctrinal formulations could be judged. Here again William was presenting a conservative point of view. It would be hard to find in earlier medieval thought any trace of the converse argument that new formulations could provide a standard for determining what "must have been" the content of ancient Tradition.

Of course the Franciscans indignantly denied that their "new traditions" were contrary to Scripture and they tried whenever possible to find patristic evidence to support their interpretations of particular Scriptural texts. But, in the last resort, they could not deny and had no wish to deny that St. Francis had introduced a radically new understanding of Christian truth into the life of the church. Bonaventure, in effect, accepted William of St. Amour's charge that the Franciscans were exponents of a "new tradition" and gloried in the fact that God had given them such a role. In defending this position he was led to develop a thesis that was to be of considerable importance for later theories of papal authority. He persistently maintained that the current teachings of the church could provide an unerring guide to the truths of faith which Christ had revealed to the first apostles—even when there was no obvious warrant for those teachings in ancient sources.

The whole logic of the Franciscan position required the development of such a theory and eventually some of the friars would come to believe that they needed also a theory of papal infallibility to complement it. Their arguments—which were sometimes essentially similar to modern arguments about development of doctrine, but sometimes highly eccentric—could be used either to justify their interpretations of Scripture or to claim for extra-Scriptural traditions (even recent ones) the same dogmatic validity as the teachings of Scripture itself. Both developments were suggested in the writings of St. Bonaventure.

Bonaventure's arguments on behalf of the Franciscan Order were set in the context of a theory of history—partly Joachimite-inspired—in which a unique role was ascribed to St. Francis and his followers. Bonaventure first discussed the position of the Franciscans in sacred history in the *De perfectione evangelica*. Replying to critics who asserted that it was safer to follow the well-tried doctors of old he wrote:

> God disposes and orders all things according to their proper times. Hence, just as in the first age of the church he brought forward men

potent in signs and miracles as were the apostles and their disciples;
and, in the middle age, men of discernment in Scripture and reasoning;
so, in the last age, he has brought forward men of voluntary mendicancy, poor in the things of the world. And this indeed was fitting, in that
through the first men idolatry and the fables of idolatry were destroyed;
through the second heresy, and through the third avarice which especially flourishes at the end of the world.[1]

Yet these new men whom God had sent to inspire the church in
its last age were also representatives of a way of life that Christ had
established at the very foundation of the church.

Nevertheless because poverty is the foundation of evangelical perfection and, so to speak its complement, therefore it flourished in the beginning of the church and it is fitting that it should flourish in the final
state of the church. ... (Jerome says) that "Omega revolved to alpha,"
that is the final state agreed with the first—and so our proposition can
be conveniently understood.[2]

Thus the "new tradition" of the Franciscans was closer to the life of
the apostles than the old traditions that William of St. Amour
defended. It is hard to describe this view of history as precisely
"linear" or "circular". Bonaventure seems to have taught that Christ
made a perfect revelation to the apostles but that the full meaning of
this revelation was almost at once lost sight of.[3] (Bonaventure did not

---

[1] *Quaestiones disputatae de perfectione evangelica*, Q. 2 art. 2 in *Opera* V, pp. 147-148,
"Deus universa disponit et ordinat temporibus suis. Unde sicut in primo tempore
Ecclesiae introduxit viros potentes et miraculis et signis, sicut fuerunt Apostoli et
eorum discipuli; et medio tempore viros intelligentes in Scripturis et rationibus
vivis: sic ultimo tempore introduxit viros voluntarie mendicantes et pauperes rebus
mundanis. Et hoc quidem recte congruebat, ut per primos destrueretur idolatria et
idolorum portenta, per secundos haeresis, per tertios avaritia, quae in fine saeculi
maxime regnat." The outstanding work on Bonaventure's theology of history is
Ratzinger's *Geschichtstheologie des hl. Bonaventura* (cited above p. 71 n.1).

[2] *Op. cit.*, p. 148, "Nihilominus tamen, quia paupertas fundamentum est evangelicae perfectionis, et ipsa est quasi complementum eiusdem; ideo viguit in Ecclesiae primordio, et congruum est, ut vigeat circa Ecclesiae statum finalem ...
Hieronymus ... dicit ibidem, quod 'omega revolvit ad alpha', id est, finalis status
concordavit cum primo."

[3] At one point he compared the life of "apostolic men" to the life of Adam before he had sinned. Again there seems an implication—not fully explained—of a
"Fall" in post-apostolic times. *Collationes in Hexaemeron XVIII* in *Opera* V, p. 415,
"*de pomis et vertice montium*, per hoc intelligitur *sublimitas apostolicorum virorum*, qui
tenent vitam, quam Deus dedit in paradiso. Si enim homo non peccasset, nulla
fuisset agrorum divisio, sed omnia communia." See also *Collatio XVI* in *Opera* V,
p. 406, "Notandum, quod Ecclesia posita fuit in paradiso, sicut primus homo, *ut
operaretur*, cum nullus *aliquid suum esse dicebat*. Incepit enim in magna perfectione
quod modo in religiosis observatur ..."

explain precisely when or how.) Then the whole subsequent history of mankind was one of progressive recovery of the lost revelation. Bonaventure believed that the process was approaching completion in his own time. (His idea of a "middle age" separating his own era from that of the primitive church is especially interesting.)

This approach to sacred history raised a set of new problems concerning the development of Christian doctrine, the role of St. Francis in this development, and—most important for our argument—the authorities competent to validate a new development and proclaim it to the whole church as revealed truth. We shall consider each of these topics in turn.

Bonaventure believed of course that the truths expressed in Holy Scripture were unchangeable, valid for all time. But he also believed that the unfolding of those truths to the understanding of men was a slow process that extended through the whole of history. He did not set out a fully-elaborated theory of "development of doctrine" in a formal train of theological argument but, over and over again, he used similes and metaphors which show that his whole approach to Scripture was conditioned by an implicit acceptance of such a theory. He wrote that the church militant was illumined by the heavenly church just as the moon was illumined by the sun; but the church developed in time and, just as the moon received the maximum of light only when it came to the full, so too the church was wholly illumined only when it was full-grown.[1] In another context he wrote that there were "seeds" of truth in Scripture which constantly grew in the understanding of men. The "seeds" could also be called "theories" (*theoriae*). That is to say the texts of Scripture gave rise to "theories" and, just as one seed grew into a tree which produced further seeds and eventually a whole forest, so the "theories" led to new understandings of Scripture which gave rise to new "theories" in almost infinite profusion.[2]

Underlying all these expressions was Bonaventure's conviction that the Bible was essentially a work of prophecy. It not only recorded the history of mankind down to the coming of Christ but foretold the

---

[1] *Collationes in Hexaemeron* XXII in *Opera* V, p. 438, "Unde sicut luna est filia solis et recipit lumen ab eo, similiter militans Ecclesia a superna Ierusalem ... Sicut enim luna plus et plus recipit lumen a sole, quousque veniat ad complementum; sic Ecclesia."

[2] *Collationes in Hexaemeron* XIII in *Opera* V, p. 388 and XV, *Opera* V, p. 400. See Ratzinger, *op. cit.*, pp. 10-11.

whole future of the human race until the Second Coming. Bonaventure wrote that the whole history of the world was like a beautiful poem. The poem could be appreciated in all its harmony only when it was seen as a whole; but no man could see the whole of history in one lifetime; therefore God gave us Holy Scripture which "describes all times and periods from the beginning of the world down to the day of judgement."[1] The prophets foretold the truth "infallibly and certainly"; but the full meanings of the prophetic texts were revealed to man only in the course of time as, one by one, the prophecies themselves were fulfilled.[2] Hence man's understanding of Scripture could constantly deepen with the passing of the ages. "He who does not understand the past cannot understand the future," wrote Bonaventure. And, again, "Scripture and its mysteries cannot be understood unless the course of history is known."[3]

Given these views it was not unreasonable for Bonaventure to believe that the men of his own day could understand Christ's revelation more perfectly than the Fathers of old. For him, the church, under the guidance of the Holy Spirit, constantly grew in the understanding of a faith that was itself eternally true. And in the unfolding of divine truth to men, Francis of Assisi played a role second only to that of Christ himself.

(ii) *Franciscan Revelation*

For Bonaventure Francis was not only a great saint but an apocalyptic figure sent by God to complete his revelation to men and, in doing so, to inaugurate a new era of world history. In Bonaventure's divisions of the ages of the world, as in Joachim's, one can find many different patterns of number symbolism. In the *Breviloquium* Bonaventure divided the whole of history into seven ages much as Augustine

---

[1] *Breviloquium* in *Opera* V, p. 203, "Habet etiam haec Scriptura sacra *longitudinem*, quae consistit in descriptione tam *temporum* quam *aetatum*, a principio scilicet mundi usque ad diem iudicii." See also p. 201, "*Progressus* autem sacrae Scripturae non est coarctatus ad leges ratiocinationum, definitionum et divisionum iuxta morem aliarum scientiarum et non est coarctatus ad partem universitatis; sed potius, cum secundum lumen supernaturale procedat ad dandam homini viatori notitiam rerum sufficientem, secundum quod expedit ad salutem, partim per plana verba, partim per mystica describit totius universi *continentiam* quasi in quadam summa ..."

[2] *Collationes in Hexaemeron* III in *Opera* V, p. 347.

[3] *Collationes in Hexaemeron* XV in *Opera* V, p. 400, "... scire non potest futura qui praeterita ignorat." *Collatio* II in *Opera* V, p. 339, "Scripturae intelligi non possunt nec mysteria, nisi sciatur decursus mundi ..."

had done; but his more characteristic pattern, presented in the *Collationes in Hexaemeron*, took the form of a "double-seven-scheme" (as Ratzinger calls it).[1] In this latter pattern the basic division was into two epochs corresponding to the Old and New Testaments. Each epoch was further divided into seven ages which (as in Joachim's work) were related to the seven days of creation and the seven seals of the Apocalypse.[2] In the single-seven scheme Christ, the perfect man, became incarnate during the sixth age, corresponding to the sixth day of creation when God made man. In the double-seven scheme Francis, a Christ-like figure, appeared during the sixth age of the second epoch to give a new example of perfection to man. Bonaventure believed that he was living in the last days of this sixth age, the age having begun in the time of Pope Hadrian (772-795), the contemporary of Charlemagne. He expected an interlude of turmoil and persecution; then the church would enter a seventh age of perfect tranquillity.[3] Bonaventure, to be sure, had no sympathy with Gerard of Borgo San Donnino's heretical view that Francis had come to proclaim a new eternal gospel which would replace the Gospel of Christ. Nor did he accept Joachim of Flora's prophecy of a coming third age of the Holy Spirit. But he did follow Gerard in identifying Francis with the Apocalypse's "angel of the sixth seal" and he followed Joachim in teaching that this angel-figure had a two-fold role in sacred history—to make a new revelation concerning the "spiritual meaning" of the Gospel and to establish a new community of religious whose way of life would be a model for the church in the last age of its existence on earth. The identification of Francis with the "angel of the sixth seal" was set out plainly in the Prologue to Bonaventure's *Legenda*:

> (Francis) is thought to be not unfitly set forth ... under the similitude of the Angel ascending from the rising of the sun, having the seal of the living God ... he was set as an example to those who follow Christ

---

[1] *Breviloquium* in *Opera* V, p. 204; *Collationes in Hexaemeron* XVI in *Opera* V, pp. 405-408. Each of the seven ages (in both series) was further subdivided into three units giving an over-all pattern of forty-two divisions (p. 408).

[2] Ratzinger rejects the arguments of earlier scholars who denied any influence of Joachim on Bonaventure. He argues that Bonaventure took his "double seven scheme" from Joachim even though he rejected the concept of a third "state" (*op. cit.*, pp. 18-20). Reeves summed up Bonaventure as "a Joachite *malgré lui*" (*op. cit.*, p. 181). The use of a "double seven" pattern by Joachim was emphasized especially in M. Reeves and B. Hirsch-Reich, "The Seven Seals in the Writings of Joachim of Fiore," *RTAM*, 21 (1954), pp. 211-247.

[3] *Collationes in Hexaemeron* XVI in *Opera* V, p. 408.

perfectly ... this is confirmed with the witness of irrefragable truth by the seal of the likeness of the living God, namely of Christ crucified that was impressed on his body.[1]

Earlier, Bonaventure had applied the imagery of the sixth angel to the Franciscan Order in his *De perfectione evangelica*. "The Holy Spirit has raised up poor religious whose sole task and care is *to sign the servants of God on their foreheads with the sign of the living God*."[2] And, again, in a sermon on St. Francis, he brought together in one passage, dense with allusions, references to Francis' stigmata, the angel of the sixth seal, and the signing of the elect with the sign *Tau* in the Book of Ezechiel.[3]

This persistent identification of Francis with the sixth angel of the Apocalypse (and hence with the sixth age of the New Testament era) provides a key to the interpretation of several difficult passages in the *Collationes in Hexaemeron*. To understand them we must remember that there were several angels in the Apocalypse who could be designated as the sixth angel. Of these, two especially interested Bonaventure. One was the angel of the sixth seal "having the seal of the living God" who "sealed one hundred and forty-four thousand out of every tribe of the children of Israel" (Apoc. 7, 2-4). The other was the angel of the sixth church at Philadelphia to whom it was written "Thus says the holy one, the true one who has the Key of David... Behold I have caused a door to open before you which no one can shut" (Apoc. 3, 7-8). Bonaventure apparently identified these angels with one another and certainly regarded both as figures of St. Francis. The opening of the sixth seal and the opening of the door both symbolized the new insight into Scripture that Francis brought (i.e., the doctrine of evangelical poverty). The sealing of the

---

[1] *Legenda Sancti Francisci* in *Opera* VIII, pp. 504-505, "... sub similitudine Angeli ascendentis ab ortu solis signumque Dei vivi habentis astruitur non immerito designatus ... positus est perfectis Christi sectatoribus in exemplum ... verum etiam irrefragabili veritatis testificatione confirmat *signaculum similitudinis* Dei viventis, Christi videlicet crucifixi, quod in corpore ipsius fuit impressum." On the subsequent widespread diffusion in the Franciscan Order of the idea that Francis was the angel of the sixth seal see S. Bihel, "S. Franciscus fuitne angelus sexti sigilli? (Apoc. 7.2)," *Antonianum*, 2 (1927), pp. 59-90; S. Clasen, *Franziskus, Engel des sechsten Siegels* (Werl-in-Westf., 1962). Pietro Olivi wrote that he had heard Bonaventure identify Francis with the angel of the sixth seal in a sermon delivered at Paris. See R. Manselli, *La 'Lectura super Apocalipsim' di Pietro di Giovanni Olivi* (Rome, 1955), p. 211 n. 1.

[2] *De perfectione* in *Opera* V, p. 164, "Spiritus sanctus religiones pauperculas suscitavit, quarum sollicitudo et cura tota esset ad *signandos servos Dei in frontibus eorum signo Dei vivi* ..."

[3] *De S. patre nostro Francisco, Sermo* I in *Opera* IX, pp. 574-575.

hundred and forty-four thousand referred to the establishment of his new Order of poor religious.

Thus, in *Collatio XVI* Bonaventure wrote that the sixth age was an age of "clear doctrine" and "prophetic life." It was necessary that in this time a new order should appear conforming to the life of Christ with, at its head "the angel ascending from the rising sun having the seal of the living God." And, Bonaventure added, this had already come to pass.[1] He repeated the phrases about clear doctrine and prophetic life a little further on, setting them in a more explicit historical framework. The sixth age, the age of clear doctrine, was also a time when the church had to endure new persecutions. Charlemagne had initiated the age by his patronage of scholars and he had exalted the church; but under his successors, Henry IV and Frederick Barbarossa, pseudo-popes appeared who tried to destroy the church. At this point the "angel ascending from the rising sun" appeared to stay the persecution until the servants of God were sealed on their foreheads. (Here the coming of Francis was fitted precisely into a temporal framework of world politics.) There remained then only the coming seventh age of peace when the church militant would be "conformed" to the church triumphant. Bonaventure concluded this passage with a reference to the "understanding of Scripture" or "revelation" which he associated with the angel of the sixth church, the angel of Philadelphia.[2]

In another reference to the transition from the sixth age to the seventh Bonaventure wrote (after referring to the sixth angel of the

---

[1] *Collationes in Hexaemeron* XVI in *Opera* V, p. 405, "Dies *humanae formae, tempus vocis propheticae, tempus clarae doctrinae*, in quo esset vita prophetica. Et necesse fuit, ut in hoc tempore veniret unus ordo, scilicet habitus propheticus, similis ordini Iesu Christi, cuius caput esset *Angelus, ascendens ab ortu solis habens signum Dei vivi*, et conformis Christo.—Et dixit, quod iam venerat."

[2] *Opera* V, p. 408, "Hoc tempore fuit *claritas doctrinae*, quia Carolus vocavit clericos et scripsit libros, ut in sancto Dionysio Biblia et in multis locis, et inceperunt legere et philosophari, et religiosos etiam dilatavit.—Hoc tempore oportuit venire vitam per ordinem, qui haberet *vitam propheticam* ... Hoc tempore similiter Carolus exaltavit Ecclesiam, et eius successores oppugnaverunt eam: tempore Henrici quarti fuerunt duo Papae, similiter tempore Frederici magni, duo. Et certum est, quod aliquis inter eos voluit exterminare Ecclesiam; sed *Angelus ascendens ab ortu solis clamavit quatuor Angelis: Nolite nocere terrae et mari, quousque signemus servos Dei nostri in frontibus eorum*. Unde adhuc restat Ecclesiae tribulatio. Et dictum est Angelo Philadelphiae, qui sextus est: *Haec dicit Sanctus et Verus, qui habet clavem David; qui aperit, et nemo claudit; claudit, et nemo aperit. Scio opera tua, quia ecce, dedi coram te ostium apertum.*—Et dixit, quod adhuc intelligentia Scripturae daretur vel revelatio vel clavis David *personae* vel *multitudini*; et magis credo, quod multitudini."

Apocalypse) "Just as the world was made in six days and Christ came in the sixth age, so after six ages of the church the contemplative Church shall be born."[1] He associated Francis and the Franciscans quite explicitly with the coming Order of contemplatives in *Collatio XX.* Here again he used the imagery of the angel of Philadelphia, explaining that the Scriptural reference to a "key of David" could be interpreted to mean, "I will give the knowledge of Scripture to this sixth angel."[2] Then Bonaventure turned to the role of the Order of the sixth age. In this age he said, God made man "in his own image and likeness." There seems to be implied here a complex reference to Adam, Christ and Francis simultaneously for Bonaventure went on to explain that this context of the sixth age defined the vocation of the Franciscans. "Behold your vocation for it is great." Then he added that this vocation was one of contemplation and introduced a direct reference to St. Francis.

> Contemplation cannot come about except in the highest simplicity; and the highest simplicity cannot come about except in the greatest poverty; and this is proper to this Order. The intention of Blessed Francis was to live in the greatest poverty.

Finally, Bonaventure declared that God allowed the present time of affliction to continue because many friars had fallen away from their proper state, the state that was to "possess the promised land."[3]

The willingness of Bonaventure to accept, at least in part, the

---

[1] F. Delorme (ed.), *Collationes in Hexaemeron* (*Bibliotheca Franciscana Scholastica Medii Aevi*, VIII) (Quaracchi, 1934), p. 265, "Isti signati describuntur stantes super montem, scilicet contemplationis, ubi etiam sextus angelus ostendit Ioanni civitatem et mensuram eius ... In quibus etiam intellige signari sex tempora; et sextum tempus habet septem tempora cum quiete. Et sicut sex diebus factus est mundus et sexta aetate venit Christus, ita post sex tempora Ecclesiae in fine generabitur Ecclesia contemplativa." (This is a different recension from that in the *Opera Omnia.*)

[2] *Collationes in Hexaemeron* XX in *Opera* V, p. 430, "Nota, quod duodecim signationes sunt sub *sexto sigillo* et sub *sexto Angelo*, et mensuratio civitatis et ostensio civitatis et apertio libri; et sexto Angelo, scilicet Philadelphiae, qui interpretatur, *conservans hereditatem*, dictum est de *clave David* ... hoc est, dabo notitiam Scripturarum isti sexto Angelo."

[3] *Loc. cit.* "Et dicebat, quod malignitatibus latrantium necesse est impleri hoc sexto tempore, in quo fecit Deus *hominem ad imaginem et similitudinem* suam. Et addebat: *Videte vocationem vestram*, quia magna est ... Contemplatio non potest esse nisi in summa simplicitate; et summa simplicitas non potest esse nisi in maxima paupertate; et haec est huius ordinis. Intentio beati Francisci fuit esse in summa paupertate.—Et dicebat, quoniam multum retrocessimus a statu nostro, et ideo permittit nos Deus affligi, ut per hoc reducamur ad statum, qui debet habere terram promissionis."

current Joachimite fantasies about the role of St. Francis in sacred history destroyed any possibility that might still have existed of the problem of Franciscan poverty being treated for what it really was— essentially a disciplinary question affecting the practices of one particular Order in the church. Bonaventure claimed that Francis had brought to men a revelation of universal significance. The whole future of the human race depended on the acceptance of this revelation by the church. We must bear in mind that medieval theologians did not use words like *revelatio* and *inspiratio* with the same technical precision as modern ones. All the same Bonaventure's attitude to St. Francis seems far removed from the judicious doctrine formulated by Thomas Aquinas—that God sent great saints to men "not for the declaration of any new doctrine but as a guide to human conduct."

Bonaventure's repeated insistence on an apocalyptic role for St. Francis, his evident willingness to see Francis as the bearer of a new *revelatio*, a new *intelligentia Scripturae*, inevitably raised the problem of how new revelation could be authenticated. The problem was complicated by the fact that, in his controversies with the secular masters of Paris, Bonaventure's task was not simply to defend the life and teachings of Francis of Assisi. No one was attacking St. Francis. What Bonaventure had to defend was a whole way of life and a structure of doctrine associated with it that had grown up in the Franciscan Order during the half century after Francis' death. Moreover, he was committed to defending the Franciscans' practice of poverty, not only as a legitimate way of life within the church, but as the exemplification of a pattern of evangelical perfection that Christ had taught to the first apostles.

In the mid-thirteenth century any attempt to authenticate a "new tradition," a new "revelation" would almost inevitably have to depend in part at least on an appeal to the authority of the Roman see. This was especially true in the case of the "new Tradition" of the Franciscans for, as we have seen, the doctrine of the absolute poverty of Christ and the apostles had emerged in the course of a complex interplay between the Franciscan Order and the papacy. St. Francis certainly believed that, by living in utter poverty, he was faithfully imitating the life of Christ. But it was Gregory IX who laid down that the essential nature of poverty consisted in a renunciation of property "singly and in common." Bonaventure in turn maintained that Christ had taught this distinction to the apostles and, to meet various objections, added more complicated distinctions of his own con-

cerning dominion, possession and use. The process reached a conclusion when Nicholas III (in the Bull *Exiit*) gave a kind of dogmatic
validity to the terminology that Bonaventure had adopted for polemical purposes by declaring that the Franciscan way of life, so defined,
was indeed the way "given by the Son to the apostles by example and
word." Bonaventure died five years before Nicholas' decree was
promulgated. But he could maintain quite convincingly that the
earlier papal bulls defining and approving the Franciscan way of life
lent support to his theory of evangelical poverty. And, naturally, he
insisted on this over and over again.

The point to be emphasized is the extra-ordinary dependence of the
Franciscans on the papacy in the sphere of doctrine as well as in the
sphere of discipline. It was not simply that they needed a strong papal
authority to authenticate a new revelation made by St. Francis.
Rather they had embraced as the authentic doctrine of their Founder a
theory that was in large part a creation of the Roman see. We can next
examine the ways in which this situation influenced Bonaventure's
ideas on the teaching authority of the church and the sovereignty of
the popes.

3. BONAVENTURE: SOVEREIGNTY AND INFALLIBILITY

(i) *Jurisdiction*

In a recent study of the Franciscans' views on papal power Ratzinger observed that, for Bonaventure, the pope was not merely a
successor to the historical Christ who had once lived on earth;
rather, he "represented a still living and ruling Lord and actualized
his presence in the church." Moreover, according to Ratzinger,
Bonaventure advanced from this conception to anticipate also "the
idea of concretizing the infallibility of the church in the pope."[1] Such
views are in accordance with those found in several earlier studies on
Bonaventure's ecclesiology. In a work published amid the controversies of 1870, Fidelis a Fanna maintained that Bonaventure had
proclaimed both the infallibility and the primacy of the Roman
pontiff.[2] And the editors of the great Quaracchi edition of Bonaven-

---

[1] J. Ratzinger, "Der Einfluss des Bettelordensstreites auf die Entwicklung der
Lehre vom päpstlichen Universalprimat, unter besonderer Berücksichtigung des
heiligen Bonaventura" in *Theologie in Geschichte und Gegenwart*, ed. J. Auer and H.
Volk (Munich, 1957), pp. 697-724 at p. 720.

[2] Fidelis a Fanna, *Seraphici Doctoris D. Bonaventurae doctrina de Romani Pontificis
primatu et infallibilitate* (Turin, 1870). For a critical discussion see P. de Vooght in
L'infaillibilité de l'église (Chevetogne, 1962), p. 105.

ture's *Opera* went out of their way to assert that Bonaventure's teaching on papal infallibility was in perfect accord with the doctrine proclaimed at Vatican Council I.[1]

Ratzinger's observations are perceptive and, at least in part, undoubtedly true. Bonaventure did go further than his predecessors in presenting the pope as the epitome of all ecclesiastical power. The canonists had commonly defined the pope's plenitude of power in terms of a supremacy and universality of jurisdiction. The pope was the head of the episcopate just as Peter had been head of the apostles. He could judge the other bishops. He could exercise the same kind of episcopal authority throughout the universal church that each bishop exercised in his own diocese. But the canonists did not maintain that episcopal authority was a mere delegation from an all-powerful pope. On the contrary they regarded the bishops as successors of the apostles, each of whom had received authority directly from Christ. Thomas of York, as we saw, advanced beyond this position by asserting that inferior members of the hierarchy derived all their authority from the supreme pontiff. Bonaventure adopted this same position and developed it in considerable detail.

He defined the papal plenitude of power thus:

> The plenitude of this power is three-fold. The supreme pontiff alone has the whole plenitude of authority that Christ conferred on the church; he has this authority everywhere in all the churches just as in his own special see of Rome; *from him all authority flows to all inferiors throughout the universal church* so far as it pertains to individuals to participate in it just as in Heaven all the glory of the saints flows from that fount of all good, Jesus Christ.[2]

Against this position it could be argued that every priest received the "power of the keys"—the power to remit sins in the sacrament of

---

[1] *Opera omnia* V (1891), p. 198 n. 3. "Manifestum autem est, doctrinam nostri doctoris ita perfecte convenire cum decretis Vaticanis, ut ipse quasi praeoccupasse videatur ea quae a Concilio illo docentur ..." J. Uhlmann, "Die Vollgewalt des Papstes nach Bonaventura," *Franziskanische Studien*, 11 (1924), pp. 179-193 also presented Bonaventure as a defender of papal infallibility (pp. 189-193). The question of infallibility is not raised in A. Blasucci, "La costituzione gerarchica della chiesa in S. Bonaventura," *Miscellanea Francescana*, 68 (1968), pp. 81-101.

[2] *Quare fratres minores praedicent* in *Opera* VIII, p. 375. Bonaventure's views on the structure of the church hierarchy were much influenced by the pseudo-Dyonisian concepts that were so fashionable at Paris in the mid-thirteenth century. For earlier canonistic views on the relations between pope and bishops see my *Foundations*, pp. 33-34, 144-148; "Grosseteste and the Theory of Papal Sovereignty," *Journal of Ecclesiastical History*, 6 (1955), pp. 1-17; "Collegiality in the Middle Ages," *Concilium*, 7 (1965), pp. 5-14.

penance—directly from Christ at the moment of his ordination. This point was of great importance for Bonaventure, for the claim of the friars to hear confessions in any parish by virtue of their papal privileges was at the heart of the conflict between mendicant friars and secular clergy. Parish priests, often supported by their bishops, asserted that they possessed an intrinsic right, inherent in their office, to hear the confessions of their own parishioners. Bonaventure wanted to argue that even the power of sacramental absolution was in some sense a mere delegation from the papacy so that the pope had an absolute right to bestow it and take it away as he saw fit.

He reached this conclusion by presenting a variation on the canonical distinction between "power of orders" and "power of jurisdiction." In explaining the difference between the pope and other bishops, the canonists had often pointed out that all were equal in orders but that the pope excelled in jurisdiction. Every priest received the power of the keys at his ordination, Bonaventure conceded, but he identified the keys simply as the power of orders. In the sacrament of Holy Orders the priest received a "character" imprinted directly by God which could never be taken away, not even by the pope. This character conferred immediately the power to consecrate the Eucharist and potentially the power to remit sins in the sacrament of penance. But the remission of sins was an act of judging; valid judgments could be passed only on penitents subject to the jurisdiction of the priest;[1] and Bonaventure maintained, all jurisdiction descended from the pope. Therefore every exercise of the power of the keys depended ultimately on papal authorization.

> Since "character" cannot be taken away, therefore de facto the power that follows from character cannot be taken away. But since jurisdiction descends in due order from superior to inferior, so that its plenitude is in the supreme pontiff, therefore he can take it away and the power that follows from it.[2]

---

[1] *Commentaria in quartum librum Sententiarum* in *Opera* IV, D. 19 art. 2 q. 1, p. 504, "Dicendum ... quod in ordine sacerdotali clavium potestas confertur." D. 19 art. 2 q. 2, p. 506, "... si loquamur de potentia solvendi quantum ad *essentiam*, sic radicaliter est in ipsa anima, sicut et character ... Alio modo possumus loqui quantum ad *usum*, et hoc modo necessario requiritur *status viatoris* et *auctoritas iurisdictionis* ... talis autem *iudicatio* non est sine aliqua iurisdictione in eum qui iudicatur, quia nemo potest aliquem iudicare, nisi qui iudex eius constituitur ab eo qui potest ... et si amittitur haec iurisdictio, cessat clavis exsecutio." On the derivation of the power of "binding and loosing" from the pope see also *Breviloquium* in *Opera* V, pp. 276, 278.

[2] *Com. in 4 Sent.* in *Opera* IV, D. 25 art. 1 q. 2, p. 645.

Bonaventure differed sharply from the earlier canonists and from his contemporary adversaries, the secular masters of Paris, above all in the status he assigned to the bishops. For the secular masters each bishop wielded an autonomous authority derived directly from Christ. Bonaventure suggested rather that bishops were mere delegates, "vicars" of the pope, just as parish priests were vicars of the bishops.[1] Although, in discussing the derivation of all jurisdiction from the pope, Bonaventure often had occasion to refer to the use of jurisdiction in the sacrament of penance, he did not limit the application of the word *jurisdictio* to that sphere. On the contrary he used this term to designate the whole power of ruling and judging that inhered in the church by virtue of Christ's commission to Peter.[2] And in all the forms of its exercise, this power of ecclesiastical government, was derived ultimately from the pope, "Ecclesiastical rulers receive all the power which they have over their subjects from him (the supreme pontiff)."[3]

It is interesting that Bonaventure never claimed that the authority of the apostles themselves was derived from Peter rather than from Christ. He never suggested that Christ bestowed a power of orders on the apostles but no power of jurisdiction. This idea came to be widely accepted by the apologists for the mendicant orders in the half century after Bonaventure's death. But his own position was different. He repeatedly asserted that all the apostles received their authority from Christ—and at one point explicitly noted that this authority conferred by Christ included both orders and jurisdiction.[4] Bonaventure's position is summed up in his phrase "The pope stands in place of Peter; nay rather of Jesus Christ."[5] For Bonaventure the

---

[1] *Quare fratres minores praedicent* in *Opera* VIII, p. 377, "... ipsi plebani sint vicarii episcoporum in suis parochiis sicut episcopi Summi Pontificis in officiis sibi commissis ..."

[2] *Jurisdictio* could co-exist with the power of orders as in a priest but could also be exercised separately as by an archdeacon. *Com. in 4 Sent.* in *Opera* IV, D. 18 p. 2 art. 1 q. 3, p. 489; D. 25 art. 1 q. 2, p. 645.

[3] *Quare fratres minores praedicent* in *Opera* VIII, p. 376, "... omnes inferiores Ecclesiae rectores curam et totam potestatem, quam habent super subditos, ab ipso accipiunt, mediate vel immediate ..."

[4] *Com. in 4 Sent.* in *Opera* IV, D. 19 art. 3 q. 1, p. 509. Referring specifically to the power of jurisdiction he wrote, "Quando ergo *Dominus* dedit clavem *et hanc potestatem*, ipse praesupposuit eius exsecutionem secundum regulam potestatis collatae Petro et eius successoribus."

[5] *Commentarius in Evangelium S. Lucae* in *Opera* VII, Cap. IX, p. 217, "... est loco Petri, immo loco Iesu Christi." On the origins of the pope's title "vicar of Christ" see M. Maccarrone, *Vicarius Christi* (Rome, 1962). The importance of the transition

pope was not merely successor to the position that Peter held during
Christ's lifetime on earth. After the ascension Peter and all subsequent
popes moved into the position of headship over the earthly church
that Christ had formerly occupied. "The bishops hold the place of the
apostles; but above the apostles is Christ; and, after Christ, Peter."[1]
Hence, just as the first apostles derived their authority from Christ, so
too the bishops of Bonaventure's own day, the successors of the
apostles, were conceived of as deriving their authority from Christ's
representative, the pope. The church, Bonaventure wrote, "needed
such a supreme ruler in whom was the state of all ecclesiastical
prelacy."[2]

So far, evidently, Ratzinger was right. Bonaventure's idea of the
pope as immediate representative of a continuing power of Christ in
the church did lead on to a doctrine that all ecclesiastical jurisdiction
was concentrated in the supreme pontiff. But so far we have considered only questions of church government. We still have to
consider whether, in the sphere of church doctrine, Bonaventure
really proclaimed "the concretizing of the infallibility of the church in
the pope."

(ii) *Magisterium*

In his writings on behalf of the Franciscan Order (and in various
other writings) Bonaventure repeatedly appealed to three sources of
Catholic truth. These were: the teaching of Scripture, the belief
of the universal church, and the pronouncements of the popes.
As to the first, one modern author has observed that "No one in the
thirteenth century spoke of the Bible with such fullness of heart, such
warmth and such conviction as St. Bonaventure."[3] Characteristically,
in the *De perfectione evangelica*, he appealed primarily to the Gospels to
prove the truth of his doctrine of apostolic poverty. One authoritative
saying of Christ counseling absolute poverty, he wrote, would be
wholly sufficient to establish the doctrine however many texts of

---

from the earlier title, "vicar of Peter," to "vicar of Christ" was strongly emphasized by W. Ullmann, *The Growth of Papal Government in the Middle Ages* (London,
1955).

[1] *Collationes in Hexaemeron* XXII in *Opera* V, p. 439, ... locum tenent (episcopi)
Apostolorum. Super Apostolos autem est Christus, et post Petrus."

[2] *Com. in 4 Sent.* in *Opera* IV, D. 19 art. 3 q. 1, p. 508, "... oportuit, unum esse
praelatum primum et supremum, in quo esset *status* omnis praelationis ecclesiasticae."

[3] P. de Vooght, *Les sources de la doctrine chrétienne* (Bruges, 1954), p. 17.

expositors and doctors might seem to affirm the contrary.[1] Bonaventure's belief in the formal infallibility of Scripture was expressed clearly in the *Breviloquium* "Nothing in Scripture should be rejected as false—for its all-perfect Author, the Holy Spirit, could say nothing untrue." And, again, "Because authority resides principally in the Sacred Scriptures all of which are inspired by the Holy Spirit—true faith may never disagree with Scripture."[2]

But how could certain truth be established when men disagreed about the meaning of Scripture? In the *De perfectione evangelica* Bonaventure argued that the Franciscan way of life had been accepted by the universal church. To deny the doctrine on which that way of life was based implied therefore that the whole church had erred. But it was "most horrible and incredible" to assert that God would so permit his holy people to err universally.[3] Similarly, in his commentary on the Sentences, Bonaventure declared, "The universal church is not deceived, nor does she err" and referred to "the usage of the universal church which cannot err."[4] He also wrote "The church can prove her authority from Scripture; this having been proved she should be obeyed...."[5]

This last text raises a difficult point. Bonaventure plainly believed that the universal church as a whole could not err in its understanding of Scriptural truth. But did he also believe that the teaching of the church could be a channel of non-Scriptural revelation? De Vooght sharply denied this, asserting that, for Bonaventure, Scripture was "the source of all Christian doctrine." He stressed Bonaventure's text "Every saving truth is either in Scripture or emanates from it or can be reduced to it,"[6] but conceded that Bonaventure also wrote (concerning the reverencing of images) "The apostles handed down

---

[1] *Opera* V, p. 130, "... ad quam sufficientissime astruendam una sola auctoritas expressa ex ore Christi, consulentis dimittere omnia, esset sufficientissima, etiam si multa Glossarum et expositorum et doctorum dicta viderentur esse contraria."

[2] *Opera* V, p. 207, "Nihil in (Scriptura) ... respuendum tamquam *falsum* ... pro eo quod Spiritus sanctus, eius auctor perfectissimus, nihil potuit dicere *falsum*." See also p. 261.

[3] *Opera* V, p. 153, "... est horribilissimum et incredibilissimum, quod Deus permitteret sic errare universaliter populum sanctum suum ..."

[4] *Com. in 4 Sent.* in *Opera* IV, D. 20 p. 2 art. 1 q. 2, p. 532, "Ecclesia universalis non decipitur nec errat." D. 18 p. 2 art. 1 q. 4, p. 490, "... hoc habet *usus* Ecclesiae universalis, quam errare est impossibile, ut videtur."

[5] *Op. cit.* D. 40 art. 1 q. 3, p. 853, "Sed ecclesia per scripturam suam potuit probare auctoritatem; qua probata oportet obedire ..."

[6] *In circumcisione Domini, Sermo* I in *Opera* IX, p. 138, cit. de Vooght, *op. cit.*, p. 18. De Vooght gives several other similar texts from Bonaventure.

many things which are not written."[1] There is another text, over-
looked by De Vooght, in which Bonaventure seems plainly to distinguish between church and Scripture and to treat them as separate,
co-equal sources of revelation. Discussing the formula used in
baptism he wrote:

> If Christ did not institute (this formula) the church instituted it by
> inspiration of the Holy Spirit, and this is as much as if Christ had
> spoken it with his own mouth. For the whole Trinity approves what
> the Holy Spirit inspires just as it approves what Christ instituted.[2]

The view that ecclesiastical tradition could justify liturgical usages
which lacked a scriptural foundation was of course commonly held.
But Bonaventure here seems to have gone beyond this common
belief to affirm that ecclesiastical tradition was co-equal with Scripture
as a source of divine truth (since both were inspired by the Holy
Spirit). His teaching on Scripture and Tradition was, to say the least,
far from clear-cut.

Bonaventure at any rate taught that the universal church was
certainly unerring in faith. There remains the problem of how the
unerring faith of the church could be expressed. We find no trace in
Bonaventure's work of the canonistic doctrine that a representative
general council was the highest authority for declaring the faith of
the church. Nor did he explore the alternative canonistic view that
belief in an "unerring church" meant only an acknowledgment that
the church was indefectible, that the truth faith would always survive,
if only in some small group or even in a single individual.[3] There is,
however, a third possibility. Did Bonaventure hold that all the
teaching authority of the church was concentrated in the pope as an
infallible teacher just as he held that all the jurisdiction of the church
was concentrated in the pope as a sovereign head? This is the question
of crucial importance for our enquiry.

In the *De perfectione evangelica*, after appealing to the authority of
Scripture and the universal church, Bonaventure condemned his
adversaries for defying the authority of the apostolic see. "It is not

---

[1] *Com. in 3 Sent.* in *Opera* III, D. 9 art. 1 q. 2, p. 204, cit. de Vooght, p. 29.

[2] *Com. in 4 Sent.* in *Opera* IV, D. 3 p. 1 art. 2 q. 1, p. 71, "... si Christus ipse non
instituit, instituit Ecclesia instinctu Spiritus sancti, et hoc tantum est, ac si ipse
proprio ore dixisset. Tota enim Trinitas approbat quod ipse Spiritus sanctus
inspirat fieri, sicut illud quod Christus instituit."

[3] He did of course affirm the doctrine of indefectibility. E.g., in *4 Sent.* in *Opera*
IV, D. 4 p. 1 art. 2 q. 3, p. 105. But he did not use it in any discussions of inerrancy.

wisdom but rashness to wish to judge the apostolic see, which is judged by God alone, and to reject its judgment and sentence." In a corresponding passage of the *Apologia pauperum* he urged the Roman church to rise up and defend itself against the imputation of error. "Arise, holy mother, and defend your cause... you who have been so long the teacher of truth are now denounced as a proponent of error...."[1] Bonaventure evidently was certain that the popes were not in error in their teaching on the immediate point at issue—the nature of apostolic poverty—but he nowhere explicitly asserted that all doctrinal decrees of the Roman church—still less of individual pontiffs—were necessarily infallible. The texts we have quoted are typical of many to be found in Bonaventure's works. For him, the Roman church was "lifted up among nations... to defend the truths of faith and morals."[2] Papal authority was "so eminent that it transcends all human power." No one was permitted to "dogmatize contrary to the definition (of the Vicar of Christ) in faith and morals."[3] These and other similar statements were collected in the old work of Fidelis a Fanna that we have already mentioned. The meaning of such texts was so obvious, the author suggested, that there was no need to demonstrate that they referred to "a personal infallibility of the Roman pontiff in matters of faith and morals." But in fact this is precisely what cannot be demonstrated. All the texts that Bonaventure used concerning the teaching authority of the popes could have been written by the twelfth century canonists—one finds precisely similar statements in their works—but the canonists who used such language certainly did not believe in papal infallibility. Bonaventure seems to have moved always within the framework of the canonical doctrine that the pope was supreme judge in matters of faith without advancing the further proposition that his judgments were necessarily infallible and irreformable.

On the question of "reformability" Bonaventure in fact explicitly repeated the juridical doctrine that a sovereign ruler was not bound by the decisions of his predecessor. In the *De perfectione evangelica*, he argued that a decree of Pope Urban commending the poverty of monks who held all things in common could not prejudice the declarations of Popes Honorius and Gregory approving the higher mode of poverty practiced by the Franciscans, for "an equal has no

---

[1] *Opera* V, p. 153.
[2] *Opera* VIII, p. 315.
[3] *Apologia Pauperum* in *Opera* VIII, pp. 235, 313, 315.

power over an equal."[1] And, in the *Apologia pauperum*, he pointed out
that, in general, no decisions of earlier pontiffs could be used to attack
the state of evangelical poverty, here citing Pope Innocent III's
decretal *Innotuit* with its classical formulation of the principle, *par in
parem non habet imperium*.[2] Similarly, the canons of general councils
could not be cited against the Franciscan position, since the Roman
church was not bound by councils. It may be that here Bonaventure
had merely matters of church discipline in mind though, as we have
seen, the question of evangelical poverty had profound theological
implications for him. In another context, discussing the controversy
with the Greeks over the *filioque* clause in the Creed, Bonaventure
seems to have asserted more plainly that the Roman church was not
bound by councils even in matters of faith.[3]

These texts emphasizing the great freedom and discretion enjoyed
by the Roman church even in the shaping of new doctrinal formulas
fit in very well with Bonaventure's ideas on progressive revelation.
But it is not so clear that they are readily compatible with a doctrine of
infallibility which would imply the irreformability of earlier dogmatic
statements. There were problems involved here that Bonaventure
never considered. According to the strict tenor of his argument it
was entirely possible that some future pope would change Gregory
IX's conception of holy poverty just as Gregory had changed Pope

---

[1] *Opera* V, p. 145, "Unde decretum Urbani Papae praeiudicare non potuit
auctoritati Innocentii, Honorii et Gregorii, qui istum modum approbaverunt tam
in iure communi quam in privatis privilegiis, quia 'non habet imperium par in
parem'."

[2] *Opera* VIII, p. 314, "Nulla etiam *praecedentium Pontificum statuta* obsistunt, ut
Extra, de Electione, *Innotuit*, ubi dicit Innocentius tertius …' non habeat imperium
par in parem'."

[3] *Com. in 1 Sent.* in *Opera* I, D. 11 art. 1 q. 1, p. 212, "*Vel* potest dici, sicut dicit
Anselmus, quod novum (symbolum) edidimus; et hoc quidem facere potuimus,
quia Romana Ecclesia plenitudinem potestatis a Petro, Apostolorum principe,
acceperat, in qua nulla Patrum sententia nec interdictum potuit nec arctare nec ei
praeiudicare nec ligare eam ad aliquid." Here, the term *Patrum sententia* seems to
refer clearly to decrees of earlier general councils. But, after this assertion that the
pope was not bound by existing canons, Bonaventure added that he did not in fact
think that the true doctrine of the procession of the Holy Spirit had been hidden
from the early Fathers. They had simply had no occasion to define it (*op. cit.*, p.
213). Bonaventure's treatment of the *filioque* clause is perhaps best understood as an
example of the theory of "development of doctrine" in its more conservative
form. That is to say that he was concerned with the church's deepening understanding, through the course of the ages, of a truth that was implied in Scripture
though not explicitly stated there. See Ratzinger, "Offenbarung, Schrift, Überlieferung. Ein Text des hl. Bonaventure," *Trierer theologische Zeitschrift*, 67 (1958),
pp. 13-27.

Urban's. Bonaventure never envisaged such a possibility. Nor did he ever concern himself with the problems concerning alleged heretical popes of the past that had so perplexed the Decretists. But a disinclination to dwell on the errors of past popes is not the same as a proclamation of a novel doctrine of papal infallibility.

That Bonaventure stopped short of formulating such a doctrine is suggested finally by his handling of the text at Luke 22.32 "I have prayed for you Peter that your faith shall not fail." Bonaventure discussed this text several times and always (in accordance with the general opinion of his age) he took it as guaranteeing the faith of the church as a whole, not the faith of the popes in particular. Commenting on Luke 9.20 he explained Christ's words to Peter with the gloss, "It was conceded to Peter that the true faith of his church would never fail."[1] In his commentary on the Sentences he wrote, after quoting the text *Ego rogavi pro te*, "It is agreed that this was said to Peter in the person of the church; but Christ 'was heard in all things because of his reverence' (Heb. 5.7); therefore in this too. And if so the universal church is not deceived nor does she err."[2] Bonaventure's most detailed explanation of the text came in his commentary on Luke 22.32. There he presented the two standard interpretations, neither of which provided any basis for a doctrine of papal infallibility. Either the words of Christ referred to Peter himself in which case they meant, not that he would never fall away from the faith, but that his faith would not fail finally and irrecoverably. Or the words of Christ referred to the whole church. In that case they meant that the universal church, "the barque of Peter" would never suffer total "shipwreck."[3]

Bonaventure's most systematic treatise on papal power was presented in a section of his *De perfectione evangelica* entitled "On the Obedience Due to the Supreme Pontiff."[4] At the outset he undertook to prove the licitness of the papal claim to universal obedience from both the Old and New Testaments. But he did not even mention Luke 22.32

---

[1] *Commentarius in Evangelium Lucae* in *Opera* VII, p. 227, "Hinc est, quod *Petrus* est vocatus, et ei concessum est, ut de Ecclesia eius nunquam deficiat vera fides; infra vigesimo secundo: 'Ego pro te rogavi, Petre, ut non deficiat'."

[2] *Com. in 4 Sent.* in *Opera* IV, D. 20 p. 2 art. 1 q. 2, p. 532.

[3] *Com. in Luc.* in *Opera* VII, p. 552, "Hic rogavit Dominus, non ut Petrus *non caderet*, sed ut *non deficeret*, quia, quamvis ceciderit, resurrexit ... Vel potest illud referri ad *Ecclesiam Petri*, pro cuius fide rogavit Dominus ... Et haec Ecclesia, quae designatur per Petri naviculam, licet concutiatur, tamen non naufragatur."

[4] *Opera* V, pp. 189-198.

among the New Testament texts referring to the authority of Peter's successors in the papacy. Nor did the ensuing exposition contain any doctrine of papal infallibility. Bonaventure wrote that the vicar of Christ received "every power that it was fitting for a mere man to be given." But it is by no means clear that he regarded the quality of infallibility as "fitting for a mere man." Indeed, he wrote "There is no one who cannot deceive and be deceived except God and the Holy Spirit."[1]

Bonaventure has been called "the principal theoretician of papal monarchy in the thirteenth century."[2] In the history of papal infallibility he is a transitional figure. His involvement in the disputes concerning the Franciscan Order led to many new emphases in his ecclesiology, emphases that we shall find recurring in the works of the first exponents of the infallibility doctrine. He was interested, for instance, in the development of Christian doctrine, in the possibility of non-Scriptural revelation, in the authentication of new doctrine by the papacy. In some ways he went beyond the canonists in his handling of the problems of papal power. His doctrine of the pope as the epitome of all ecclesiastical authority could certainly have led to the conclusion that, since the universal church was unerring, its head was unerring too. But Bonaventure never reached that conclusion. His interest remained focused on the traditional problems of papal sovereignty. He re-iterated, in an extreme form, the old doctrine that the pope was a supreme judge. He never asked the new question—whether the pope was infallible in his judgements.

---

[1] *Com. in 4 Sent.* in *Opera* IV, D. 20 p. 2 art. 1 q. 5, p. 539, "... Dominus vicario suo plenitudinem potestatis contulit et tantam utique potestatem, quanta debebat homini puro dari ..." *Breviloquium* in *Opera* V, p. 207, "... nullus autem est, qui falli non possit et fallere nesciat, nisi Deus et Spiritus sanctus ..."

[2] Y. Congar, *L'église de saint Augustin à l'époque moderne* (Paris, 1970), p. 222.

CHAPTER THREE

PIETRO OLIVI

Pietro Olivi was probably the most influential Franciscan master in the decades immediately after Bonaventure's death.[1] He was certainly a figure of the highest importance in the development of the doctrine of papal infallibility. Olivi was, indeed, the first major medieval thinker who posed—and answered affirmatively—the question, "Whether the Roman pontiff is... unerring in faith and morals." The title under which Olivi's *Quaestio* is presented in its printed edition, *De infallibilitate Romani pontificis*, is not Olivi's own but was supplied by the modern editor.[2] The title is not misleading however. Olivi's *Quaestio* really was concerned with the precise problem of papal infallibility. It is important therefore for us to grasp the nature of his argument and to understand how he came to formulate it.

1. The Enigma of Pietro Olivi

(i) *The Novelty of Olivi's Doctrine*

Olivi was a most prolific writer and discussions on various aspects of papal authority can be found scattered throughout the vast corpus of his work. His most explicit treatment of papal infallibility was presented in a treatise, *Quaestiones de perfectione evangelica*, which dealt with various issues concerning the religious vows of poverty, chastity and obedience. In this work the discussion on papal authority was included as a problem concerning obedience. Bonaventure, in similar fashion, had included a section on the particular obedience due to the pope when considering the obligations of religious obedience in

---

[1] The fundamental study, upon which all subsequent research has been based, is F. Ehrle, "Petrus Johannis Olivi, sein Leben und seine Schriften," *ALKG*, 3 (1887), pp. 409-552. For a detailed bibliography of later work on Olivi see Servus Gieben, "Bibliographia Oliviana (1885-1967)," *Collectanea Franciscana*, 38 (1968), pp. 167-195. Gieben provides a list of editions of Olivi's writings made since 1885 at pp. 168-173.

[2] M. Maccarrone, "Una questione inedita dell' Olivi sull' infallibilità del papa," *Rivista di storia della chiesa in Italia*, 3 (1949), pp. 309-343. Olivi's text is printed at pp. 325-343 under the heading "Petri Johannis Olivi quaestio de infallibilitate Romani pontificis."

general in his homonymous treatise on evangelical perfection.[1] But whereas Bonaventure posed a merely conventional question, "On the obedience due to the supreme pontiff," Olivi went further and asked "Whether the Roman pontiff is to be obeyed by all Catholics as an unerring standard (*tamquam regule inerrabili*) in faith and morals."

Olivi is an enigmatic figure. Throughout his career as a theology teacher he was repeatedly accused of heresy and repeatedly professed himself to be a loyal and orthodox Catholic. Although he formulated the first systematic argument in favor of papal infallibility he was posthumously condemned for having despised and rejected the authority of the Roman church. Some of his works are charged with a radical Joachimism. Others contain only conventional scholastic argumentation. After his death his followers identified him with the seventh angel of the Apocalypse;[2] his enemies called him Antichrist.[3] Modern scholars disagree as to his essential orthodoxy or heterodoxy. They concur at least in acknowledging the brilliant originality of his work in various branches of metaphysics, physics and ethics. Yet, strangely, the novelty of his theological doctrine on papal infallibility has hardly been recognized at all in modern writings.

Ehrle wrote that "in this matter Olivi did not depart from the common opinion of his contemporaries." Oliger quoted the title of Olivi's *Quaestio* in abbreviated form as, "whether the pope is to be obeyed in faith and morals by all Catholics." without even noticing that it contained a novel argument about infallibility. Similarly Leff and Ratzinger mentioned Olivi's text on papal inerrancy without apparently observing anything new in it.[4] Even Maccarrone himself, who edited Olivi's *Quaestio*, claimed no great originality for its

---

[1] Bonaventure, *Quaestiones disputatae de perfectione evangelica*, *Opera* V (1891), p. 189, "De obedientia summo Pontifici debita."

[2] F. Ehrle, "Zur Vorgeschichte des Concils von Vienne," *ALKG*, 2 (1886), pp. 353-416 and *ALKG*, 3 (1887), pp. 1-195, citing an accusation presented by Olivi's opponents in 1311 (p. 371), "Et aliqui dixerunt, quod doctrina dicti fratris P(etri) erat defendenda sicut articulus fidei. Et aliqui dixerunt, quod ipse frater P(etrus) erat ille angelus, de quo dicitur in apocalipsi, qui veniebat post illum angelum, qui habebat signum dei vivi."

[3] "Zur Vorgeschichte," *ALKG*, 3 (1887), p. 10, "... Frater Petrus Johannis Olivi, qui caput fuit rebellium in Provincia, in scolis et alibi in statu et in ordine vocabatur Antichristus."

[4] Ehrle, "Olivi," p. 500; L. Oliger, "Petri Iohannis Olivi de renuntiatione papae Coelestini V quaestio et epistola," *AFH*, 11 (1918), pp. 309-373 at p. 329; G. Leff, *Heresy in the Later Middle Ages*, 2 vols. (Manchester, 1967), I, p. 120; J. Ratzinger, *art. cit.* (supra p. 82 n. 1), p. 721.

central thesis. In introducing Olivi's text, he observed that the doctrine of papal infallibility was being widely discussed in the 1270's and that the Greek emperor, Michael Paleologus, had professed his belief in the "infallible magisterium of the Roman Pontiff" in his confession of faith presented to the Council of Lyons. Moreover, according to Maccarrone, Thomas Aquinas and Bonaventure both adhered to the same teaching; and, finally, the doctrine of infallibility, which was "always maintained and pre-supposed" in the church had been widely proclaimed in the canonical works of the preceding century.[1] All these views are mistaken of course. Michael Paleologus' profession of faith contains no reference to any "infallible magisterium" of the pope.[2] Neither Thomas nor Bonaventure taught such a doctrine.[3] And the whole idea of papal infallibility was alien to the canonists' way of thinking. Maccarrone did claim that Olivi went further than his predecessors and contemporaries in that he was the first scholastic theologian to provide "a separate and exhaustive

---

[1] Maccarrone, *art. cit.*, pp. 315-316.

[2] The emperor merely repeated the standard canonical doctrine, "Ipsa quoque sancta Romana ecclesia ... sicut prae ceteris tenetur fidei veritatem defendere, sic et si quae de fide subortae fuerint quaestiones, suo debent judicio definiri," J. D. Mansi, *Sacrorum conciliorum nova et amplissima collectio*, 24 (Venice, 1780), col. 71. These words were included in the 1870 definition of papal infallibility.

[3] For Bonaventure see above pp. 88-92. Thomas Aquinas' position was not significantly different from Bonaventure's. The modern scholars, from Döllinger to Küng, who have pointed out that later defenders of papal infallibility often appealed to the authority of St. Thomas are quite correct of course. But it is far from clear that the later theologians were interpreting Thomas correctly. In fact he claimed almost every conceivable power for the pope in church affairs—except infallibility. The relevant texts were presented in R. Bianchi, *De constitutione monarchica ecclesiae et de infallibilitate Romani pontificis iuxta S. Thomam* (Rome, 1870). None of them actually asserted that the pope was infallible. The principal loci in St. Thomas are the *Summa Theologiae*, IIa-IIae q. 1. art. 10, the *Contra errores Graecorum*, and *Quodlibet* 9 q. 8. The last text has been especially emphasized by scholars who regard Thomas as an exponent of papal infallibility. There he argued that the universal church could not err in faith, that it pertained to the pope to determine in matters of faith, and that, accordingly, the judicial sentences of the pope in such matters were to be preferred to the opinions of any private doctors. But this is exactly the doctrine of the twelfth-century decretists; and we have seen that, for them, the doctrine in no way implied the infallibility of the pope. Döllinger was quite right to point out that the teaching of St. Thomas was essentially that of the preceding canonists. The point is that the canonists had never taught a doctrine of papal infallibility. For modern discussions of Thomas' position see the remarks of B.-D. Dupuy and P. de Vooght in *L'Infaillibilité de l'église* (Chevetogne, 1962), pp. 94-96, 103-104 and E. Ménard, *La tradition, révélation, écriture, église selon Saint Thomas d'Aquin* (Paris, 1964), pp. 147-164, 214-228 (with additional bibliography at p. 221 n. 1). See also infra, p. 245 n. 4.

treatment of this doctrine." But Hödl apparently thought even this was going too far.[1]

Virtually all the scholars who have written on Olivi's attitude to the papacy have been misled by the widespread but quite unfounded assumption that papal infallibility was a generally received doctrine of the church in the second half of the thirteenth century. And this assumption in turn seems to rest on a common pre-supposition that texts which affirmed the supreme juridical authority of the pope in matters of faith necessarily implied that the pope's judgments were unerring; whereas, as we have tried to show, the whole canonical tradition of the twelfth and thirteenth centuries tended to reject this implication. Olivi was deliberately raising a new and delicate question when he added to Bonaventure's conventional *Quaestio* "On the obedience due to the supreme pontiff," the further query whether obedience was owed to the pope as an unerring teacher. In a fumbling and hesitant way perhaps, and yet quite explicitly, Olivi was trying for the first time to formulate a viable theory of papal infallibility.

(ii) *Olivi and the Franciscan Order*

Olivi's doctrine of papal power was inextricably bound-up with his attitude to the teaching of St. Francis and the authentication of that teaching by the Roman church. To understand his thought, therefore, it is necessary to know something concerning the course of his relationship with his Franciscan superiors and with the papacy.[2] Olivi lived at a time when the Franciscans were beginning to split into two mutually antagonistic groups. The party of the "Community", containing the bulk of the members and the most respected leaders of the Order, was prepared to accept relaxations in the strict provisions

---

[1] L. Hödl, *Die Lehre des Petrus Johannis Olivi O.F.M. von der Universalgewalt des Papstes* (Munich, 1958), p. 17 n. 53, "Der Titel, unter dem M. Maccarrone die Quaestio ediert hat, ist nicht gerechtfertigt. Erst recht kann Olivi nicht als scholastischer Zeuge der Lehre von der päpstlichen Unfehlbarkeit in Anspruch genommen werden." Hödl saw Alexander III's decree *Cum Christus* as a "landmark" in the development of the doctrine of papal infallibility and referred to the work of Landgraf (supra p. 13 n. 1). But Landgraf did not find any assertions of papal infallibility in the literature stimulated by *Cum Christus*. Hödl also referred to the texts assembled in his own work on the power of the keys (supra p. 40 n. 1). But again none of them affirms a doctrine of papal infallibility.

[2] Two good modern surveys of Olivi's life and of the doctrinal controversies in which he was involved are C. Partee, "Peter John Olivi: Historical and Doctrinal Study," *Franciscan Studies*, 20 (1960), pp. 215-260 and G. Leff, *Heresy*, I, pp. 100-139.

of the Rule in order to make the Order a more flexible instrument for the service of the universal church and the papacy. The "Spirituals" believed that Franciscans could play a useful role in the church only if they adhered rigorously to the primitive ideals of their founder—especially the ideal of poverty.[1] Olivi, like Bonaventure, believed that Franciscan poverty was far more than merely a salutary form of religious discipline. Rather, it exemplified the one perfect pattern of Christian life, made known to St. Francis by divine revelation, that Christ had taught to the first apostles. This view was commonly held by Franciscans of all persuasions. However, the theologians of the Community generally taught that the one really essential element in a vow of apostolic poverty was the renunciation of property rights. Against this position Olivi argued vehemently that "poor use"—the practice of severe frugality in actual day-to-day living—was just as important. "Poor use is to renunciation of right as form is to matter," he wrote.[2]

Olivi's fervor for apostolic poverty, his defense of the *usus pauper*, and his compelling personality marked him out from the beginning of his teaching career as a leading spokesman for the Franciscan Spirituals. This helps to explain his frequent troubles with the leaders of the Order. Olivi's teachings were first condemned during the generalate of Jerome of Ascoli (1274-1279) who later became Pope Nicholas IV. This censure (which concerned certain teachings of Olivi on the Blessed Virgin) seems to have been a trivial affair that did not seriously damage Olivi's reputation for, in 1279, he was one of the Franciscan masters consulted by a papal commission engaged in drafting the Bull, *Exiit*, which we have already mentioned in discussing the growth of Franciscan ideas on apostolic poverty.

This Bull, promulgated by Nicholas III in August 1279, was welcomed by Olivi with the warmest approval and, indeed, his enthusiasm for it was an important factor in shaping his attitude to the authority of the Roman see for the rest of his life. In *Exiit*, Pope Nicholas III not only approved the Franciscan way of life as his predecessors had done. For the first time he affirmed as an official teaching of the Roman church the Franciscans' assertion that their way of life was the very way of perfection that Christ had revealed to

---

[1] The conflict and Olivi's part in it are discussed in all the standard histories of the Franciscan Order cited above (p. 59 n. 3).

[2] Ehrle, "Olivi," *ALKG*, 3, p. 508. Cf. Lambert, *Poverty*, pp. 149 ff.

the apostles. *Exiit* was a document of major importance in later debates over papal infallibility. We shall therefore give its principal provisions here. On Franciscan poverty the pope declared:

> Now since this rule expressly stipulates that the friars should appropriate nothing to themselves ... and since it was decreed by our predecessor Gregory IX ... that they should observe this both individually and in common ... we say that renunciation of property in all things in this fashion, not merely individually but also in common for the sake of God, is meritorious and holy and that Christ, showing the way of perfection, taught this by word and confirmed it by example, and that the first founders of the church militant, wishing to live perfectly, channeled it on as they had drawn it from that source.[1]

Exiit, moreover, specifically affirmed that the Franciscan Rule was directly inspired by the Holy Spirit, a view that Olivi held with passionate intensity.

> This is the way of religious life, pure and immaculate before God the Father which, descending from the Father of lights, handed on by his Son to the apostles by word and example, and finally inspired in blessed Francis and his followers by the Holy Spirit, contains, as it were, the testimony of the whole Trinity in itself ....[2]

To rebut the arguments of theologians who held that total, permanent renunciation of all dominion was legally and practically impossible—a view that Olivi had to contend with in his polemical writings—the pope presented a series of distinctions similar to those of Bonaventure.

> In temporal things we have to consider especially property, possession, usufruct, right of use and simple factual use; the life of mortals requires the last as a necessity but it can do without the others. Hence there can be no profession which excludes the use of things necessary for sustenance. But it was truly suited to that profession which willing-

---

[1] *Liber Sextus*, ed. E. Friedberg in *Corpus Iuris Canonici*, II (Leipzig, 1879), *Sext.* 5.7.3, col. 1112, "Porro, quum ipsa regula expresse contineat, quod fratres nihil sibi approprient, nec domum, nec locum, nec aliquam rem, sitque declaratum per eundem praedecessorem nostrum Gregorium IX. et nonnullos alios, hoc servare debere tam in speciali quam etiam in communi ... dicimus, quod abdicatio proprietatis huiusmodi omnium rerum non tam in speciali, quam etiam in communi propter Deum meritoria est et sancta, quam et Christus, viam perfectionis ostendens, verbo docuit et exemplo firmavit, quamque primi fundatores militantis ecclesiae, prout ab ipso fonte hauserant, volentes perfecte vivere, per doctrinae ac vitae exempla in eos derivarunt."

[2] col. 1110, "Haec est apud Deum et Patrem munda et immaculata religio, quae, descendens a patre luminum, per eius filium exemplariter et verbaliter Apostolis tradita, et deinde per Spiritum sanctum beato Francisco et eum sequentibus inspirata, totius in se quasi continet testimonium Trinitatis."

ly vowed to follow the poor Christ in such poverty to renounce ownership of all things and to be content with the necessary use of things
conceded.[1]

Finally, in defining Franciscan poverty, *Exiit* did not neglect to
mention the manner of using goods as well as the renunciation of
property rights.

> They shall not accept utensils nor other things which they can licitly
> use … (for they ought not to have the use of all things as has been said)
> in any superfluity or copiousness or abundance which derogates from
> poverty ….[2]

Olivi regarded such phrases as a complete vindication of his own
doctrine of *usus pauper*. In subsequent controversies he appealed to
Exiit over and over again; and when, toward the end of his life, a
group of radical Spirituals began to attack the Bull, he vigorously
rebuked them.[3]

It would seem that Olivi was over-optimistic in his appraisal of

---

[1] col. 1113, "Nam quum in rebus temporalibus sit considerare praecipuum
proprietatem, possessionem, usumfructum, ius utendi, et simplicem facti usum, et
ultimo tanquam necessario egeat, licet primis carere possit vita mortalium: nulla
prorsus potest esse professio, quae a se usum necessariae sustentationis excludat.
Verum condecens fuit ei professioni, quae sponte devovit Christum pauperem in
tanta paupertate sectari, omnium abdicare dominium, et rerum sibi concessarum
necessario usu fore contentam."

[2] col. 1114, "Insuper nec utensilia, nec alia praeter eorum usum ad necessitatem
et officiorum sui status exsecutionem, (non enim omnium rerum usum habere
debent, ut dictum est,) ad ullam superfluitatem, divitias seu copiam, quae deroget
paupertati, vel ad thesaurizationem, vel eo animo, ut ea distrahant sive vendant,
recipiant."

[3] Examples of Olivi's appeals to the authority of *Exiit* can be found in Ehrle,
"Zur Vorgeschichte …," *ALKG*, 2, p. 401; Ehrle, "Olivi," *ALKG*, 3, p. 531; D.
Laberge, "Fr. Petri Ioannis Olivi, O.F.M. tria scripta sui ipsius apologetica," *AFH*,
28 (1935), pp. 115-155, 374-407 at p. 391. The rebuke to the Spirituals on this
point is in Olivi's letter to Conrad of Offida (1295) printed by Oliger, "De Renuntiatione," *AFH*, 11 (1918), pp. 309-373 at pp. 366-373, "Dicunt autem presump-
tores prefati declarationem domini Nicolai errare … in hoc quod testamentum
beati Francisci cassat … Attendant igitur, isti vesani et ceci et scripturarum sanc-
tarum nimis ignari quod papalis declaratio non cassat sancti Patris litteram, que a
quibusdam dicitur testamentum, ymo potius ipsam commendat … papa vere dicit
quod si sanctus Pater ibidem intendisset ultra precepta regule imponere nova et
regularia precepta ordini et successoribus suis, quod hoc facere non poterit, *cum
non habet imperium par in parem*." (p. 371). The text incidentally shows that Olivi
was familiar with the Roman law doctrine of sovereignty. Even Francis could not
bind future heads of the Order to his wishes because "an equal has no authority
over an equal." The question whether the approval of the rule by the Roman
church could be binding on future popes raised a whole new set of problems that
are discussed below.

Exiit. In fact the section on use proved vague enough to satisfy all parties in the Order and the promulgation of the Bull certainly did not end Olivi's troubles with his superiors. In 1283 a commission of seven theologians, appointed by the Franciscan minister-general, Bonagrazia of S. Giovanni in Persiceto, drew up a *Rotulus* containing numerous excerpts from Olivi's writings which the theologians considered worthy of censure. Olivi was not at first permitted to see the *Rotulus* but he was compelled to profess his adherence to twenty-two affirmative propositions correcting his "errors." (Later he complained that he was made to subscribe to them "as if they were words of Holy Scripture or definitions of the Roman pontiff."[1]) In 1285 Olivi obtained a copy of the *Rotulus* and wrote a vigorous *Defensio*. In 1287 he was allowed to argue his case before a general chapter of the Order and he succeeded in satisfying the assembly of his orthodoxy. Olivi was then sent as lector to the Franciscan studium of S. Croce in Italy and here he first came into contact with the Italian Spirituals. In 1289 he returned to his native Provence as an honored teacher. The minister-general was by then Raymund Gaufredi, a friend of the Spirituals, and the pope was Nicholas IV, the former Jerome of Ascoli. Both of these superiors seem to have been well disposed toward Olivi. In 1290 he was again denounced to the pope but no action was taken against him. In 1292 he once more explained his doctrine of *usus pauper* before a general chapter of the Order. He died, uncondemned and unmolested in 1298. Almost at once he was accepted as a kind of patron saint by the most radical Spirituals of Provence and Italy.

The most damaging attacks on Olivi's orthodoxy came after his death. In 1299 a new minister-general, John de Murrovalle (appointed by Boniface VIII), ordered all his writings to be burned. At the Council of Vienne (1311) the leaders of the Community made the most strenuous efforts to procure a solemn condemnation of Olivi's works. After an elaborate investigation the Council affirmed as true three dogmatic propositions that Olivi was held to have denied. It was a thin harvest for Olivi's adversaries to have culled from the vast field of his writings. Moreover it is not clear whether in fact any proposition that Olivi had dogmatically affirmed was even by implication condemned.[2]

Modern scholars disagree on the question whether the attack on

---

[1] Laberge, *art. cit.*, p. 132.

[2] For a discussion on this point, defending Olivi's orthodoxy and reviewing the modern literature on the question, see Partee, *art. cit.*, pp. 241-253.

Olivi in 1282—and the other attacks during his lifetime—were motivated simply by the opposition of the Community to his doctrine of Franciscan poverty or whether they stemmed from a genuine concern on the part of his opponents over the various theological and philosophical novelties that they found in his works.[1] It seems quite obvious however that the continuing assault on Olivi's reputation after his death was stimulated by his role as "the head of a superstitious sect"[2] rather than by any possible errors he may have made on fine points of speculative theology. Olivi had the misfortune to attract the fanatical devotion of men who were more radical and rebellious than himself and his posthumous reputation suffered accordingly. When the papacy turned decisively against the Spiritual Franciscans during the pontificate of John XXII it became essential to discredit Olivi's work. Once again, in 1319, the minister-general (now Michael of Cesena) condemned all of his writings. In the same year a commission of theologians appointed by the pope denounced numerous errors in Olivi's *Lectura* on the Apocalypse, his last major work, completed in 1297. The fundamental charge was that Olivi had utterly rejected the authority of the Roman church by denouncing the papacy as the "whore of Babylon."[3] Olivi's *Lectura* was finally condemned by John XXII in 1326.

(iii) *Olivi and the Roman Church*

Modern defenders of Olivi's orthodoxy have argued that the condemnation of 1326, based solely on ambiguous texts excerpted from Olivi's most obscure work, gives a totally false impression of his real attitude toward the Roman see. To this question we must now

---

[1] Olivi has sometimes been regarded as a precursor of fourteenth-century nominalism. Cf. J. Koch, "Die Verurteilung Olivis auf dem Konzil von Vienne und ihre Vorgeschichte," *Scholastik*, 5 (1930), pp. 489-522 and Leff, *Heresy*, I, pp. 107-111.

[2] The words were used by Arnold of Rochafolio, provincial-minister of Provence. (Ehrle, "Zur Vorgeschichte," *ALKG*, 3, p. 14.) The wild aberrations of Olivi's more eccentric disciples are well-illustrated in W. H. May, "The Confession of Prous Boneta," in *Essays in Medieval Life and Thought Presented in Honor of A. P. Evans*, ed. J. H. Mundy, R. W. Emery, and B. N. Nelson (New York, 1955), pp. 3-30. Other examples, drawn from the works of the inquisitor Bernard Gui, are given by Leff, *Heresy*, I, pp. 212-230.

[3] E. Baluze, *Miscellanea*, II (Lucca, 1761), p. 259, art. 3, "... per illam meretricem intelligat sicut inferius apparebit ecclesiam Romanam ..." art. 4, "... in toto tractatu per Babylonem ipse intelligit ecclesiam Romanam et universalem ei obedientem, quam nos ecclesiam catholicam appellamus." The charge was repeated over and over again throughout the sixty articles of the accusation.

turn. There are certainly many passages in Olivi's writings which express his devotion and filial obedience to the papacy. A good example is this statement in his *Defensio* of 1285:

> In order that, without any schism or error or doubt over ambiguities, (the eternal truth) might be observed more stably, more openly and more infallibly she chose for herself and established by irrefragable sanction a universal see of orthodox faith ... namely the Roman church; concerning which church no Catholic can or should doubt that she is the mother and teacher of all the churches and that it is for her alone, through her plenitude of authority, to determine and define the greater causes of the church especially those touching articles or questions of faith.[1]

One can find similar affirmations of papal primacy, not only in Olivi's polemical writings, where he had an obvious interest in insisting on his own orthodoxy, but also in his formal scholastic treatises. In a commentary on the Sentences he wrote that the Roman church was the head from which jurisdiction flowed to all the other churches.[2] His gloss on Matthew 16.19, "I will give you the keys of the kingdom of heaven", presented an entirely conventional doctrine of Petrine primacy.[3] Most striking of all, in the last years of his life, Olivi vigorously defended the licitness of Pope Celestine V's abdication (December, 1294) and the consequent validity of Boniface VIII's election as pope. This *Quaestio, De renuntiatione papae*, was appended to the *Quaestiones de perfectione evangelica* (the treatise which also contains our text on papal infallibility). In the course of his argument Olivi commented,

> Many canons and indeed almost the whole canon law of the church cry out by word and deed that the supreme power of settling doubts and questions concerning the faith and all major causes of the church resides with the pope.[4]

The pope's decisions were always to be obeyed unless they ran directly counter to the law of Christ, Olivi maintained. Christ's law did not forbid a pope to abdicate.[5] Therefore Celestine's renunciation

---

[1] Laberge, *art. cit.*, pp. 130-131.

[2] Hödl, *op. cit.*, p. 11.

[3] *MS New College, Oxford 49.* fol. 107ra, "Dicit tamen *tibi* singulariter ut ostendat quod isti soli et eius successoribus summam et singularem auctoritatem committit. Quare autem Christus unum voluit esse caput totius ecclesiae multas habet notabiles rationes, quas quia alibi tradidi hic ommitto."

[4] Oliger, *art. cit.*, p. 347.

[5] Oliger, *art. cit.*, p. 351, "Constat enim ex omnibus predictis, quod papa potest novam legem condere de quocunque, quod non est contra Christi fidem et legem

of the papacy was licit and Boniface was a true pope. This was a striking affirmation of Olivi's loyalty, not only to the Roman see in the abstract, but to an actual reigning pontiff in particular, and it is the more noteworthy since Boniface's election was vehemently challenged by the Italian Spirituals who had been Olivi's allies in earlier conflicts within the Franciscan Order.

The texts we have considered so far are entirely consistent with Olivi's role as the first champion of papal infallibility. But they represent only one side of his thought. The attacks on the institutional structure of the church for which Olivi was condemned after his death do really exist in his work. They are not mere distortions invented posthumously by his enemies; and at first glance they may seem irreconcilable with the passages on papal authority that we have just quoted. Olivi's whole position was based on his fidelity to the Rule of St. Francis—or, more accurately, on his fidelity to his own understanding of the Rule. Bonaventure, for all his dedication to the Franciscan way of life, had never lost sight of the fact that the Friars Minor constituted a relatively small group, a spiritual élite within a universal church whose hierarchical structure enjoyed its own undoubted legitimacy. Olivi at times wrote as though the true followers of St. Francis alone constituted the real church in the eyes of God. Certainly he juxtaposed the ideals of the Franciscans and the actual practices of the church in such a way as to imply a condemnation of almost the whole existing hierarchy. For example, when Bonaventure considered the perfection proper to bishops (who were universally regarded as successors of the apostles), he tactfully observed that there were different kinds of perfection, and that the forms of perfection appropriate for a public official were different from those of a private individual. Olivi simply declared that, if bishops wanted truly to fill the role that Christ had prescribed for the apostles, they ought to live in Franciscan poverty. In actual practice, he observed, this was not required of them. On the contrary, they lived so idly and pompously, were so much given over to trifling diversions and to the passions of anger and concupiscence that any Franciscan who lived in such a fashion would be considered on the road to damnation. The argument implicitly cast doubt on the claim of the bishops to be true successors of the apostles.[1]

---

et quod in omni tali et etiam in omni sententiali et autentica expositione dubiorum cristiane legis et fidei est sibi credendum et obediendum, nisi aperte esset contraria fidei Christi et legi."

[1] Ehrle, "Olivi," *ALKG*, 3, p. 511, "... nunquam status ille (episcopalis) habetur

For Olivi the Franciscan ideal constituted a standard against which
the conduct of the whole church could be judged—and his judgments
were often harsh. Moreover, he did not hesitate to apply this exacting
standard of judgment to the papacy itself. Olivi's horror at the corrup-
ting power of material wealth in the church, and especially in the
Roman see, was very evident in one of his *Quodlibeta* in which he
discussed the question "Whether the pope has universal power."
Olivi's purpose here was to rebuke those among his contemporaries
who held that the pope was, by divine right, temporal lord of the
world. After stating the usual Scriptural and canonical arguments in
favor of this position he replied simply that such a doctrine was
contrary to the counsels of Christ and to the way of life he had laid
down for the apostles. If Christ had wished to establish the pope as
temporal lord and king of the world, then he would have endowed
Peter with immense riches instead of prescribing for him a life of utter
poverty. Olivi maintained that "Spiritual and ecclesiastical power is the
more noble and holy the more it is separated from all worldly affairs."
This is a far cry from the actual practice of the papacy in the late
thirteenth century. Olivi even wrote that those who wished to plunge
the papacy into the mire of secular affairs were striving to build up the
power of Antichrist; and this in an age when the popes themselves
were more and more overtly claiming a universal temporal dominion.
Indeed, in this passage, Olivi presented Peter, the true pope, almost as
an antitype of the typical thirteenth century pontiff.[1]

Moreover, Olivi set strict limits to the sovereign power of the pope
even in the sphere of internal church government. In a lengthy
argument included in the *Quaestiones de perfectione evangelica* he maintained that the pope had no authority to dispense a Franciscan from

in plena decentia et perfectione sua, nisi simul cum perfectionis evangelice observantia teneatur—in cuius signum salvator perfectionem evangelicam et maxime
paupertatis et potissime quoad eius pauperem usum apostolis imposuit ..."; p. 512,
"Quia unus frater minor vivens ita laute et otiose et pompose et in tot et tantis
passionibus ire et concupiscentie et in tot solatiis et trufis seu ludis et fabulis sicut
unus episcopus secularis, qui tamen hodie iudicabitur communiter esse in statu
salutis, credo communi omnium iudicio iudicaretur esse in statu dampnationis."

[1] *Quodlibeta Petri Ioannis Provinzialis* (Venice, 1509), *Quodl.* 1, q. 18, fol. 8vb-9ra,
"Si enim papa ex absoluto iure evangelico et ex absoluta Christi commissione esset
temporalis rex et dominus mundi, tunc Petro apostolorum principi non commisisset
statum et consilium altissime paupertatis, sed potius summarum divitiarum et ter-
rene temporalitatis cuius oppositum patet ex textu ... tanto potestas spiritualis et
ecclesiastica est nobilior et sanctior et spiritualior quanto est a terrenis omnibus
amplius segregata ... ergo qui ... volunt eam in lutum terrenorum demergere
potestatem antichristi conantur erigere."

his vow of poverty. "The evangelical state is absolutely immutable," he wrote.[1] Similarly Olivi maintained that a pope could not change the substance of the Franciscan life by decreeing that evangelical poverty should consist solely in renunciation of property rights (i.e., without mendicancy and "poor use"). The popes of the thirteenth century certainly did not regard themselves as bound by the Franciscan Rule in this way. Nor did the canonists or the papalist theologians. Olivi's position was highly idiosyncratic.

The locus classicus for Olivi's alleged anti-papalism is his Joachimite-inspired *Lectura* on the Apocalypse for, in this work, he envisaged a future in which Antichrist would sit enthroned in Rome itself. The *Lectura* was written toward the end of Olivi's life; but it would be incorrect to suppose that the obsession with the threat of a coming Antichrist, served by a pseudo-pope, which finds expression in this work, was an aberration of Olivi's last years. We saw that he referred to the danger of building up the power of Antichrist at Rome in his *Quodlibet* on temporal power (written c. 1285). And the same concern was expressed in the two *Quaestiones* on the immutability of the Franciscan Rule that we have just mentioned. A pope who dispensed against the Franciscan vow of poverty, according to Olivi, would not merely exceed his authority. He would hasten the coming of Antichrist, "the mystical Antichrist... to whom the name and number of the Beast belong." And any papal relaxation of the Rule would lead on to "the perversion of the whole faith, the introduction of Antichrist and all the final temptations and the dissipation of every perfect good."[2]

These *Quaestiones* were written during the years 1279-1283 at just the time when Olivi was composing the *Quaestio* on papal infallibility which he incorporated into the same treatise, *De perfectione evangelica*. Similarly Olivi was vigorously defending the legitimacy of Pope Boniface VIII's election at the same time that he was working on the Joachimite *Lectura* to the Apocalypse. There can be no simple explanation of his attitude to the Roman see in terms of a transition

---

[1] Ehrle, "Olivi," *ALKG*, 3, p. 528, "Quantum ad primum dicendum quod status evangelicus est et esse debuit omnino immobilis et indissolubilis." In the *Quodlibet* cited above (p. 104 n. 1) Olivi declared again that the pope could not dispense "in consiliis et votis evangelicis" (fol. 8ra).

[2] Ehrle, "Olivi," *ALKG*, 3, p. 532, "Iste modus ... est precursor novissimus Antichristi, propter quod numerus et nomen bestie merito competit sibi ..." Cf. p. 530, "... ex ea (laxatio) sequatur denigratio totius fidei, introductio antichristi et omnium temptationum finalium et dissipatio omnis perfecti boni ..."

from an earlier pro-papal to a later anti-papal position. At every stage of Olivi's life one finds the same tension in his work—expressions of total fidelity to the Roman church and even affirmations of papal infallibility combined with severe reservations concerning the more extreme theories of papal sovereignty that were current in the late thirteenth century and dire forebodings concerning an impending betrayal of the church by a heretical pseudo-pope.

Olivi's scheme of church history, as set out in his *Lectura* to the Apocalypse, was in many ways similar to Bonaventure's. Like Bonaventure, Olivi divided the whole history of the world into two sequences of seven ages or successive "states." (He usually employed the word *status*.) Olivi's scheme was characterized by a description of the fifth age of the church as a time of deepening corruption, by an emphasis on the survival of the forces of evil into the beginning of the sixth age and, above all, by a conviction of the imminent coming of a "mystical Antichrist." Olivi believed that he was living in a period of transition from the fifth age to the sixth. For him, as for Bonaventure, St. Francis was the "angel of the sixth seal."[1] Olivi saw the whole thirteenth century as a time of struggle between the forces of the coming sixth age, already heralded by St. Francis, and the surviving evil forces of the fifth age typified in the abuses of the actual existing church. This conflict could also be described as a struggle between the "true church" and the "carnal church." The true church was represented by those Franciscans who remained faithful to the practice of poverty along with their supporters. The carnal church was typified by wealthy prelates and by university masters who sought to substitute pagan philosophies for Christian revelation.[2] (Here

---

[1] On Olivi's Joachimism see especially R. Manselli, *La "Lectura super Apocalipsim" di Pietro di Giovanni Olivi* (Rome, 1955). Again, there is a good summary in Leff, *Heresy*, I, pp. 122-139. Excerpts from the *Lectura* are printed in E. Baluze, *Miscellanea*, II, pp. 258-270; I. von Döllinger, *Beiträge zur Sektengeschichte des Mittelalters*, II (Munich, 1890), pp. 527-585; Hödl, *op. cit.*, pp. 23-26; and in the works of Manselli and Leff just cited. For Francis as the angel of the sixth seal see Döllinger, p. 540, "... constat etiam per indubitabile testimonium S. Francisci ineffabili sanctitate et innumeris Dei miraculis confirmatum et praecipue gloriosissimis stigmatibus sibi a Christo impressis patet, ipsum vere esse angelum apertionis sexti signaculi habentem signum Dei vivi ... prout a fratre Bonaventura ... fuit ... me audiente solemniter praedicatum." p. 548, "Hic ergo angelus est Franciscus evangelicae vitae et regulae sexto et septimo tempore propagandae et magnificandae renovator et summus post Christum et matrem ejus observator." For other references to the role of St. Francis and his Order in the last ages of the church see Döllinger, pp. 532, 552, 561, 571.

[2] Hödl, *op. cit.*, p. 24 n. 73.

Olivi neatly bracketed together the two principal sources of opposition to the Franciscans.) The conflict between the forces of good and evil would reach a climax with the appearance of the "mystical Antichrist." Under him almost the whole church would be corrupted and transformed into a "great Babylon." But then the ten kings of the Apocalypse would arise and destroy this evil Babylon. And, finally, the true church would be exalted, the Jews and pagans would be converted, and the seventh age of the church, the age of peace and joyous tranquillity would be inaugurated.[1]

Manselli and other scholars have pointed out that Olivi did not explicitly identify the whole existing church hierarchy headed by the pope with his carnal church. But, while this is true and important, it is also true that Olivi regarded nearly all the rulers of the church in his own day if not quite all of them as "carnal" and corrupt.[2] "'The seat of the beast' principally designates the carnal clergy who reign and preside over the whole church in this fifth age," he wrote. Moreover, he was convinced that the forces of evil would soon subvert the Roman see itself. In his picture of the coming climactic struggle between the carnal church and the true church he assigned a major role to a pseudo-pope through whom the work of Antichrist would be accomplished. According to a prophecy that Olivi attributed to Brother Leo (the companion of St. Francis) the pseudo-pope would be appointed by a prince of the house of Frederick II who would appear at the time of the mystic Antichrist. This prince would conquer the Roman Empire and France and gain the support of "the other five kings of the Christians." Then he would seek to dominate and pervert the church.

> He will establish as pseudo-pope a certain false religious who will plot against the evangelical rule ... promoting as bishops professors of the said rule who acquiesce to him ... and persecuting all those who wish to preserve and defend the rule purely and fully.[3]

---

[1] Döllinger, *op. cit.*, pp. 582-585.

[2] Manselli, *op. cit.*, p. 219. Cf. Leff, p. 128. Döllinger, p. 575, "... in eodem quinto tempore ... sublimata est sedes bestiae, i.e. bestialis catervae, ita ut numero et potestate praevaleat et fere absorbeat sedem Christi, cui localiter et nominaliter est commixta, unde et sic appellatur ecclesia fidelium sicut et illa, quae vere est per gratiam sedes et ecclesia Christi ... Per hanc autem sedem bestiae principaliter designatur carnalis clerus in hoc quinto tempore regnans et toti ecclesiae praesidens ..."

[3] Döllinger, *op. cit.*, p. 573, "Statuet in Pseudopapam quendam falsum religiosum qui contra regulam evangelicam excogitabit et faciet dispensationem dolosam,

On this whole prophecy Olivi cautiously commented, "Which of these things shall be or shall not be I leave to the divine disposition." But other passages in his work make it clear that it could only have been the fantasies about the Hohenstaufen prince that he doubted. Olivi repeatedly affirmed his own belief in the coming of a pseudo-pope who would malevolently attack the theory and practice of apostolic poverty.[1]

In the face of these dire predictions, what are we to make of Olivi's protestations of undying devotion to the Roman church? Above all, how can we reconcile Olivi's proclamation of papal infallibility with his prognostication that a false pope would soon occupy the Roman See and would pervert almost the whole church by his evil teaching? As is so often the case where Olivi is concerned there are almost as many answers to these questions as there are scholars who have discussed them. Ehrle held that, in defending Boniface VIII's election and in rebuking the extreme Spirituals who attacked it, Olivi was "hiding the true opinions of his heart." Oliger declared simply that Olivi possessed a split mentality. One half of his mind was "perspicacious, profound and penetrating"; the other half was "mystical, abstruse, irreparably snared by Joachimism." Without going so far as Oliger, Leff also thought that the *Lectura* on the Apocalypse reflected "a subterranean side of Olivi's mind." Manselli, Partee and Callaey on the other hand, have maintained that, if Olivi's various writings are interpreted as he himself intended them, and not as they were understood by his enemies it is not impossible to reconcile them with one another and to interpret them in an orthodox sense. Benz treated Olivi as a radical Joachimite without seriously considering the "conservative" elements in his thought.[2] Ratzinger assumed that Olivi's experiences produced a sharp change in his attitude to the papacy toward the end of his life. In his earlier work he defended papal infallibility but later, as he became more deeply committed to the struggle of the Spiritual Francis-

---

promovens in Episcopos professores regulae praefatae sibi consentientes ... ac persequens omnes qui regulam praedictam ad purum et plene voluerint observare et defensare."

[1] Hödl, *op. cit.*, p. 23 n. 73, "Puto ego de huiusmodi pseudopapa quod ipse veniat tenere locum Antichristi." p. 25 n. 75, "Facient etiam quod imago bestiae, id est pseudo-papa, a rege bestiae primae sublimatus adoretur. ..." Cf. Manselli, p. 225 n. 2, n. 3; Döllinger, p. 559.

[2] Ehrle, "Olivi, *ALKG*, 3, p. 439; Oliger, *art. cit.*, p. 323; Leff, *op. cit.*, p. 123; Manselli, *op. cit.*, p. 219; Partee, *art. cit.*, pp. 241-253. Callaey, "Olieu" in *DTC*, XI (Paris, 1931), cols. 982-991; Benz, *Ecclesia Spiritualis* (Stuttgart, 1934), pp. 256-357, 404-432.

cans, he was led to denounce the pope as Antichrist. De Vooght expressed the same opinion and Hödl too held that Olivi intended to designate the reigning pope, Boniface VIII, as a pseudo-pope.[1]

The point of view we wish to present is different from all of these. We would maintain that the *Lectura* on the Apocalypse is not only formally reconcilable with Olivi's other writings on ecclesiology but is essential to the right understanding of them. In particular, we would argue, Olivi's teaching on papal infallibility would be unintelligible if we did not possess the *Lectura* on the Apocalypse as a guide to his inmost thought.[2]

2. DOCTRINAL DEVELOPMENT AND THE ROMAN SEE

(i) *Progressive Revelation. The Role of St. Francis*

Before we turn to the *Quaestio* on infallibility itself we need to consider certain underlying principles of Olivi's ecclesiology. His theology of the church was built around three themes that had all been important for Bonaventure too. These were: the progressive revelation to the church throughout the course of the ages of the inner meaning of Sacred Scripture; the supreme importance of St. Francis of Assisi in this process; and the need for a papal *magisterium* to validate new revelations of divine truth. (When discussing papal teaching authority, Olivi used the words *magisterium* and *magistralis* in much the same sense as modern theologians.)[3] In handling these themes Olivi sometimes took ideas that were implicit in Bonaventure's work and made them crisply explicit. Sometimes, as in the matter of papal infallibility, he started out from Bonaventure's premises but reached new conclusions more radical than those of his predecessor.

---

[1] Ratzinger, *art. cit.* (supra p. 82 n. 1), pp. 721-722; de Vooght, *Les pouvoirs du concile et l'autorité du pape* (Paris, 1965), p. 23; Hödl, *op. cit.*, pp. 24-25. This last opinion seems certainly mistaken. As Partee writes, "To uphold such a view is to interpret the clear by the obscure." Olivi quite plainly defended Boniface's legitimacy. He never clearly denied it. It should be remembered that Boniface VIII (as Benedict Gaetani) had been a member of the commission that drafted *Exiit*. Also, as a leading member of the papal legation sent to France in 1290, he had vigorously defended the rights of the mendicant friars against sharp attacks from the French bishops and the secular masters of Paris. Olivi was hardly likely to cast a man with such a record for the role of Antichrist. In fact he never denounced the legitimacy of the popes who reigned during his lifetime. At times they must have seemed to him to lack some of the perfections proper to a successor of St. Peter, but essentially they were upholders of sound doctrine and still true popes.

[2] Hödl seems to be the only modern author who has discerned an organic connection between the two works. See his brief, penetrating remarks in *op. cit.*, p. 19.

[3] Infra, p. 112 n. 1, p. 120 n. 1.

Olivi's tendency to tease out of Bonaventure's thought all its most extreme implications is evident above all in his attitude to Scripture and to St. Francis' revelation of the inner meaning of the Gospels. Olivi's theology was characterized both by an intense devotion to Scripture and by a marked subjectivity in his interpretations of it. He deplored the application of merely human categories of thought (especially the fashionable Aristotelian categories) to the elucidation of divine truth.[1] This left him with a sort of arbitrary freedom of interpretation which, when he went outside the bounds of traditional exegesis, could lead to mere eccentricity. The best known example of this trait is his interpretation of John 19.33-34. Here the Gospel narrative records quite plainly that a soldier thrust a spear into the side of Christ *after* Christ's death on the cross. But Olivi knew of a certain holy man to whom it had been revealed in a vision that Christ was still living when he received the spear thrust. Olivi found various theological grounds for regarding this account as a persuasive one and presented it as a new interpretation of John's text.

This point was of only peripheral importance for Olivi though it provided his enemies with a charge against him that they never allowed to be forgotten.[2] Far more important was the fact that Olivi's willingness to accept private revelation as a guide to Scriptural truth colored his whole approach to the teaching of St. Francis. In his *Lectura* on the Apocalypse, Olivi, like Bonaventure, presented Francis as the bearer of a new revelation to the church. During the first five ages of the church, he wrote, it was not given to any of the saints, however enlightened, to open the inmost secrets of Scripture. Then, just as Christ himself had appeared in the sixth age of the Old Testament, so the Christ-like figure of Francis came to herald the sixth age of the Christian era. Francis brought a "singular clarification" of the life of Christ and, with twelve followers (like the twelve apostles), established a truly evangelical way of life suited to the impending new age of the church.[3] In emphasizing the central importance of

---

[1] See his *De perlegendis philosophorum libris*, ed. F. Delorme, "Fr. Petri Joannis Olivi tractatus 'De perlegendis Philosophorum libris'," *Antonianum*, 16 (1941), pp. 30-44. See also E. Stadter, "Das Problem der Theologie bei Petrus Johannis Olivi," *Franziskanische Studien*, 43 (1961), pp. 113-170 and *idem*, "Die spiritualische Geschichtstheologie als Voraussetzung für das Verstandis von fides und auctoritas bei Petrus Johannis Olivi," *Franziskanische Studien*, 48 (1966), pp. 243-253.

[2] On this dispute see Partee, *art. cit.*, pp. 244-245.

[3] Döllinger, *op. cit.*, p. 561, "Nam in prioribus quinque ecclesiae statibus non fuit concessum sanctis quantumcunque illuminatis aperire illa secreta hujus libri.

Francis' teaching for the future life of the church, Olivi, if possible, went even further than Bonaventure. Bonaventure had maintained, in a quite different context, that the Holy Spirit could speak through the church as authoritatively as through Scripture. Olivi applied this principle explicitly to the teaching of Francis in his argument denying to the pope the right to dispense against the Franciscan Rule. The pope's power was dependent on Christ and subject to Christ's laws, he wrote. But, "The laws of Christ are not only those that he has expressed in sacred Scripture, but also, those that he has instilled in the hearts of the faithful through the Holy Spirit."[1] For Olivi the Franciscan Rule was like another Gospel, not replacing the old one of course but completing it by revealing its inmost meaning. As such it had a cosmic significance in opening the way for the church to advance to its final "state" of perfection. The relevance of all this for Olivi's teaching on infallibility of course lies in the fact that the Rule itself derived its canonical authority from the confirmation of the popes.

(ii) *Papal Magisterium: The* Quaestio de renuntiatione

Olivi was saved from mere irresponsible subjectivism in his interpretation of Sacred Scripture by his constant emphasis on the supreme authority of the Roman church where actual truths of faith were involved. "The Roman church is the highest authority after God in settling doubts concerning the faith," he wrote, and he applied this doctrine specifically to the new (for him all-important) revelation of St. Francis. We have seen how he often appealed to the authority of the Roman see in defending his own position against the attacks of his adversaries within the Franciscan Order.[2] Even in the supposedly

---

quae in solo sexto et septimo statu erant apertius reseranda, sicut nec in primis quinque aetatibus veteris testamenti fuit concessum prophetis clare aperire secreta Christi et novi testamenti in sexta aetate saeculi reseranda et reserata." p. 532, "Sicut in sexta aetate rejecto carnali judaismo et vetustate prioris saeculi venit novus homo Christus cum nova lege, vita et cruce, sic in sexto statu rejecta ecclesia carnali et vetustate prioris saeculi renovabitur Christi et vita et crux, propter quod in primo ejus initio Franciscus apparuit, Christi plagis characterizatus et Christo totus concrucifixus et configuratus." p. 539, "... vita Christi erat in sexto et septimo statu ecclesiae singulariter clarificanda ..." p. 552, "Sicut synagoga propagata est ex XII patriarchis et ecclesia de gentibus ex XII apostolis est specialiter propagata, sic finalis ecclesia reliquiarum Judaeorum et gentium est per XII viros evangelicos propaganda, unde et Franciscus habuit XII filios et socios, per quos et in quibus fuit fundatus et initiatus ordo evangelicus."

[1] Hödl, *op. cit.*, p. 20 n. 63, "Leges autem Christi non solum sunt illae quas in scripturis sacris expressit sed etiam illae quas in corde fidelium per spiritum sanctum insinuit."

[2] Supra, p. 99 n. 3.

anti-papal *Lectura* on the Apocalypse, he cited the papal confirmation
of Francis' Rule to prove that the Franciscan way of life was indeed
the evangelical way that Christ himself had followed. And he submitted this whole work to the "universal magisterium" of the Roman
church.[1]

Olivi's most interesting treatment of the pope's teaching authority
(apart from the *Quaestio* on infallibility itself which we shall consider
separately) occurs in his discussion on the abdication of Pope Celestine.
In this work the three themes that we have mentioned as common to
Bonaventure and Olivi—progressive revelation, the central role of
St. Francis, and papal authentication of new revelation—occur once
again. But, whereas Bonaventure had treated these themes mostly in
cloudy metaphors or obscure allusions, Olivi here brought them
together in one tersely explicit passage. After emphasizing the supreme
authority of the Roman see he argued that even decisions of the pope
introducing new explanations of the faith had to be accepted as binding
because, if the pope lacked this authority,

> ... there would be no new explication in the holy church of God—
> more and more through the course of time—of the sublime truths of
> the Catholic faith; the opposite of which we can prove through the
> whole progress of the church. Thus in this thirteenth century of the
> incarnation of Christ there has flourished in Francis and his way of life
> (*statu*) an evangelical rule and order, introduced through the mediacy
> of the Roman see and its papal power.[2]

Here, more clearly than in any other passage, Olivi defined the role
of the papacy as the essential organ of church government through
which new understandings of divine truth could be authenticated for
the universal church.

The *Quaestio de renuntiatione* is also interesting and important because it brings together in one short work the two aspects of Olivi's

---

[1] Döllinger, *op. cit.*, p. 539, "Ex quo igitur per Romanae ecclesiae authenticam
testificationem et confirmationem constat, regulam minorum per b. Franciscum
editam esse vere et proprie illam evangelicam, quam Christus in se ipso servavit, et
apostolis imposuit et in evangeliis suis conscribi fecit ... patet, ipsum vere esse
angelum apertionis sexti signaculi ..."; Manselli, *op. cit.*, p. 220 n. 2, "Si autem
velox vocatio Domini subtraxerit ex hac luce, Romana ecclesia, cui datum est
universale magisterium, si qua indigne perspexerit dignetur, obsecro emendare."

[2] Oliger, *art. cit.*, p. 362, "... alias nulla nova explicatio sublimium veritatum
fidei catholice esset magis ac magis per successionem temporum in ecclesia Dei
sancta; cuius oppositum per totum decursum ecclesie comprobamus. Unde et in
hoc XIIIo centenario Christi incarnati floruit in Francisco et eius statu evangelica
regula et religio, mediante ducatu romane sedis et sue papalis potestatis."

thought that we emphasized in describing his "enigmatic" attitude to the papacy—his real reverence for the authority of the Roman church and his deep concern about the individual persons who might come to preside over it. The very nature of the problem that Olivi was discussing in this *Quaestio* required him to make a distinction between the office of the papacy and the persons of the individual popes, for one of the arguments that he had to answer took the form, "A power conferred by God can be taken away only by God." The obvious response was to point out that, although the power inherent in the papal office came from God alone, individual popes were appointed through human agency and so could be removed by human agency.[1] Olivi, however, went further than his argument about papal abdication strictly required and insisted that a pope could be removed from office even against his own will if his rule became harmful to the church.

The person of the pope, he wrote, could more easily be corrupted than the Roman see, for all mortal men were prone to corruption.[2] Hence papal jurisdiction had to be regarded as "removable" from any particular person. A pope might grow unfit for his office in many ways. He might become physically incapable—blind, deaf and dumb for instance. He might go mad, or degenerate into a shameless public sinner. He might also become a pertinacious heretic.[3] In such cases, according to Olivi's argument, there was no necessity for a general council to be summoned to sit in judgment on the pope. It was sufficient for the cardinals to remove a guilty or incapable man from office. At one point Olivi suggested that the cardinals, in a sense, acted as a superior judge in condemning an erring pope. But later he explained that "since all ecclesiastical jurisdiction is taken away by manifest heresy," their sentence was essentially declaratory. The pope had, in effect, renounced his own power by becoming a heretic or notorious

---

[1] Oliger, *art. cit.*, p. 359. The same distinction is found in the discussions of John of Paris and Giles of Rome on Celestine's abdication. See my *Foundations*, p. 161.

[2] Oliger, *art. cit.*, p. 359, "... persona pape potest facilius corrumpi aut ad regimen ecclesiarum inutilis reddi quam sedes romana."

[3] *Art. cit.*, p. 356, "Constat autem, quod omnis persona huius vite corruptibilis et variabilis potest communiter incidere in tales defectus mentis et corporis, quod fiat etiam omnino inutilis et nociva et etiam periculosa ad regimen, ad quod est assumpta, puta si in perpetuam amentiam, aut in pertinacem heresim cadat, aut si omnem impudicitiam imprudenter et ribaldice et incorrigibiliter prosequatur aut ecclesiam lupina rabie vastet et exterminet, aut si fiat cecus et mutus et surdus et sic de aliis consimilibus."

sinner.[1] Olivi seems to have followed the doctrine of the canonist
Huguccio precisely, both in regarding a heretical pope as self-deposed
and in extending the meaning of the word heresy to include notorious
crime.

For Olivi, then, the pope was the supreme judge in matters of faith.
In the sphere of divine truth he could "explicate what had been implicit." He could even add to the content of the faith in the sense of
authenticating new revelations (as the papacy had done in the case of
St. Francis). But Olivi insisted with equal force in the *Quaestio de
renuntiatione* that the pope could not overturn truths of faith that were
already established. If he attempted to do this he became a heretic
and a pseudo-pope. In making this point at considerable length Olivi
quoted several of the rather ambiguous canons of the Decretum which
stated that, in matters of faith, a pope was bound by the decrees of
preceding "fathers."[2] Indeed his whole exposition of papal power in
this *Quaestio* relied very heavily on canonical authorities and it raised
once again the same central problem or paradox that we have already
encountered in the works of the Decretists. The ruler whom God had
established as supreme judge of the church in matters of faith might
himself become a heretic. But for Olivi the problem was much more
real and urgent than it had been for the canonists. In their work the
problem of a heretical pope arose merely as a scholastic dilemma
inherent in the collection of texts they had to expound. Olivi believed
that the pope, as supreme arbiter of the faith, had recently authenticated a new revelation of the Holy Spirit which was destined to re-shape
the whole life of the church; and he also believed in the coming of
a heretical pseudo-pope who would attack that revelation, not as a
mere abstract possibility, but as an impending calamity, an imminent
threat to the life of the church. Our next task will be to explain how this
tension in Olivi's thought led him to formulate his novel non-canoni-
cal doctrine of papal infallibility.

---

[1] *Art. cit.*, pp. 357, 358, "Omnis autem iurisdictio ecclesiastica tollitur per heresim manifestam," pp. 358-359, "Rursus, sicut supra ostensum est, cardinales gerunt
vicem superioris in eligendo papam et in preceptorie cogendo ipsum consentire
electioni et in ipsum consecrando et in eius renuntiationem acceptando. Si autem
papam propter aliquod crimen deponerent, credo quod hec depositio potius modum renuntiationis haberet quam iudiciarie condempnationis, nec differ(r)et a
simplici renuntiatione nisi solum pro quanto referretur ad crimen commissum."

[2] *Art. cit.*, pp. 349, 355, citing C. 25 q. 1 c. 6-9, C. 25 q. 1 c. 3, C. 25 q. 2 c. 4.

3. Olivi and Papal Infallibility

(i) *The Doctrine of Infallibility*

First, we must examine the actual content of Olivi's doctrine as set out in his *Quaestio* on papal infallibility. His argument was presented in a common scholastic form. He intended to give an affirmative response to the question that he posed. "Whether the pope is to be obeyed by all Catholics as an unerring standard in faith and morals." At the beginning of his *Quaestio*, however, he presented a series of arguments that favored a negative answer. These were followed by arguments in favor of the affirmative position, arguments asserting that the pope was indeed infallible. Then Olivi gave his own affirmative answer to the question and moved on to a more detailed discussion of the problems raised by this response. Presumably the *Quaestio* would have concluded in the usual fashion with refutations of the negative arguments posed at the outset. Unfortunately, however, Olivi's text breaks off, uncompleted, in the course of a discussion on the exact nature of the inerrancy he had attributed to the pope.

Most of the thirteen negative arguments set out at the beginning of the *Quaestio* were objections to the doctrine of papal primacy in general rather than to the thesis of papal inerrancy in particular and they are of no great interest from our point of view. Bonaventure included a somewhat similar list in his parallel *Quaestio*, "On the obedience due to the Roman pontiff." Many of these objections were standard arguments of the schools and there were standard answers to them. E.g., "All bishops are equal to the pope." Answer: They are equal in orders but not in jurisdiction. "Christ gave authority to all the Apostles." Answer: He gave authority to all but not in the same degree. "General councils conferred authority on the papacy and so they can take it away." Answer: The councils merely acknowledged an authority originally conferred by Christ. And so on. In a few cases we must regret that Olivi did not provide the answers to his own objections, notably those in which he observed that the pope could be deposed for heresy; that the pope could err in faith and morals like anyone else; that Pope Anastasius had in fact favored heretics and so did not deserve to be obeyed as unerring. Detailed replies to these objections would have required a careful explanation of the precise circumstances in which papal pronouncements were to be regarded as infallible.

After his negative arguments Olivi presented five arguments in favor of papal infallibility, all of them following essentially the same form and each based on a foundation of familiar quotations from canon law. In each argument he considered some particular aspect of papal power, presented a substantial body of canonistic references to prove that the power in question was indeed universally attributed to the pope, and then—here going beyond anything that the canonists had envisaged—argued that the attribution of such power to the pope would be unintelligible or impossible unless the pope was also regarded as unerring. The best argument, perhaps is the one that he placed third:

> It is impossible for God to give to any one the full authority to decide about doubts concerning the faith and divine law with this condition, that He would permit him to err. And anyone who, we agree, is not permitted to err is to be followed as an unerring rule. But God has given this authority to the Roman pontiff, whence it is said in *Dist.* 17 c. 5 (of the Decretum) that "greater and more difficult questions are to be referred to the apostolic see."[1]

The other arguments were basically similar. Thus, the higher and more independent a power was, the more it was indefectible; but the pope was supreme and independent of all powers in the church as *mater* and *magistra* of all. Again it was impossible for God to bind a man to follow fixedly an erring rule; but all men were bound to follow and believe what the pope handed down. Also, since God had immediately established the Roman see, it would seem that he would always immediately protect and direct it. Finally, everyone in the church who was liable to error could be judged and corrected. But the pope could be judged by no man and, accordingly, it was to be assumed that he could not err.[2] Throughout this sequence of arguments Olivi used canonical texts like, "The Roman church has never erred" and assumed that they referred to the unfailing faith of the pope as an individual

---

[1] Maccarrone p. 328, "Item, impossibile est Deum dare alicui plenam auctoritatem diffiniendi de dubiis fidei et divine legis cum hoc, quod permitteret eum errare; de quocumque autem constat quod nullo modo permitteretur errare; ipse sequendus est tamquam regula inerrabilis; sed romano pontifici dedit Deus hanc auctoritatem. Unde XVIIa distinctione, *Denique*, dicitur quod 'maiores et difficiliores questiones ad sedem apostolicam semper debent referri'. Et Innocentius *Extra De baptismo et eius effectu* dicit 'maiores ecclesie causas, presertim articulos fidei contingentes, ad Petri sedem referendas intelligit, qui, eum querenti Domino quem discipuli dicerent ipsum esse, Petrus respondisse notatur: Tu es Christus filius dei vivi; et pro eo Dominum exorasse ne deficiat fides eius'." References to C. 24 q. 1 cc. 7, 9, 10, 11 and 12 followed.

[2] *Art. cit.*, pp. 326-330.

although the canonists themselves had generally explained that such texts referred rather to the whole body of the faithful.

Olivi next set out his own opinion—"It is to be said that all Catholics are to obey the pope in faith and morals"[1]—and proposed for further exploration four topics related to the position he had adopted. These were: (1) The necessity for a single supreme pontiff in the church. (2) The necessary authority of the Roman see. (3) The manner in which inerrancy should be attributed to the pontiff and his see. (4) The measure of the obedience necessarily required from the Catholic people.[2] Olivi's exposition broke off in the middle of his treatment of the crucial third topic. His discussions on the first two, the necessary primacy of the pope and of the Roman church, were for the most part merely conventional with only an occasional flash of Olivi's individual quirkishness.[3] But with his third question—*quis sit modus sue inerrabilitatis*—he came to the heart of the problem he had posed. "Concerning the third topic," Olivi wrote, "it is necessary, firstly, to consider in general the inerrancy of the church and, secondly, to consider in particular the inerrancy of the Roman see and of him who presides in it, namely the pope."[4] The indefectibility of the faith of the whole church could be proved directly from Scripture, he pointed out, citing texts like Matthew 28.20, where Christ said to his disciples "I will be with you all days even to the end of the world."[5] Moreover,

---

[1] *Art. cit.*, p. 331, "Ad primam questionem dicendum quod ab omnibus catholicis est romano pontifici in fide et moribus obediendum." It will be noted that Olivi did not here repeat the phrase "tamquam regule inerrabili." This does not seem significant, however. The whole argument continued to be directed to the precise point of papal inerrancy.

[2] *Ibid.* The text continued, "Ad cuius intelligentiam quatuor sunt inspicienda: primo scilicet que fuit in ecclesia necessitas unius generalis capitis seu pontificis; secundo, que fuerit necessitas et auctoritas romane sedis; tertio quoad utrumque, quis sit modus sue inerrabilitatis; quarto, quanta sit obediendi mensura et necessitas ex parte catholice plebis."

[3] *Art. cit.*, pp. 331-338. Olivi argued that the church needed a single supreme pontiff to maintain unity of faith and order; it also needed a single head so that the earthly hierarchy of the church could parallel the divine hierarchy of heaven. As for the Roman see; a fixed see was needed to ensure stability of succession and ready access to the head. Peter chose Rome because it ruled over the whole world. Also the western Latin people were more robust, more fitted to sustain the faith stably than the oriental peoples who were always prone to schism and heresy. And the fact that Latin emerged last among "the three principal languages" made it fitting that Latin should be the language of the last age of the world down to the second coming of Christ.

[4] *Art. cit.*, p. 338.

[5] *Ibid.* Olivi also cited here Luke 22.32 and Matthew 24.24.

the majesty of God required that his church militant should never be utterly vanquished by the forces of the devil. The clemency of God ensured that his grace would at all times be bestowed at least on some people. The justice of God forbade the total triumph of the wicked for God tolerated evil men only for the sake of the good scattered among them. (He would have spared even Sodom if there had been ten good men there to save.) And the wisdom of God excluded the possibility of any "discontinuity" in the life of his church. (God had made all things for the use of men and especially for those who served him faithfully. If at any time God had no true servants then the whole purpose of creation would be frustrated.) But men could serve God unswervingly only if they held to a stable faith; and, considering the foolishness and simplicity of many believers, such a faith could be maintained only if there existed in the church an authority capable of guiding and ruling all its members.[1] Obviously Olivi regarded the papacy as this "authority." These texts provide a second set of arguments in favor of papal infallibility different from those presented earlier in the *Quaestio*. In his first group of arguments Olivi asserted that the primacy of jurisdiction conferred on Peter necessarily included the attribute of infallibility. In this second group of arguments he maintained that the indefectibility of the universal church necessarily implied the inerrancy of its head. The problem remained of proving— preferably from Scripture—that the unfailing faith of the church was indeed expressed infallibly in the teachings of the pope.

In this regard, Olivi's treatment of the text at Luke 22.32—"I have prayed for you Peter that your faith shall not fail"—is of the highest importance. In his argument on the indefectibility of the church Olivi cited this text with the explanation that Christ spoke to Peter "in the person of the church."[2] This was the traditional interpretation derived from St. Augustine which, in thirteenth century theology and canon law, was commonly taken to mean that, even though individual popes might err in doctrine, the faith of the whole church would never fail completely. But this was not what Olivi was trying to prove. He

---

[1] *Art. cit.*, pp. 339-342.

[2] *Art. cit.*, p. 338, "Et Petro, in persona ecclesie, dixit 'Ego rogavi pro te, ut non deficiat fides tua.'" Olivi also wrote here that the words of Christ referred, not to Peter alone, but to "the office and authority of his see." Earlier Olivi had quoted a canonical text which used Luke 22.32 to establish that "greater causes of the church, especially those touching articles of faith, are to be referred to the see of Peter" but without any further explanation of his own understanding of the gospel text (supra p. 116 n. 1).

was seeking to show that the generally accepted doctrine of the indefectibility of the church implied the existence of an infallible pope.
Perhaps if he had completed his *Quaestio* he would have explained
more clearly how the text, "Ego rogavi pro te …" supported this
conclusion. It is quite certain at any rate that he did regard Christ's
words as applying specifically to Peter and his successors (as well as
to the whole church and to the Roman see as an institution) for he
explained this elsewhere in a detailed commentary on the Gospel text.
To understand the whole range of meanings that Olivi attached to
Luke 22.32 we must turn aside for a moment from his *Quaestio* on infallibility to consider his unpublished commentary on Luke. Here he
departed notably from the standard Augustinian interpretation to
offer an explanation that strongly emphasized the personal role of
Peter as guardian of the faith. The words "Ego rogavi pro te …," he
wrote, were to be understood in three ways. In the first place they
applied to Peter personally in his future role as prelate of the whole
church. Such a prelate needed to be "strong and indefectible" in the
faith so that he could confirm and sustain the faith of others. Secondly
Christ's words applied to all Peter's successors in the papal office
and to his apostolic see. A human body could function only if it
possessed a sound heart. But Christ chose the apostolic see as the
heart of the whole church. Hence it was fitting that he should pray
for the indefectibility of its faith. Thirdly Christ's words applied to
all the apostles and all the elect in the sense that all who were to be
saved needed the grace of final perseverance in the faith.[1]

To return to the *Quaestio* on infallibility. Here too Olivi was arguing
for the unfailing faith of the pope as an individual and not just

---

[1] *MS Vat. Ottob. lat.* 3302, fol. 106v, "Nota quod haec verba sub triplici respectu feruntur … Primo scilicet respectu sue persone et prelationis pro ut solum
esset in eo, eo enim ipso quo Christus finaliter elegerat eum ut esset ecclesie sue
caput et fundamentum, habuit secundum quod homo rogare totam trinitatem ut
eius fides pro tempore sue future prelationis esset sic fortis et indefectibilis quod
posset ceteros in fide corroborare et eorum infirma et debilia supportare. 2o.
Feruntur ad eum pro omnibus successoribus suis in papali offitio successuris seu
feruntur ad eum pro apostolica sede eius. Sicut enim cor, quia est prima et radicalis
sedes anime, oportet in vita conservari ad hoc quod corpus in vita continuetur, sic
ex quo Christus apostolicam sedem Petri finaliter elegerat quasi pro corde, oportuit
quod secundum quod homo pro sue fidei indefectibilitate rogaret per quam suf-
fraganeorum ecclesias aliquando in fide nutantes aut a fide ruentes ad fidem redu-
ceret aut in fide plenius confirmaret. 3o. Feruntur ad ipsum pro tota universitate
Christi apostolorum et omnium electorum. Nam non solum prima gratia est omnibus electis per Christi precem promerita sed etiam omne eius augmentum eiusque
finalis perseverantia et indeficientia.

repeating the standard platitudes of the schools about the integrity of the faith of the church as a whole. But he could not simply assert without any qualification that it was impossible for the pope to err in faith for the common doctrine of the time held that several popes (most notably Anastasius) had in fact erred. Olivi therefore proposed a series of distinctions in a page of densely packed argumentation that concludes the text of his *Quaestio*. To understand the nature of the inerrancy that inhered in the Roman see and in the supreme pontiff, he wrote, it was necessary first to distinguish between different kinds of error. An error could be merely personal or it could be "magisterial," i.e., it could be merely an individual opinion or it could be proposed as a public teaching which would affect the faith of others. Again, some errors were entirely incompatible with sincere faith while others concerned matters of human knowledge which had little relevance for the truths of religion. Finally a pope might be pertinacious in error or willing to accept correction.[1]

In the second place, Olivi proposed a distinction concerning the Roman see and its bishop. An institution might be the Roman see only in name and appearance or it might be the Roman see in true fact. The same was true of the pope.[2]

Last of all, Olivi considered the meaning of the term "inerrancy" itself. The pope or the Roman see could be called "unerring" either absolutely or only conditionally. For instance, one could add a condition by stating that the Pope could never err so long as he remained true pope and true head of the church (and the same could be said of the Roman see). Granted this condition it was quite clear that neither the pope nor the Roman see could err pertinaciously in a matter of faith, at any rate not by propounding an error "magisterially." The whole church could not err and so it could not be united to an erring head. Hence, if the pope did err magisterially in exercising his office as head of the church he would thereupon cease to be a true pope.

---

[1] *Art. cit.*, p. 342, "Ad quod attendendum triplex distinctio est premittenda. Quarum prima est de errore. Est enim quidam error personalis et quoad se; quidam vero communis et quasi magistralis et quoad alios; iterum, est quidam error qui cum sinceritate fidei non se compatitur, pro eo quod directe et evidenter ei contrariatur, sicut est error in fide pertinaciter edoctus aut defensus. Alius est error contra aliqua scientialia vel humana, qui ad veritatem fidei non multum pertinet. Iterum, est error in fide pertinax, et est etiam error in fide non pertinax, sed levis et corrigi promptus."

[2] *Ibid.* "Secunda distinctio est de ipsa sede et eius presule. Est enim sedes secundum nomen seu secundum solam apparentiam, et est sedes romana secundum rem et existentiam aut secundum utrumque. Et idem potest dici de papa."

As a heretic he would lose all power over the church, for any faithful Christian was superior to him. At this point Olivi's argument breaks off.[1]

It will be evident that, in several respects, Olivi's discussion anticipated the ways in which the doctrine of papal infallibility would develop for centuries to come. The phrase he used to define the sphere within which the pope was unerring—"in faith and morals"—was the same as that employed in the nineteenth century definition of Vatican Council I. His assertion that a man established by God as supreme judge in questions of faith had to be regarded as necessarily unerring in his judgments, his application of the text "Ego rogavi pro te Petre …" to the persons of Peter and his successors, his insistence on a necessary link between the indefectible faith of the church and the inerrancy of doctrinal pronouncements made by its head—all of these arguments became commonplaces of ultramontanist apologetics in later times.

And yet, at the very end of his argument, Olivi seems to have been shaping a conclusion radically different from that of more recent defenders of papal infallibility. His last sentences disclose his full awareness of the complexity of the problem that he had posed. For Olivi it was not sufficient to distinguish between the pope's private and public capacities, to maintain that a pope could err in his private opinions but not in his "magisterial" pronouncements, because there always remained the possibility that the person making a magisterial pronouncement from the papal throne might be a pope "only in name and appearance." Nor could this difficulty have been evaded by the invention of a special class of ultra-official decrees proceeding from an "extra-ordinary magisterium" (to use the language of modern

---

[1] *Ibid.* "Tertia distinctio est de ipsa inerrabilitate, seu de impossibilitate errandi. Hec enim impossibilitas potest inesse aliquibus per se aut per alterum, et potest inesse simpliciter aut solum quoad quid; utpote si dicatur quod sedes romana existens sedes vera non potest errare, aut quod papa existens verus papa et verum capud ecclesie non potest errare; et talis impossibilitas est secundum quid, et de hac clarum est quod nec papa nec sedes romana potest in fide pertinaciter errare, saltem errore communi seu magistrali. Cum enim ecclesia generalis errare non possit, et sic per consequens nec capiti erroneo seu falso veraciter coniungi et inniti possit. Papa autem sic errans, errore scilicet communi, cum habeat rationem capitis erronei, et non solum persone singulariter et quoad se errantis, impossibile est quod papa sic errans sit verus papa et verum capud ecclesie. Et ideo secundum iura nullus hereticus publicus seu in quantum hereticus, quod idem est in proposito, habet potestatem benedicendi et maledicendi in ecclesia, quia omnis fidelis est maior eo."

theology). In the last resort the man who claimed to be wielding such an authority might still not be the true pope in whom it really inhered. A further exploration of Olivi's thought on this question will help us to understand the final topic we need to consider—why Olivi felt moved to develop a theory of papal infallibility at all.

(ii) *The Necessity for Infallibility*

It is certain that Olivi's interest in the question of infallibility was stimulated by the problems of the Franciscan Order rather than by the problems of reunion with the Greeks as Maccarrone suggested.[1] This is clear from the fact that his discussion on the subject was presented in the *Quaestiones de perfectione evangelica*, a work devoted wholly to problems concerning the Franciscans and their way of life.[2] Several of the *Quaestiones* touched on issues that arose out of the bull *Exiit* and it seems very likely that the *Quaestio* on papal infallibility was written immediately after the appearance of the bull in August 1279, and was stimulated directly by Olivi's enthusiasm for the doctrine proclaimed by the pope. It is impossible to date the *Quaestio* with precision but its relationship to the *Quaestiones* that can be dated tends to confirm this hypothesis.

The *Quaestiones* were first described in detail by Ehrle on the basis of the text in MS Vat. 4986. He argued—and all subsequent scholarship has confirmed this judgment—that the first ten *Quaestiones*, which form a coherent treatise on the religious life, were probably completed before 1279.[3] The first four dealt with topics concerning the active and contemplative lives. Q. 5 introduced the theme of vows in general. Then Olivi seems to have embarked on a systematic treatment of the three monastic vows of chastity, poverty and obedience, Qq. 6-7

---

[1] Maccarrone, *art. cit.*, p. 315. Maccarrone also mentioned the Franciscan disputes in this connection.

[2] This is true even of the *Quaestio, De renuntiatione papae* since Celestine's abdication was denounced as invalid by some of the Spirituals. Cf. supra p. 102.

[3] Ehrle, "Olivi," *ALKG*, 3, p. 498. For further studies on the dating of particular *Quaestiones* see A. Maier, "Per la storia del processo contro l'Olivi," *Rivista di storia della chiesa in Italia*, 5 (1951), pp. 326-339; F. M. Delorme, "Fr. P. J. Olivi Quaestio de voto regulam aliquam profitentis," *Antonianum*, 16 (1941), pp. 131-164; D. Pacetti, *Quaestiones quatuor de domina* (Quaracchi, 1954); A. Emmen and F. Simoncioli, "La dottrina dell' Olivi sulla contemplazione, la vita attiva e mista," *Studi Francescani*, 60 (1963), pp. 382-445. V. Doucet, "De operibus manuscriptis Fr. Petri Ioannis Olivi in biblioteca Universitatis Patavinae asservatis," *AFH*, 28 (1935), pp. 156-197, 408-442 maintained (p. 413) that the whole treatise was intended by Olivi to form part of a Summa on the *Sentences*. For criticism of this view see Emmen and Simoncioli, pp. 386-387.

dealt with chastity and Qq. 8-10 with poverty. (Maier referred to these first ten *Quaestiones* as "an organic whole."[1]) In Ehrle's manuscript Q. 11 asked "Whether to vow obedience to another man in all things is of evangelical perfection" and Q. 12 is our *Quaestio* on infallibility, "Whether the Roman pontiff is to be obeyed in faith and morals as an unerring standard." None of the first ten *Quaestiones* referred to the Bull, *Exiit* and this is the main reason for supposing that they were completed before August, 1279 since Nicholas' decree would have been highly relevant at several points in the discussion. We know, moreover, that Olivi was writing on poverty earlier in 1279. He himself recorded that he traveled to Rome in that year and that, while there, he wrote a little treatise *De paupertate*. This he inserted between Q. 8 and Q. 9 of the *De perfectione evangelica*. (Q. 9 had already been written by then.)[2]

The first ten *Quaestiones* of the *De perfectione* are found in the same order and in substantially the same form in the two best manuscripts which present Olivi's final recension of their text, MSS Vatican Lat. 4986 and Vatican Borgh, 357.[3] There is, however, no coherent manuscript tradition that could enable us to establish with certainty the order in which the remaining seven *Quaestiones* were composed. We have to deal with a collection of scattered questions on Franciscan themes written at various times (one of them as late as 1295) and presented in different sequences in the two best manuscripts. Both manuscripts, however, presented a group of questions on obedience (including the question whether the pope was to be obeyed as an "unerring standard") immediately after those on poverty.[4] It seems clear that, by

---

[1] Maier, *art. cit.*, p. 329. Emmen and Simoncioli, who provide the best discussion of the question, conclude that Qq. 1-11 were completed by 1279 and that all of the rest were probably written between 1279 and 1282, except only the *Quaestio, De renuntiatione* (which refers to the abdication of Pope Celestine V on 12 Dec. 1294). The authors also confirm Ehrle's judgment in basing his account on MS Lat. 4986, arguing that this manuscript contains Olivi's final ordering of the text (p. 385). Pacetti preferred *MS Borgh*. 357, but this judgment seems based on a misunderstanding of Maier's work and on a confusion between Q. 15 and a sub-section of Q. 10 (See Emmen and Simoncioli, p. 386 n. 15.)

[2] Ehrle, "Olivi," p. 415. Olivi wrote that the *De paupertate* was written in Summer, 1279 during the deliberations on the drafting of *Exiit*. Q. 9, on the *usus pauper*, was definitely written before August 1279 because Olivi declared subsequently that he had not quoted *Exiit* in this *Quaestio* since the decree was not promulgated at the time he wrote it. (Cf. Ehrle, p. 531.)

[3] Maier, *art. cit.*, p. 330.

[4] In *MS Borgh*. 357 the sequence is as follows. Q. 11 "Whether to vow obedience to another man in all things ... is of evangelical perfection." Q. 12 "Whether one

Summer, 1279, Olivi had just completed the sections of his treatise
dealing with chastity and poverty. It would have been natural for
him to turn next to the third monastic vow of obedience. Most
probably Q. 11 and Q. 12 (in Ehrle's enumeration) were conceived
of and written together, for the latter *Quaestio* is, in effect, a sub-ques-
tion arising out of the former one. (Q. 11 dealt with obedience in
general, Q. 12 with the special obedience owed to the pope. As we
have noted, the two questions were arranged in the same way in
Bonaventure's homonymous treatise.) It thus seems probable that
both *Quaestiones* were written in late 1279 or shortly thereafter. Q. 11
was definitely completed before 1283[1] and, if the *Questiones* on obedience had been composed earlier in the 1270s, before those on chastity
or poverty, one would expect to find them embedded in the "organic
whole" formed by the first part of the treatise.[2]

   To sum up. The internal structure of the *Quaestiones* suggests a
probable date of c. 1280 for Qq. 11 and 12. Q. 12 introduces a novel
doctrine on papal inerrancy "in faith and morals." And, in August,
1279, the pope had promulgated a decree which Olivi regarded as a
triumphant vindication of his own views on a major disputed point of
faith (the poverty of Christ) and a major disputed point of morals
(the obligations imposed by the Franciscan vow of poverty). There
seems no reason to resist the obvious inference that Olivi's affirmation

---

vowing to obey the gospel or any Rule ... is bound to obey all things in them." Q.
13 "Whether the pope can dispense in any vow." Q. 14 "Whether the Roman pontiff is to be obeyed in faith and morals ... as an unerring standard." Cf. Pacetti, *op.
cit.*, p. 22.

   [1] Q. 11 is referred to in Q. 17 (Ehrle's enumeration). Q. 17 in turn can be dated
to the period 1279-1283 since it mentioned *Exiit* and was itself mentioned by the
commission of Franciscan theologians which was set up to examine Olivi's works
in 1282 and made its response in 1283. Cf. Delorme, *art. cit.*, p. 139.

   [2] Maccarrone, *art. cit.*, pp. 313-315, preferred an earlier date but presented no
convincing evidence for his point of view. Stressing the close connection between Q. 11 and Q. 12 he pointed out that Q. 17 (which mentioned Q. 11) was
composed between 1279 and 1283, and, he thought, "closer to the former than the
latter date because the argument presented attracted most interest immediately
after the Bull of 1279." This argument establishes a *terminus ante quem* for Q. 11 of
1283 with the probability that that date is a little late. Maccarrone's argument,
however, makes a sudden leap at this point. He simply assumed that 1279 (not
1283) was a definite *terminus ante quem* for Q. 11 and looked for a *terminus post quem*
in the period when Olivi began to teach, 1270-1274. There seems no rational basis
for this approach except Maccarrone's inclination to relate Olivi's discussions of
papal infallibility to the debates of the Council of Lyons held in 1274. In fact no
shred of evidence suggests that either Q. 11 or Q. 12 was composed before August
1279. Most probably Q. 11, Q. 12 and Q. 17 were all written together in late 1279.

of papal infallibility was a direct response to the promulgation of
Exiit.

But, still, why infallibility? Why could Olivi not have been content
to reaffirm the existing canonical and theological doctrine that the
pope was supreme judge in matters of faith? After all, Bonaventure
too had seen the need to exalt papal power in arguing that the decrees
of the popes provided unimpeachable authentication for the doctrine
of Franciscan poverty. But he had not found it necessary to elaborate
a doctrine of papal infallibility. The difference in the thought of the
two great Franciscans can be explained by a difference in their expectations concerning the papacy. Bonaventure never envisaged the possibility that a Roman pontiff might seek to pervert the faith of the church.
Olivi not only envisaged the possibility over and over again. He was
obsessed with the fear that such a calamity was about to happen.
From his point of view, therefore, it was essential that the papal
decrees already enacted in support of the Franciscan way of life—the
decrees of true, orthodox popes—should be regarded as, not only
authoritative for the present, but immutable, irreformable for all time
to come.

The evidence for Olivi's pre-occupation with the coming of a heretical pseudo-pope is not limited to the predictions in his *Lectura* on the
Apocalypse. We have found persistent hints of the same concern expressed in his *Quaestio* on Celestine's abdication, in his *Quaestiones* on the
indispensability of the Franciscan vow of poverty, and in his *Quodlibet*
on the pope's temporal power. And the whole argument of the *Quaestio
de infallibilitate* itself led up to a crucial distinction between a true
pope and a pontiff who was pope "only in name and appearance."
It was of course the true pope who could not err. "The pope is unable
to err so long as he is true pope and head of the church."[1] The full
significance of this statement becomes apparent only when it is taken
in conjunction with Olivi's frequently expressed fears concerning
the future of the Roman church. Taken in the whole context of Olivi's
writings his argument that inerrancy was an essential attribute of the
pope evidently could never have been intended to mean that all
solemn teachings from the papal throne were necessarily true. The
man occupying the throne might well be a pope in "mere appearance."
Rather, Olivi meant to assert here, as he had done elsewhere (especially
in the *Quaestio de renuntiatione*), that a pontiff who erred incorrigibly

---

[1] Maccarrone, *art. cit.*, p. 342.

in his official teaching automatically ceased to be pope. Olivi's doctrine of infallibility also implied—and this was new—that any pontiff who departed from the doctrinal decisions of a predecessor would, by doing so, automatically fall into heresy and so cease to be the true head of the church.

For Olivi, of course, the doctrinal decisions that especially needed to be safeguarded were those concerning Franciscan poverty for, in his view, the major perversity of the carnal church of the fifth age was precisely its attack on true poverty—and especially on the *usus pauper*—both by word and by example.[1] The coming reign of Antichrist and the pseudo-pope would be marked by an intensification of these evils. Indeed the pesudo-pope would be identifiable as such primarily because he would attack the doctrine of apostolic poverty. "The pseudo-pope will be pseudo because he will err in heretical fashion against the evangelical truth of poverty and perfection."[2] The forces of Antichrist would rise up against precisely the doctrine that Nicholas III has proclaimed in the decretal *Exiit*.[3]

Olivi was not alone in anticipating that a future pope might turn against the Franciscan doctrine of evangelical poverty. This fear was widespread among the more radical friars toward the end of the thirteenth century. As early as 1274 a rumor spread through Italy (a false rumor as it turned out) that Pope Gregory X was determined to impose the obligation of property-ownership on all the mendicant orders. His right to do so was vigorously challenged by a group of Spirituals from the March of Ancona (a group that later came under Olivi's influence during his lectorship at Florence). Their leaders declared that such a decree would be

---

[1] Döllinger, *op. cit.*, p. 542, "... sentiant et doceant, statum evangelicum mendicitatis non esse statum perfectionis, vel esse statum minimae perfectionis, et quod habere aliquid in communi est perfectius et magis evangelicum quam non habere." p. 555, "... quidam eorum dicunt, paupertatem altissimam non esse de substantia perfectionis ejus, et quod ejus est habere sufficientia aut saltem necessaria in communi; quidam vero, quod usus paupertatis i.e. altissimae paupertatis secundum debitas circumstantias proportionatus non est de substantia ejus."

[2] *Op. cit.*, p. 573, "... tunc fere omnes discedent ab obedientia veri Papae et sequentur illum pseudopapam, qui quidem erit pseudo, quia haeretico modo errabit contra veritatem evangelicae paupertatis et perfectionis, et quia forte ultra hoc non erit canonice electus, sed schismatice introductus."

[3] *Op. cit.*, p. 571, "Insurrexerunt item alii non modice contra evangelicam paupertatem errantes, contra quos est declaratio sive decretalis D. Nicolai IV. in eadem generatione edita."

... not only inappropriate but damnable and leading to apostacy and not falling under his power and so impossible.[1]

This was precisely Olivi's position. The final point we wish to make—and it is all-important for understanding Olivi's thought—is that this was not a position that could possibly have been sustained within the traditional framework of the canonical doctrine on papal sovereignty.

In the canonists' theory no pope could be bound by the decree of his predecessor because *par in parem non habet imperium*. For them, it would have been impossible to recognize a pseudo-pope as "pseudo" simply because he chose to take a different line from his predecessors in dealing with the problem of Franciscan poverty. According to the canonists a future pope would have every right to do this. Even Bonaventure had cheerfully acknowledged that a pope could freely change the decision of his predecessor concerning the meaning of perfect poverty (though it never occurred to him that this papal power might one day be turned against the Franciscans). Olivi declared that each pope was bound "by the commands of God... and the authentic dogmas of the Catholic faith written in Sacred Scripture and held by the Catholic church ..."[2] This was entirely conventional. The novelty in Olivi's position was that, from his standpoint, individual papal definitions (because they were infallible) could become parts of the "authentic dogma" of the church. And this in turn explains his account of the relationship between the popes and the Franciscan Rule. According to Olivi the Rule was authenticated by past decrees of the Roman see but it could not be changed by future decrees of the same authority. Viewed from the standpoint of the canonical theory of sovereignty such a position is simply nonsensical. Given the presupposition of papal infallibility it becomes entirely coherent and reasonable for, on that theory, the decrees of earlier pontiffs acknowledging that Francis' way of life was the way of Christ and the apostles could be seen as establishing an "authentic dogma" that was binding on future popes.[3]

---

[1] Ehrle, "Die 'historia septem tribulationum ordinis minorum' des fr. Angelus de Clarino," *ALKG*, 2 (1886), pp. 249-336 at p. 302.

[2] The words occur in the *Quodlibet* on papal temporal power. *Quodlibet* 1, q. 18, fol. 8rb, "Dicendum quod potestas papalis ... potest referri ad dei mandata a solo deo dispensabilia et ad sue catholice fidei autentica dogmata in scripturis sacris scripta aut per catholicam ecclesiam pro indubitabili fide habita. Et de his etiam clarum est quod papa ... non potest ... prefata dogmata in puncto infringere seu falsificare."

[3] Significantly, after stating that the pope was bound by "authentic dogma" in

Olivi's whole position pre-supposed the inviolability of the papal decrees approving the Franciscan way of life. Above all he relied on *Exiit*, which treated the Franciscan doctrine of poverty as a matter of divinely revealed truth and not simply as a matter of church discipline. Olivi himself was so conscious of this fact that, in his *Lectura* on the Apocalypse, he appealed to the authority of the Roman church and paraphrased the words of *Exiit* when he presented Francis as the angel of the sixth seal and the fount of a new revelation.[1] If the papal decrees in favor of Franciscan poverty were to be repealed—and Olivi thought this likely to be attempted—then the whole Franciscan position would crumble. But, once again, according to the accepted doctrine of papal sovereignty, a future pope would be entirely competent to repeal the decrees of his predecessors. The existing doctrine, therefore, was inadequate for Olivi's purposes. Only if the papacy were infallible would the decision of one pope on Franciscan poverty be binding on all his successors.

Olivi himself believed of course that his doctrine of evangelical poverty was firmly grounded on a right understanding of Holy Scripture. But his bitter denunciations of contemporary prelates and university masters show how sharply aware he was that his own interpretation of Scripture was not supported by any considerable body of theological opinion outside the Franciscan Order nor even by all the Franciscan masters themselves. Olivi had no doubt that the coming pseudo-pope would enjoy the support of almost the whole church and of nearly all the learned and respectable opinion of his day.[2] In this connection we may note yet another significant parallel between Olivi's apocalyptic speculations and the arguments he presented at the conclusion of the *Quaestio* on infallibility. In the latter context he

---

the passage cited above, Olivi referred the reader to his *Quaestio* on infallibility for a fuller treatment of the question. *Op. cit.*, fol. 9ra, "Si etiam christus commisit sibi simpliciter totum posse suum, ergo potest sicut christus omnia sacramenta destruere et condere nova, et in tot preceptis dispensare in quot potest et deus: que omnia falsa sunt et absurda. Est ergo vicarius eius universalis non sic sed modo superius pretaxato: quem in questione an Pape in omnibus tanquam regule inerrabili sit credendum plenius explicavi."

[1] Döllinger, *op. cit.*, p. 539 (cited supra p. 112 n. 1).

[2] Döllinger, *op. cit.*, p. 570, "... surgent enim tunc pseudochristi et pseudo-prophetae, qui facient ab omnibus adorari cupiditatem et carnalitatem seu terrenam bestiae gloriam secularis, dabuntque ad hoc signa magna. Primo scilicet suae ecclesiasticae authoritatis, cui contradicere videbitur inobedientia, contumacia, rebellio schismatica. Secundo universalis sententiae omnium magistrorum et doctorum suorum et totius multitudinis seu communis opinionis omnium, cui contradicere videbitur stultum et insanum et haereticum."

wrote, "Since the whole church cannot err ... it cannot be united to an erring head." It seems clear that, in the last resort, the faith of the universal church was the "unerring rule" by which individual occupants of the Roman see were to be judged and not vice-versa. But the whole of the immediately preceding argument had been based on a doctrine of indefectibility which asserted only that , in every generation, some of the elect would survive to constitute a true, unfailing church. The true pope would obviously have to be united in faith with this true church. Olivi's argument implied then that the beliefs of an unspecified group of "the elect"—perhaps a very small group— constituted the standard by which a true pope could be distinguished from a pseudo-pope. And this was precisely the situation whose coming he foretold in the *Lectura*.[1]

It will be obvious now why we wrote that a knowledge of Olivi's *Lectura* on the Apocalypse is essential for an understanding of his meaning and purpose in formulating a doctrine of papal infallibility. In the *Lectura* Olivi finally set down plainly his conviction—which he had hinted at often enough in earlier works—that a future pontiff would seek to overturn an established papal teaching which expressed an immutable truth of the Catholic faith. That truth could be safeguarded only if the earlier papal teaching were regarded as irreformable. But a papal teaching could be considered irreformable only if the pope himself were regarded as, not only a supreme judge, but also an infallible teacher. Only then would a pope who went against the teaching of a predecessor be recognizable by the vigilant faithful as a pseudo-pope, a pope "only in name and mere appearance," one who had automatically degraded himself from the papal office. Thus the predictions of a coming pseudo-pope in Olivi's *Lectura* on the Apocalypse dove-tail precisely with the distinction presented in the *Quaestio* on infallibility between a man who was "pope only in name and appearance" and a true pope who was head of the true, unfailing church. The two texts shed light on one another and we need both to understand all the dimensions of Olivi's thought.

Olivi never abandoned the orthodox doctrine of Petrine primacy that he proclaimed in so many of his works. (Even in the coming time of trial, there would always be a "true pope" to lead the scattered remnant of the faithful.) But, by the standards of the late thirteenth

---

[1] Döllinger, *op. cit.*, p. 547, "Tunc enim totus status ecclesiae in praelatis et plebibus et religiosis funditus subvertetur, praeter id quod in paucis electis remanebit occulte."

century, Olivi was never an extreme papalist. He denied to the popes any divine right to temporal power and he severely limited their discretionary authority even within the ecclesiastical sphere. This attitude is entirely consistent with his development of a theory of papal infallibility. To attribute infallibility to the papacy is to limit the sovereignty of each individual pope. The canonists perceived this and so did Olivi. (Bonaventure seems never to have faced the problem at all.) The canonists wanted to maintain the maximum freedom of maneuver for the papacy in the face of the ever-changing needs of the church so they emphasized the very broad discretionary authority of the pope as supreme judge and legislator. Olivi wanted to diminish the capacity of future occupants of the Roman see to injure the church so he insisted on the infallibility—and consequent irreformability—of doctrinal decisions already established by preceding popes. The new theory of papal infallibility was designed to limit the power of future popes, not to loose them from all restraints.

CHAPTER FOUR

MENDICANTS AND SECULARS, 1280-1320

In the forty years after Pietro Olivi first formulated the idea of papal infallibility a sort of hiatus occurred in the development of the doctrine. Theologians did not hasten to attack or defend Olivi's thesis; they seem for the most part to have been content to ignore it as merely an eccentric and unimportant novelty. This is the more noteworthy in that a great body of new writing on papal power appeared in the early years of the fourteenth century, stimulated both by the continuance of the old secular-medicant disputes and by a new series of conflicts between the spiritual and temporal authorities in Christian society. The subject of ecclesiology, treated as a separate branch of theology with its own distinctive literature, first emerged (so it is often asserted) in the numerous treatises of this period bearing titles like *De potestate ecclesiastica* or *De potestate papae*. But, surprisingly perhaps, in all this literature the question of papal infallibility was virtually ignored.

There are several possible reasons why the most avid partisans of papal power in the conflicts of church and state—Giles of Rome, Henry of Cremona, James of Viterbo, Alvarus Pelagius, Augustinus Triumphus—should have been so indifferent to the doctrine of papal infallibility. Perhaps they sensed that the idea of infallibility, with its necessary corollary of irreformability, was incompatible with the theories of papal sovercignty which they were propounding. Probably they had no wish to consecrate as infallible all the decrees of earlier popes that were to be found in Gratian's Decretum (for some of them were hard to reconcile with the papal publicists' own ideas on the right relations between church and state).[1] In any case, at the beginning of the fourteenth century, no one doubted that some popes of the past had indeed erred in faith and, to most thinkers, this still seemed to preclude the possibility of developing any theory of papal infallibility.

Although there was no major debate on the doctrine of papal infallibility itself in the period 1280-1320, important developments

---

[1] At this time the Decretum was emerging from the technical preserve of the of the canonists to be used as a convenient armory of texts by polemicists of all shades of opinion in the controversies concerning papal power.

occurred in several related fields of ecclesiology. New speculations appeared concerning the relationship between Scripture and ecclesiastical Tradition; concerning the inerrancy of the church and the teaching authority of the pope; and concerning the right relationship between pope, bishops and *congregatio fidelium*. In our first chapter we reviewed the teachings of the canonists on Tradition, infallibility and sovereignty in the years around 1200. It will be useful now to survey the developments of theological thought that were taking place in each of these areas a century later. This will help us to understand the ways in which theologians and canonists reacted when the doctrine of infallibility was re-asserted in a new and radical fashion during the 1320s.

1. TRADITION: CHURCH AND SCRIPTURE

In discussing the problem of an "unerring magisterium" in the church it is important to consider the object of infallibility as well as the subject. That is to say we have to ask not only, "Who can define infallibly?" but also, "What can be defined?" If the object of infallibility is taken to be Christian truth concerning faith and morals then our question becomes, "What are the possible sources of Christian truth?" Scripture alone? In that case the scope of an infallible magisterium is limited to the resolution of doubts concerning the meaning of Scriptural texts. Unwritten apostolic traditions as well as Scripture? The infallible authority then has a much broader scope. Post-apostolic revelations as well as the initial "deposit of faith"? The scope of infallibility then becomes illimitable.

Various new trends of thought concerning Scripture and church as founts of revealed truth appeared in the years around 1300. They were characterized above all by a tendency to treat as separate, juxtaposed, authorities these two sources of revelation which earlier centuries had seen as "co-inhering" in a single indissoluble whole. The new trends can be best illustrated from the writings of the secular master, Henry of Ghent and from those of the eminent Franciscan philosopher, Duns Scotus, In Henry of Ghent's work we find a new kind of pre-occupation with the unique authority of Scripture. This led Henry to consider the possibility of a conflict between Scripture and church— a sharp break with preceding ways of thought. Duns Scotus emphasized the importance of non-Scriptural revelation and the unerring authority of the church as exponent of all the truths of faith, written and unwritten.

(i) *Henry of Ghent*

The possibility of envisaging a conflict between the teaching of the church and the teaching of Scripture was inherent in the nature of the mendicant-secular disputes of the 1270s and 1280s. The Franciscans claimed that the approval of the Franciscan Rule by the papacy, the canonization of their founder, and the acceptance of Francis as an undoubted saint by the whole Catholic world established beyond doubt the truth of their teaching on evangelical poverty. Their argument was, in effect, that by accepting Francis and the Franciscan Order the universal church had implicitly accepted the truth of the doctrine that Christ and the apostles owned nothing "singly or in common." The opponents of the Franciscans held that this doctrine was evidently opposed to the plain words of Scripture.

The question, "Whether we should believe the authority of Scripture rather than that of the church or vice-versa" was first raised by Henry of Ghent, the leading opponent of the friars during the 1280s, in his *Summa Quaestionum*.[1] He approached the question by first discussing another, related, topic—whether the whole of Christian revelation was set down perfectly in the Old and New Testaments. It might seem, he argued, that a further divine revelation was needed, for Christ himself said "Many things yet I have to say to you, but you cannot bear them now. But when he, the Spirit of truth, has come he will teach you all the truth ..." (John 16.12-13). And Paul wrote, "We know in part and we prophesy in part ..." (1 Cor. 13. 9), implying the need for a more perfect revelation. Moreover, wrote Henry, some masters (including it was said, Abbot Joachim) had taught that there were to be three ages and three Testaments corresponding to the three persons of the Trinity and that, at his coming, the Holy Spirit would promulgate a new Gospel.[2]

To all this Henry of Ghent replied that belief in post-Scriptural revelation was no part of the true Christian faith but an error of dissident sects like the Manichees and the Mohammedans. Christ said that

---

[1] Cf. supra p. 65 n. 1. The *quaestio* on the relative authority of Scripture and the church was discussed by J. Beumer, "Heilige Schrift und kirchliche Lehrautorität," *Scholastik*, 25 (1950), pp. 40-72 at pp. 51-53; B. Smalley, "Gerard of Bologna and Henry of Ghent," *RTAM*, 22 (1955), pp. 125-129; P. de Vooght, "La méthodoligie théologique d'après Henri de Gand et Gérard de Bologne," *RTAM*, 23 (1956), pp. 61-87; idem, "L'évolution du rapport Église-Écriture du XIIIe au XVe siècle," *Ephemerides theologicae Lovanienses,* 38 (1962), pp. 71-85; G. H. Tavard, *Holy Writ or Holy Church* (London, 1959), pp. 23-26.

[2] *Summae quaestionum ordinarium ... tomos prior* (Paris, 1520), fol. LXVIIIr.

he had come to "fulfil" the law and he would not have carried out this task if something still remained to be fulfilled. Moreover, Christ had promised to send the Holy Spirit *to the apostles*, and he had kept this promise. Above all, when Christ replaced the Old Testament's eye-for-an-eye morality with the perfect law of charity he made a complete and final revelation, which called for no addition or completion. The Old Testament might be called imperfect in comparison with the New Testament, Henry wrote, but together the two books formed a complete and perfect whole. There were, to be sure, three states of man but they were defined by the law of nature, the law of Moses, and the law of the Gospel. The law of the Gospel would endure to the end of time. When Christ promised to the apostles that the Holy Spirit would teach them all truth he did not mean that the Spirit would teach some different or more perfect truth but that he would explain more fully the truths already revealed. Similarly when Paul wrote "We know in part ..." he was not referring to any need for a new revelation but to the need for a more perfect understanding of the existing one.[1]

For Henry of Ghent Scripture was perfect in itself but our perception of its meaning was imperfect.[2] This consideration led him on to a most interesting discourse on the progress of man's understanding of divine truth from the time of Moses down to his own day. God had first revealed himself to men in the Old Testament. Then the Gospel of Christ completed the teaching of the Old Testament in two ways. So far as ceremonial precepts were concerned Christ abolished the literal observance of them and revealed their spiritual meaning; so far as moral precepts were concerned he perfected what was imperfect by supplying omissions and extending the application of Old Testament texts. (The Decalogue said only, "Thou shalt not kill" but Christ said, "Be slow to anger.")

The writings of the Apostles in the New Testament continued the work of Christ, again in two different ways. So far as the Old Testament was concerned the apostles continued the task or reinterpreting ceremonial precepts and supplementing moral ones. The whole "perfect art and science" of doing this had been revealed in the

---

[1] *Op. cit.*, fol. LXVIIIv, "Non enim promisit spiritum docturum aliquam aliam veritatem aut perfectiorem quam ipse docuerat, sed potius explanaturum illam quam in veteri testamento et in sua doctrina evangelica inexpositam reliquit."

[2] *Op. cit.*, fol. LXVIIIv, "Hoc modo scripture sacre scientia est imperfecta respectu visionis aperte ..."

Gospel message of Christ. Thus the whole of Christian revelation was "formally" implicit in the Gospels.[1] The apostles, under the guidance of the Holy Spirit, added to the store of revealed truths "materially" in the sense that they applied Christ's "art" to new areas of subject matter.

The relationship of the apostles to the evangelical teaching of Christ himself was quite different. Here there could be no question of abolishing a literal sense in favor of a spiritual one, nor of supplying what was lacking, nor of perfecting what was imperfect.[2] The Gospel of Christ was complete and perfect in itself. The task of the apostles was therefore purely expository. Christ had himself explained some of his own difficult sayings but not all of them. The apostles continued the work of explanation.

The fathers of the church in turn—Augustine and Ambrose and the rest—continued the work of the apostles. But their writings were of less authority since the church could not be sure that the Holy Spirit spoke through the Fathers as he spoke through the apostles.[3] Finally, even the Fathers did not bring to an end the task of explaining divine truth. Christ's words "Many things yet I have to say ..." were directed not only to the apostles but to their successors. Therefore:

> Just as the apostles expounded the Scriptures not expounded by Christ on the model of those that he did expound, so too down to the end of the world Catholic doctors should expound those that Christ and the apostles did not expound on the model of those that they did expound— nor should they be content with old expositions.[4]

Henry concluded his argument with a paragraph of complex scriptural and patristic imagery. The temple of God would be built up throughout the ages. The task of understanding and expounding Scripture

---

[1] *Op. cit.*, fol. LXIXr, "... artem exponendi obscura et supplendi omissa traditam in doctrina evangelica, doctrina apostolica applicat ad plures materias. Et sic ex evangelio Christi formaliter habetur omnis veritas ..."

[2] *Op. cit.*, fol. LXIXr, "Doctrina vero apostolica ad doctrinam evangelicam nullo modo se habet ut eius impletiva, imperfectum aliquid existens in ipsa supplendo vel addendo vel expositione spirituali aliquid literale evacuando ..."

[3] *Op. cit.*, fol. LXIXv, "... non aequale pondus auctoritatis obtineat, quia non constat ecclesiae doctores aliquos catholicos in spiritu sancto fuisse loquutos, sicut constat ipsi apostolos in eo fuisse locutos."

[4] *Op. cit.*, fol. LXIXv, "Unde illud, 'Adhuc multa habeo etc.' dictum erat apostolis non tam pro ipsis quam pro suis successoribus ... Sicut ergo apostoli exposuerunt scripturas non expositas a Christo ad exemplar eorum quae ipse exposuit: sic catholici doctores ea quae nec Christus nec apostoli exposuerunt, ad exemplar illorum quae ipsi exposuerunt, debent usque in finem mundi exponere, nec antiquis expositionibus contenti esse."

would continue until the consummation of all things. Knowledge of Scripture would grow more and more with the passing of time.

Henry of Ghent thus contrasted the total adequacy of Scripture with the incompleteness of the church's understanding of Scripture at any given time. His discussion on this point provides a necessary background for understanding his response to the further question that he posed, "Whether we should believe the authority of Scripture rather than that of the church or vice-versa." Henry began his argument by quoting Augustine's text, "I would not believe the Gospels unless the authority of the Catholic church moved me to do so." This might be taken to mean, he pointed out, that the authority of the church was greater than that of Scripture. Henry responded to this argument at first rather conventionally. A Christian was to believe equally in Scripture and the church for the two necessarily agreed in everything concerning the faith. But then he introduced a distinction. The "church" whose authority was compared with Scripture might be the true church (in which case no problem arose) or a church "only in reputation." (It could happen that multitudes would depart from the faith through ignorance or malice; yet the church would always live on in a few just men.) in the second case Scripture was "simply and absolutely "more to be believed than such a church, for the truth of Scripture was immutable and no one was permitted to add to it, subtract from it, or change it.[1]

As for Augustine's text, Henry conceded that an unbeliever, not yet converted, would necessarily believe in the church more than in Scripture, for the preaching of the church was needed to convince him of the truth of the Gospels. But once he was so convinced he had to hold to the Scriptures at all costs even if those who had taught him the faith themselves fell away from it, even if—*per impossibile*—the whole church, as it was constituted in others, abandoned the faith.[2]

---

[1] *Op. cit.*, fol. LXXIIIr, "Aut enim intelligitur comparatio scripturae ad ecclesiam quae vere est ecclesia et merito et reputatione. Aut reputatione tantum. Primo modo omnino credendum est aequaliter scripturae et ecclesiae quia in nullo discrepare possunt. Secundo autem modo dicendum quod simpliciter et absolute magis credendum est sacrae scripturae quam ecclesiae: quia veritas ipsa in scriptura immobiliter et impermutabiliter semper custoditur, nec permittitur cuique addere, subtrahere, vel mutare ... In personis autem ecclesiae mutabilis est et variabilis ut dissentire fidei possit multitudo illarum et vel per errorem vel per malitiam a fide discedere, licet semper ecclesia in aliquibus iustis stabit."

[2] *Op. cit.*, fol. LXXIIIv, "... quo ad primam notititiam eorum quae credenda sunt plus ecclesiae quam scripturae credendum est ... Ad fidem autem iam genitam

This whole section of Henry of Ghent's *Summa* has usually been regarded as a mere display of dialectical dexterity, an ingenious exploration of a hypothetical problem that he never expected to arise in practice. But there was more to it than that. Henry returned to the problem of "Scripture versus Church" in one of his *Quodlibeta* and there he revealed a genuine concern that the institutional church of his own day was in danger of straying from the true faith His argument dealt with the question whether the church could change the essential nature of a sacrament, with especial reference to the sacrament of penance. The church could not do this, Henry declared, observing that "the church is subject to the law of the Gospel" and "We should not depart from Scripture for any authority whatsoever." And here again Henry wrote, repeating the argument of his previous *Quaestio* "In matters of faith we should adhere to Scripture rather than the church, understood as any members erring from the truth of Scripture."[1]

The papal regulation of the administration of penance was of course a burning issue in the conflict between the mendicant orders and the

---

confirmandam ... maxime valet auctoritas intellecta sacrae scripturae; cui fidelis adhaeret etsi videret illos per quod fidem acceperat a fide resilire et per impossibile totam ecclesiam in aliis a fide discedere ..." Henry's view on this point was criticized by Gerard of Bologna in his *Summa*, ed. P. de Vooght in *Les sources de la doctrine chrétienne* (Bruges-Paris, 1954), pp. 269-483 at pp. 357-359. Scripture and church were so inseparable, he argued, that even the neophyte should believe in both equally from the beginning. Gerard agreed with Henry, however, that Scripture was to be preferred to the Church "si ecclesia sumeretur pro hominibus a fide discedentibus." He added "... si omnes a fide et sacra scriptura discederent, uno excepto, plus illi uni credendum esset quam ceteris ..." De Vooght has maintained (in *Ephemerides theologicae Lovanienses*, cited above p. 133 n. 1) that Gerard's view was radically different from Henry's but his argument is not very convincing. He fails to see that Henry emphasized exactly the same distinction that de Vooght finds in Gerard, i.e., the "church" that can depart from scriptural truth is not the real church at all but a church only in reputation.

[1] *Quodlibeta Magistri Henrici Goethals a Gandavo*, I (Paris, 1518), *Quodl*, 5. q. 36, fol. CCXIIr, "Cum ergo legi Evangelicae subiecta est ecclesia ... dico simpliciter quod ecclesia circa essentialia sacramentis nihil potest immutare." fol. CCXIIv, "... nullo modo a scriptura sane intellecta propter cuiuscunque auctoritatem recedendum est ..." "... contra ea que sunt veritatis evangelice non est potestas in terris." "In eis enim quae sunt fidei magis adhaerendum esset scripturae quam ecclesiae quo ad aliqua membra a veritate scripturae aberrantia secundum quod determinavimus alibi in quaestionibus nostris ordinariis de auctoritate scientiae theologicae." Henry also mentioned in his *Quodlibet* unwritten traditions handed down by the apostles which the church was required to maintain, but he referred to them constantly as *observantia*—ritual practices apparently.

secular clergy which engaged so much of Henry's attention. He concluded in the *Quodlibet* under discussion that the pope had touched only the "accidents" of the sacrament. Henry did not press his argument to the conclusion that the pope had actually broken "the law of the Gospel" but, throughout the discussion, he made plain his real aprehension that the church was in danger of going seriously astray. "We should beware," he wrote, "lest the power given to the church be abused so as to prejudice the knowledge of God." Christians could be sure that there would always be some faithful men in the church and that they would preserve the integrity of the Christian religion (for Christ had said, "I have prayed for you Peter that your faith shall not fail"). But Christians ought also heed the warning of Paul "In the last days some will depart from the faith..."[1]

These words of Paul had provided the central text for William of Saint Amour's *De periculis novissimorum temporum*. William had argued that almost the whole church including the pope might err in faith. He had further maintained that this catastrophe had actually happened in the days of St. Hilary and suggested that the erring pope of that time was perhaps the notorious Anastasius mentioned in the Decretum.[2] Henry of Ghent offered a conspectus of the dangers facing the church as gloomy as that of William. He recalled the text of Augustine stating that, after the age of persecutions there came a more dangerous age of scandal and deceit, "Our enemy then was a lion who raged openly; now it is a serpent who plots secretly ... Then he compelled Christians to deny Christ; now he teaches Christians to deny Christ." All this Henry presented as a warning to the church of his own day.[3] It was no mere hypothetical danger that he feared. These are the words of a man so bitterly hostile to the current policies of the popes that he was silenced by a papal legation a few years later.

At this point we may note a peculiar convergence between the thought of Henry of Ghent and that of his principal adversary,

---

[1] *Loc. cit.*, "Unde cavendum est in hoc multum ecclesiae ne potestate sibi concessa abutatur quoquo modo in prejudicium scientiae dei ... Etenim quamvis securi sumus quod per bonos in ecclesia in quibus proprie est ecclesia, hoc numquam fiet; sed semper in eis stabit ecclesia intemerata et fide integra, assecurante nos Christo, qui in Petro dixit ecclesiae Luc. xxii, 'Ego rogavi pro te ut non deficiat fides tua,' timendum est tamen multum de malis de quibus dicit Apostolus 1 Timoth. iiii, 'In novissimis temporibus discedent quidam a fide.'"

[2] E. Faral, "Les 'Responsiones' de Guillaume de Saint-Amour," *AHDL*, 26 (1951), pp. 337-394 at p. 347.

[3] *Op. cit.*, fol. CCXIIv.

Pietro Olivi, with whom he disagreed about almost everthing else. Each theologian was utterly convinced of the rightness of his own interpretations of Scripture; each saw a danger that his position would be condemned by the ecclesiastical authorities, and each went on to speculate that, if the official church fell into error, the true church might live on in a small minority of faithful Christians separated from the visible ecclesiastical institution. The great difference between the two thinkers was that Olivi was able to support his position by appealing to recent papal enactments. Henry, on the other hand, was sharply critical of the legislation of contemporary popes and was most anxious to see their decretals repealed. Hence, in his work, there is no trace of any doctrine of infallibility or irreformability.

Indeed, a striking feature in Henry of Ghent's ecclesiology is a general lack of trust in the public teaching authority of the church as a whole and a corresponding emphasis on the role of the private theologian. This appeared first in his *Quodlibet* on the perfection of Scripture, where Henry wrote that the task of interpreting Christ's teaching was entrusted not only to the apostles but to "their successors." One would expect this to have been followed by some discussion on the role of bishops as "successors of the apostles" and on the teaching authority of councils of bishops (especially since Henry was a staunch episcopalist so far as the problem of jurisdiction in the church was concerned). But instead, in a quite different fashion, Henry went on to assert that the task of expounding the Scriptures belonged to "Catholic doctors."[1] Apparently the doctors were successors of the apostles in this sphere. Again, in the *Quodlibet* on the immutability of sacraments that we have just discussed, Henry offered a peculiar interpretation of the power of the keys, which once more emphasized the role of the private theologian. The "key of power," he wrote, belonged to the rulers of the church while the "key of knowledge" belonged to the doctors. Each group had to be careful not to abuse its authority.[2] Henry was indeed an outstanding exponent of the thirteenth century phenomenon that Yves Congar has called "a magisterium of doctors."

The implications of his arguments on indefectibility and inerrancy

---

[1] Supra p. 135 n. 4.

[2] *Op. cit.*, fol. CCXIIIr, "... opporteat summe solitam Ecclesiam esse circa ea quae sunt fidei et sacramentorum ne nimium extendendo clavem scientiae in doctoribus aut clavem potestatis in rectoribus, excedat limites et terminos circa ea quae sunt fidei et sacramentorum."

were really very radical. The doctrine that the church could not completely "fail" that it would always live on, if only in a small surviving band of Christians, was of course very ancient and, as we have seen, it was deeply embedded in the canonical tradition of the Middle Ages. But Henry of Ghent (like Olivi) deployed the idea in a fresh way. The true church, he argued, was by definition faithful to Scripture. But the theologian could not on that account accept all the doctrines publicly proclaimed by the church as certainly true. Rather it was his task to scrutinize them, to measure their orthodoxy against his own understanding of the immutable truths of Scripture. In the last resort, he might have to decide that the visible, institutional church was not the true church at all but only a mass of apostates. Every little dissident, heretical sect of the Middle Ages must have held to some such belief explicitly or implicitly. Henry of Ghent was the first to draw it into the mainstream of orthodox, scholastic ecclesiology.

(ii) *Duns Scotus*

The Franciscan master, Duns Scotus, stood at exactly the opposite pole from Henry of Ghent. No major figure in the history of medieval thought displayed a more complete, unreserved confidence in the public teachings of the universal church than the *doctor subtilis*. In his writings the church was presented over and over again as the one certain guide to all the truths of Christian revelation both Scriptural and non-Scriptural; and, for Duns, this authoritative unerring church was very plainly the institutional church, speaking through its popes and councils, not some small hidden group of the elect.[1]

On the problem whether Scripture was the sole source of revelation Duns Scotus expressed himself with ambiguity. At one point he wrote, "Our theology concerns only things that are contained in Scripture or that can be deduced from them. ..."[2] But, in many other contexts,

---

[1] On Duns Scotus' ecclesiology see E. Longpré, "Le B. Jean Duns Scot. Pour le Saint Siège et contre le gallicanisme," *La France franciscaine*, 11 (1928), pp. 137-162; A. Dietershagen, "Kirche und theologisches Denken nach Duns Scotus," *Wissenschaft und Weisheit*, 1 (1934), pp. 273-288; A. M. Vellico, "De regula fidei iuxta Joannis Duns Scoti doctrinam," *Antonianum*, 10 (1935), pp. 11-36; J. Finkenzeller, *Offenbarung und Theologie nach der Lehre des Johannes Duns Skotus* (Münster i. West., 1961).

[2] *Ordinatio (Opus Oxoniense)*, prol. n. 204 in *Ioannis Duns Scoti ... opera omnia*, ed. C. Balić et al. (Vatican City, 1950-), I, p. 138, "Igitur theologia nostra de facto non est nisi de his quae continentur in Scriptura et de his quae possunt elici ex eis."

he referred to extrascriptural sources of divine revelation. This problem has been perceptively discussed by Leo Rosato who also presented an excellent selection of texts from Scotus bearing on the question of Scripture and Tradition.[1] Responding to the question whether all necessary supernatural truth was contained in Sacred Scripture, Duns wrote that Scripture sufficed to teach man what was his true end and how to attain it. He added that many of these necessary truths were not expressly stated in Scripture but were implicit in it, like conclusions in premises.[2] His position then was that Scripture taught all necessary truths (at least implicitly) in that it taught what was essential for man's salvation. But, as Rosato noted, there could be a whole realm of supernatural, revealed truths beyond the bare necessities essential to salvation; and Duns Scotus plainly believed that such truths existed.[3] "The church holds many things that were promulgated by the apostles orally, without writing," he wrote. The point that remains unclear is whether he held that the church had continued to receive new revelations through the inspiration of the Holy Spirit in post-apostolic times. At one point Duns declared that "general revelation" ended with the Scriptures.[4] But he also wrote (discussing the *filioque* clause in the Creed), "We must believe not only what is found (in the New Testament) but also what the apostles wrote and taught *and what the church has learned through revelation*." In another comment he added, "The church holds and teaches many things *which the apostles did not hand down* but which the church has ordained at the command of the Holy Spirit."[5] He further explained that, when the church issued

---

[1] L. Rosato, "Ioannis Duns Scoti doctrina de Scriptura et Traditione," in *De Scriptura et Traditione*, ed. C. Balić (Rome, 1963), pp. 233-252, discussing the views of H. Lennerz, "Scriptura sola," *Gregorianum*, 40 (1959), pp. 38-53; J. R. Geiselmann, *Die Heilige Schrift und die Tradition* (Freiburg-Basel-Vienna, 1962); P. de Vooght, *op. cit.* (supra p. 136 n. 2).

[2] *Ordinatio*, prol. n. 120, n. 123, ed. cit., I, pp. 85, 87. Cf. Rosato, *art. cit.*, pp. 234-235.

[3] *Ordinatio*, IV, d. 17 q. 1 n. 17 in *Joannis Duns Scoti ... opera omnia*, ed. L. Vivès (Paris, 1891-1895), XVIII, p. 519, "... multa alia tenet ecclesia, oretenus per apostolos sibi promulgata sine Scriptura ..." Similar statements occur at IV, d. 7 q. 1 n. 3 (Vivès, XVI, p. 690); IV, d. 8 q. 2 n. 6 (Vivès, XVII, p. 43), cited by Rosato, pp. 239-240.

[4] *Ordinatio*, prol. n. 204 in *Opera* (Vatican City), I, p. 137, "Terminus autem praefixus a voluntate divina, quantum ad revelationem generalem, est illorum quae sunt in Scriptura divina ..." (Rosato, p. 235).

[5] *Lectura*, I, d. 11 n. 17 (cited Rosato, p. 236), "Unde non tantum tenendum est quod ibi [scil. in N.T.] invenitur, sed [etiam] quod apostoli scripserunt et docuerunt et quod Ecclesia per revelationem didicit. Unde dixit Christus quod *multa habeo vobis dicere, quae non potestis portare modo*." *Reportatio examinata*, I, d. 11 n. 18

a fresh Creed, it was not to proclaim a different faith but to combat some novel heresy.[1] The new truth that was proclaimed had always been a part of the faith; but previously no occasion had arisen for explicitly formulating it because it had never been challenged. Perhaps Duns Scotus meant to argue that all post-apostolic revelations were revelations of truths already implicit in the first "deposit of faith."

However that may be, there is no doubt of his total unwavering commitment to the authority of the visible church in all matters touching sacred doctrine. Repeatedly he quoted the text of Augustine, "I would not believe the Gospel unless the authority of the church moved me to do so."[2] using the text to establish, not only that the church was an indispensable witness to the authenticity of Scripture but also that its authority was decisive in every dispute over revealed truth. His attitude was clearly expressed in a comment on the Trinitarian doctrine of Peter Lombard. Hugh of St. Victor had ridiculed Peter because the Master of the Sentences presented many patristic arguments against his own position but then dismissed them all and maintained his personal view without adequate authority. For Duns Scotus the only significant point in the controversy was that Peter's doctrine had been approved by the Fourth Lateran Council. Far from lacking support, therefore, it was sustained by the greatest authority of all, that of the universal church. Referring to Augustine's text, Duns wrote here that, just as the church had decided which books belonged to the authentic canon of the Bible, so it determined what writings were authentic among the books of the Doctors.[3] (He seems

---

(Rosato, *loc. cit.*), "Spiritus Sanctus postea—qui habuit tantam auctoritatem quantam Christus—docuit apostolos. Sic etiam est de sacramentis aliquibus et de multis aliis. Multa etiam sunt quae Ecclesia tenet et docet, quae non tradiderunt apostoli, sed Ecclesia eodem Spiritu dictante ordinavit. Et ideo credo quidquid Ecclesia tradidit, ut articulus fidei in universali, in eadem auctoritate; unde credo in Spiritum Sanctum, sanctam Ecclesiam catholicam; et ideo Augustinus 'Evangelio non crederem nisi Ecclesia me docuisset.'" Duns Scotus was arguing here against the Greeks who maintained that the *filioque* clause could not be an article of faith since all articles of faith were contained in the New Testament and the *filioque* clause was not included there. Duns' comment in the *Ordinatio* (I, d. 11 n. 20, Rosato, p. 236) was more moderate. There he apparently presented the *filioque* clause as apostolic teaching, not post-apostolic revelation. His argument concluded, "Multa ergo docuit eos Spiritus Sanctus, quae non sunt scripta in Evangelio: et illa multa, quaedam per scripturam, quaedam per consuetudinem Ecclesiae, tradiderunt."

[1] *Ordinatio*, I, d. 11 n. 21 in *Opera* (Vatican City), V, p. 8 (Rosato, p. 237).

[2] See, e.g., Rosato's citations, Nos. 2, 6, 6a, 7b, 9, 9a, 11, *art. cit.*, pp. 234-238.

[3] *Ordinatio*, I, d. 5 n. 26 in *Opera* (Vatican City), IV, p. 24 (Rosato, p. 235), "... non autem nullam habet pro se auctoritatem, sed habet illam universalis Ecclesiae

here implicitly to have attributed to the church the same authority over the canon of Scripture as over the writings of private theologians.) An alternative form of his comment, preserved in the *Reportatio examinata* even stated, "Peter (Lombard) has canonical authority on his side, namely that of the church, which is perhaps greater than that of Scripture, as Augustine says."[1]

In considering the doctrine of transubstantiation Duns Scotus wrote, "I hold this principally on account of the authority of the church which does not err in faith and morals" and he added a reference to Luke 22 "I have prayed for you Peter, that your faith shall not fail." Here again the specific authority that he had in mind was a decree of the Fourth Lateran Council. The old Petrine text now served to establish the inerrancy of Innocent III's great synod.[2] In a further discussion on transubstantiation Duns asked why the church should accept such a difficult doctrine when alternative explanations of the words of Scripture were more simple and even, apparently, more true. It sufficed that the church in a general council had declared transubstantiation to be a truth of faith, he replied. The church, it must be supposed, was guided by the Holy Spirit. God determined what was true and not true; the church only made explicit what God handed down through the Spirit.[3]

Though Duns Scotus clearly maintained that divine truth itself was unchanging he also believed that God constantly granted to men new insights into the truth and that these insights could be established as truths of faith through the authority of the church. Tradition was what

---

in capitulo praeallegato, quae maxima est, quia dicit Augustinus *Contra epistolam Fundamenti*: 'Evangelio non crederem nisi Ecclesiae crederem catholicae',—quae Ecclesia sicut decrevit qui sunt libri habendi in auctoritatem in canone Bibliae, ita etiam decrevit qui libri habendi sunt authentici in libris doctorum, sicut patet in canone ..."

[1] *Reportatio examinata*, I, d. 5 n. 24 (cit. Rosato, p. 235), "Magister Petrus habet hic auctoritatem canonicatam, scilicet Ecclesiae, quae forte maior est quam Scripturae, sicut dicit Augustinus *Contra epistolam Fundamenti*: 'Evangelius (sic) non crederem, nisi Ecclesiae credidissem, etc.'."

[2] *Reportata parisiensia*, IV, d. 11 q. 3 n. 13 in *Opera* (Vivès), XXIV, p. 120 (Rosato, p. 239), "Hoc principaliter teneo propter auctoritatem Ecclesiae, quae non errat in his quae sunt fidei vel morum, cuius Vicario primo dixit Christus: *Ego rogavi pro te, Petre, ut non deficiat fides tua, et tu aliquando conversus, confirma fratres tuos.*"

[3] *Ordinatio*, IV, d. 11 q. 3 n. 15 in *Opera* (Vivès), XVII, p. 376 (Rosato, p. 240), "... et ideo hunc intellectum eligit, quia verus est: non enim in potestate Ecclesiae fuit facere istud verum vel non verum, sed Dei instituentis: sed intellectum a Deo traditum Ecclesia explicavit, directa in hoc, ut creditur, Spiritu veritatis."

God "handed down" *(a deo traditum)*. New tradition, it would seem, was as good as old tradition. In all this Duns' thought was essentially a development of that of Bonaventure. Both doctors had abandoned the old criterion of Vincent of Lérins for determining Catholic truth— "What has been believed everywhere, always, by everyone." In their arguments the temporal, historical, dimension simply vanished. For Bonaventure and Duns Scotus, Catholic truth was not what the church had demonstrably always proclaimed but what the church was proclaiming then and there, in their own time. The Franciscan thinkers had traveled a long way toward the doctrine of "living Tradition" which, in modern theology, has often been associated with theories of papal infallibility.

2. INFALLIBILITY: CHURCH AND POPE

At the beginning of the fourteenth century probably every orthodox theologian and canonist held that, in some sense, the church was unerring though many of them, in making such a statement, would have intended only to affirm the old doctrine of indefectibility. To many modern thinkers the step from the unerringness of the church to the infallibility of the pope has seemed a small one. But in the years around 1300, the gap between the two doctrines seemed enormous. The nature of the church's inerrancy was still ill-defined. The idea that the pope might be personally infallible was too novel, too contrary to all traditional teaching, to find any widespread acceptance. The major publicists of papal power in the conflicts of church and state hardly considered the possibility of developing a theory of papal infallibility at all—for understandable reasons as we have noted. But certain eminent doctors of the mendicant orders did give some attention to the issue, the most important contributions coming from Duns Scotus again and from two leading Dominican theologians, Hervaeus Natalis and Peter de la Palu. Each of these authors seems to have come to the very brink of formulating a doctrine of papal infallibility but then (perhaps regretfully) to have turned away from it as an obviously unsound and indefensible theory.

(i) *Duns Scotus*

Duns Scotus—like most of the great scholastics— has been claimed[1]

---

[1] *Art. cit.* (supra p. 140 n. 1), pp. 156-157.

by a modern admirer as an ardent champion of papal infallibility. Ephraim Longpré writes "De fait, aux yeux de Duns Scot, le Souverain Pontife est le Vicaire du Christ ... Infaillible et indéfectible en raison des paroles du Christ a S. Pierre, il fonde la stabilité de l' Eglise dans la vérité." But in fact the words of Christ to Peter "I have prayed for you Peter that your faith shall not fail," which Longpré cited in support of his views from Duns Scotus' *Reportata parisiensia*, were used there to prove the infallibility of the universal church, not that of the pope.[1] The same is true of all the other citations given by Longpré in so far as they deal with the principle of inerrancy at all.

There exists in Duns Scotus' work, however, another series of texts which come closer to an affirmation of the pope's personal infallibility. These texts dealt with the question of whether a "character" was imprinted on the soul at baptism. The presence of such a character could not be proved by Scripture, reason, or the authority of the saints, wrote Duns Scotus, yet he accepted its existence solely and simply on the authority of a pronouncement made by Pope Innocent III.[2] In this case the text of Innocent to which Duns referred was not promulgated in a general council but was a papal decretal addressed to the archbishop of Arles. There could hardly be a more striking affirmation of Duns Scotus' total confidence in the authority of the pope as supreme judge in matters of faith. But, although Innocent's decretal provided the sole documentary support for his position, Duns never stated that he held the doctrine involved "on the authority of the pope" but always "on the authority of the church." The actual phrases he used were "Propter ergo solam auctoritatem Ecclesiae ... est ponendum characterem imprimi ...," "Propter auctoritatem ecclesiae sub Innocentio III ... ," "... ponendi necessitas est haec, quia Ecclesia ponit ...," "... auctoritate Ecclesiae solum tamquam fidei probatus est ..."[3] Innocent's decretal was included in the *Liber Extra*, one of the volumes of *Corpus Iuris Canonici* which was accepted

---

[1] *Reportata parisiensia*, IV d. 11 q. 3 n. 13. The text is quoted above (p. 143 n. 2).

[2] *Reportata parisiensia*, IV d. 6 q. 8 n. 14 in *Opera* (Vivès), XXIII, p. 646 (Rosato, p. 239), "... nihil inveniatur de charactere scriptum ad propositum, nec possit probari per rationem, vel auctoritatem Sanctorum; tamen auctoritate Ecclesiae *solum*, tanquam fidei probatur esse, sicut patet supra per dictum Domini Innocentii Papae III. Et ideo propter declarationem Ecclesiae hoc teneo."

[3] *Ordinatio*, IV d. 6 q. 9 n. 14 in *Opera* (Vivès), XVI, p. 604; *Reportata parisiensia*, IV d. 6 q. 8 n. 11 in *Opera* (Vivès), XXIII, p. 643; *Ordinatio*, IV, d. 6 q. 9 n. 17 in *Opera* (Vivès), XVI, p. 606; *Reportata parisiensia*, IV, d. 6 q. 8 n. 14 in *Opera* (Vivès), XXIII, p. 646 (Rosato, pp. 238-239).

throughout the universal church and this may explain Duns Scotus' terminology.[1] At any rate he seems here to have studiously refrained from asserting the pope's personal infallibility even in a context where his own theological position was based entirely on a papal decretal.

The reason for this reticence was made plain in another context when Duns Scotus discussed the power of the keys. Here Duns made it clear that he did not adhere to a doctrine of papal inerrancy by distinguishing sharply between the authority of Christ, which, he said, was unerring and so could make "irrevocable" pronouncements, and the lesser authority which Christ conferred on Peter and the apostles. Duns referred here to three levels of power—a "first and principal power" which belonged to God and could not be alienated, a "pre-eminent" power of the keys which was committed to Christ, and a "ministerial" power of the keys which Christ conferred on Peter and the apostles. The pre-eminent power of Christ was distinguished from the ministerial power of Peter precisely by its infallibility.

> A power whose judgment is sure and firm and irrevocable can be committed only to one who adheres inseparably to the laws of the divine will and who cannot err in reaching decisions. ... And in this sense I say that the power of judging pertains only to the soul of Christ, which is inseparably united with the Word.[2]

Duns Scotus had in mind here primarily the common sacerdotal power of the keys. But his words seem plainly to exclude the possibility of attributing an unerring authority to any person other than Christ.

(ii) *Hervaeus Natalis*

Hervaeus Natalis, who was elected master-general of the Dominicans in 1318, came closer than Duns Scotus to formulating a doctrine of papal infallibility, at least verbally. In his treatise *De iurisdictione*,[3] Hervaeus set out to prove that papal power was instituted by God alone. One of his arguments ran thus:

---

[1] X. 3.42.3.

[2] *Reportata parisiensia*, IV, d. 19 q. 1 n. 6 in *Opera* (Vivès), XXIV, p. 294, "Potestas autem commissaria, cujus judicium sit ratum et firmum et irrevocabile, potest committi illi soli, qui inseparabiliter adhaeret legibus divinae voluntatis; nec potest errare in sententiando de aliquo, quia conformiter agit suae regulae primae iustae, divinae scilicet voluntati. Et illo modo dico quod potestas judicandi de aliquo tantum convenit animae Christi, quae est inseparabiliter unita Verbo ..."

[3] Ed. L. Hödl, *De iurisdictione. Ein unveröffentlichter Traktat des Herveus Natalis O.P. (+1323) über die Kirchengewalt* (Munich, 1959). On this work see P. E. Elter, "Un ouvrage inconnu de Hervé Nédellec," *Gregorianum*, 4 (1923), pp. 211-240 and,

What should be altogether infallible in itself should not be instituted by a fallible understanding, but the papal power should be altogether infallible in itself ... that the papal power should be altogether infallible I prove thus: That power which extends to things of salvation should be infallible in itself, that is which extends to the things of salvation and not their opposites; but the papal power is of this kind.[1]

On the face of it nothing could be clearer. Not only the concept but the very word "infallible" was here applied to the papal power. The difficulty is that, throughout this section of his treatise, Hervaeus was operating with a distinction between the "state" of an office and the individual person who occupied the office. He concluded that the "state" of the papacy was instituted by God alone but that the choice of individual pontiffs required human consent.[2] There was obviously room for a similar distinction between "state" and person in connection with infallibility. When he returned to the question in another work Hervaeus explained that he had just such a distinction in mind.[3]

His fuller discussion of the question was presented in the treatise, *De potestate pape*, in the course of which Hervaeus set out to prove

---

for a general sketch of Hervaeus' life and writings (with full bibliography), F. J. Roensch, *Early Thomistic School* (Dubuque, 1964).

[1] *Ed. cit.*, pp. 21-22, "Secunda ratio sumiter ex infallibilitate quam debet habere talis potestas et est; quae debet esse omnino in se infallibilis, non debet institui ab intellectu multipliciter possibili fallibili ... quod potestas papalis debet esse omnino infallibilis probo: Quia ista potestas quae se extendit ad ea quae sunt salutis debet esse in se infallibilis, scilicet quae se extendat ad ea quae sunt salutis et non ad contraria; sed potestas papalis est huiusmodi ..."

[2] This distinction between person and office was of course well established in medieval legal thought by the early fourteenth century. It received special emphasis from theologians at this time because the issue was involved in the debates concerning the abdication of Celestine V. The subject is explored in all its intricacy in E. Kantorowicz, *The King's Two Bodies* (Princeton, 1957) and in G. Post, *Studies in Medieval Legal Thought* (Princeton, 1964).

[3] M. Wilks, *The Problem of Sovereignty in the Later Middle Ages* (Cambridge, 1963), p. 500 n. 2 has pointed to a doctrine in Augustinus Triumphus that is essentially similar to the doctrine of Hervaeus Natalis discussed above. Augustinus held that the papal power could not err *per se et formaliter* but that individual popes might well do so, "Sed per accidens et materialiter papa et in clave potentie potest excedere et in clave scientiae potest errare." Wilks also discerns a theory of infallibility in Augustinus' presentation of the papacy as a corporation sole. "... the papacy is a corporation and since a corporation can do no wrong, the pope in possession of the papal office is infallible." (*Op. cit.*, p. 469). The last words of course are Wilks' not Augustinus'. The argument seems rather far-fetched. According to this line of reasoning all corporations would be infallible and not only the corporation of the Roman see. Actually, of course, medieval doctrine never held that a corporation could not err in its corporate decisions and pronouncements. It held that a corporation (lacking a soul) could not *sin* and hence could not be excommunicated.

that the pope had the power to resolve doubts in matters of faith. His argument began with a distinction. Any man learned in a particular science could resolve doubts by applying his specialized learning to a controverted question. But this was not the role of the pope. The pope's function was to settle doubts, *cum auctoritate*, in such a fashion that, once he had spoken, it was no longer licit to hold the opposing opinion. This power necessarily resided "solely and simply with the supreme pontiff" because the unity of the church's faith could not be maintained unless the whole community could have recourse to one single head when doubts arose.[1]

Hervaeus introduced the specific problem of infallibility by posing an objection to this position. It might be argued that the pope could sin and err and that one who could err ought not to have the authority to make decisions concerning the faith. To this Hervaeus replied:

> Although the pope is a single person and, acting according to his own will, can err, as is said of Pope Leo against whom St. Hilary went to a general council, nevertheless, when he uses counsel, availing himself of the help of the universal church, he cannot err by the ordinance of God who said to Peter, "I have prayed for you Peter that your faith shall not fail."[2]

Hervaeus' further comment makes it plain that, for him, it was the universal church that was divinely preserved from error, not the individual pope.

> The universal church as a whole cannot accept anything erroneous, and if the pope decrees an error as a single person it is not binding nor does his authority oblige (others) to hold his opinion.[3]

Hervaeus concluded this argument with a novel variation. He argued that, when the pope pronounced falsely in a matter of faith, he did not automatically strip himself of his judicial power in the case (as some scholars maintained). His pronouncement was without binding force,

---

[1] *Hervei Natalis ... De potestate papae* (Paris, 1647), p. 365.

[2] *Loc. cit.*, "... licet Papa sit singularis persona et proprio motu agens possit errare sicut dicitur de illo Leone contra quem iuit Hilarius pictauiensis, ad consilium Generale, tamen Papa utens consilio, requirens adiutorium uniuersalis Ecclesiae Deo ordinante qui dicit Petro *Ego rogavi pro te (ut) non deficiat fides tua*, non potest errare."

[3] *Loc. cit.*, "... nec potest esse quod universalis Ecclesia tanquam unum accipiat aliquod erroneum, nec tamen si Papa ut singularis persona sententiat errorem teneat; vel sequitur quod auctoritas eius obliget ad illam sententiam tenendam."

not because the pope lacked authority, but because he had applied his authority to an improper object. We would not say that a man lacked the power of sight because he could not see a taste. A taste is not a proper object of sight. So too, Hervaeus implied, a false doctrine was not a proper object for a papal definition.

The whole argument is interesting because of its juxtaposition of a very strong emphasis on the pope's judicial authority in matters of faith with a very explicit acknowledgment that the judgments rendered by a pope might well be in error. In essence, Hervaeus was re-stating the old doctrines of the canonists. The pope was supreme judge in matters of faith. His judgments were not infallible. Only the universal church was necessarily unerring. When the pope erred the church ought not to obey him. Far from anticipating the doctrine of Vatican Council I, Hervaeus had really anticipated one form of the Gallican position that the infallibilists of 1870 were determined to eradicate.[1]

(iii) *Peter de la Palu*

There is a rather different emphasis in the works of Hervaeus' Dominican contemporary, Peter de la Palu. In his writings, we find a strong insistence on the doctrinal authority of the corporate Roman church rather than on that of the universal church or the individual pope. Peter was also much concerned with the irreformability of dogmatic decrees, a subject that was soon to become a matter of burning controversy. To understand his position we must describe briefly the disputes in which he was involved. Peter was the principal spokesman of the mendicants against John de Pouilli, who presented the episcopalist case against the friars' privileges with such vigor and indiscretion that his views were condemned as heretical in 1318.[2] The controversy between mendicants and seculars had come to center on a peculiar technicality which had first arisen in the disputes of the 1280s. John de Pouilli maintained that, when a penitent had confessed his sins to a friar and received absolution, he was still bound to confess the same sins a second time to his own parish priest (for the Fourth

---

[1] *Loc. cit.*, "... nec etiam (sequitur) quod auctoritas illa sibi erranti subtrahatur, scilicet quod auctoritas sua non habet locum obligandi in tali casu, sed quod de est obiectum aptum natum autenticari: sicut non sequitur quod careat visu ille qui non videt saporem qui non est obiectum visus."

[2] F. J. Roensch, *op. cit.*, pp. 124-131; J. Koch, "Der Prozess gegen den Magister Johannes de Polliaco und seine Vorgeschichte (1312-1321)," *RTAM*, 5 (1933), pp. 391-422; J. G. Sikes, "John de Pouilli and Peter de la Palu," *English Historical Review*, 49 (1934), pp. 219-240.

Lateran Council had decreed that every Catholic must confess once a year "to his proper priest"). Peter de la Palu argued that this view was incompatible with the intrinsic nature of the sacrament of penance and so was heretical.

The state of papal legislation on the question was very confused. Boniface VIII's Bull, *Super cathedram* (1300) significantly curtailed the friars' privileges but it made no reference to the question of a second confession. Benedict XI's Bull, *Inter cunctas* (1304) conferred much broader privileges on the friars and specifically decreed that sins were not to be confessed a second time. Then Clement V, in the Council of Vienne, promulgated the Bull, *Dudum* (1312) which annulled Benedict's decree and re-enacted Boniface's, but again without any reference to the question of a second confession. The issue to be decided was whether the Council of Vienne, in revoking the privileges conferred by Benedict XI, had intended implicitly to condemn his view on repeated confessions as well. It was essential to Peter de la Palu's position to demonstrate that this was not the case.

John de Pouilli argued that popes could very well err in matters of faith, that Benedict XI had so erred, and that the council had properly corrected his blunder. An obvious line of counter-argument would have been to assert that papal decisions were infallible and so irreformable. Peter de la Palu at times came close to formulating this argument but in fact always stopped short of doing so. His most detailed discussion of the question is contained in a *Quodlibet* of 1312.[1] First he emphasized the authority of the pope to judge questions of faith and morals. Disputes on such matters were to be referred to the see of Peter. What the Roman church determined and declared concerning them was to be held by all. Anyone who scorned a judgment of the supreme pontiff automatically excommunicated himself. Once the apostolic see had pronounced judgment no one could retract its sentence—at any rate no inferior.[2] But this left open the question whether an equal, a subsequent pope, could reverse the judgment of his predecessor. Peter's whole argument was designed to prove that the provision of *Inter cunctas* which he was defending had not been

---

[1] MS Toulouse, Bibliothèque de la Ville, 744. (I am grateful to Charles Zuckerman for calling my attention to this work.) Some of the arguments from the *Quodlibet* were repeated in Peter's *Articulis de audientia confessionum* (Paris, 1506).

[2] MS Toulouse 744, fol. 89rb, "Et tunc illud quod romana ecclesia iudicat et determinat et declarat ab omnibus est tenendum, nec ex tunc licet aliter opinari nec in dubium revocare nec aliter iudicare ... Et intelligo nemini inferiori."

so annulled. He approached the question delicately. Concerning Benedict's Bull, he wrote in a later work

> Although it is totally annulled in so far as it is an act of legislation, in so far as it is a true declaration of the faith it is irrevocable.[1]

The argument here seems to be, not that papal legislation was necessarily unerring but that, when a papal decree incorporated a truth of faith, that truth was, by its own intrinsic virtue unchangeable. Elsewhere Peter expressed himself more emphatically about the unerring authority of the Roman church, distinguishing clearly between decrees of positive law that could be changed and definitions of faith that ought to remain immutable:

> Although statutes of the Roman church are often changed because what is just at one time may become unjust as times and persons change, nevertheless, because the truth of faith is immutable, it has never been heard and by the grace of God never will be heard that the Roman church should retract a decree made by itself in such matters, for then it would confess itself to have erred or to be erring.[2]

Peter also wrote in another context that if the Roman church held to one doctrine and all the rest of the church to another, the Roman church was to be followed.[3]

Evidently he had the utmost respect for the dogmatic definitions of the papacy. But two points should be noted. In the first place Peter never specifically stated that the local Roman church could not err even though he wrote that such error was unheard-of and not to be anticipated. (One can find precisely similar statements among the earlier canonists who still maintained that, in the last resort, only the universal church was certainly preserved from error.)[4] Secondly, Peter set these comments about the authority of the Roman church in the

---

[1] *De audientia* (Paris, 1506), fol. 65vb, "... licet sit omnino cassata in quantum constitutio est, in quantum tamen est declaratio vera fidei irrevocabilis est."

[2] *Quodl.* fol. 92ra, "... et quamvis statuta romane ecclesie sepe mutentur quia quod iustum est aliquando mutatione aliqua temporum vel personarum sit iniustum, tamen quia veritas fidei est immutabilis nunquam auditum est nec per dei gratiam audietur quod ecclesia romana retractaret declarationem a se alias factam in talibus quia tunc confiteretur se aliquando errasse vel tunc errare."

[3] *Op. cit.*, fol. 94vb, "... si tota ecclesia residua teneret unum et romana ecclesia oppositum ipsi est adherendum ..." For the same doctrine in Huguccio, see above, p. 50. We noted there that the doctrine can refer only to judicial supremacy and has no connotation of infallibility.

[4] See e.g. the comments of Johannes Teutonicus *ad* C. 24 q. 1 c. 6 and *ad* C. 24 q. 1 c. 9, cited in *Foundations*, p. 253.

context of a very sharp distinction between the corporate Roman see and the individual popes who presided over it. (Here again his thought closely paralleled that of the Decretists.)

The issue of the relationship between pope and Roman church arose in Peter de la Palu's reply to one of John de Pouilli's arguments. John maintained that *Inter cunctas* was contrary to divine law and, apparently, accused Peter of holding that all papal pronouncements concerning the faith had to be accepted unquestioningly, however dubious their content. In fact, John de Pouilli wrote, popes could err in faith, and for the church to follow an erring pope would be like the blind leading the blind. It was intolerable that an erring rule should bind the defenders of the true faith. We ought to obey God rather than man.[1] Peter did not reply to all this by defending a theory of papal infallibility in any form. Rather he indignantly denied that he had ever taught any such doctrine as the one John imputed to him. He had not written that the pope could not err in faith and morals, Peter declared. Evidently popes could err, he went on. Anastasius had erred, and Marcellinus, and "Pope Leo in the time of blessed Hilary." And an erring pope was not to be followed, but was to be corrected, just as Paul had corrected Peter. (One has to bear in mind with Peter de la Palu, as with the canonists, that he acknowledged the pope's liability to err in an official capacity without having any conception of an "extra-ordinary magisterium" that would have guaranteed the infallibility of a particular class of papal decisions.) But the fact that individual popes erred did not prove that the whole Roman church erred, Peter continued; and the decree he was defending, *Inter cunctas*, was not made up by the pope "out of his own head" but was approved "by the counsel of all his brothers." Moreover, it was not to be presumed in doubtful cases that the pope was in error; and certainly no individual could take it upon himself to judge the pope. Only a general council had the authority to pronounce on the orthodoxy of papal decrees and, if necessary, to depose an erring pope as a heretic.[2] Peter

---

[1] *Op. cit.*, fol. 89va, "Dogmatizans contra doctrinam pape est excommunicatus. Verum est si papa non errat in fide nec in moribus nec ordinat aliquid contra scripturam vel contra evangelium. Alias non est audiendus nec sequendus ne *si cecus cecum ducet ambo in foveam cadent*, quia obedire oportet deo magis quam hominibus. Sic enim sententia canonis haberet errorem intollerabilem expressum si ligaret defendentes fidem ..."

[2] *Op. cit.*, fol. 89vb, "notandum quod papa possit errare et in fide et in moribus sicut quidam leo papa tempore beati hylarii narratum fuisse hereticus et sicut Anastasius favens hereticum divino nutu fulmine percussus est ... et Marcel-

concluded his argument by maintaining that the doctrine he defended concerning repeated confessions had been held by the whole Roman church for many years with no other church in the world dissenting and had been tacitly accepted by the general council of Vienne. If the pope had indeed erred against divine law in his solemn decree—and Peter admitted the possibility—then it was remarkable, he wrote, that no one had previously pointed this out and that the general council had not explicitly corrected the pope's teaching.[1] In the end then his argument leads us back to the common opinion of the age, that ultimate authority in matters of faith resided with the universal church or with a general council—which was competent to judge the faith of a pope suspected of error. Even though his whole case rested on maintaining the irrevocability (or, at least, the unrevoked status) of a particular papal decree—and here he was in somewhat the same position as Olivi had been —Peter could not bring himself to formulate a doctrine of the pope's personal infallibility. The idea was apparently too eccentric to appeal to a cautious, curial theologian.

When we considered the broad problems of Scripture and Tradition, we found important new ways of thought arising in the years around 1300. But, when we turn to the specific problem of the pope's teaching authority, we can only note that the theologians, with the exception

---

linus ... Sed propter hoc ecclesia romana non errat que favente deo omnium ecclesiarum capud est et magistra. Si autem capud haberet occulos erutos reliqua membra corporis nihil viderunt. Illam autem constitutionem non solus papa fecit de capito suo imo de consilio omnium fratrum sicut in ea dicitur. Item, etsi papa errare possit nec in suo errore sequendus sit sed corrigendus sicut dicitur Gal. 2 *In faciem resisti quia reprehensibilis erat*, tamen in dubio non praesumitur nec est cuiuslibet iudicare papam errantem sed concilii quod propter heresim ipsum deponere potest, 40 di. *si papa* ... Unde non sunt sequendi clave errante, sed non presumuntur errare in dubia nec pertinet ad aliquem citra concilium ipsorum iudicium erroneum appellare." In his *De potestate papae*, ed. P. T. Stella (Zürich, 1966) Peter explained that the sentence of the general council against a heretical pope was merely declaratory. In becoming a heretic he automatically forfeited his role as head of the church. "Et tunc magis deponitur de facto quam de iure quia qui non credit iam iudicatus est, de iure scilicet." (p. 195). Peter also distinguished carefully in this work between formulations of divine law included in conciliar decrees and merely human regulations. The pope could change the latter but not the former because "... ibi fides sicut in evangeliis declaratur." (p. 201).

[1] *Op. cit.*, fol. 89vb, "Unde cum tota ecclesia romana, nulla ecclesia mundi aperte contradicente, multis annis, immo usque hodie in illa declaratione perstiterit, mirum est si tamdiu erravit. Mirum est etiam si evidenter erravit quod nullus ei contradixit, et si hoc erat contra ius naturale et divinum et error in fide quomodo sacrum concilium istum errorem clare non revocaverit quod quosdam alios errores ammovit ..."

of Olivi, had made strikingly little progress since the days of the twelfth-century Decretists.

3. SOVEREIGNTY: POPE, BISHOPS AND GENERAL COUNCIL

Any theory of papal infallibility must depend, implicitly or explicitly on a set of assumptions concerning the relationship between the pope and the rest of the church. As modern theologians say, the infallibility of the pope can not be "other than" the infallibility of the church. The significant relationships moreover are the permanent divinely-willed ones, not those defined merely in the positive constitutional law of the church which has changed from age to age. A major problem then, in any theology of infallibility, is it explain the structure of the church that Christ established in the first place; the relationships that really matter are the relationships between Christ, Peter, the apostles, and the faithful.

In the early fourteenth century various tensions in ecclesiastical life stimulated new enquiries into such questions. Conciliarists and episcopalists appealed to the New Testament to prove that Peter shared power with the whole college of the apostles. The more extreme papalists among the Dominicans deduced precisely opposite conclusions from the same passages of Scripture. The Franciscans, obsessed with their own role as the only practitioners of perfect evangelical poverty, raised new questions about the continuance of the apostolic life in the church and about the theory of apostolic succession in the episcopate. This whole background of debate would influence the new discussions on papal infallibility that began in the 1320s.

(i) *Conciliarists*

Duns Scotus, we have seen, held that the universal church was unerring in faith and that the faith of the church could be expressed with certainty in the canons of general councils. For Scotus himself this doctrine most certainly held no antipapal implications. Indeed, he adhered to a doctrine of papal sovereignty essentially similar to Bonaventure's. But, around 1300, other scholars were emphasizing the authority of general councils in the church precisely in order to limit the centralized power that was commonly attributed to the popes. (They were encouraged, of course, by the actual appeals to a general council launched by Philip the Fair against Boniface VIII.)[1] The expo-

---

[1] There is a good narrative of events in T. S. R. Boase, Boniface VIII (London,

nents of the conciliar position relied on two basic lines of argument. Firstly, they maintained that Christ had originally conferred jurisdiction on all the apostles, whose successors were the bishops, so that the fullness of jurisdiction of the church resided in a general council, conceived of as an assembly of the whole episcopate, rather than in the pope alone. Secondly, they held that a general council could effectively represent the universal *congregatio fidelium*, the whole body of the faithful, whose integrity in the faith had been guaranteed by Christ himself. When these premises were combined with the universally held belief that individual popes could sin and err in faith they led to the conclusion that the whole church (or its representatives) could depose an unworthy pope. The arguments concerning the deposition of a pope that were used around 1300 were essentially similar to those advanced by the twelfth century Decretists and were, in large part, derived from their works directly or indirectly; but now, for the first time, they were presented in coherent treatises intended for wide circulation rather than in scattered legal glosses.

A good example is the *De potestate regia et papali* of John of Paris (c. 1302). John maintained that the apostles received the power of binding and loosing *with* Peter, not *from* him and that, in the existing church, a prelate's power was not derived through the mediacy of the pope but "from God immediately, and from the people who elect or consent."[1] John conceded and indeed emphasized that the pope was head of the church by divine right. But, to the argument that the

---

1933). See also H.-X. Arquillière, "L'appel au concile sous Philippe le Bel," *Revue des questions historiques*, 45 (1911), pp. 23-55 and V. Martin, *Les origines du Gallicanisme* (Paris, 1939). Two older words of synthesis remain valuable: R. Scholz, *Die Publizistik zur Zeit Philipps des Schönen und Bonifaz VIII* (Stuttgart, 1903); J. Rivière, *Le problème de l'église et de l'état au temps de Philippe le Bel* (Louvain-Paris, 1926). On John of Paris, besides the works of Rivière and Scholz, see my *Foundations*, pp. 157-178; J. Leclercq, *Jean de Paris et l'ecclésiologie du XIIIe siècle* (Paris, 1942); and, for more recent literature, F. Bleienstein, *Johannes Quidort von Paris. Über königliche und päpstliche Gewalt Textkritische Edition mit deutscher Übersetzung* (Stuttgart, 1969), pp. 61-65.

[1] Cap. X, Bleienstein, *ed. cit.*, p. 109, "Item eandem potestatem acceperunt omnes Apostoli cum Petro, Matthaei XVIII (18), et habetur XXI D., 'In Novo', ubi dicitur quod Petrus ligandi solvendique potestatem primus accepit, ceteri vero apostoli cum eodem, non dicitur 'ab eodem', pari consortio honorem et potestatem acceperunt. ..." Cap. X, p. 114, "Sed potestas praelatorum non est a Deo mediante papa, sed immediate, et a populo eligente vel consentiente." There was, however, some equivocation about the precise nature of the *jurisdictio* which the apostles received from Christ in John's Cap. XII (pp. 127-134). In his *De confessionibus audiendis*, ed. L. Hödl (Munich, 1962) John seems to have adopted a more papalist position.

papacy was the "highest created power" and so immune from all judgment, he replied that there existed a power equal to or greater than that of the pope in the college of cardinals or in the whole church.[1] He stated repeatedly that a criminal or heretical pope could be deposed by a general council or by the cardinals acting on behalf of the universal church.[2]

The central theme of the *De potestate* was John's argument that the pope had not established and could not establish his own temporal supremacy over kings and princes as an article of Catholic faith. (He was writing either immediately before or immediately after the appearance of the Bull, *Unam sanctam*.)[3] John's pre-occupation with this matter led him to a series of considerations on the role of Scripture, pope and general council in the establishment of truths of faith. If, John wrote, the pope, without consulting a general council, were to condemn as heretics those who asserted that the king of France was not subject to the Roman pontiff in temporalities, his words were to be understood in an orthodox sense if possible. They might, for instance, mean only that the king was subject to the pope *ratione peccati* and *in foro conscientiae*. If the pope meant anything more than this then his decree would be manifestly contrary to Scripture and the common doctrine of the church. In any case the pope could not introduce novelties of doctrine without a general council.[4] Discussing particularly the doctrine of the "two swords" John declared that to claim both swords for the pope was close to heresy for this claim was not to be found in Scripture, "the rule of faith," and the Lord had commanded "Do not add or take away from the words I speak to you" (Deuteronomy, 4.2). Likewise the councils of Ephesus and Chalcedon

---

[1] *Ed. cit.*, Cap. XXV, p. 207, "Licet sit summa virtus in persona, tamen est ei aequalis vel maior in collegio sive in tota ecclesia."

[2] *Loc. cit.*, "Vel potest dici quod potest deponi a collegio vel magis a generali concilio auctoritate divina, cuius consensus supponitur et praesumitur ad deponendum ubi manifeste apparet scandalum et incorrigibilitas praesidentis." Similarly Cap. VI, p. 95; Cap. XIII, p. 140; Cap. XXIV, p. 201.

[3] On the dating of the work see Bleienstein, pp. 13-14.

[4] *Ed. cit.*, Cap. XXII, p. 195, "Sed quid si papa dicat quod reputat illum haereticum qui tenet aliquid de quo sunt opiniones litteratorum, et dicat hoc sine concilio generali, ut si dicat quod reputat haereticum omnem hominem qui asserit regem Franciae vel aliquem huiusmodi non esse ei subiectum in temporalibus? ... Hoc enim esset contra Scripturam et contra communem doctrinam et novitas quaedam, quam non proferret summus pontifex nisi cum multa maturitate et habito prius concilio generali et discussione facta ubique per litteratos, et ideo debet intelligi in sensu sano, scilicet ratione delicti ..."

had decreed that no faith was to be professed save that of the Nicene Creed. In these passages John seems to have hesitated between two opinions—that a pope could not introduce novelties of doctrine at all and that he could do so only with the support of a general council. At any rate he was quite clear that the pope could not define an article of faith for the whole church without consulting a council. "The world is greater than the City," he wrote (quoting Jerome). And, again, "The pope with a council is greater than the pope alone."[1]

Similar ideas occur in the *Tractatus de modo generalis concilii celebrandi* of Gulielmus Durandus (1309).[2] Here the episcopalist theme was especially stressed. The author argued at length from both Scripture and canon law that the apostles received their authority directly from Christ and that bishops succeeded to this apostolic authority.[3] He also maintained vehemently that the centralizing of all power in the Roman curia was undermining the status of the bishops and disturbing the good order of the whole church. The "Roman church" that was "without stain or wrinkle", "mother and teacher of the faithful", was the universal church.[4] The local Roman church was bound by the decrees of general councils and could change them only by summoning a new council. Indeed, the author held, councils ought to participate regularly in the government of the church, meeting every ten years to consider important issues of legislation and taxation.[5]

---

[1] *Ed. cit.*, cap. XX, pp. 184-185, "... nam papam habere utrumque gladium non continetur in sacra scriptura quae est regula fidei, et Deut IV (2) dicat Dominus: 'Non addetis ad verbum quod vobis loquor neque auferetis ab eo.' Et in *Gestis primae Ephesinae synodi* dicitur quod perlecto symbolo Nicaenae synodi decrevit sancta synodus aliam fidem nulli licere proferre ... Amplius, cum fides Christiana sit catholica et universalis, non potest summus pontifex hoc ponere sub fide sine concilio generali quia non potest papa destruere statuta concilii, XIX D., 'Anastasius.' Nam licet concilium non possit papae legem imponere, *Extra, De electione*, 'Significasti', et XXXV, q. vi, 'Veniam', tamen non intelligitur in his quae fidei sunt, eo quod orbis maior est Urbe et papa cum concilio maior est papa solo, XCIII D., 'Legimus'.

[2] On his views see my *Foundations*, pp. 180, 190-198 with references to the earlier literature.

[3] *Tractatus de modo generalis concilii celebrandi* (Paris, 1545). See e.g., Part I, Tit. 5, p. 16, "Ceteri vero apostoli cum eodem Petro pari consortio honorem et potestatem acceperunt a Christo ... Ipsis vero apostolis decedentibus in loco eorum successerunt episcopi ..."

[4] Part III, Tit. 27, p. 188, "... videretur quod ipsa Romana ecclesia quae non debet habere maculam vel rugam et quae mater est fidei et magistra debet esse universalis ecclesia, et ad quam omnis sanctae religionis relatio debet referri ..."

[5] Part I, Tit. 3, pp. 10-11, "... contra dicta concilia et iura nihil possent de novo statuere vel condere nisi generali concilio convocato. Cum illud quod omnes tangit,

A little later on, Marsilius of Padua presented a far more radical statement of the conciliar thesis in his *Defensor pacis* (1324).[1] According to Marsilius all the apostles received from Christ exactly the same power as Peter, and this power was simply the sacramental "power of orders." The primacy of jurisdiction of the papacy was of merely human institution.[2] The general council was the sovereign body in the church and the pope merely its delegate. The council was infallible in its definitions of faith while individual popes could err. An erring pope could be deposed by the council.[3]

Many strands of doctrine were interwoven in these treatises of the early fourteenth century—terminology derived from Aristotle's *Politics*, Roman law ideas on popular sovereignty, canonistic corporation concepts, theological interpretations of the Scriptural texts referring to Peter and the apostles. But, underlying all these layers of thought, was the fundamental assertion of the twelfth century Decretists that an erring pope could be judged by a general council. This is no place to attempt a detailed analysis of conciliar ideology at the beginning of the fourteenth century. But we cannot understand the development of the idea of papal infallibility in later times unless we bear in mind that the very core of the conciliarist position was the assertion of Johannes Teutonicus, embedded in the *glossa ordinaria* to the Decretum, "Where matters of faith are concerned ... a general council is greater than a pope." For a century past every young canonist, plodding his way through the Decretum and its Gloss in law school, had been taught this doctrine. In the days of Boniface VIII and John XXII it had spread from the technical writings of the canonists to widely read treatises on ecclesiology and political theory.

---

secundum iuris utriusque regulam ab omnibus debeat communiter approbari." Part III, Tit. 27, p. 190, "Item quod nulla iura generalia deinceps conderet nisi vocato concilio generali quod de decennio in decennio vocaretur. ..."

[1] For recent literature on Marsilius see G. de Lagarde, *La naissance de l'esprit laïque*, III *Le Defensor pacis* (Paris, 1970); J. Quillet, *Le défenseur de la paix* (Paris, 1968). The major work of synthesis in English is A. Gewirth, *Marsilius of Padua*, 2 vols. (New York, 1951-1956).

[2] *The Defensor Pacis of Marsilius of Padua*, ed. C. W. Previté-Orton (Cambridge, 1928), *Dictio* II, cap. 6, pp. 159-174; cap. 16, pp. 273-288; cap. 22, pp. 342-358.

[3] Marsilius presented his doctrine of conciliar authority mainly in *Dictio* II, caps. 18-22, pp. 304-358. On the errancy of the pope and the infallibility of the council see especially Cap. 20, p. 323, "... semel determinata circa Scripturam per concilium generale ... praesertim quae ad salutem aeternam vera credere necessarium sit, immutabilis et infallibilis veritatis existant ..." Marsilius argued here that both Boniface VIII and John XXII had promulgated false interpretations of Scripture.

Finally, when powerful kings and emperors began to appeal to the principle of conciliar supremacy in their political struggles with the popes, that principle ceased to be a mere abstract theory of the schools and became a real threat to the independence of the papacy. Slowly, papalist theologians began to realize that the doctrine of the *glossa ordinaria* would have to be defeated if the popes were to rule securely as sovereign heads of the church.

(ii) *Anti-conciliarists*

In later centuries, when the doctrine of the medieval canonists was being defended principally by Gallican doctors against the theologians of the Roman school, the most effective way of refuting it seemed to be to assert the principle of papal infallibility. If the pope was personally infallible then, obviously, a general council was not greater than an individual pope in matters of faith.

In 1300 the situation was quite different. Long ago Arquillière observed that the medieval church's defective formulation of the doctrine of papal infallibility encouraged the growth of conciliarist ideas. But the problem was more than one of mere "defective formulation." As we have seen the idea of papal infallibility was blankly unacceptable even to the most ardent defenders of the Roman see in the first decades of the fourteenth century. The idea was too novel, too radical, too sharply opposed to the juridical conception of papal sovereignty, too alien to the theological tradition of the church, to command support among respectable theologians. They therefore developed a quite different approach to the problems of conciliarism and episcopalism.

Everyone agreed that the pope was required to adhere to dogmatic definitions of the great councils of the early church. But this did not in itself cause too great a difficulty for the papal theologians. They could argue that the pope was bound by, say, the doctrinal definitions of Chalcedon because of the acknowledged, intrinsic, permanent truth of the dogmas defined, not because the defining body possessed an authority superior to that of the pope. This seems to have been the position of Peter de la Palu. The more serious problem was that some canonists had in fact associated the binding force of conciliar decrees with the idea that a supremacy of jurisdiction inhered in the council. This idea, we have seen, could be expressed in two ways. In its more moderate formulation it asserted that pope-and-council together possessed a greater authority than the pope acting alone. A pope who went against the decisions of an earlier council, presided over by one of his predecessors, could then fall under a sentence of excommunication decreed in advance by that council. In its more extreme formulation the conciliar thesis asserted simply that the members of a council separated from the pope possessed greater authority than he did and could judge and depose him if necessary. The defenders of papal theocracy in the fourteenth century were anxious to prove that the conciliar doctrine in either form was false, untenable and probably heretical.

They could not or would not propound a theory of papal infallibility. Instead they developed in a variety of ways the doctrine that had been advanced earlier by Bonaventure asserting that all inferior jurisdiction in the church was derived from the pope. Bonaventure had taught that every bishop received the power of the keys from Christ but that the "keys" conferred only the sacramental power of orders. The Franciscan theologian, Richard of Middletown, took the next logical step by applying Bonaventure's distinction to the New Testament texts referring to Peter and the apostles. All the apostles received the "power of binding and loosing." the "power of the keys" immediately from Christ, he wrote, but this power did not include the jurisdiction which was essential to the use of the keys. Jurisdiction came from Christ through the mediacy of Peter; and, Richard concluded, "I say the same concerning the power of bishops in relation to the pope."[1]

Hervaeus Natalis, who provided the most detailed treatment of this problem among the controversialists of the early fourteenth century presented a different set of arguments. He conceded that, when Christ said to Peter "I will give you the keys of the kingdom of Heaven... Whatsoever thou shalt bind on earth it shall be bound in Heaven," the words did indeed refer to jurisdiction, and to jurisdiction in both

---

[1] *Super quatuor libros Sententiarum*, IV (Brixiae, 1591), Dist. 24 art. 5 q. 1, p. 375, "Ad primum in oppositum dicendum quod potestatem ligandi et solvendi in foro poenitentiae acceperunt tam apostoli quam alii discipuli a Christo immediate ..." q. 3, p. 377, "Petrus enim summus fuit inter alios apostolos quia quamvis potestatem clavium omnes immediate receperint a Christo, tamen potestatem iurisdictionis acceperunt mediante Petro ..." Richard presented a more nuanced view in his *Quaestio disputata de privilegio Martini papae* IV, ed. F. Delorme (Quaracchi, 1925), pp. 75-77. In his work, as in that of John of Paris (and in several other authors of the period), there is some hesitancy as to the precise authority conferred by a grant of *jurisdictio*. The grant could confer directly a right to govern that did not exist beforehand. It could also be taken to mean merely the assigning of subjects to one already fully qualified to govern. On this see Congar, "La querelle," pp. 89 ff. The question needs further study.

the internal and the external forums.[1] But, he argued, these words did not confer any actual authority on Peter. They were merely a promise of an authority that Christ would confer after the Resurrection in the words spoken at John 22.15-17, "Feed my sheep."[2] So long as Christ lived as a man among men, himself ruling and guiding the church, he had no occasion to confer jurisdiction on others, not even on Peter.[3] All the texts which, according to the episcopalists, proved that Christ conferred authority immediately on the apostles could be taken as assigning to the apostles some mission or duty or sacramental function—but not the actual power of jurisdiction.[4] Even after the Resurrection, when Christ said to the apostles, "Receive the Holy Spirit, whose sins you shall forgive they are forgiven them," he still conferred only the power of orders.[5] Only when Christ finally said to Peter "Feed my sheep" did he make a grant of jurisdiction—and he spoke these words to Peter alone. Hence he conferred jurisdiction only on Peter;[6] and subsequently all jurisdiction in the church was derived from Peter and his successors. Augustinus Triumphus, in a variation on this argument, insisted that Christ's words to Peter at Matt. 16.18-19 did indeed confer jurisdiction on Peter then and there

---

[1] *De potestate papae* (Paris, 1647), p. 366, "Nam Mathei 16 dicit: Tu es Petrus ... Quod quidem referri potest et quantum ad ligamentum et solutionem sentendiando in utroque foro, scilicet interiori et exteriori et quantum etiam ad ligamentum in statuendo ..."

[2] *De potestate*, p. 368, "Secunda conclusio, patet et per illam auctoritatem Math. 16. Tibi dabo claues regni caelorum, ubi secundum Doctores sanctos Christus promisit Petro determinate se daturum potestatem praedictam, etiam per illam auctoritatem Ioannis 21. Pasces oues meas, et pasce Agnos meos, ubi secundum expositores sanctos collata est praedicta potestas Petro," Similarly at pp. 367, 375, 389. See also *De iurisdictione*, ed. cit., p. 22. The view that Christ actually conferred power on Peter by the words spoken at John 22.15-17 was widely held.

[3] *De potestate*, p. 385, "... in praesentia autem Christi conuersantis cum hominibus, nec oportuit nec decuit quod esset unus talis vicarius generalis, et ideo sic Christo praesente non fuit alius Papa praeter ipsum." *De iurisdictione*, p. 22, "... vivente Christo non debuit habere vicarium generalem."

[4] The authorities cited by Hervaeus' opponents are given in the *De potestate*, pp. 378-379. His replies, denying in every case a grant of jurisdiction to the apostles by Christ, are at pp. 393-394.

[5] *De potestate*, p. 370, "Nam sicut infra dicetur id quod habetur Ioannis 20 'Insufflavit etc.' potest referri ad potestatem characteris." See also p. 394 where the argument is repeated.

[6] *De potestate*, p. 389, "Quarta conclusio est, quod omnes potestates inferiores quae sunt in Ecclesia, et personae in potestatibus sunt institutae a vicario generali Christi et successore Petri, non prout Petrus accipitur pro persona singulari, sed ut accipitur pro illo cui talis vicaria est commissa Ioan. 22 'Pasce oves meas etc.'" Similarly *De iurisdictione*, pp. 26-27.

and established him in the papal office. Subsequently the power of jurisdiction received by the other apostles came to them through this office already established in Peter.[1]

For Hervaeus Natalis the argument that Peter alone received jurisdiction immediately from Christ was only, so to speak, a first line of defense. Even if it were granted that Christ conferred jurisdiction on all the apostles, he argued, it still did not follow that bishops succeeded to this apostolic jurisdiction.[2] A theologian could prove that Christ's commission of supreme power to Peter necessarily applied to all Peter's successors in the papacy for it was evident that Christian society needed a single head to maintain its order and unity. But there was no convincing argument to prove that Christ had established a host of lesser permanent jurisdictions in the church. If then Christ did confer authority directly on the apostles, the grant could be seen as merely a personal one, limited to those particular individuals.[3] Finally, Hervaeus argued, even if we were to concede that Christ gave jurisdiction directly to the apostles and that bishops succeeded to this apostolic authority, it still would not follow that, in the existing church, bishops received jurisdiction immediately from Christ. In the days of the apostles Christ was, so to speak, his own pope *(non erat aliquis papa nisi Christus)*; and, just as all power then flowed from Christ, so too, in later ages of the church, all power flowed from Christ's successor, the pope.[4]

---

[1] *Summa de potestate ecclesiastica* (Rome, 1584), XX. 5, p. 125, "Unde Christus eligendo Petrum pastorem ecclesiae dedit sibi singularem potestatem clavium ut dicit iurisdictionem quando dixit Matth. 16, 'Tibi dabo etc.'" For Augustinus' views on this whole question see M. Wilks, *The Problem of Sovereignty* (Cambridge, 1963), pp. 530-537.

[2] *De potestate*, p. 389, "... dato quod Christus immediate contulisset Apostolis et discipulis potestatem iurisdictionis, et cum hoc supponatur quod Episcopi et curati successerint in loco eorum, non sequitur quod potestates quae nunc sunt in ecclesia, et personae in ipsis potestatibus non sunt institutae a Papa." There is a similar argument in Alexander de Sancto Elpidio, *De ecclesiastica potestate*, ed J. T. Rocaberti, *Bibliotheca Maxima Pontificia*, II (Rome, 1698), pp. 6-10. Alexander argued that the apostles received jurisdiction from Christ but that subsequent bishops received it through the mediacy of the pope.

[3] *De potestate*, p. 366, "... oportet in tota communitate Christiana ponere aliquem praesidentem ad quem pertineat per se vel per alium sententiare de quolibet ..." p. 372, "... nulla est necessitas quod particularis vicaria instituatur vel conferatur immediate a principali Domino sicut est de vicaria generali ... non sic succedunt episcopi apostolis sicut papa Petro ..." The argument denying that a permanent episcopate was established by Christ is pursued in detail at pp. 388, 394.

[4] The argument is most clearly stated in the *De iurisdictione*, p. 28, "Ad primum dicendum quod magis deberet dici, quod sicut apostoli ad Christum ita etiam

The practical conclusions of this argument were that most probably the whole state of episcopacy was established by the papacy and that certainly each individual bishop derived his jurisdiction from the pope, not immediately from Christ. Hervaeus was at pains to point out that bishops did not stand to the pope in the same relationship as princes or barons to a secular king. (The princes had some inherent right to their positions.) Rather bishops were like royal bailiffs or servants.[1] "They have as much jurisdiction as pleases the pope." To the objection that, if all this were true, a general council would have no more authority than a pope alone, Hervaeus cheerfully replied that this was indeed the case. It did not follow that general councils should never be held. They could usefully be convoked "not to have greater authority but fuller deliberation."[2] The same argument about conciliar authority was put in an interesting form by Hervaeus' contemporary, Gulielmus Petrus de Godin. He pointed out that the council was not simply a collection of individuals but a corporate body truly representing the universal church. And yet still all its authority came from the pope, since all jurisdiction in the church was derived from him; and so the council could not limit the papal power. (Like Hervaeus, this author held that Christ conferred jurisdiction on the church solely through Peter.)[3]

---

episcopi ad papam, et tempore isto quo Christus dedit potestatem apostolis non erat aliquis papa nisi Christus, sed post successit Petrus Christo, quem tunc successurum instituit. Et ideo non oportet, quod si tunc apostoli non habuerunt potestatem a Petro, quod episcopi postea non recipiant potestatem a papa ..."

[1] *De iurisdictione*, p. 28, "Unde magis est simile de comparatione iuris papalis ad ius temporale et de comparatione iuris regalis ad ius ballivorum et consulum qui instituuntur a rege in ordine ad populum immediate subiectum quam de comparatione iuris papae ad ius regale et ius baronum."

[2] *De iurisdictione*, p. 34, "Ad sextum dicendum quod auctoritas totius concilii et auctoritas papae non sunt aliquid maius, ut mihi videtur, quantum ad ipsam auctoritatem, nec sequitur, quod aliquando non convocetur concilium generale in aliquibus casibus, quia hoc non fit ad habendum maiorem auctoritatem, sed ad habendum pleniorem deliberationem et etiam ad maiorem solemnitatem et concordiam ecclesiae."

[3] *De causa immediate ecclesiastice potestatis* (Paris, 1506), fol. 24r. The argument was intended to prove that papal power could not be derived from general councils, "... tota ecclesia non congregatur nisi in conciliis generalibus in quibus ipsa est tota in virtute per hoc quod ibi quilibet episcopus representat totum dyocesim suam vel solus vel cum procuratoribus collegiorum. Unde proprie dicitur tota ecclesia facere quod que ibi fit sicut canonici omnes dicuntur facere quod faciunt in capitulo ad hoc congregato non quod quilibet per se faciat ut sunt singulares persone ... Sed papa dat auctoritatem et robur omnibus consiliis generalibus ergo ab ipsis non accipit ipse potestatem." The authorship of this work is disputed. I have followed the opinion of P. T. Stella, *op. cit.* (supra p. 152 n. 2), pp. 27-35. Exactly the

The arguments we have considered all led to the same conclusion. The pope was everything; the bishops almost nothing. Unfortunately the arguments contradicted one another and none of them, considered individually, was altogether satisfactory. If the "power of the keys" was merely a power of orders (in which all the apostles were equal) then Matt. 16.18 "I will give you the keys of the kingdom of Heaven" could have no relevance for the doctrine of Petrine primacy, which then had to be based entirely on other texts. But this contradicted a tradition of exegesis going back to St. Augustine, a tradition that the popes themselves had frequently invoked. Again, if the words at Matt. 16.18 designated Peter as the source of all jurisdiction in the church it was really impossible to explain (on the theory of either Hervaeus or Augustines Triumphus) why Christ himself subsequently addressed to all the apostles the same words that he had originally spoken to Peter "Whatsoever you shall bind on earth it shall be bound in Heaven." The texts of Scripture were really plain enough—or, at any rate, their meaning had seemed plain enough for centuries. Over and over again the Gospels describe occasions when Christ conferred authority on the whole group of apostles (or on a still broader group); and of course the Scriptural texts themselves did not discriminate between a power of orders and a power of jurisdiction. (That technical distinction was an invention of the medieval canonists).

It is impossible to believe that the papalists of the early fourteenth century arrived at their novel forms of Scriptural exegesis by deep disinterested meditations on the mysteries of Holy Writ. The views they held about papal and episcopal power were forged in the heat of disputes that involved the status and privileges of their own mendicant orders. They turned to the Bible to seek justification for positions they had already found it convenient to adopt in the course of those disputes. All theologians of the early fourteenth century paid lip-service to the awesome authority of Sacred Scripture but too many of them displayed an almost frivolous subjectivity in twisting Scriptural texts to suit their own polemical purposes. There was a fourteenth century saying, "the law has a nose of wax", implying that a strong ruler could twist it any way he pleased. Scripture did not fare much better in the hands of the more contentious theologians of the period.

---

same text is presented by Peter de la Palu in his *De potestate papae* (ed. Stella, p. 183) but it is set there in a different framework of argument. Peter conceded in this work that episcopal authority was derived directly from Christ and maintained only that it was subjected to papal authority by divine will.

(iii) *The* De perfectione statuum

A striking feature of the thought of Hervaeus Natalis is his evident willingness to abandon the whole ancient doctrine of apostolic succession in the episcopate if this would help him to score a useful debating point in his arguments against the adversaries of the friars. Something of the same attitude appears in the final work to be considered here, the Franciscan treatise *De perfectione statuum*.

This work has commonly been attributed to Duns Scotus. He is named as the author in the surviving manuscripts (though they are late manuscripts) and the treatise was included in Vivès' edition of his *Opera omnia*. The attribution has been vigorously attacked by Longpré, but the only significant argument he could bring against it was that the work is different in tone and style from Scotus' other writings.[1] The point is not without substance even though, often enough, the polemical treatises of the period differed in tone from their authors' more formal academic writings.[2]

The *De perfectione statuum* is certainly a strange work. Its author was concerned to establish that the way of life professed by the Franciscan Order constituted the most perfect "state" in the church.[3] Thomas Aquinas had taught that the bishops, as successors of the apostles, held the most perfect state. Bonaventure, discussing the same question, maintained that Franciscan poverty represented the highest form of perfection but distinguished between the perfection proper to a public official, like a bishop, and that which a private individual was free to

---

[1] E. Longpré, *La philosophie du B. Duns Scot* (Paris, 1924), pp. 19-22.

[2] Duns' authorship was defended by G. J. Kirby, "The Authenticity of the *De perfectione statuum* of Duns Scotus," *The New Scholasticism*, 7 (1933), pp. 134-152. Apart from his general argument concerning the tone and content of the work Longpré maintained that the *De perfectione* must have been written after 1322 (Duns Scotus died in 1308). This point is discussed below p. 169 n. 3. Longpré also argued that the *De perfectione* never cited Nicholas III's decree *Exiit* when discussing Franciscan poverty, while Duns Scotus often cited it in this connection. He gives six references to prove the point. In one of them Scotus cited the Bull *Exigit* (not *Exiit*). The other five have no connection with Franciscan poverty. Two of them present a peculiar mariological doctrine. Pope Nicholas III, Scotus argued, had laid down that dominion could be permanently separated from use. It could properly be maintained therefore that Mary conceded the dominion of her body to Joseph but not the use of it. (*Opera*, ed. Vivès, XIX, p. 279; XXIV, pp. 410-411.) To some scholars it may seem that Scotus' capacity for this kind of tasteless nonsense makes it more likely rather than less that he also perpetrated the eccentricities of the *De perfectione statuum*.

[3] On the whole controversy see K. Schleyer, "Disputes scolastiques sur les états de perfection," *RTAM*, 10 (1938), pp. 279-293.

pursue. Pietro Olivi was less tender toward episcopal sensibilities and was very willing to attack abuses in the lives of contemporary bishops. The author of the *De perfectione statuum* went a step further and embarked on a frontal assault on the whole "state" of episcopacy.

His arguments were directed against a series of theses advanced by Henry of Ghent in the 1280s, theses which sought to establish the superior perfection of prelacy as opposed to mendicancy.[1] In particular, the Franciscan author attacked a proposition advanced in Henry's *Quodlibet XI* which asserted that a man who preached by virtue of his ordinary jurisdiction was "greater and more truly a father" than one who preached by virtue of a privilege. To prove this point Henry argued that prelates, possessing ordinary jurisdiction over their flocks, actually brought into existence the congregations of Christian people. Friars, armed with their privileges, merely preached to congregations that already existed and so played a lesser role in the church.[2] The author of the *De perfectione statuum* simply turned this argument upside down. The state of prelacy, he argued, was by its intrinsic nature incapable of generating spiritual sons, of creating Christian communities. Infidels could be converted to Christianity only by the example of men living the perfect life of the apostles.[3] But the episcopal "state" did not require such a way of life. On the contrary bishops could live as luxuriously as the infidels themselves. They could have greater wealth and power than the kings and princes of the world. They could delight in sensual pleasures like the pagans of old.[4] The very existence of prelates presiding over Christian flocks therefore presupposed the

---

[1] *Quodlibeta Magistri Henrici Goethals a Gandavo* (Paris, 1518), *Quodl.* VII, q. 29 (1282); *Quodl.* XI, q. 27 (1286-1288); *Quodl.* XII, q. 29 (1288). On the dating see P. Glorieux, *La littérature quodlibétique de 1260 a 1320* (Kain, 1925).

[2] *Quodl.* XI q. 27, fol. CCCCLXXVII.

[3] *De perfectione statuum* in *Joannis Duns Scoti ... opera omnia,* ed. L. Vivès (Paris, 1891-1895), XXVI, pp. 499-561 at p. 501, "Quod status praelatorum ecclesiasticorum praesupponit statum alium, probatur, quia status praelatorum respectu subditorum est status secundum quid generantis patris ... respectu quorum subditorum status alius se habet ut status per se generantis patris ... Et quod hoc possunt soli illi qui vitam tenent apostolorum. ..."

[4] *Op. cit.,* pp. 509-510, "Non repugnat essentialiter statui praelatorum tot habere et tantos vel majores honores, divitias et delicias, potentiam et familiam tantam, sicut infideles, reges eorum et principes terrae, et sicut ipsi, sic isti post electionem pro praedictis obtinendis laborare, litigare, exercitum ducere et infinitum populum ducum, comitum, baronum, militum et aliorum nobilium sub dominio suo habere. Et quantum Stoici, qui felicitatem ponebant in voluptatibus gustus et tactus, in cibis et potibus delicatis, et cum uxoribus quibus ratione essentiali status non repugnat delectari."

existence of a higher, more perfect way of life in the church. This way was represented by the mendicant friars.

As always, the author's views on the structure of the church in his own day had to be somehow justified by reference to the New Testament texts on the church of the apostles. He argued therefore that Christ had conferred two roles or statuses on the apostles. First he sent them out as evangelical preachers to make converts. Then he gave them authority as prelates to rule over the flocks that their preaching had created. The apostles continued to fill both roles but, in the post-apostolic period, the roles separated. Friars succeeded to the role of evangelical preaching, bishops to the role of prelacy.[1] Much of the treatise was devoted to contrasting the two "states" or ways of life that ensued. The friars' "state" required a penitential life of asceticism, humility, and total poverty; the episcopal "state" permitted every kind of worldly self-indulgence. The work of the friars was to convert infidels, move sinners to repentance, urge the imperfect to achieve perfection; the work of the bishops was to administer sacraments to the converted and supervise the acts of external observance required by the church.[2] In effect, the friars carried on the evangelical work of Christ and the bishops performed routine administrative chores. Understandably, the author concluded that the state of the friars was "more arduous, more perfect and more essential to the existence and perfection of the church" than that of the bishops.[3] All this amounts to a radical attack on the ancient conception of the bishops as the principal bearers of ecclesiastical tradition, as the indispensable transmitters of the faith that Christ had handed down to the apostles. For our author, an essential, indeed *the* essential, part of the Christian heritage was not transmitted by bishops but by friars.

---

[1] *Op. cit.*, pp. 527-528, 558-559, "... aliis autem Apostolis succedunt episcopi alii, non inquantum erant apostoli ad conversionem populorum missi, sed inquantum super populum fidelem erant praelati ecclesiastici, pastores et episcopi ... Christo autem et Apostolis et discipulis ... missis succedunt modo qui pro salute Christianorum ... Spiritu sancto inspirati vitam perfectam et poenalem ... tenent Christi et apostolorum ..." The idea that the apostles had two roles, as evangelical preachers and as prelates, was derived from Bonaventure, *Expositio super Regulam, Opera* VIII, p. 416.

[2] *Op. cit.*, pp. 528, 559.

[3] *Op. cit.*, p. 559, "... quae vita sive qui status statu praelatorum ecclesiasticorum, ut superius est probatum, est prior, mundo necessarior, difficilior et perfectior ad purgandum, illuminandum et perficiendum, in ecclesiastica hierarchia pars principalior, sine qua ecclesiastica nec fuisset, nec perfecta esse posset ..." The claim was repeated over and over throughout the work.

In real life the friars were totally dependent on the continued good will of the popes. But it was not at all easy to fit the papacy into this account of church government and church history. After all, the pope was a bishop! The author of the *De perfectione statuum* argued, however, that the pope's position was different from that of all other bishops. The apostles had two roles, but Christ had three. As God he was lord of the world, as an evangelical preacher he was the model of perfection, as prelate he was ruler of the church.[1] Peter, "the perfect and universal vicar of Christ"[2] inherited all three roles; accordingly the friars were inferior to Peter's successors in the sense of being ruled and governed by them.[3]

Peter, it will be noted, inherited the role of evangelical perfection—the role of the friars—along with his other two roles. Our author evidently believed that Jesus Christ was a good Franciscan and he insisted that Peter was a good Franciscan too. Also he made no secret of his belief that, ideally, all other popes ought to be good Franciscans. "It is fitting for the supreme hierarch ... to be of the highest perfection," he wrote.[4] He had to admit, however, that, in practice, supreme power and supreme perfection could be separated so that they did not always exist together in the same office. This led him to the conclusion that, in the last resort, the Franciscan "state" was "more perfect and more meritorious" than the papal "state."[5] Inevitably, therefore, his acknowledgment that the friars were "ruled and directed" by the papacy was hedged with significant reservations. His real thought seems to have been that the papacy existed to serve Franciscans and not vice-versa. Since the pope, as vicar of Christ, was concerned with the salvation of all men, the author wrote, it was the pope's duty to put the needs of the friars before those of the prelates and to

---

[1] *Op. cit.*, pp. 525, 557-558.

[2] *Op. cit.*, pp. 545, 558, "Inter quos erat beatus Petrus tanquam Christi perfectus et universalis vicarius ..."

[3] *Op. cit.*, p. 547, "... status ille statu episcoporum omnium est perfectior; idem tamen status ad potentiam vicarii Christi comparatus est ea inferius, sicut ab ea regulandus et dirigendus."

[4] *Op. cit.*, p. 547, "Decet enim principalem hierarcham et omnium gubernatorem et regulatorem summae esse perfectionis; sic enim fuit de Christo et consequenter de beato Petro, ejus perfecto et universali vicario."

[5] *Op. cit.*, pp. 545-546, 553, "... status ille, qui ratione status requirit perfectiora et difficiliora opera bona quam status papalis, perfectior et magis est meritorius simpliciter quam status papalis; sed status praedictorum religiosorum est hujusmodi ..."

cherish and care for them especially.[1] Certainly the author did not
believe that it lay within the competence of the popes to frustrate or
radically change the Franciscan way of life. (In this he was faithful
to the doctrine of Pietro Olivi.) One of the arguments he had to
counter pointed out that, if the friars held no dominion over their
goods and the pope did not retain dominion, then anyone could licitly
plunder the Order at will. The author of the *De perfectione statuum*
replied to this by asserting that a pope *could* not renounce his responsibility for Franciscan property and still remain the vicar of Christ.[2]
His work—like all the polemical Franciscan treatises—contained many
passages exalting the majesty of papal authority but he was really
making the pope a mere figure-head, assigning to him a role like
that of some oriental god-king who is accorded inexhaustible deference
but no real power of decision making. The real work of the church
was to be carried on by the true successors of the apostles, the friars.
Such a role was not likely to commend itself to hard-headed pontiffs
like Boniface VIII and John XXII.

It is of no great significance for our argument to determine whether
or not the *De perfectione statuum* was in fact written by so great a theologian as Duns Scotus,[3] but it is of some importance to note that
the views expressed in it were not merely eccentric aberrations. On
the contrary, when the popes began to attack some of the characteristic

---

[1] *Op. cit.*, p. 559, "... ergo ad Papam Christi vicarium summe pertinet illum
statum fovere et nutrire, et de illo sollicitari et curare, per quem perfectissime potest in praedicta, et magis quam alium quemcumque, per quem non potest praedicta
excercere ..."

[2] *Op. cit.*, p. 533, "Ad tertium decimum, si tales non possunt nec volunt habere
dominium, nec dans sibi retinet, nec Papa habet, ergo res talibus datas quisque
capere posset qui vellet ... Tunc dico quod si renuntiet dominio talium, de necessi-
tate cedet in dominium Christi immediate, et per consequens ejus dispensatio solum pertinet immediate ad ejus vicarium, et sic nulli alteri licitum est eas accipere
nec auferre, et non potest Papa manens Papa tali potestati renuntiare."

[3] In 1322 Pope John XXII renounced all "ius seu dominium" in Franciscan
property. Referring to the text cited in the previous note Longpré argued, "Ces
mots *nec papa habet* ne se conçoivent pas si la bulle *Exiit* de Nicolas III est encore en
vigueur ..." (*Op. cit.*, p. 20) He concluded that the *De perfectione* must have been
written after 1322 and so after the death of Duns Scotus. Kirby (*art. cit.*) pointed
out that the words *nec papa habet* referred only to a hypothetical possibility that
could easily have been envisaged while *Exiit* was in force. This is true but it still
misses the main point. After 1322 the author could hardly have answered the objection in the way that he did without holding that the reigning pontiff had become an anti-pope. There is no trace of any such attitude in the *De perfectione statuum*. Most probably then the work was composed before 1322.

theses of the treatise concerning the relationship between the papacy and the Franciscan Order, the most respected leaders of the Order moved promptly to their defense.

At the beginning of the fourteenth century the whole field of Catholic ecclesiology was in a state of considerable disarray. Theologians were not certain whether Scripture was the sole fount of revealed truth or whether Tradition also was a source of divine revelation. The old doctrine of indefectibility was giving way to a different theory of ecclesiastical inerrancy, but this had not yet been given any clear, definitive expression; it could be twisted in different ways, either to attack the public insitutions of the visible church or to exalt them more than ever before. The proper structure of ecclesiastical institutions—the right form of government for the church—was again a matter of vigorous debate, with no agreement in sight. Conciliarists were attacking the principle of papal sovereignty. Dominicans, seeking to defend the papacy, were deploying Scriptural arguments that were bound to offend influential sections of the episcopate and that were very vulnerable to attack from traditionally-minded theologians. Franciscans were developing a theory of papal power that, although it was couched in deferential terms, could hardly in the long run be acceptable to the popes themselves. This was the situation when a new round of controversies thrust the problem of papal infallibility into the forefront of theological controversy.

CHAPTER FIVE

JOHN XXII AND THE FRANCISCANS

During the reign of Pope John XXII (1313-1334) Pietro Olivi's doctrine of papal infallibility was vigorously revived and re-asserted. This re-assertion of the doctrine, like Olivi's first formulation of it, emerged in the course of a complex struggle over Franciscan poverty. In 1322 John XXII undertook to revoke the provisions of Nicholas III's decree *Exiit* which had regulated the life of the Franciscan order since 1279. Then, in 1323, he promulgated a new dogmatic statement concerning the poverty of Christ and the apostles. The leaders of the Franciscans maintained that the doctrine contained in *Exiit* was intrinsically irreformable. From this assertion they advanced to a theory of papal infallibility based on a novel interpretation of the Petrine "power of the keys."

Pope John XXII strongly resented the imputation of infallibility to his office—or at any rate to his predecessors. The theory of irreformability proposed by his adversaries was a "pestiferous doctrine," he declared; and at first he seemed inclined to dismiss the whole idea as "pernicious audacity."[1] However, through some uncharacteristic streak of caution or through sheer good luck (or bad luck) the actual terms he used in condemning the Franciscan position left a way open for later theologians to re-formulate the doctrine of infallibility in different language. This is the tangled situation that we have next to explore.

1. The Franciscans and the "Key of Knowledge"

The intricacies of the Franciscan poverty disputes of the fourteenth century have been recounted often enough.[2] Our purpose is to tell

---

[1] The phrases *pestifera doctrina, perniciosis ausibus* are taken from the introductory clauses of John's Bull, *Quia quorundam*, which is discussed below.

[2] D. Lambert provides a convenient outline, *Franciscan Poverty* (London, 1961), pp. 184-246. G. Leff, *Heresy in the Later Middle Ages*, I (Manchester, 1967), pp. 139-255 gives a more detailed discussion of the doctrinal issues involved. See also D. Douie, *The Nature and Effect of the Heresy of the Fraticelli* (Manchester, 1932); F. Tocco, *La quistione della povertà nel secolo XIV* (Naples, 1910) (valuable documentation); K. Balthasar, *Geschichte des Armutsstreites im Franziskanerorden bis zum Konzil*

the story from a fresh point of view, to pass over so far as possible the subtleties of the arguments about dominion and use and right of use in order to concentrate on the changing conceptions of papal authority that the various participants brought into play during the course of the controversies.

In the first years of the fourteenth century the long-simmering disputes between the "Conventual" and "Spiritual" parties in the Franciscan Order boiled up into an open and violent conflict. The central issue in dispute was still the *usus pauper*. The Conventuals, the official "establishment" of the Order, maintained that the one essential feature of evangelical poverty was the abandonment of all legal rights to property "singly and in common"; the Spirituals, following Olivi, insisted that "poor use" was essential too. Pope Clement V (1305-1314) remained on the whole neutral in the dispute. He could not condone the excesses of the more radical Spirituals but he evidently felt some sympathy for their charge that the Conventuals had abandoned the real substance of poverty while still claiming to follow a more perfect way of life than any other Order in the church.[1] The situation changed abruptly with the advent of the next pope, John XXII (1316-1334). John was a professional canonist, an expert administrator, a strict disciplinarian; and, to him, the one outstanding characteristic of the Spirituals was precisely their indiscipline. He had some reason for his attitude. The desire of the most fanatical Spirituals to publicize their devotion to poverty sometimes expressed itself in mere eccentricities of dress and conduct; passive disobedience to the commands of superiors was giving way in some places to violent resistance; above all, the most extreme Spirituals had convinced themselves that they were actually living in the Joachimite fantasy-world whose coming Pietro

---

von Vienne (Münster-in-Westf., 1911). Again, the disputes of this period are discussed in the standard histories of the Franciscan Order already cited.

[1] F. Ehrle's studies are of basic importance for the Spiritual movement, "Die Spiritualen, ihr Verhältniss zum Franciscanerorden und zu den Fraticellen," *ALKG*, 1 (1885), pp. 509-569; 2 (1886), pp. 106-164, 249-336; 3 (1887), pp. 553-623; 4 (1888), pp. 1-90. For a more recent account see R. Manselli, *Spirituali e Beghini in Provenza* (Rome, 1958). Clement's Bull *Exivi*, promulgated after detailed discussions in the Council of Vienne, rebuked the abuses of the Conventuals but did not grant to the Spirituals the permanent exemption from the Order's superiors that they sought. On the discussions leading up to *Exivi* see F. Ehrle, "Zur Vorgeschichte des Concils von Vienne," *ALKG*, 2 (1886), pp. 353-416; 3 (1887), pp. 1-195; E. Müller, *Das Konzil von Vienne 1311-1312* (Münster-in-Westf., 1934); G. Fusseneger, "Relatio commissionis in concilio Viennensi institutae ad decretalem *Exivi de paradiso* praeparandum," *AFH*, 50 (1957), pp. 145-177; J. Lecler, *Vienne* (Paris, 1964).

Olivi had predicted. They believed that almost the whole church had apostatized, that they alone constituted the true church, that the apparent pope was Antichrist. John XXII did not take kindly to such ideas. From the beginning of his pontificate he waged a bitter campaign against the Spirituals in association with the new minister-general of the Franciscans, Michael of Cesena. The Spirituals' doctrines were condemned, their houses suppressed, their leaders driven into exile. A new papal commission, set up to investigate the works of Pietro Olivi, the patron saint of the Spirituals, soon discovered numerous errors and heresies in his writings. In 1318 four poor wretches who refused to submit to the pope were burned at the stake in Marseilles.

By 1320 the Conventuals seemed completely triumphant. The pope's next move came as a startling shock to them. Having demolished the position of the Spirituals he next turned to attack the central doctrine of the Conventuals themselves, their teaching on the absolute poverty of Christ and the apostles. In 1321 John XXII invited theologians to debate publicly the question "Whether it is heretical to say that Christ and the apostles had nothing individually or in common." A few months later, to facilitate the discussion, he annulled the prohibition of Nicholas III which had forbidden all discussion of the contents of the decretal, Exiit. John's Bull, promulgated in March 1322, introduced at once the theme that he would maintain throughout the ensuing controversy, i.e., the pope's absolute freedom to revoke the decrees of his predecessors whenever he saw fit.

> Because sometimes what conjecture believed would prove profitable subsequent experience shows to be harmful, it ought not to be thought reprehensible if the founder of the canons decides to revoke, modify or suspend the canons put forth by himself or his predecessors.[1]

To the Franciscans Exiit was almost a second foundation charter, the very Magna Carta of their Order. John XXII made no secret of the fact that he regarded it as a highly dispensable document.

The traditional account of how John XXII came to reopen the question of apostolic poverty is presented in the fourteenth century chronicle of Nicholas the Minorite. According to Nicholas the issue first

---

[1] Extravagantes D. Ioannis XXII in E. Friedberg (ed.), Corpus Iuris Canonici, II (Leipzig, 1879), Tit. 14 c. 2, col. 1224, "Quia nonnumquam, quod coniectura profuturum credidit, subsequens experientia nocivum ostendit: non debet reprehensibile iudicari, si canonum conditor canones a se vel suis praedecessoribus editos, vel aliqua in eisdem contenta canonibus revocare, modicare vel suspendere studeat."

came to light in a heresy trial at Narbonne where a Dominican inquisitor, John of Belna, condemned a Beguin for teaching that Christ
and the apostles had nothing individually or in common. A Franciscan
who was present, Berengar Talon, protested that, far from being heretical, this proposition was an orthodox doctrine of the church, defined
in *Exiit*. Both parties appealed to the papacy and so the contest
began.[1]

Joseph Koch has offered a more devious explanation for the opening
of the dispute. He pointed out that the commission which had recently
investigated the works of Pietro Olivi took a rather equivocal position
on Olivi's assertion that the Franciscan Rule was "truly and properly
the evangelical rule that Christ observed." If these words were taken
"according to the understanding and declaration of the decretal *Exiit*"
they were acceptable, the commission reported. But, if they meant that
the Rule of St. Francis was identical with the Gospel of Christ in the
sense that the pope had no power over it, they were evidently heretical. According to Koch's thesis, John XXII was unwilling to accept
even the very partial endorsement of Olivi's view contained in the
commission's report. He conceived the idea that Nicholas III's *Exiit*
stood in the way of a really thorough-going condemnation of Olivi's
Lectura and it was for this reason that he launched an attack on his
predecessor's decretal.

Gordon Leff has rightly pointed out that this hypothesis is mere
"speculation" unsupported by any evidence.[2] One might add that the
commission found no difficulty at all in condemning Olivi on many
grounds without also condemning *Exiit*. (This was what the Franciscan Conventuals wanted of course.) Koch's thesis, however, does at
least have the merit of reminding us that the existence of a routine
appeal to the curia would not in itself explain the pope's eagerness to
turn the affair into a cause célèbre. The appeal of John of Belna was

---

[1] Baluze, *Miscellanea*, III (Lucca, 1762), p. 207.

[2] J. Koch, "Der Prozess gegen die Postille Olivis zur Apokalypse," *RTAM*, 5
(1933), pp. 302-315. Cf. Leff, *op. cit.*, p. 161 n. 2. The commission's qualified condemnation of Olivi's text is given in Baluze, *Misc.* II, p. 261, art. 22, "Ubi videtur
de regula beati Francisci, quam vere et proprie illam evangelicam et caetera quae
de ipsa adjungit, quod si haec verba capit secundum intellectum et declarationem
decretalis *Exiit qui seminat*, verum dicit. Si autem intelligit, sicut ipse alibi declarat,
et sui sequaces asserunt, quod regula beati Francisci sit vere et proprie idem et
idipsum quod Christi evangelium et e converso, et quod Dominus Papa non habet
potestatem super eam sicut nec super evangelium, vel quicquid est in regula beati
Francisci, totum Christus ad litteram servaverit et Apostolis imposuerit obser-
vandum, hoc totum simpliciter reputamus haereticum et ridiculum et insanum."

at most the occasion, not the reason for the pope's action. The reason itself seems plain enough. In the course of his intimate dealings with the Franciscan Order between 1315 and 1320 John had come to see that the friars' most wounding criticism of the official, hierarchical church did not arise from any eccentric perversion of Franciscan doctrine; rather it was implicit in that very doctrine itself, as the most respected, conservative leaders of the Order understood it. The Franciscans taught that the perfect way of life which Christ had shown to Peter and the apostles required the abdication of all dominion, all usufruct, all right of use. If this were true then pope and bishops had long ago abandoned the ideal of Peter and the apostles. It was not simply that individual prelates failed to live up to the ideal. Rather, the ordered, visible structure of the hierarchical church failed to exemplify the Christian ideal at all. If the Franciscans were right about the essence of the evangelical life then John XXII and his bishops were not "successors" of Peter and the apostles in any full and meaningful sense of the word. And yet the Franciscan doctrine seemed to be supported by the plain words of the decretal *Exiit*. John XXII evidently came to the conclusion that his predecessor, Nicholas III, had made radical blunders in his dealings with the Franciscans—blunders concerning both church discipline and church doctrine. John was determined to use his sovereign authority as head of the church to correct those blunders.

The Franciscans reacted to the pope's pronouncement of May 1322, reopening the discussion of *Exiit*, with indignation as well as dismay. A general-chapter of the Order, meeting at Perugia in June, approved two encyclical letters defending the Order's doctrine which were addressed to all the faithful and widely distributed.[1] (John XXII, as he revealed years later in an angry interview with Michael of Cesena, regarded them as heretical in content and insolent in form.) The letters presented essentially the same arguments in two formats—a "long version" and a "short version." The long version of the Perugia encyclicals began with the assertion that it was no heresy but sound Catholic doctrine to affirm that Christ and the apostles, when showing the way of perfection, had no right of property or dominion singly or in common. The first argument to prove this ran as follows. No assertion could be heretical which was founded on the repeated determinations and confirmations of the holy Roman church; but the Franciscan

---

[1] Both versions are printed in Baluze, *Misc.* III, pp. 208-213.

assertion was so founded; therefore it could not be heretical. The major premise was proved by the texts of the Decretum asserting that the Roman church had never strayed from the path of the true faith and by St. Augustine's declaration that he would not believe in the Gospels unless the authority of the church moved him to do so. The minor premise was proved by the promulgation of *Exiit* and by the incorporation of Nicholas' decree in the official canon law of the church. (It was included in Boniface VIII's collection, the *Liber Sextus*.) Moreover *Exiit* was approved in a decree of the general council of Vienne which in turn was incorporated into the next volume of the *Corpus Iuris Canonici* and approved by the universal church.[1]

In a subsequent variation on this argument the Franciscans went on to maintain that no proposition ought to be called heretical unless its opposite was expressed either in Scripture (in the words of Scripture themselves or in the interpretations of Scripture by the Fathers) or else in the declarations of the holy Roman church. It was unnecessary, the authors observed, to add "unless its opposite is declared in the articles of faith" for articles of faith were themselves derived either from Scripture or from the declarations of the church.[2]

The Franciscan leaders were using the same conception of the sources of Christian truth that we have traced in some detail in the writings of Duns Scotus. Their arguments display the same kind of ecclesiastical fideism that one finds in his work. Scripture and church were equiparated as sources of Christian doctrine. Then it was further argued that, since the church could not err, a doctrine once accepted by the church

---

[1] *Op. cit.*, p. 209, "Major est evidens cuilibet Catholico, cui et concordant multa c. Decreti ut XXIIII. q. 1 c. *a recta*, et c. *pudenda* in fine. Et Augustinus contra Epistolam fundamenti dicens: 'Ego evangelio non crederem, nisi me Ecclesiae authoritas commoncret.' Minor probatur per decretalem extra *de verbor. sign.* c. *Exiit* § *porro* lib. VI. ubi sic habetur. 'Dicimus quod abdicatio proprietatis omnium rerum tam in speciali, quam etiam in communi propter Deum meritoria est, et sancta, quam Christus viam perfectionis ostendens verbo docuit, et exemplo firmavit: quam quoque primi fundatores Ecclesiae militantis, prout ab ipso fonte hauserant in volentes perfecte vivere per doctrinae ac vitae ipsorum alveos derivarunt.' Quae quidem Decretalis per aliam, quae incipit *Exivi de Paradiso* in Viennensi Concilio promulgatam, et in VII. lib. sub titulo *de verbor. signif.* insertam, est ab Universali Ecclesia approbata."

[2] *Op. cit.*, p. 210, "Nulla propositio debet dici haeretica, cujus oppositum non exprimitur evidenter in Sacra Scriptura, nec secundum se, nec secundum expositiones Sanctorum, vel cujus oppositum secundum determinationem Sacrosanctae Romanae Ecclesiae non apparet evidenter Catholicum ... Nec oportet addere, nec supra articulos fidei, quia omnes, vel ex Sacra Scriptura, vel ex determinatione Ecclesiae evidenter habentur et expresse."

could never subsequently be condemned as heretical. However, the Franciscan claim that their doctrine had in fact been approved by the universal church was very vulnerable to attack. Several popes had indeed referred in vaguely approving terms to the provisions of *Exiit*; but Nicholas' Bull had been more concerned with discipline than with doctrine and no subsequent pope or council ever affirmed that the doctrinal statements that it did contain had to be accepted as dogmatic truths of faith. Hence, although the Franciscan polemicists never abandoned the claim that their teaching had been accepted, for a time at least, as valid dogma by the universal church, they did not continue to rest their case wholly on this assertion. More and more they came to assert that, in any case, a single pronouncement by an individual pope could establish a dogma binding on all his successors. As their argument developed in this direction they deployed, as proofs of the irreformability of particular papal pronouncements, all the old Decretist texts which had originally been employed to establish the indefectibility of the church or the permanence of the ancient, central doctrines of Christian faith.

Something of this appeared already in the shorter version of the Perugia encyclicals. After stating that both *Exiit* and the decretal *Exivi* of the Council of Vienne (which referred approvingly to *Exiit*) had been incorporated into the canon law of the church this document added a further argement:

> And, as *Dist*. 19 c. 1 of the Decretum witnesses, what the apostolic see has approved as sound dogma is always to be adhered to and may not in any way be abandoned.

The interesting point here is that *Dist*. 19 c. 1 was introduced into the Decretum precisely to establish the point that individual papal decrees possessed binding force even when they were not incorporated in approved collections of canon law.[1] (Of course the original canon as it appears in the Decretum made no reference to the infallibility or irreformability of such decrees but merely asserted their legal validity.) Another Franciscan pamphlet of the time, perhaps by Bonagratia of Bergamo the proctor of the Order at the papal curia, put the case for the irreformability of papal definitions even more explicitly.

---

[1] *Dist*. 19 *dictum ante* c. 1, "De epistolis vero decretalibus quaeritur, an vim auctoritatis obtineant cum in corpore canonum non inveniantur." *Dist*. 19 c. 1, "Restat nimirum quod decretales epistolae Romanorum pontificium sunt recipiendae etiam si non sunt codici canonum compaginatae." Cf. Baluze, *Misc*. III, p. 208.

> If a pope revokes what one pope or several has determined concerning the faith ... the church falters and there is doubt concerning the faith .... If the declaration of faith varies the faith itself will vary and there will be many faiths, which is an error, for there is one God and one faith.[1]

The argument continued by asserting that the predecessors of John XXII, especially Nicholas III in the decretal *Exiit*, had defined the absolute poverty of Christ and the apostles as an article of faith and that, accordingly, a subsequent pope could not decree the contrary.[2]

To all of these arguments, which so plainly raised the question of the irreformability of dogmatic definitions, John XXII replied with the cold language of juridical sovereignty in his Bull, *Ad conditorem* (December, 1322);

> There is no doubt that it pertains to the founder of the canons, when he perceives that statutes put forward by himself or his predecessors are disadvantageous rather than advantageous, to provide that they no longer be disadvantageous ....[3]

At this point of the controversy John XXII seems to have viewed the issues involved in very simple terms. The idea that any decisions of his predecessors might be irreformable presented itself to the pope

---

[1] Alvarus Pelagius, *De planctu ecclesiae* (Ulm, 1474) (unpaginated) II, c. 60, "Item diversitas personarum Romanorum pontificum et cardinalium non facit ecclesie diversitatem quia una est ecclesia vetus et nova ... Nam si ea que unus vel plures papa determinat de fide vel fidei adiacentibus vel de declaratione evangelii alter revocat iam ecclesia nutat et dubia est circa fidem ... Nam si fidei declaratio variatur et fides variabitur et multiplex erit fides, quod est error, quia unus deus, una fides, Eph. IIII, XXIV q. 1 *Loquitur* ..." Much of c. 60 of Alvarus' work (though not the above passage) is copied verbatim from Bonagratia of Bergamo's *De paupertate* (1322), ed. L. Oliger, "Fr. Bonagratio de Bergamo et eius Tractatus de Christi et apostolorum paupertate," *AFH*, 22 (1929), pp. 292-335, 487-511. Bonagratia may be the source of the quoted passage also or it may be from some unidentified Franciscan controversialist. The whole of the material in Alvarus' c. 60 certainly comes from the period 1322-1323 since it discusses the question that John XXII posed for discussion in March, 1322—whether Christ and the apostles had anything singly or in common—without any reference to the pope's decision on the matter promulgated in *Cum inter* (November, 1323).

[2] Alvarus Pelagius, *loc. cit.* "Sed iste articulus declaratus est a predecessoribus domini papa Io. XXII, maxime a Nicolao III in decret. *Exiit* ... Ergo circa eum non videtur quod alius papa possit contrarium declarare per ea que not. XXV q. I *Que ad perpetuam* in glo. *ex hoc patet*." The author went on to argue once again that the doctrine he defended had been promulgated by a series of popes whose decrees were accepted by the universal church.

[3] *Extrav. Ioann. XXII*, Tit. 14 c. 3, col. 1225, "Ad conditorem canonum non est dubium pertinere, quum statuta, a se vel praedecessoribus suis edita obesse percipit potius quam prodesse, ne ulterius obesse valeant providere."

simply as a threat to his own sovereign authority. He was not entirely mistaken of course. The head of an ancient church may be an infallible teacher with the power to promulgate irreformable doctrines or he may be a sovereign ruler with the power to revoke all decrees of his predecessors. Perhaps, in a sensibly ordered church, the individual head would not be regarded as either sovereign or infallible. What is certain is that he cannot be sovereign and infallible at the same time. In so far as he perceived the dilemma at all John XXII was evidently determined to opt for sovereignty.

The Bull *Ad conditorem* was concerned mainly but not wholly with disciplinary matters. It declared that papal ownership of Franciscan property had proved useless to the papacy and harmful to the Order. Instead of removing from the hearts of the friars all solicitude for worldly things (as the Franciscans claimed) the arrangement tended to make them greedy, vain and quarrelsome. John XXII therefore relinquished papal dominion of Franciscan property and required the Order to assume the ownership of the goods that it held. The theoretical portions of the Bull, which are more important for our enquiry, attacked the Franciscan distinction between "right of use" and "simple use of fact." In the long version of the Perugia encyclicals the Order, following the language of *Exiit*, had proclaimed as an established truth of faith that Christ and the apostles, when showing the way of perfection, exercised only a *simplex usus facti* devoid of all *ius utendi*. John XXII declared that such a distinction could not lawfully exist. So far as goods consumable in use were concerned, the distinction was obviously absurd, he argued. A man exercised not only a right of use but actual dominion over a commodity when he consumed it.[1] But, even in relation to non-consumable goods, the Franciscan doctrine was still invalid. It was impossible for a donor to confer the actual use of an article; he could only confer the right of using it.[2] If I lend

---

[1] Col. 1226, "Dicere siquidem, quod in talibus rebus usus iuris vel facti, separatus a proprietate rei seu dominio, possit constitui, repugnat iuri, et obviat rationi ..." John continued that it was absurd to suppose his predecessor had ever intended to reserve dominion for the Roman see and use for the friars in such things as an egg or a piece of cheese or a loaf of bread. But that was exactly what Nicholas had intended. In *Exiit*, following the doctrine of Bonaventure, he explicitly mentioned food among the commodities of which the Franciscans had only the use. *Sext.* 5.12.3. "Ex quibus omnibus satis claret, ex regula ad victum, vestitum, divinum cultum et sapientiale studium necessarium rerum usum fratribus esse concessum."

[2] *Extrav. Iaonn. XXII*, Tit. 14 c. 3, col. 1227, "Licet autem quis re usibili absque iuri iutendi aliquo uti possit: ipsum tamen uti etiam in re tali absque iure utendi,

a man my horse, the pope pointed out, I do not confer on him the act of riding on the horse but rather the right to do so. To use anything without having a right to use it is simply to perform an illicit act.[1] It is important to follow John's argumentation on this point in order to understand the significance of the language he would employ in his subsequent dogmatic definition concerning the poverty of Christ.

The publication of *Ad conditorem* evoked a passionate protest from Bonagratia of Bergamo. In an appeal delivered to the papal curia Bonagratia repeated all his former arguments about the irreformability of the doctrinal decrees of the Roman see. He added, with a reference to the inevitable text of St. Augustine, that the authority of Scripture itself depended on the authority of the Roman church. And, just as the whole authority of Scripture would falter if the Bible were found to contain one single falsehood, so the whole authority of the church would falter if the Roman church once erred in faith or morals.[2] Bonagratia also maintained that the pope, as head of the church, was inescapably bound by divine law to support the Franciscans from the goods offered by the faithful in their behalf.[3] Finally, he declared that he and the whole Franciscan Order were enormously aggrieved by *Ad conditorem* and appealed against the Bull to the pope himself and to holy mother church, ending with the words, "And if the apostles can

---

separato a domino vel coniuncto, nec ab aliquo potest constitui, nec a quoquam haberi."

[1] Col. 1228, "Praeterea si simplex usus absque iure utendi haberi possit ab aliquo: constat, quod non iustus esset actus utendi huiusmodi reputandus ..."

[2] Baluze, *Misc.* III, pp. 213-221 at 219, "Et sicut non licet contradicere Scripturae Sacrae, sic nec auctoritati Sanctae Romanae Ecclesiae, cui ipsius Sacrae Scripturae auctoritas innitur; dicente Augustino contra Epistolam fundamenti: 'Ego evangelio non crederem, nisi me ad hoc catholicae Ecclesiae auctoritas commoveret': et sicut non est fas dicere, quod in Sacra Scriptura falsum aliquod, aut erroneum reperiatur, alioquin totius Sacrae Scripturae auctoritas vacillaret IX. di. c. *Si ad scripturas*: Sic non est licitum dicere, vel sentire, quod semel Sancta Romana Ecclesia praecipue in his, quae tangunt vitam, et regulam evangelii pro sana dogmate comprobavit, fore falsum, vel figmentum, quia pari modo tota Ecclesiae authoritas vacillaret."

[3] *Op. cit.*, p. 214. The argument was essentially similar to that of the *De perfectione statuum* (see above, p. 169). Anything given to poor religious who could not have ownership themselves was given "to God and the mystical body, the church." But the head of the church by divine law was the Roman pontiff. Dominion stemming from divine law could not be renounced. The pope as *universalis dispensator et administrator* was required by divine law to provide for the friars. Bonagratia did not openly state to the pope's face that if he attempted to renounce the Roman church's dominion he would cease to be head of the church but his argument certainly had that implication.

and should be appealed to in this case I do appeal to them, urgently and most urgently."

All the Franciscan protests of this period served only to increase the pope's exasperation with the Order and Bonagratia's indiscreet language earned him a year's imprisonment. Meanwhile the theological discussions in the curia were proceeding and at last, in November 1323, John gave his considered judgment concerning the doctrine of Christ's poverty in the Bull, *Cum inter nonnullos*. On the surface at least, this Bull constituted a flat condemnation of the whole Franciscan theory of evangelical poverty. It declared:

> Since among various men of learning it is often doubted whether it should be judged heretical to affirm with pertinacity that our redeemer and lord Jesus Christ and his apostles did not have anything singly or in common ... we ... declare that a pertinacious assertion of this kind shall henceforth be judged erroneous and heretical since it expressly contradicts holy Scripture from which undoubtedly the articles of orthodox faith are demonstrated ... and so, taking away all faith in Scripture (as far as it can), renders the Catholic faith doubtful and uncertain by removing its proof. Further, we declare, it shall henceforth be judged erroneous and heretical to assert pertinaciously that our aforesaid Redeemer and his apostles in nowise had a right of using those things which holy Scripture testifies they had ... since such an assertion plainly defines as unjust the practices and acts of Christ and the apostles in connection with the aforesaid things.[1]

The Franciscans' hostility to this Bull eventually led the leaders of the Order to insist on the irreformability of *Exiit* to the point where

---

[1] *Extrav. Ioann. XXII*, Tit. 14 c. 4, col. 1225, "Quum inter nonnullos viros scholasticos saepe contingat in dubium revocari, utrum pertinaciter affirmare, Redemptorem nostrum ac Dominum Iesum Christum eiusque Apostolos in speciali non habuisse aliqua, nec in communi etiam, haereticum sit censendum, diversa et adversa etiam sententibus circa illud: nos, huic concertationi finem imponere cupientes, assertionem huiusmodi pertinacem, quum scripturae sacrae, quae in plerisque locis ipsos nonnulla habuisse asserit, contradicat expresse, ipsamque scripturam sacram, per quam utique fidei orthodoxae probantur articuli quoad praemissa fermentum aperte supponat continere mendacii, ac per consequens, quantum in ea est, eius in totum fidem evacuans, fidem catholicam reddat, eius probationem adimens, dubiam et incertam, deinceps erroneam fore censendam et haereticam, de fratrum nostrorum consilio hoc perpetuo declaramus edicto. Rursus in posterum pertinaciter affirmare, quod Redemptori nostro praedicto eius Apostolis iis, quae ipsos habuisse scriptura sacra testatur, nequaquam ius ipsis utendi competierit ... quum talis assertio ipsorum usum et gesta evidenter includat, in praemissis non iusta ... deinceps erroneam fore censendam merito ac haereticam declaramus."

they condemned John's doctrine as a heretical denial of an established article of faith. This position was not, however, first formulated by the official leaders of the Order. For several years after the appearance of *Cum inter nonnullos* they busied themselves in attempts to prove that, in spite of all appearances to the contrary, the pope's language was not irreconcilable with their own position as set out in the Perugia encyclicals. The first overt condemnation of the pope's Bull came from a different quarter, from a group of dissident Franciscans who had taken refuge at the court of the excommunicated Emperor Lewis of Bavaria. Their protest, included as a sort of excursus in the emperor's Sachsenhausen Appeal of May 24, 1324, not only defended the doctrine of evangelical poverty and denounced John XXII as a heretic for attacking that doctrine, but also presented a novel formulation of the theory of papal infallibility. In this work, for the first time, the ancient teaching that one of the keys conferred on Peter had been a "key of knowledge" was used to support a doctrine that the pope was personally infallible when he used this key to define truths of faith and morals. It was a major theological break-through.

The central thesis of the excursus was presented after a lengthy argument designed to show that John XXII had indeed contradicted the decrees of his predecessors in the matter of Franciscan poverty. It should be noted that, in the following passage, there is no distinction between the decrees of individual pontiffs and the doctrines of the unerring "Roman church" such as one commonly encounters among the canonists. On the contrary it is precisely the decrees of "the supreme pontiffs" that establish immutable truths of faith for the church.

> What the Roman pontiffs have once defined in faith and morals through the key of knowledge is immutable because the Roman church is unerring ... what is once defined through the key of knowledge by the supreme pontiffs, the vicars of God, to be of the truth of faith can not be called into doubt by any successor nor can the contrary to what is defined be affirmed without the one doing this being manifestly adjudged a heretic ... what is once defined in faith and morals is true for all eternity and unchangeable by any one. It is otherwise in things that are established with the key of power. For often what it is fitting to do at one time, it is fitting to prohibit at another time.[1]

---

[1] *Die Appellation König Ludwigs des Baiern von 1324*, ed. J. Schwalm (Weimar, 1906), p. 28, "Quod enim per clavem sciencie per Romanos pontifices semel determinatum est in fide et moribus recte vite, est immutabile, eo quod ecclesia Romana est inerrabilis in fide ... Nam quod semel per summos pontifices Dei vicarios per clavem sciencie est diffinitum esse de fidei veritate, non potest per successorem ali-

The author of this doctrine has never been identified with certainty. The name of the Spiritual leader, Ubertino of Casale, has been proposed but without real supporting evidence. Franz of Lauten, Heinrich of Thalheim and Ulrich Wild have all been put forward as possibilities. It has also been suggested that Bonagratia of Bergamo wrote the "excursus", which appeared in the Sachsenhausen Appeal, as a separate tractate and had it smuggled from Avignon to Germany. This is an attractive suggestion, for there are many close parallels between the Franciscan excursus and Bonagratia's writings of 1322 (his *De paupertate* and his appeal to the papal curia). But the Sachsenhausen document also made use of *Quaestio* 8 of Pietro Olivi's *De perfectione evangelica* in defending apostolic poverty. Bonagratia had been an enthusiastic persecutor of the Spirituals before his quarrel with the pope and it has been argued that he would not have used Olivi's work approvingly.[1] In spite of this objection Bonagratia seems the most likely author of the Sachsenhausen excursus. Michael of Cesena and his friends embraced the excursus' rather eccentric doctrine concerning the pope's key of knowledge immediately after Michael's breach with the papacy in 1329. This is easier to understand if the doctrine had emanated from Michaelist circles in the first place.

The fact that the author of the Sachsenhausen excursus knew *Quaestio* 8 of the *De perfectione evangelica* suggests that he may well have known *Quaestio* 12 too—Olivi's *Quaestio* on papal infallibility. The intention of the author was certainly exactly the same as that of Olivi, to ascribe to the pope the novel attribute of infallibility in order to undercut his traditional claim to sovereignty so far as the decrees of his predecessors were concerned. However the specific argument about the key of

---

quem in dubium revocari vel eius quod diffinitum est contrarium affirmari, quin hoc agens manifeste hereticus sit censendus ... Et ideo quod semel est diffinitum verum esse in ipsa fide vel moribus, in eternum verum est et inmutabile per quemcunque. Secus autem in hiis, que statuuntur per clavem potencie. Nam sepe quod uno tempore expedit fieri, alio tempore expedit prohiberi." On the political background of the Sachsenhausen Appeal see especially R. Scholz, *Unbekannte Streitschriften aus der Zeit Ludwigs des Bayern 1327-1354* (Rome, 1911-1914).

[1] Ubertino's authorship was suggested by E. Knoth, *Ubertino de Casale* (Marburg, 1903). His arguments were criticized by F. Callaey, *L'Idealisme franciscain spirituel au XIVe siècle. Étude sur Ubertin de Casale* (Louvain, 1911), pp. 242-250. The use of Bonagratia's writings and of Olivi's in the Sachsenhausen Appeal has long been recognized. On Bonagratia see C. Müller, *Der Kampf Ludwigs des Baiern mit der Römischen Curie*, I (Tübingen, 1879), p. 86 and, on Olivi, F. Ehrle in *ALKG*, 3 (1887), pp. 540-552. For a modern discussion see F. Hofmann, *Der Anteil der Minoriten am Kampf Ludwigs des Bayern* (Münster-in-Westf., 1959), pp. 54-60.

knowledge was not taken from Olivi;[1] nor is it to be found in the writings of other theologians of the late thirteenth or early fourteenth centuries. In an earlier chapter we traced the evolution of the doctrine of the key of knowledge down to the middle of the thirteenth century and saw that it was quite unrelated to any theory of papal infallibility. Little significant development had taken place since then. The canonists continued to argue that in truth only one key existed, a key of power. Among the theologians, Henry of Ghent treated the key of knowledge as conferring an authority to expound divine truth but this was an unusual position and, in any case, Henry attributed the key of knowledge (understood in this sense) to private theologians rather than to the popes. The nineteenth-century author, Fidelis a Fanna, to be sure, asserted that Bonaventure taught a doctrine of papal infallibility when he attributed to the pope the "plenitude of the keys" and included among the keys of Peter a key of knowledge. But this is mere imagination. Bonaventure in fact gave an entirely conventional account of the common theological doctrine of his time, maintaining that the key of knowledge did not confer any *habitus*, any quality of intellect, but rather a form of juridical authority—the authority to inquire into the facts of a case as distinct from the authority to pronounce judgment.[2] This had become a theological platitude by the beginning of the fourteenth century. One finds the same doctrine in other Franciscans like Duns Scotus and Alvarus Pelagius. Augustinus Triumphus was of the same opinion and he offered a particularly interesting discussion because (probably writing after 1324) he overtly raised the question of papal infallibility in connection with the papal key of knowledge. He suggested that a theologian might argue thus. "The church cannot err. But the pope is head of the church. Therefore

---

[1] Olivi offered a merely conventional account of the key of knowledge in his commentary on Matt. 16.19 and, in his commentary on Luke 11, no discussion at all of the *clavis scientiae* mentioned there. For the Matthew text see MS New College, Oxford 49, fol. 107ra, "Secundum autem Rabanus per claves has intelliguntur potestas et discretio, potestas qua liget et solvat, discretio qua dignos vel indignos discernat. Secundum quosdam tamen discretio non habet rationem clavis nisi in quantum includitur in potestate ligandi et solvendi. Quia qui habet plenam potestatem iudicandi eo ipso habet potestatem inquirendi et examinandi et discernendi et tandem diffiniendi."

[2] Fidelis a Fanna, *op. cit.* (above p. 82 n. 2), pp. 15-16, 44, "Ideo etiam personalem Rom. Pontificis infallibilitatem adstruit dicens: Petro collatam esse clavem scientiae seu discernendi auctoritatem in sua plenitudine." For Bonaventure's real teaching see above p. 45 n. 1. Bonaventure actually used the term "power of the keys in its plenitude" to indicate that Peter received both orders and jurisdiction from Christ. (*Com. in 4 Sent.*, D. 18 p. 2 art. 1 q. 3, p. 489).

he cannot err in using the key of knowledge."[1] Augustinus rejected this argument as any orthodox theologian of the time would have done. The interesting point is that, in responding to the argument he had proposed, he reported on the common opinion of the age.

> Against this is the common opinion of the Doctors—that the pope can do all things when the key of power is not used to excess and when the key of knowledge does not err.[2]

The idea that the pope's key of knowledge *could* not err seems to have been an entirely novel contribution made by the Franciscan author of the Sachsenhausen excursus. It is a little disconcerting that such a significant development of doctrine cannot be attributed to any of the great theologians or canonists of the age but must be ascribed to some unknown, rebellious friar. The importance of his contribution lies in the fact that, for the first time, it drew the discussion of papal infallibility into the mainstream of Catholic ecclesiology. Olivi had indeed presented an earlier version of the doctrine. But Olivi's teaching had been generally ignored and there was a real possibility that it would have been forgotten altogether as a mere minor eccentricity of a theologian who, by the 1320s, was coming to be regarded as very eccentric indeed. The Sachsenhausen excursus, on the other hand, gave rise to a major controversy concerning irreformability and infallibility in which the pope and some of the leading canonists and theologians the age became involved. Naturally, orthodox scholars and the popes

---

[1] Augustinus Triumphus, *Summa de potestate ecclesiastica* (Rome, 1584), Q. 20 art. 6, p. 125, "Praeterea Ecclesia non potest errare ... Sed papa est caput Ecclesiae. Ergo non potest errare in clave scientiae." On the dating of Augustinus' work see Wilks, *Problem of Sovereignty* (Cambridge, 1963), p. 6 (following Ministeri). Augustinus presented a copy of his treatise to John XXII. It seems likely that, after the exchanges of 1324, he would have retouched anything he might have written earlier about the key of knowledge.

[2] *Loc. cit.*, "In contrarium est commune dictum Doctorum quod papa omnia potest, clave potentiae non excedente, clave scientiae non errante." Cf. Peter de la Palu, MS Toulouse 744, fol. 89va, "(Papae) non sunt sequendi, clave errante." Augustinus concluded his argument with a distinction similar to that of Hervaeus Natalis. Considered *formaliter*—i.e., as God intended it to be used—papal power could not err. But *per accidens*—as it existed in a particular pope—it might well err. "Sed per accidens et materialiter papa ... in clave scientiae potest errare." Again, this is an anticipation of a particular line of Gallican thought, not of modern infallibility. On earlier usages of the term *clave non errante*, referring to the sacerdotal power of absolution, see F. Gillmann, "Clave non errante?" *Archiv für katholiches Kirchenrecht*, 110 (1930), pp. 451-465. Gillmann shows how the phrase was invariably used to mean that there could be an error in the use of the power of the keys (against Sohm, who saw an implication of priestly infallibility in it).

themselves were slow to embrace such a novel and revolutionary doctrine; but from 1324 onward the idea that the pope might be personally infallible was never altogether absent from Catholic ecclesiology.

2. THE REACTION OF JOHN XXII

Pope John XXII reacted to the Sachsenhausen Appeal with all the glee of a wily old tactician who sees his adversary stumble into an unnecessary blunder. Good canonist that he was, John knew very well that the idea of the pope's possessing an unerring key of knowledge was a novelty, probably nonsensical and certainly unacceptable to all sound Catholic opinion. He proceeded to explain this at length in his Bull, *Quia quorundam* (November, 1324). The "father of lies" had so blinded the pope's enemies, John wrote, that they maintained:

> "What the Roman pontiffs have once defined in faith and morals with the key of knowledge stands so immutably that it is not permitted to a successor to revoke it ...."

This proposition was utterly erroneous, John declared. In the first place, it was erroneous, according to those who held that the "spiritual key" did not consist of knowledge at all but was simply a power of binding and loosing.[1] In favor of this view was the fact that every priest received the keys at his ordination, but evidently not all of them possessed any gift of knowledge. This argument restated the common opinion of the canonists and, most probably, reflected the personal point of view of the pope. However, he did not insist on it. Instead he argued that, even according to the doctrine of those who held that there were truly two keys, one of *scientia*, one of *potestas*, his adversaries were again in error. For if these keys could be used to define articles of faith then every simple priest (who received both keys at his ordination) could make such definitions—and this was absurd.[2]

---

[1] *Extrav. Ioann. XXII*, Tit. 14 c. 5, col. 1231, "Quod autem ... prorsus sit contrarium veritati, patet ex sequentibus evidenter. Primo quidem secundum illos, qui tenent, clavem spiritualem nequaquam esse scientiam, sed ligandi atque solvendi potestatem, patet, assertores, praedictos, ponendo esse scientiam, eravisse."

[2] *Loc. cit.*, "Adhuc secundum illos qui ponunt unam clavem spiritualem esse scientiam ... noscuntur evidenter errasse. Supponunt enim, per claves huiusmodi circa ea, quae fidei sunt, et alia, posse per constitutionem aliquam diffiniri. Claves autem, quae in sacerdotali conferuntur ordine, ad talia minime se extendunt; alias sequeretur, quod circa praemissa possent constitutionem sacerdotes simplices facere: quod falsum est evidenter."

There remained a third possibility. The term 'keys' could be used, not generally to describe the sacramental power of orders received by all priests, but specifically to designate the powers conferred on Peter and his successors for the discharge of their supreme pastoral office in the church. But even if this interpretation were accepted there was still no substance in the arguments of pope's opponents. They maintained that papal enactments made by virtue of the key of knowledge had a different effect from those made by virtue of the key of power. (Their position, it will be recalled, was that enactments made with the key of knowledge were irreformable but those made with the key of power were not.) This was evidently false, the pope continued. The key of knowledge (if we were to call it a key at all) was merely an *auctoritas cognoscendi*, an authority to enquire into an issue as distinct from the authority to pronounce a final sentence. No definitive decree could be promulgated with the key of knowledge. Either both keys were required or, if only one sufficed, then the essential key was the key of power.[1] Thus, at the end of his argument, the pope returned to his preferred position. He added (assuming now that *scientia* was not a divinely conferred "key") that a judge would of course be guided by the light of his knowledge in using the key of power and that Christ had been content to let this be assumed when he said, "Whatsoever you shall bind on earth it shall be bound in Heaven," without any reference to *scientia*.[2]

The exchanges of 1324 are of fascinating interest for a historian of the doctrine of papal infallibility. Here, for the first time, a doctrine of infallibility based on the Petrine power of the keys was overtly propounded. But the doctrine was fathered by anti-papal rebels not

---

[1] *Loc. cit.*, "Si autem intendant claves istas extendere ad generalem potestatem, attributam beato petro, suisque successoribus in personam eiusdem in commissione officii pastoralis ... adhuc claret ipsos errasse. Dicunt enim, alium affectum habere illa, quae per clavem scientiae, et alium illa, quae per clavem potentiae statuuntur, supponentes, alia per clavem scientiae, et alia per clavem potentiae statui, seu etiam diffiniri: quod evidenter est falsum. Per clavem enim scientiae, sive per auctoritatem discernendi seu cognoscendi inter lepram et lepram, (si ipsam dixerimus esse clavem,) nil aliud per ipsum illi cui datur, tribuitur, nisi auctoritas cognoscendi."

[2] *Loc. cit.*, "Quare restat, quod ad convenienter statuendum, seu aliquid diffiniendum, utraque clavis, scilicet cognoscendi et diffiniendi necessario requiratur; vel quod soli clavi potentiae statuere competat, et etiam diffinire; sed, sicut lumen materiale clavigerum in usum clavis materialis dirigit, et quasi quantum ad hoc obtineat scientia vicem lucis. Et hoc Salvator noster in promissione clavium facta beato Petro sensisse videtur expresse, quum post illam immediate subiunxerit: 'Et quodcunque ligaveris super terram, erit ligatum et in coelis, et quodcunque solveris super terram, erit solutum et in coelis,' nulla de scientia habita mentione."

by curial theologians. And, far from embracing the doctrine, the pope indignantly denounced it as a pernicious novelty. Some modern scholars have apparently found it so hard to conceive of a pope or his more extreme supporters rejecting the idea of an unerring power of the keys that they have precisely reversed the meaning of the relevant texts. Gordon Leff persistently asserted that John XXII claimed for himself a key of knowledge which gave him the power to decide matters of doctrine. But this is just the doctrine that John rejected. Leff attributed to John's enemies the view that "John XXII had illicitly made himself the guardian of the key of wisdom, when such a thing did not exist..."[1] But the view of John's Franciscan opponents was exactly the opposite. They did not say that John illicitly claimed the key of knowledge; they charged him with heresy for denying its existence. De Vooght made a similar mistake in discussing the work of John's ardent supporter, the Carmelite theologian John Baconthorpe. "Jean Baconthorpe (+1348) a consacré...un *quodlibetum* à la question de savoir si la 'clé de la science' permet a un pape de remettre en question ou de déjuger ce qu'un de ses prédécesseurs a défini. La réponse est négative, car 'il est impossible...que le pape et toute l'église se trompent.'"[2] Baconthorpe certainly held that, by the "ordained power" of God (as distinct from his "absolute power") the pope *and the whole church* could not err. But he plainly declared that a pope could revoke decisions of individual predecessors in matters of faith if they were in error. "There are four cases in which the pope can and ought to revoke (a decision) even if his predecessor established it. The first is in a matter of faith as if someone should say Christ was not consubstantial with the Father...As to the view that a pope can not revoke...what a predecessor has established in morals through the key of knowledge, he ought to do so when it contains intolerable error..."[3]

---

[1] *Op. cit.* (above p. 171 n. 2), pp. 241, 246, 249.

[2] P. de Vooght, "Esquisse d'une enquête sur le mot 'infaillibilité'," *L'infaillibilité de l'église* (Chevetogne, 1962), p. 120.

[3] *Quodlibeta Joannis Bachonis Anglici* (Venice, 1527), fol. 63v, "... dico primo quod esset impossibile de ordinata potentia dei quod papa et quod tota ecclesia erraret ... Unde sciendum quod quatuor sunt casus in quibus dominus papa debet, decet, et potest revocare etiam si predecessor statuit. Primus de fide ut si aliquis diceret Christum non consubstantialem patri ... Quartus si sit contra legem morum ... Contra hoc quod dicitur quod papa non potest dispensare aut revocare aut irritare in his que pertinent ad mores quod predecessor fecerit per clavem scientie quantum ad claves excommunicationis debet quando continet intollerabilem errorem ..." On Baconthorpe's life and work see B. M. Xiberta, *De scriptoribus scholasticis saeculi XIV ex ordine Carmelitarum* (Louvain, 1931), pp. 167-240 and, for his

Most commonly John's teaching on the power of the keys has been simply ignored by authors who have considered his pontificate. Noel Valois, who wrote the best general account of John's reign, made no reference to it although he gave an analysis of the other parts of the Bull *Quia quorundam*.[1] The controversialists of the nineteenth century paid some attention to John's decretals but only because the anti-infallibilists sought to prove that the pope had contradicted a dogmatic decree of his predecessor, while the infallibilists tried to demonstrate that this was not really the case. Neither side seems to have emphasized that the really important issues involved in the controversy of 1324 were the emergence of a doctrine of papal infallibility based directly on the Petrine power of the keys, and the vehement denial of that doctrine by the pope.[2] The whole situation was perhaps hard to grasp. It contained ironies within ironies. Not only did the pope's opponents rather than the pope himself advance the doctrine of infallibility. Further, that doctrine had been created by Pietro Olivi; and the men who gave it a new currency were not Olivi's followers in the Franciscan Order but their most bitter enemies, the Michaelists.

Let us return to the situation in 1324. Although *Quia quorundam* rejected so decisively the idea of an unerring key of knowlege, this Bull marked a change in John's attitude to the whole problem of irreformability. Previously he had been content to assert that, as a sovereign legislator, he could revoke any decrees of his predecessors whenever he saw fit. While he never withdrew this assertion, from 1324 onward John began to rely principally on another argument—that in fact he never had revoked any decree of a predecessor containing an article of faith.

It is impossible for us to know with certainty the reasons for John's change of opinion or (if his opinions did not change) the reasons for the shift in his debating stance. Perhaps he began to see—even if confusedly—that to exclude every possibility of attributing to the pope a

---

views on papal power, B. Smalley, "John Baconthorpe's Postill on St. Matthew," *Mediaeval and Renaissance Studies*, 4 (1958), pp. 91-145.

[1] N. Valois, "Jacques Duèse, pape sous le nom de Jean XXII," *Histoire littéraire de la France*, 34 (1915), pp. 391-630 at pp. 458-460.

[2] Döllinger, however, noted correctly that the Fraticelli "were among the first champions of that theory (papal infallibility), then still new to the church." See Janus, *The Pope and the Council* (Boston, 1870), p. 49. For a reply to Janus see J. Hergenröther, *Anti-Janus* (Dublin, 1870), p. 87. Other references in Lambert, *op. cit.*, p. 145 n. 4. The modern controversy is discussed in R. M. Huber, *A Documented History of the Franciscan Order* (Milwaukee, 1944), pp. 228-231.

power of making infallible, and so irreformable, dogmatic decrees could have disadvantages for the Roman see in the long run. The most obvious reason why the pope might have had such second thoughts lies in the fact that the conciliarists of the past thirty years had frequently stressed the erringness of individual popes in arguing that the pope was subject to the council in matters of faith. And the relationship between pope and council was a very live issue in John's pontificate. Marsilius of Padua's *Defensor pacis*, which once again contrasted the erring pope with the infallible council appeared in the same year as John's Bull *Quia quorundam*. The Sachsenhausen Appeal itself, to which John was replying in that Bull, was an appeal to a general council against the pope on the ground that the pope had fallen into heresy. Although he was a sound professional canonist, John was merely an irresponsible amateur as a theologian;[1] but he had good theologians at the curia. It seems that, between 1322 and 1324, someone conveyed to him that the issues involved in his problems were too delicate to be resolved purely and simply by a dogmatic reassertion of the canonical doctrine of sovereignty.

At any rate, while John never ceased to denounce the doctrine of an unerring key of knowledge, he refused to pronounce any further on the question whether the solemn dogmatic decrees of one pope could be revoked by another one and he persistently maintained that he had not in fact contradicted any doctrinal definition of Nicholas III. When, in 1328, John was accused of heresy for having declared in *Quia quorundam*

> That the supreme pontiff can revoke decrees of his predecessors in matters pertaining to faith and morals

he maintained that he had never asserted this proposition.[2]

But, instead of stating explicitly that he rejected it, he merely repeated the words of his earlier decretal *Quia quorundam*, and those words were very ambiguous indeed. The latter part of *Quia quorundam* was devoted to arguments which sought to prove that John's definition of apostolic poverty did not in fact contradict any established teaching of the church, while simultaneously maintaining that the pope could freely

---

[1] This became evident especially in John's erroneous teaching concerning the Beatific Vision which came as a boon to those who had already denounced him as a heretic. On this affair see T. Kaeppelli, *Le procès contre Thomas Waleys, O.P.* (Rome, 1936).

[2] Baluze, *Misc.* III, p. 309. The accusation was made by Michael of Cesena (see below p. 203).

revoke the decrees of his predecessors if he saw fit to do so. But each time that John attempted this delicate feat of intellectual tightrope walking his argument shifted so evasively from the doctrinal defini-tions of earlier popes to their disciplinary decrees that it is hardly possible to extract any coherent meaning from them at all. John began by stating the position of his adversaries. They maintained that he could not change the definitions of earlier popes concerning the pover-ty of Christ and the apostles. Actually, John declared, his predecessors had not defined the doctrine that his opponents were upholding. But even if Nicholas III had done so and even if a pope were bound by the decrees of his predecessors, the opponents' case would still fall to the ground; for if Nicholas' Bull contained the doctrine that they claimed to find in it, then Nicholas had contradicted *his* predecessors, and so, on the Franciscans' own premises, his Bull was null and void from the beginning. The argument is reasonably straightforward so far. It is at any rate entirely clear that we are dealing with a sequence of papal declarations concerning a matter of faith—the poverty of Christ. But at this point John's argument took a sudden twist. The main conten-tion of his adversaries was in any case mistaken, he wrote, for a pope was not bound by the decrees of his predecessors. To prove this John pointed out that, although Innocent III had decreed in a general council that no new religious Orders were to be instituted, his succes-sors had permitted the founding of such Orders.[1] Now this last point plainly concerned church discipline. The argument has moved in-explicably from dogma to discipline. If we assume that a clear distinc-tion can be drawn between the two kinds of decrees, the end of the argument has nothing to do with the beginning. The pope's conclusion was simply a non-sequitur.

John next produced another argument designed to prove that his Bull denying the absolute poverty of Christ was not contrary to the established faith of the church. (This was the argument he repeated in 1329 in order to prove that he had never asserted he could revoke the

---

[1] *Extrav. Ioann. XXII*, Tit. 14, c. 4, col. 1235, "... constitutiones illas, quibus se adiuvant, ostendunt, (si eorum falsae assertiones verae exsisterent,) fore invalidas, erroneas et infirmas. Si enim nobis non licuit contra constitutionem Nicolae IV (!) praedecessori nostri, in qua se fundant praecipue, aliquid statuere commune: nec sibi licuit contra statuta Gregorii, Innocentii et Alexandri praedictorum statuere aut aliquid declarare ... Adhuc patet, quod asserunt, esse falsum. Licet enim Inno-centius III. praedictus in generali concilio interdixisset, novas religiones institui: tamen successores ipsius, (non obstante interdicto huiusmodi,) plures leguntur ordines confirmasse."

decrees of his predecessors in matters "pertaining to faith and morals.") Addressing his adversaries John wrote, "Let them tell us where they read that it pertains to faith and morals to assert that Christ and the apostles had only simple use of fact." This proposition did not "pertain" to the faith directly in the sense of being defined as an article of faith in the orthodox creed. Nor did it pertain to the faith implicitly in the sense that, if it were denied, the truth of Scripture (on which the articles of faith were based) would be called into doubt. So far John seems to have been arguing that he had not contradicted a predecessor in a matter of faith because no issue pertaining to the faith was involved in the matter under discussion. But then, referring to the Franciscan teaching on Christ's "simple use of fact," he added, "This cannot be found in holy Scripture but the contrary can." Also, John wrote, holy Scripture did not assert that a pope could not renounce dominion of Franciscan poverty. Therefore he was free to do so and to revoke his predecessor's decision on this matter.[1]

Once again the argument was a tangled one. In this discussion John seems to have played on an ambiguity in the word "pertain." First he asserted that his opponents' views on the poverty of Christ (which he had condemned) did not "pertain" to faith and morals in order to prove that his own definition could not be contrary to any established article of faith whatever his predecessors had decreed. But, if the issue did not "pertain" to the faith at all, John had no grounds for denouncing as heretics those who disagreed with him. He therefore threw in the observation that their position was contradicted in Scripture. But if a doctrine is contradicted in Scripture then evidently either to affirm it or deny it "pertains" to the faith. John could not really have it both ways. (William of Ockham pointed this out in a later critique

---

[1] Col. 1236, "Praeterea dicant nobis, ubi legunt assertiones huiusmodi, quod ad fidem vel mores pertineat, Christum et Apostolos non habuisse in his, quae habuerunt, nisi simplicem usum facti? Profecto directe hoc ad fidem non pertinet, quum de hoc articulus non sit aliquis, nec sub quo valeat comprehendi, ut patet in symbolis, in quibus articuli fidei continentur, nec etiam reducte, ne quasi hoc sacra scriptura contineat, quo negato tota scriptura sacra redditur dubia, et per consequens articuli fidei, qui habent per scripturam sacram probari, redduntur dubii et incerti. Hoc enim in scriptura sacra non poterit, sed contrarium reperiri. De fratribus autem Minoribus praedictis constat, quod de ipsorum paupertate et simplici usu facti seu de dominio eorum, quae ipsis offeruntur, quod summus Pontifex illud sibi et Romanae ecclesiae reservaverit vel potuerit reservare. Nec, quod illud reservatum successori abiicere non liceat, si hoc expedire viderit, seu quod procuratores constitutos auctoritate summi Pontificis pro negotiis ordinis praedicti successor revocare non valeat, in praedictis symbolis, evangelio, neque Actibus Apostolorum et epistolis mentio aliqua non habetur."

of the pope's words.) And once again, it will be noted, the argument moved uneasily from a question about the irrevocability of doctrinal definitions to a conclusion asserting merely that the pope could revoke an administrative arrangement of his predecessor.

It may be that John's imprecision of argument grew out of a failure to come to grips with the whole system of ecclesiology that his opponents had adopted. Significantly, the Franciscans, in their Perugia declaration, maintained that articles of faith were derived "either from sacred Scripture or from the determination of the church." John XXII declared more simply "articles of faith have to be proved by sacred Scripture." The whole theology of "ecclesiastical fideism" that had dominated Franciscan theology since the days of Bonaventure, the belief that the church was a second source of divine revelation, supplementary to Scripture, was alien to Pope John. He had no sympathy with such a system and perhaps little understanding of it. He had been brought up in the canonist tradition that saw Scripture as the unique source of Christian faith. When his arguments slipped uneasily from the doctrinal decisions of his predecessors to their disciplinary decrees it was perhaps because he did not regard the two classes of pronouncements as essentially different in their intrinsic authority (at any rate in relation to a subsequent pontiff) in the same way that his opponents did. He seems never to have fully grasped the point of view of his adversaries who held that a papal decretal could constitute an article of faith that was just as certainly inspired by the Holy Spirit as the texts of sacred Scripture themselves. John's canonistic theory of papal sovereignty left no room for a theology of papal infallibility. He understood very clearly that he, as pope, was bound by the articles of faith set out in Scripture. He stood below them; he could not change them. But he would never acknowledge that a pronouncement of the church, still less a decretal of one of his own predecessors, could create a new, non-Scriptural article of faith that would likewise be binding on him.[1] When he tried to cope with the problem in any terms other than the

---

[1] Baconthorpe certainly understood the pope to be affirming without qualification that he could revoke the decrees of his predecessors on faith and morals. See his *Postill on St. Matthew* 16.18, MS Trinity College, Cambridge, B. 15.12, fol. 157ra, "*Et tibi dabo claves* ... De clavibus ecclesie tempore Ioannis XXII fuit ortus error magnus ut patet in constitutione sua, *quia quorundam*. Dicebant enim quidam filii mendacii quod papa sequens non potuit per clavem potestatis revocare quod predecessor suus firmaverat in fide (et) moribus, et sic falsificaretur quod hic dicitur, *quodcumque ligaveris* etc."

simplistic terms of juridical sovereignty his arguments became indecisive and unsatisfactory.

We can gain some further insight into John XXII's views concerning these complex questions by considering the glosses that the canonist Zenzellinus de Cassanis wrote on his decrees.[1] These glosses were carefully scrutinized by the theologians of the curia and one of them at least was rewritten at the pope's command. In their final form they were approved by John XXII. (Michael of Cesena later complained that, although Zenzellinus' glosses were filled with heresies, the pope did not condemn them but rather loaded Zenzellinus with honors.)

In the first version of his glosses Zenzellinus quoted approvingly a comment of the canonist Alanus on Alexander III's decretal, *Cum Christus*:

> Thus the pope can make new articles of faith, which is true in one meaning of the term "article of faith", that is (as meaning) something which has to be believed when formerly it would not have to be believed.[2]

John XXII's reaction to this text again illustrates his hostility to the idea that a pope could create articles of faith in the sense that he could add to the body of scriptural teaching declarations that would be binding on subsequent pontiffs. He found Alanus' comment unacceptable and insisted on a much more cautious form of words. In its final, approved version Zenzellinus' gloss omitted the above passage and stated:

> The pope can make an article of faith if "article" is understood, not properly, but in a broad sense as meaning something which has to be believed when earlier it would not necessarily have to be believed *by command of the church* .... You are not to understand through these words that the pope can make a new article through which new faith is introduced or the truth of faith is taken away from or added to as regards its substance.[3]

---

[1] On Zenzellinus see P. Fournier, "Jesselin de Cassagnes canoniste," *Histoire littéraire de la France*, 35 (1921), pp. 348-360.

[2] The text of Alanus is given above, p. 24. Zenzellinus knew it through Guido de Baysio's *Rosarium* where it was reproduced. The original and revised texts are printed side by side in Fournier, *art. cit.*, pp. 359-360. John XXII's letter absolving Zenzellinus from the censures incurred by the first version of his gloss is given in G. Mollat, ed., *Jean XXII (1316-1334). Lettres Communes* (Paris, 1904-1946), VI, p. 483, No. 28199.

[3] *Glossa ordinaria* in *Extravagantes Ioannis XXII* (Antwerp, 1573), Gloss *ad* Tit. 14 c. 4 (*Cum inter nonnullos*) s.v. *Declaramus* (col. 163), "Potest etiam articulos fidei facere si sumatur articulus non proprie sed large pro illo quod credere oporteat cum

These passages of Zenzellinus were presented in the course of a lengthy discussion concerning the pope's dogmatic constitution on apostolic poverty, *Cum inter nonnullos*. Zenzellinus was particularly concerned with the question whether the pope had propounded a new doctrine in this decree. He pointed out that, in defining the true faith, John had used the word *Declaramus*, implying that he was declaring a faith that had always existed. But in condemning the opposing point of view he had written *Deinceps*. (*Henceforward* it would be heretical to assert the doctrine of Christ's absolute poverty.) Zenzellinus explained the apparent discrepancy by referring to Pope Nicholas' decretal *Exiit* which, he said, seemed expressly to affirm that Christ and the apostles had nothing. Objectively, to be sure, this view was contrary to Scripture, and the doctrine Pope John XXII defined had always been the true faith. That was the meaning of the word *Declaramus*. But, subjectively, men who had held the false doctrine before the appearance of *Cum inter nonnullos* were excused from the charge of heresy because they were merely asserting a view that seemed to be justified by an earlier papal decretal.[1] That was the significance of the word *Deinceps*. In effect Zenzellinus was arguing thus. The true faith is unchanging; but a pope can make a misleading statement about the faith which will cause the faithful to fall into error; they will not be formally guilty of heresy, however, until a subsequent pope uses his sovereign power as head of the church to correct publicly his predecessor's false teaching. This was the quintessence of the position that the canonists had always held. It was most probably the personal view of John XXII. It was quite alien to the new theology of infallibility that the rebellious Franciscans were propounding.

On the power of a pope to revoke or reform the decrees of his predecessors Zenzellinus expressed himself vigorously and explicitly, without distinguishing between dogmatic and disciplinary enact-

---

prius ex praecepto ecclesiae necessario non opporteret ... Per iam dicta vero non credas papam posse facere novum articulum per quem nova fides inducatur aut veritati fidei detrahatur aliquid vel accrescat quo ad substantiam ...."

[1] Gl. *ad* Tit. 14 c. 4 (*Cum inter nonnullos*) s.v. *Deinceps* (col. 162), "Quod Christus et apostoli nihil habuerunt in speciali vel in communi, videretur ante expresse comprobari per decre. Nicolaii III, *exiit* ... Quid enim peccavit antiquitas huius constitutionis inscia pristinam secuta observationem? Nihil, ut videtur ... verbum 'declaramus' expresse denotat ante hanc decre. etiam tenendum fuisse quod Christus et apostoli aliqua habuerunt: non autem quod aliter tenere haereticum censeretur, et licet in veritate sacrae scripturae contradiceret, tamen illa interpretatio sumenda videri poterat per decret. *exiit*, ab haeresi quem excusans ante hanc decret. Alias frustra esset hic oppositum istud verbum 'deinceps'."

ments. Thus, John's adversaries plainly referred to doctrinal decrees when they wrote, "It is not permitted to a successor to revoke what the Roman pontiffs have once established in faith and morals with the key of knowledge." On these words Zenzellinus commented:

> I do not see how they have the insolence to say such things, for the Lord himself is found to have changed some things in the New Testament that he established in the Old .... And things defined by the Roman pontiffs are found to have been changed by the pontiffs themselves or their successors as in *Extra, De consanguinitate*, c. *non debet* ....[1]

As for the unerring key of knowledge, Zenzellinus wrote that the pope's enemies had created it as a fantasy of their own imaginations, since its origin could not be traced to any law, divine or human, at least in the sense in which the dissident friars employed the term.[2] Zenzellinus was equally scathing in discussing the Franciscan doctrine on the absolute poverty of Christ. The doctrine was plainly contrary to Scripture. To assert it was to assert that holy Scripture lied. And this was to destroy the only means of authenticating the Christian faith for,

> The faith cannot be proved among men except through sacred Scripture ....[3]

In all these explanations of John XXII's texts we may well suppose that Zenzellinus was merely stating without inhibition the meanings that the pope himself had intended to convey but had expressed more enigmatically.

3. Michael of Cesena

The final stages of the dispute between John XXII and the Franciscans culminated in an open rebellion led by the minister-general of the

---

[1] Gl. *ad* Tit. 14 c. 5 (*Quia quorundam*) s.v. *Non licet* (col. 170), "Sed qua fronte hoc dicere ausi sunt non video, cum et dominus per se ordinata in veteri testamento aliquando reperiatur mutasse in novo ... Et definita per Romanos pontifices ipsi iidem et eorum successores mutasse reperti sunt, ex. de consangui. c. *non debet* ..."

[2] *Loc. cit.*, s.v. *Clavem scientiae*, "Hanc clavem scientiae isti ex capite proprio sive phantasia adinvenire sunt moliti, cum a nulla lege divina vel humana originem sumpsisse reperiatur, saltem quantum ad hoc quod ipsum inducunt ..."

[3] Gl. *ad* Tit. 14 c. 4 (*Cum inter nonnullos*) s.v. *Per consequens* (col. 162), "Dicas quod cum scriptura sacra asserat Christum et apostolos aliqua habuisse, assertio contrarium astruens ex se dicit scripturam sacram mentiri et sic per mendacium quod illa impingit fidem eius tollit ... fidem nisi per scripturam sacram probari penes homines non possit ..."

Order, Michael of Cesena.[1] A few high officials of the Order joined Michael in his protest and subsequent exile but the vast majority of the friars submitted to the pope. Moreover, little that was new in the way of theoretical argumentation appeared in the exchanges between Michael and John XXII. Yet their dispute was important in the development of the doctrine of papal infallibility for two reasons. In the first place Michael accepted and re-stated vigorously the theory that a true pope possessed an unerring key of knowledge, thus giving a wider currency to a doctrine that earlier had found supporters only among the most radical, not to say lunatic, fringes of the Franciscan Order. In the second place, between 1327 and 1328 Michael recruited to his cause the brilliant young English bachelor of theology, William of Ockham. Ockham probably influenced late medieval ecclesiology more than any other one man; and he embarked on his career as a polemicist against the Avignon papacy wholly committed to the positions that his leader, Michael of Cesena, had adopted in the course of his quarrel with John XXII.

At the end of 1323 Michael of Cesena found himself in an agonizing dilemma. For years he had enthusiastically cooperated with John XXII in the persecution of the Spirituals in his own Order. He had hounded many of his brothers into exile; a few of them had been burned to death. Their basic offense was indiscipline, a refusal to obey the commands of their lawful superiors in the church, above all their assertion that the pope was a heretic, an anti-pope. From the time when John's dogmatic constitution *Cum inter nonnullos* appeared, Michael had to face the ugly possibility that his victims had been right all along in their central contention. John had apparently condemned as heretical the most cherished doctrine of the Franciscan Order, a doctrine that Michael himself had officially formulated as minister-general in the Perugia encyclicals. Perhaps then the pope was a heretic after all? Perhaps he was an anti-pope? Perhaps he was a fore-runner of Antichrist?

Michael of Cesena eventually came to assert all these things; but, understandably, he was deeply reluctant to be forced to such conclusions. The immediate reaction of the Franciscan leaders to *Cum inter nonnullos* was to devise intricate arguments trying to prove that the pope's Bull was after all consistent with *Exiit* and with the doctrine of the Perugia encyclicals. Pope John himself, we have noted, in-

---

[1] The principal sources for this dispute are the letters and manifestos of Michael of Cesena, printed in Baluze, *Misc.* III.

sisted that he had not contradicted any doctrine of faith defined by his predecessor so it might seem that a possibility existed of a mutual understanding emerging from the debate. The trouble was that the arguments which John XXII used to reconcile his position with that of Nicholas III were totally incompatible with the ones that the Franciscans brought forward.

John presented a number of arguments of varying persuasiveness; they are essentially the arguments that have been used by all subsequent controversialists who have tried to reconcile the two Bulls. Firstly John maintained that Nicholas had never expressed the view that Christ and the apostles exercised only a simple use of fact in the goods that they had.[1] This seems a mere verbal quibble. Nicholas declared that Franciscan poverty was the way of perfection shown by Christ and then went on to define the essence of that poverty as the retention of a simple use of fact divorced from all right of using. He quite plainly intended to convey the meaning that Christ and the apostles also retained only simple use of fact. On any other interpretation his arguments become nonsensical.

Secondly, John pointed out that Nicholas had described Christ and the apostles as abandoning dominion singly and in common only when they were showing the way of perfection and had plainly conceded that they held dominion—even of money—at other times.[2] This was a point of major substance. John's dogmatic definition left intact the whole Franciscan theory of condescension. The pope condemned a simple, unqualified assertion that Christ and the apostles had nothing; he did not exclude the possibility that they might have had things at some times but not at others. If the Franciscans had been content to adhere to Bonaventure's doctrine of apostolic poverty they could probably have reconciled it with the pope's pronouncement. But, basing themselves on *Exiit* and going beyond Bonaventure, the Franciscans had made it a cardinal point of their doctrine to assert that perfect evangelical poverty required not only the abandonment

---

[1] *Extrav. Ioann. XXII*, Tit. 14 c. 5, cols. 1232-1233, "Adhuc non apparet, ipsum dixisse, sustentationem Christi et Apostolorum eius in solo et nudo simplici consistere usu facti, quum quoad Christum et Apostolos nullam praefatus praedecessor noster Nicolaus in sua declaratione fecerit mentionem."

[2] Col. 1233, "Nam sic ipse Christus, cuius perfecta sunt opera, in suis actibus viam perfectionis exercuit, quod interdum, infirmorum imperfectioni condescens, et viam perfectionis extolleret, et imperfectorum infirmas semitas non damnaret: sic et infirmorum personam Christum asserit in loculis suscepisse."

of all dominion but also of all right of use.[1] And this Pope John XXII explicitly denied. His dogmatic definition maintained that use without right of use was simply illicit. Such a practice could not then be ascribed to Christ and the apostles even (or especially) when they were showing the way of perfection.

All the Franciscan attempts to reconcile John's Bulls with their own position broke down over this point. A typical example was the so-called *Concordia* of c. 1324 which was later incorporated into Alvarus Pelagius' *De planctu ecclesiae*. The author distinguished various meanings of the verb "to have." It could refer to simple use of fact, or to a prelate's right of administration over the goods of his church, or to dominion by divine law or to dominion by human law. Now Nicholas III had plainly taught that Christ and the apostles had only simple use of fact; and it was not to be presumed that John XXII wished to contradict the definition of his predecessor; therefore his declaration was to be interpreted in the same sense. When John XXII condemned the view that Christ and the apostles "had" nothing, he was quite right, for evidently the pope meant to assert that they "had" simple use of fact.[2] But of course this was exactly what John XXII did not mean to assert. His own way of reconciling his words with those of Nicholas went in just the opposite direction. Since a distinction between use of fact and right of use was impossible in the case of consumables and illicit in the case of other goods it was to be assumed that his predecessor had never intended to make such a distinction. But of course this distinction was precisely what Nicholas III had insisted on. The views of John XXII and Nicholas III on this point were in fact starkly irreconcilable with one another. Every attempt at a reconciliation ended with an elaborate pretence that one

---

[1] It is quite obvious that John XXII disagreed with Bonaventure's doctrine of poverty, e.g., in the matter of consumables. But he refrained from branding that doctrine as heretical in the dogmatic constitution *Cum inter*. On the other hand *Cum inter* did reject a distinction of Nicholas III by stating that use of fact separated from right of use was "unjust." John's radical disagreement with the whole Franciscan theory of poverty, even in its more moderate forms, became evident in his later decretals.

[2] *De planctu ecclesiae* (Ulm, 1474) (unpaginated), II, c. 59. The author is unknown. It may have been Alvarus himself. Bonagratia of Bergamo has been suggested. See J. Hofer, "Der Verfasser und die Entstehungszeit der 'Responsiones ad oppositiones'," *Franziskanische Studien*, 4 (1917), pp. 93-98; L. Oliger, "Fr Bonagratia de Bergamo et eius Tractatus de Christi et apostolorum paupertate," *AFH*, 22 (1929), pp. 292-335 at pp. 315-316; E. Hofman, *op. cit.*, pp. 66-68. Hofer's argument on the dating of the treatise is more convincing than Oliger's.

pope or the other had not maintained the position that he actually did maintain.

It was John's refusal to accept the equivocations by which the Franciscans sought to twist the words of his decretals to fit their own doctrine that finally drove Michael of Cesena into open rebellion. "He would not accept any concord that was made between his *Cum inter* and *Exiit* but rather persecuted those who did not agree with him," Michael complained after the breach.[1] At the chapter-general of 1325 the minister-general evidently still hoped for an accommodation and urged his friars not to show disrespect for the pope or his decrees. In 1326 John summoned him to Avignon to discuss the affairs of the Order; probably in the same year, Michael entered into secret negotiations with the excommunicated Lewis of Bavaria. Michael's journey to the curia was postponed because of ill-health and he did not arrive at Avignon until December 1328. He took up residence at the Franciscan house and there met William of Ockham who had been summoned to Avignon four years previously to defend his writings against various charges of unorthodoxy. John received the minister-general with apparent cordiality; but the pope had been informed by ambassadors from Perugia of Michael's contacts with the emperor and he was probably seething with suppressed rage from the beginning of the interviews. His anger burst out openly at a meeting held on April 9. The pope called Michael a supporter of heresy for his role in drafting and circulating the Perugia encyclicals of 1322.[2] Michael replied that the encyclicals were entirely in accord with Nicholas III's decretal *Exiit* and that to denounce them as heretical was to denounce Pope Nicholas as a heretic. (He later recalled with satisfaction that he had resisted the pope to his face, as Paul resisted Peter.) John ended the interview by forbidding Michael to leave Avignon on pain of excommunication. Michael returned to the Franciscan convent and

---

[1] Baluze, *Misc.* III, p. 273. Zenzellinus de Cassanis reproduced the arguments of the concord of 1324 and vigorously condemned them. *Gl. ad Extrav. Ioann. XXII*, Tit. 14 c. 4 (*Cum inter nonnullos*) s.v. *Declaramus* (col. 168), "Videtur etiam ... excusari non posse illos qui secundum praemissam modorum habendi distinctionem nituntur nodum praesentis constitutionis evadere; ex quo enim per decre. *ad conditorem* reprobatus est et confusus simplex usus facti absque aliquo iure utendi substinens in persona Christi et apostolorum ... asserere extunc contrarium qualiter quem ab imperitia poterit excusari non videtur cum (ut supra dixi) peccatum ariolandi sit non obedire et scelus idolotriae non acquiescere ..."

[2] Baluze, *Misc.* III, p. 238, "Dominus Ioannes ... asseruit me fautorem haereticorum et specialiter increpavit me de quadam littera Capituli ... quam litteram Capituli generalis frequenter dixit fuisse et esse haereticam ..."

there drew up an indictment in the form of a letter to the Franciscan Order which accused "the Lord John who calls himself Pope John XXII" of manifest heresy and appealed against him "to the apostolic see." A few weeks later, accompanied by Bonagratia of Bergamo and William of Ockham, Michael escaped from Avignon and took refuge with the emperor at Pisa. From there he issued a series of manifestos denouncing the pope. John promptly excommunicated him and replied to his charges in the Bull, *Quia vir reprobus* (1329).[1]

Michael's manifestos are enormously repetitive and they make tedious reading. It is impossible to extract a coherent system of ecclesiology from them. The author simply threw together in a kind of jumbled heap every possible argument that might tend to incriminate John XXII. He relied heavily on the doctrine asserting that a pope who became a heretic automatically ceased to be head of the church.

> From the very fact that a pope manifestly errs in faith he incurs a sentence of excommunication at once, nor is it necessary to await any other sentence of condemnation.[2]

This principle commanded widespread though not universal assent at the beginning of the fourteenth century. Michael's real problem was to prove that the pope was indeed a heretic. John XXII had declared that his teaching on apostolic poverty did not violate any established article of faith. Michael responded with repeated assertions that it plainly violated the article of the Apostles' Creed which declared "I believe in one holy, catholic and apostolic church," for this article implied that the Roman church could not err in faith and John had denounced the teaching of the Roman church.[3] If there is one central

---

[1] *Op. cit.*, pp. 323-341.

[2] The same arguments are repeated over and over again with a wealth of citations to the Decretum, e.g., *op. cit.*, p. 252, "Et illud quod semel Sancta Romana Ecclesia pro fide, et fidelium moribus approbavit, semper teneri debeat acceptum, et quod reprobavit pro reprobato teneri, XIX. di. *Si Romanorum* in prin. et XV. di. *Canones*, et c. *sicut Sancti*, et XXV. q. 1. *ad perpetuam* in tex. et glos. et c. *nulli*, et c. *Contra statuta*." p. 275, "Et eo ipso quod Papa manifeste errat in fide, sententiam Excommunicationis statim incurrit: nec est necesse sententiam damnationis alicujus alterius expectare." This argument was repeated with many Decretist references at p. 299.

[3] *Op. cit.*, p. 245, "Et considerans quod dictum pronunciamentum in articulum fidei 'In unam sanctam Catholicam et Apostolicam Ecclesiam' enormiter impingebat; sub quo fidei articulo continetur quod Romana ecclesia non potest errare in fide, quia Christus rogavit pro ea ut non deficeret fides ejus ... ad sanctam Romanam Catholicam et Apostolicam Ecclesiam appellavi." The argument recurred frequently, e.g., at pp. 250, 252, 273, 297, 307.

theme in Michael's letters it is this reiterated appeal to the faith of the Roman church. He was inclined to set the authority of the church even above that of Scripture. To go against Scripture was to offend against the article of faith, *unam sanctam catholicam ecclesiam*, "because the holy Roman church which is ruled by the Holy Spirit received and approves the divine Scripture of the Old and New Testaments..." The church was of such authority that Augustine had written "I would not believe the Gospels unless the authority of the Church so moved me."[1]

Michael gave no simple, clear answer to the question of how the faith of the church could be articulated with certain truth, preferring to accumulate authorities that favored his own side of the case rather than to discriminate between them. He asserted that the doctrine of absolute poverty had been defined in Scripture, asserted by a long line of popes, accepted by the whole church, and approved by a general council which could act on behalf of the church.[2] (John had already rejected all these assertions in his earlier bulls and he did so again in *Quia vir reprobus*.)

According to Michael, Pope John had also contradicted the holy doctors of the church, whose authority in expounding Scripture, according to Gratian, was greater than that of the popes. Michael here referred to *Dist.* 20 of the Decretum.[3] This was the text where

---

[1] *Op. cit.*, p. 247, "Quia quicumque contrarium Scripturae divinae a Spiritu Sancto promulgatae asserit, sive docet haereticus est censendus ... Et haeresis hujusmodi obviat articulo fidei, 'Credo in sanctam Catholicam, et Apostolicam Ecclesiam.' Quia sancta Romana Ecclesia, quae a Spiritu Sancto regitur, Scripturam divinam novi, et veteris Testamenti recipit, et approbat." p. 252, "... determinatio Sanctae Matris Ecclesiae, cujus tanta est auctoritas, ut de ea Augustinus ... dicat, 'Ego evangelium non crederem, nisi auctoritas Ecclesiae me commoveret.'"

[2] E.g., *op. cit.*, p. 251, "... sancta Romana ecclesia ... solemnem edidit Decretalem, quae incipit *Exiit, qui seminat*, quae in VI. lib. Decretalium sub tit. *de verbor. signif.* est inserta: et ab universali Ecclesia tanquam veram, sanam, et Catholicam Doctrinam continens accepta, quae etiam fuit postmodum in generali Viennensi Concilio approbata, et confirmata, sicut patet per solemnem Decretalem, quae incipit, *Exivi de Paradiso* in Lib VII." p. 252, "Cum igitur dicta determinatio sit in Scriptura divina fundata, et cum diffinitionibus Sanctorum Patrum, institutorum religionum approbatarum per Ecclesiam, ac Sanctorum Doctorum, Canonum, quod Ecclesiae concordet, ut superius est probatum: Et hoc pro sano dogmate in moribus ab universali Ecclesia sit acceptum ..." p. 266, "Nicolaus III ... non dixit quasi aliquid novum statuendo, sed quod erat a suis praedecessoribus Romanis Pontificibus doctrinae, et vitae Evangelicae, et Apostolicae, et Sanctorum Doctorum et Patrum Sanctae Romanae Ecclesiae auctoritatibus, et divinis testimoniis innitentibus dictum, diffinitum, et approbatum." p. 267, "... quod per Concilium universali fit, per totam Ecclesiam fieri censetur ..."

[3] *Op. cit.*, p. 277, "Secundo incidit in haeresim, determinando contra illud, quod

Gratian had attributed a gift of knowledge to doctors and a gift of power to pontiffs. A little further on, however, Michael used the same text to prove the existence of an unerring key of knowledge belonging to the popes. Here he came closest to the central question that concerns us, the irreformability of specific decretals of individual popes, for he re-stated and accepted as sound doctrine the contention of the Sachsenhausen Appeal, "What has been defined in faith and morals by the supreme pontiffs through the key of knowledge cannot be called into doubt by their successors." John was a heretic for denying this principle, Michael wrote, for what he really meant to deny was that the Roman church was unerring in faith and morals; and if one single error were admitted the whole authority of the church would be shaken.[1] John was also a heretic for questioning the existence of a key of knowledge since by doing so he cast doubt on the veracity of holy Scripture which plainly referred to such a key at Luke 11.52.[2] (John replied to this that he had never denied the existence of a key of knowledge and that the key of the Pharisees mentioned in Luke 11 had nothing to do with the keys of the kingdom that Christ gave to Peter.) Finally, according to Michael, John was a heretic because he stated dogmatically that he could revoke the definitions of preceding popes in matters of faith and morals.[3] (As we have seen, John denied that he had made this assertion though he would never simply affirm the contrary—that he was indeed bound by the dogmatic decisions of his predecessors.) This error, according to Michael, threatened the whole faith and authority of the church. If a pope

---

Sancti Doctores Ecclesiae de scriptura sacra divina sentiunt, asserunt, et exponunt, quorum Doctorum auctoritas in expositione Sacrae Scripturae praefertur, ut dictum est, Romanorum Pontificum institutis, XX di."

[1] *Op. cit.*, p. 287, "... non est licitum dicere quod Ecclesia Romana semel in fide vel moribus erraverit, quia sic tota auctoritas et fides Ecclesiae vacillaret." Here again Michael gave a long list of references to the Decretum to establish the irreformability of papal decrees. He cited 24 q. 1 c. *A recta* (c. 9), 24 q. 1 c. *Pudenda* (c. 33), 24 q. 1 c. *Haec est fides* (c. 14), Dist. 19 § *Hoc autem* (*dictum post* c. 7) and § *Qui ergo* (*dictum post* c. 8), 25 q. 1 c. *Contra statuta* (c. 7), 25 q. 2 c. *Si ea* (c. 4), 25 q. 2 c. *Ecclesiasticae* (c. 12), 24 q. 1 *Majores* (c. 2), 25 q. 1 c. *Sunt quidam* (c. 6), Dist. 15 c. *Sicut sancti* (c. 2), Dist. 19 c. *Ita dominus* (c. 7), Dist. 19 c. *Sic omnes* (c. 2).

[2] *Op. cit.*, p. 288, citing Luke 11.52, "Vae vobis legis periti quia tulistis clavem scientiae." Michael also noted that the ordinary gloss to the Bible interpreted the "key of David" at Apoc. 3 as a *clavis scientiae*.

[3] *Op. cit.*, p. 309, "Nonus error est, quia ipse in dicto Statuto, *Quia quorundam*, etiam dogmatizat, quod Summus Pontifex in his, quae ad fidem, et mores pertinent, potest suorum Praedecessorum difinitiones, et dicta revocare, et ejus contrarium statuere."

could change what his predecessors had defined in faith and morals the teaching of the church would become unstable and unfirm. Hence in this matter once again John had violated the article of faith professing belief in "one holy catholic church."[1]

In insisting that an individual pope like John XXII could fall into heresy while persistently affirming that the Roman church was unerring in faith, Michael of Cesena was restating an old problem of the canonists. In the course of the debates over Franciscan poverty, however, the problem had grown much more acute. The Franciscan polemicists found it essential to maintain that certain papal decretals, promulgated with the key of knowledge, could establish infallible truths of faith, immutable for all time. *Exiit* was such a decree. They also had to maintain, however, that other decretals, solemnly promulgated by the pope as dogmatic definitions in his official capacity as head of the church, were heretical aberrations from the true faith. Such a decree was *Cum inter*. How was a Catholic to know when the pope was being infallible and when he was being heretical? This was the dilemma that William of Ockham inherited.

---

[1] *Op. cit.*, p. 309, "Quia sequeretur, quod quivis Romanus Pontifex possit revocare, et destruere omnia in fide et moribus a suis praedecessoribus diffinita; Et sic tota auctoritas Ecclesiae vacillaret, et in fide, et moribus foret instabilis, et infirma. Unde dicta Doctrina est haeretica judicanda: Quia in articulum fidei: 'Et in unam Sanctam Ecclesiam Catholicam, etc.' evidenter impingit."

CHAPTER SIX

ANTI-PAPAL INFALLIBILITY: WILLIAM OF OCKHAM

William of Ockham is a difficult thinker. In his age, one might say, it was a complex fate to be a Franciscan. For fifty years the Friars Minor had been simultaneously exalting the authority of the popes and developing a theory of evangelical perfection that made an eventual clash with the papacy well-nigh inevitable. When a particular Franciscan possessed the sharpest logical mind in Europe and was possessed by an abiding conviction that the pontiff sitting on the chair of St. Peter had become an obdurate heretic, one would not expect his work to be lacking in subtlety. In fact Okham's writings on ecclesiology are so complex that modern critics have often reached diametrically opposed interpretations of them.[1] For Georges de Lagarde the *Venerabilis Inceptor* was "un éveilleur du monde modern"; for John Morrall he was "an interpreter and defender of the achievements of the past."[2] Some call Ockham a fore-runner of Martin Luther; others admire his Catholic orthodoxy. But, in all the extensive modern literature on Ockham's thought, no one seems to have considered the aspect of his work that is most important for our present enquiry— that is, Ockham's role as an early champion of the doctrine of papal infallibility.

---

[1] The best biographical study is L. Baudry, *Guillaume d'Occam, sa vie, ses oeuvres, ses idées*, I (Paris, 1950). Several recent works of synthesis discuss Ockham's ecclesiology in detail and provide full bibliographies of modern work. See C. Vasoli, *Guglielmo d'Occam* (Florence, 1953); W. Kölmel, *Wilhelm Ockham und seine kirchenpolitischen Schriften* (Essen, 1962); G. de Lagarde, *La naissance de l'esprit laïque*. Vol. V, *Guillaume d'Ockham: Critique des structures ecclésiales* (Louvain-Paris, 1963); J. Miethke, *Ockhams Weg zur Sozialphilosophie* (Berlin, 1969). H. Junghans provides a useful survey of modern controversies concerning Ockham's thought from a Lutheran standpoint in *Ockham im Lichte der neueren Forschung* (Berlin, 1968).

[2] De Lagarde, *op. cit.*, p. 337; J. B. Morrall, "Some Notes on a Recent Interpretation of William of Ockham's Political Philosophy," *Franciscan Studies*, N.S. 9 (1949), pp. 335-369 at p. 369. See also Morrall's "Ockham and Ecclesiology" in *Medieval Studies Presented to Aubrey Gwynn S.J.* (Dublin, 1961), pp. 481-491 and, for a similar point of view, C. C. Bayley, "Pivotal Concepts in the Political Philosophy of William of Ockham," *Journal of the History of Ideas*, 10 (1949), pp. 199-218.

1. Ockham's Ecclesiology: Form and Content

The difficulties in understanding Ockham's ecclesiology arise from the form of his works as well as from the complexity of their content. His most important writings on the structure and teaching authority of the church are not cast in the conventional scholastic form of his early writings on theology and philosophy; nor do they display the relative coherence and lucidity of his later treatises on problems of church and state. Ockham never wrote any really systematic treatise on the nature and structure of the church. His ideas were expressed principally in five works, all written between 1333 and 1338, the *Epistola ad Fratres Minores,* the first part of the *Dialogus,* the *Opus nonaginta dierum,* the *Contra Iohannes* and the *Contra Benedictum.*[1] None of these works provides a coherent exposition of Ockham's own views on the central problems of ecclesiology. The *Epistola* is useful for a brief summary of some of Ockham's major theses but it provides no detailed explanation of them. In the *Dialogus* Ockham deliberately adopted a mask, hiding his own opinions in the disquisitions of a *Magister* who expounded all the possible answers to problems proposed by a *Discipulus,* without committing himself to any particular solutions.[2] The other works were polemical treatises which took their form from the arguments of Ockham's opponents, often refuting them word by word for chapter after chapter. The *Dialogus* is particularly hard to use. One can prove anything about Ockham by simply ascribing to him the opinions expressed by the *Magister* in this treatise. We shall therefore follow the rule of never attributing to Ockham the views expressed in the *Dialogus* unless there is evidence from his other writings that he actually held an opinion presented there.

When one turns from the form of Ockham's writings to their content, one can discern two main lines of argument running through all the various modern interpretations of his thought. Those scholars who approach Ockham's ecclesiology by way of his nominalistic

---

[1] *Dialogus* in M. Goldast, *Monarchia S. Romani imperii* II (Frankfurt, 1614), pp. 392-957; *Opus nonaginta dierum* in J. G. Sikes etc. (eds.), *Guillelmi de Ockham opera politica,* 3 vols. (Manchester, 1940-1956), I, pp. 287-374, II, pp. 1-858; *Epistola ad Fratres Minores, Opera politica,* III, pp. 1-17; *Tractatus contra Ioannem, Opera politica,* III, pp. 19-156; *Tractatus contra Benedictum, Opera politica,* III, pp. 157-322. On the dating of these works see Junghans, *op. cit.,* pp. 94-98.

[2] In the *Opus nonaginta dierum* also Ockham declared that he was merely presenting the arguments of Michael of Cesena and his supporters against John XXII. But, at the time he wrote, Ockham had publicly identified himself with the Michaelist party.

philosophy and find a close interconnection between the two spheres usually regard him as a radical innovator—e.g., Dempf, de Lagarde, Wilks. Those who seek to explain Ockham's theology of the church by seeking out sources for his ideas in earlier juristic and theological writings often succeed in convincing themselves of his essential conservatism—e.g., Boehner, Morrall, Kölmel.

Neither approach seems altogether satisfactory. In the first place, none of the various modern attempts to derive Ockham's ecclesiology from the premises of his nominalistic philosophy has proved entirely convincing. To be sure, Ockham's theology and his philosophy are not inconsistent with one another; in reading Ockham's work it is one mind that we have to deal with, not two. Modern scholars need feel no temptation to postulate schizophrenia in order to explain his varied literary output, as in the case of Pietro Olivi. Yet Boehner was certainly correct when he wrote, "Ockham's political ideas ... could have been developed from ... any of the classical metaphysics of the 13th. century,"[1] and the same is true of Ockham's ecclesiology. In the course of late medieval thought as a whole there seems to be no correspondence between an acceptance of philosophical nominalism and an espousal of the doctrines most characteristic of Ockham's theory of the church. For example, Ockham's ecclesiology was animated through and through by a conviction that virtually the whole body of Christians might apostatize from the truths of Scripture. The closest approximation to Ockham's treatment of this question that we have encountered in earlier literature was in the work of Henry of Ghent. His philosophy has been described as a form of *Aristotélisme platonisant*[2]—and in any case Henry's argument seems to have been inspired more by his concern over practical problems of church governance than by his metaphysical presuppositions. Some later nominalists were extreme conciliarists, which Ockham certainly was not, while Wyclif and Hus, who shared Ockham's skepticism about the definitive authority of a general council, are usually regarded as metaphysical realists. Moreover, it is by no means clear in principle that any valid argument can be constructed which proceeds exclusively from a given set of

---

[1] P. Boehner, "Ockham's Political Ideas," in *Collected Articles on Ockham*, ed. E. M. Buytaert (St. Bonaventure, N.Y., 1958), pp. 442-468 at p. 446. Boehner continued "... for, as will be shown, they coincide with a sound Catholic political theory." On this see Junghans, *op. cit.*, pp. 275-277.

[2] De Lagarde, *La naissance*. Vol. II, *Secteur social de la scolastique* (Louvain-Paris, 1958), p. 161. On the views of Henry of Ghent see above, p. 136.

metaphysical premises to reach necessary conclusions concerning the structure of the church.[1]

As to the argument that Ockham's work contains many traditional elements of thought, this is true enough in itself. But it does not establish that Ockham's position as a whole was conservative. Ockham was in fact a radical, even revolutionary, critic of the structure of the medieval church. Almost every strand of doctrine that we have traced out so far will be found interwoven at some point into the fabric of his thought—Bonaventure's teaching on the inerrancy of the universal church, Henry of Ghent's development of the doctrine of indefectibility, Olivi's insistence on the infallibility of a true pope. But Ockham wove the old strands into new patterns. In general, his ecclesiology can best be understood as an attempt—not altogether successful—to combine in a novel synthesis the two major traditions of Catholic thought that we have already explored in some detail: the classical canonistic tradition which emphasized the indefectibility of the universal church while acknowledging that any individual Catholic, even the pope, could fall into heresy (a tradition continued by the episcopalist theologians); and the Franciscan theological tradition which emphasized the infallibility of the church, the progressive revelation of Christian truth through the course of the ages, and the necessary role of the pope as the authenticator of newly revealed truth.[2]

The importance of this last aspect of traditional Franciscan ecclesiology in the thought of William of Ockham has not been sufficiently emphasized. Even the writers who have argued most strongly for Ockham's Catholic orthodoxy have not thought to present the *Venerabilis Inceptor* as a defender of papal infallibility. Yet Ockham did insist

---

[1] This is the essential point. One can raise doubts about the metaphysical stance of almost any medieval thinker (most obviously about that of Ockham himself). J. Paulus succeeded in finding elements of nominalism blended with extreme platonic realism in the work of Henry of Ghent. See his *Henri de Gand. Essai sur les tendances de sa métaphysique* (Paris, 1938) and de Lagarde, *op. cit.*, pp. 164-170. M. Wilks has denied that Wyclif was a philosophical realist. M. J. Wilks, "The Early Oxford Wyclif: Papalist or Nominalist?" *Studies in Church History*, 5 (1969), pp. 69-98. The truth is that all medieval philosophers were eclectics, even if sometimes unconsciously so. For us, to repeat, the essential point is that, in the case of all the authors mentioned, their ecclesiological conclusions did not follow as necessary deductions from their metaphysical premises.

[2] These two sources of Ockham's thought are discussed in my articles, "Ockham, the Conciliar Theory and the Canonists," *Journal of the History of Ideas*, 15 (1954), pp. 40-70; "From Thomas of York to William of Ockham," in the forthcoming proceedings of the conference *De historia sollicitudinis omnium ecclesiarum*.

on the infallibility of the church and on the irreformability of decrees promulgated by the pope as head of the church on matters of faith and morals; and these were the essential elements of the doctrine of papal infallibility that came to be defined in 1870. A widely held point of view suggests that, when Ockham insisted on the proneness to error of a pontiff occupying the Roman see, he was explicitly attacking an old doctrine of papal infallibility. The truth is just the opposite. We should say rather that, when Ockham insisted on the irreformability of a true pope's doctrinal decrees, he was implicitly affirming a new doctrine of papal infallibility. What he was attacking was the old doctrine of papal sovereignty.

It may still seem that to call Ockham a champion of papal infallibility is willfully to use the language of paradox. We know, after all, that his whole concern over problems of ecclesiology grew out of a conviction that popes could err in faith and that, indeed, the reigning pope was a heretic. Accordingly, modern writers of all shades of opinion have insisted that Ockham rejected any idea of papal infallibility. "Il nie résolument l'infaillibilité du pape." "Ockham does not believe in the infallibility of the Pope." "... ist auch nicht zu erwarten dass er ein unfehlbares Lehramt anerkennt." "... egli potrà subito rivolgersi contro i sostenitori dell'infallibilità pontificia..."[1] But, if Ockham's doctrine was paradoxical, it was no more paradoxical than the modern theology of infallibility. Modern doctrine does not assert that a pope cannot err; it presumes the possibility of error in virtually all of a pope's official pronouncements. Modern theologians typically assert only that certain very rare and hard-to-identify papal documents express catholic truth infallibly. The criteria for determining that a given statement is indeed infallible are very exacting. Theologians assign to themselves the task of deciding which particular papal pronouncements meet these exacting criteria. Ockham claimed the same role for himself. The failure of modern scholars to emphasize the fact perhaps arises from the widespread assumption that any early defender of papal infallibility (in any form of the doctrine) must necessarily have been an ardent partisan of some extreme theory of papal sovereignty. But, as we have so often noted, this is a fallacy.

Infallibility can be a corrosive concept in Catholic ecclesiology if all its implications are explored both rigorously and audaciously.

---

[1] A. van Leeuwen, "L'église, règle de foi, dans les écrits de Guillaume d'Occam," *Ephemerides theologicae Lovanienses*, 11 (1934), pp. 249-288 at p. 288; P. Boehner, *op. cit.*, p. 453 n. 19; W. Kölmel, *op. cit.*, p. 191; C. Vasoli, *op. cit.*, p. 280.

Ockham's work demonstrates this truth in the highest degree. We have suggested that the principal elements of his doctrine were derived from two earlier traditions of ecclesiology—essentially a canonistic legal tradition and a Franciscan theological tradition. But the way in which Ockham combined those traditions to reach his own novel conclusions becomes comprehensible only when we remember the actual historical circumstances in which he lived and wrote. Ockham believed that he and his friends constituted a tiny minority who held fast to the Catholic faith at a time when almost the whole organized church had abandoned it. There are no traces of Joachimite fantasy in his work and no evidence that he was directly influenced by Pietro Olivi but he was concerned with the same problem of defending the true church against a heretical pseudo-pope that Olivi had so vividly envisaged. Olivi's nightmare had become Ockham's everyday, waking world. Ockham's task, as he himself saw it, was to uphold the sound, Catholic definitions of the past against the heretical aberrations of his own day. Accordingly, he argued in his first polemical treatise, the *Opus nonaginta dierum* that the authentic papal definitions of the past were immutable and irreformable. They established Catholic truth for all time. He devoted substantial sections of this and succeeding works to showing how, in the hands of a sufficiently skilled logician, this principle of irreformability could become subversive of all existing ecclesiastical order.

2. Irreformability and the "Rule of Faith"

We can perhaps best pick our way through the shifting arguments of Ockham's polemics by asking persistently a question that Ockham himself asked often enough. How can a Christian know with certitude the truths of faith that he is bound to know in order to attain salvation?

Ockham gave a first answer to our question in his *Opus nonaginta dierum* (1333). "What the supreme pontiffs have once defined with the key of knowledge stands immutably." Ockham denounced Pope John XXII as a heretic for rejecting this principle. Similarly in his letter to the Franciscan general chapter of 1333 he denounced John for asserting that the Roman pontiff could revoke the decisions of his predecessors in matters of faith and morals.[1] Ockham had, so to speak, inherited these arguments from his leader, Michael of Cesena, who

---

[1] *OND*, p. 833; *Epistola ad Fratres Minores*, p. 14. Similarly *Contra Ioannem*, p. 118.

in turn had borrowed them from the Sachsenhausen Appeal of 1324. Ockham made them his own and defended them in a long intricate passage of the *Opus nonaginta dierum*. Like all the Franciscans of his party he relied heavily on Nicholas III's decretal, *Exiit* in discussing the problems of Franciscan poverty. To establish the immutability of this decree was essential to his position. Accordingly, Ockham committed himself from the outset to the doctrine that authentic papal decrees expressed Catholic truth with unfailing certainty. On the other hand he displayed an evident uneasiness in using the concept of an unerring "key of knowledge" to defend that doctrine. As a young bachelor of theology he had studied the Sentences and written his own commentary on them. He must have known perfectly well that Michael of Cesena's use of the term *clavis scientiae* was an unsanctified novelty, with no roots in preceding theological tradition. Ockham was determined to prove that Michael's doctrine was entirely free from actual error and he was anxious to prove, if at all possible, that the terms in which John XXII had condemned it were heretical. But the main thrust of his argument was to prove that the doctrine of the irreformability of papal decrees on faith and morals could be expressed just as well without the argument from the key of knowledge as with it.

In order to follow Ockham's arguments we must remind ourselves of John XXII's position. John's adversaries had declared that a pope could not revoke anything his predecessors had established "with the key of knowledge" although he could revoke what they established "with the key of power." John explicitly condemned this teaching. But, when challenged on the point, John would not admit that his condemnation was equivalent to a simple assertion that he could revoke the dogmatic decrees of earlier popes. His technical argumentation had in fact been based on the view that no decree could be promulgated "with the key of knowledge." Probably the pope did not possess any key of knowledge, the pope maintained in *Quia vir reprobus*, and certainly the key of knowledge mentioned at Luke 11.52 was not one of the keys of the kingdom of heaven that Christ conferred on Peter. The text of Luke could be interpreted as referring simply to faith in Christ or to the humility that was necessary for a clear understanding of Scripture. And of course Peter possessed faith and humility before he ever received the gift of the keys. In any case, even if the pope did in some sense possess a key of knowledge, that key had nothing to do with the defining of doctrine.

Any scholar who takes the trouble to compare Ockham's arguments point by point with the assertions of John XXII will probably feel that the pope had the best of this particular controversy. Ockham found that he could not defend the arguments of Michael of Cesena without radically reformulating them. Moreover, in order to prove John XXII guilty of heresy, he had constantly to impute to the pope a view that John may well have held but that he had carefully refrained from formulating explicitly—the view that he could revoke at will any dogmatic decrees of his predecessors. At one point Ockham showed himself aware of the difficulty. It might be argued, he admitted, that the pope did not actually hold the position that his writings seemed to imply. To this Ockham replied: Let the pope express his mind clearly! It was not for an appellant to search the secret heart of his adversary. If the pope would plainly and simply profess that he was bound by the decrees of his predecessors in matters of faith Ockham would not hold him guilty of heresy on this particular count![1] Pope John, of course, never took advantage of this invitation to clarify his position.

We shall not present here all the twists and turns of Ockham's arguments. Briefly, they ran like this. Even those doctors who denied that, in a strict sense, a key of knowledge was conferred on all priests at their ordination admitted that the knowledge a priest possessed beforehand could become a key after he received holy orders.[2] So too Peter had possessed faith and humility beforehand, but they became "keys of the kingdom of Heaven" after Christ said to him "Tibi dabo claves...."[3] In any case it was not necessary to prove that the *clavis scientiae* was one of the keys of the kingdom of Heaven in order to uphold Michael of Cesena's position. One had only to prove

> that a matter pertaining to faith and morals can be defined by the Roman pontiffs through some kind of key of knowledge, whether it is called a key of the church or not, and that anything rightly so defined cannot be called into question.[4]

---

[1] *OND*, p. 836.

[2] *OND*, pp. 827-828, citing Johannes Teutonicus and Peter Lombard.

[3] *OND*, pp. 830-831, "*Hanc clavem, scilicet fidem, habebat Petrus, antequam Dominus sibi promitteret regni caelorum claves*: Hoc concedi potest; et tamen illa fides Petri, quae erat aliquo modo clavis, non erat clavis regni caelorum, sed postea facta fuit clavis regni caelorum, sub fide includendo scientiam discernendi inter lepram et lepram."

[4] *OND*, p. 834, "... sufficit ostendere quod per aliquam clavem scientiae, sive debeat vocari clavis regni caelorum sive ecclesiae, sive non, aliquid potest in fide et

John XXII himself had admitted that a key of knowledge existed which could be defined as faith in Christ. Obviously a pope could define in matters of doctrine by virtue of his Christian faith. Therefore, he could define with the key of knowledge. And so, when John denied that papal definitions made with the key of knowledge were irreformable, he was actually intending to deny the whole principle of irreformability.[1] The phrase *per clavem scientiae* was not essential to the argument of John's adversaries. It was, in a sense, superfluous and if it were omitted a lot of "frivolous" objections to their position would disappear.[2] What John's adversaries really meant to affirm was simply this:

> What the Roman pontiffs have once defined in faith and morals—whether through the key of knowledge or the key of power or through the papal authority or through any power whatsoever—stands so immutably that a successor cannot call it into question or affirm the contrary.[3]

This proposition, which Ockham vigorously defended, provides us with an explicit definition of an extreme doctrine of papal infallibility—more extreme, indeed, than the doctrine defined in 1870. Ockham had still one objection to consider, however, and in meeting it he introduced some significant refinements of thought. If the key of knowledge was simply faith, and if irreformable definitions could be promulgated with the key of knowledge, it seemed that any Christian could promulgate such definitions. But in fact, Ockham admitted, only the pope or a general council could definitively settle disputes concerning the faith. To be sure, any theologian could "define" in the sense of asserting the truth. But to define in the strict sense of the word required also the "authority and power of jurisdiction."[4] It

---

moribus a Romanis pontificibus diffiniri, et quod sic diffinitum rite non potest in dubium revocari, nec debet eius contrarium diffiniri."

[1] *OND*, p. 835, "Quare, cum iste impugnatus neget illam propositionem cum dicta additione, debet eam negare absolute sine illa additione."

[2] *OND*, p. 835, "... tamen ista adiectio 'per clavem scientiae' quodam modo videtur superflua, et sine ipsa ita haberent intentum impugnatores istius impugati, sicut cum ea. Et si illam adiectionem 'per clavem scientiae' dimisissent, multae instantiae frivolae contra processum eorum exclusae fuissent."

[3] *OND*, p. 835, "Quia intentio eorum fuit asserere quod illud, quod in fide et moribus semel diffinierunt sive per clavem scientiae sive per clavem potentiae sive per auctoritatem papalem sive per quamcunque potestatem Romani pontifices, adeo immutabile perseverat, quod illud successori non licet revocare in dubium nec contrarium affirmare."

[4] *OND*, p. 834, "... ad solum concilium generale et Romanorum pontificem pertineat diffinire dubia, quae circa fidem emergunt ... Non autem potest quilibet

might seem then that, when a pope defined a doctrine of faith, he defined with the key of power, which was precisely what John XXII had insisted all along. Ockham had to concede that in a sense this was true.[1] (Earlier he had explained that the key of knowledge was "distinct" from the key of power but not "separate" from it, just as the soul was distinct from the body but not separate from it.[2])

But why then had Michael of Cesena written that decrees promulgated with the key of knowledge were irrevocable and then added "It is otherwise in things ordained with the key of power"? The distinction which John's adversary intended to draw, Ockham explained, was simply a distinction between doctrinal decrees and disciplinary decrees. No doubt both keys were used in all decisions. But it was proper to point out that power was especially important in disciplinary decrees and knowledge in doctrinal decrees. Thus the pope could use his power to promulgate a ruling on some point of discipline indifferent in itself. Then, even if he acted against his knowledge of what was good for his subjects, still the decree had legal force (though the pope imperiled his immortal soul in so acting). The situation was quite different with doctrinal decisions. There, everything depended on right knowledge. If the pope used his power to define a doctrine of faith and morals *contra illud quod scientia dictat diffiniendum* then the decree was null and void from the beginning. Indeed, it was the duty of any Christian who knew the truth of the matter to detest the pope's decree and reject it and rebuke it as heretical.[3]

These last words bring us to the heart of Ockham's argument. He

---

diffinire sicut modo accipimus 'diffinire'; quia licet habeat notitiam, quae potest vocari clavis scientiae ... deficit ei tamen auctoritas et potestas iurisdictionis, quae ad talem diffinitionem requiritur." Ockham repeated the distinction between a definition *auctoritate officii* and one made *per modum doctrinae* in the *Dialogus*, p. 399. The distinction was commonly drawn in the early fourteenth century. We have noted a similar argument in Hervaeus Natalis (above, p. 148).

[1] *OND*, pp. 834-835.

[2] *OND*, p. 825.

[3] *OND*, pp. 836-837, "... in diffinitione eorum, quae diffiniuntur circa fidem et mores, quodam modo principalius se habet scientia, et in constitutione eorum agibilium, quae de se indifferentia sunt, quodam modo principalius se habet potentia. Quia in diffinitione eorum, quae pertinent ad fidem et bonos mores, nichil debet potentia, nisi quod decernit scientia, ita quod in illis potentia debet omnino sequi scientiam; quia si in minimo potentia adversaretur scientiae, diffinitio esset omnino nulla; quia, si papa per quamcunque potentiam diffiniret aliquid contra illud, quod scientia dictat diffiniendum in fide et bonis moribus, diffinitio sua nulla penitus esset, immo liceret cuilibet Christiano hoc scienti ipsam detestari, respuere et sicut haereticam reprobare."

was genuinely interested in building up a theory of the irreformability of dogmatic decrees. One of his major contributions was indeed to suggest that the doctrine of irreformability could be defended without an appeal to the dubious argument concerning a key of knowledge on which it had originally been based. But of course Ockham had no intention of using such a theory to buttress the power of the Avignon papacy. The whole of the preceding argument was intended to prove that John XXII was a heretic because he had revoked the irreformable definitions of his predecessor. And, at this point, Ockham interrupted his technical argumentation about the power of the keys to point out at some length that Nicholas III's decree *Exiit* had established irrevocably one truth of morals and four truths of faith and that John XXII had heretically rejected all of them.[1] Returning to his main theme he faced the central problem inherent in this kind of a theory of infallibility. How could he possibly assert on the one hand that papal decrees on doctrine were irreformable, and on the other, that a pope could officially promulgate heretical teachings (and that the contemporary pope had indeed done so)? Ockham's answer was exactly the same as Pietro Olivi's:

> Whatever (John) defined with the key of knowledge, *while he was supreme pontiff*, should not be called into question. But what he defined against the definitions of the Roman pontiffs was not defined through the key of knowledge but through heretical depravity.[2]

For Ockham, of course, John ceased to be a true pope when he became guilty of heretical depravity. The doctrine that a pope who persisted in heresy automatically ceased to be pope was widely held in the fourteenth century. But Ockham was particularly insistent that a pope who erred in pronouncing on a question of faith became at once a heretic; and this seems to have been a novel position. Earlier

---

[1] *OND*, pp. 837-844. Ockham brushed aside John XXII's assertion that it did not "pertain" to the faith to assert that Christ and the apostles had only "simple use of fact." A statement could "pertain" to the faith, Ockham wrote, either by affirming or denying Catholic truth. The doctrine about simple use of fact belonged to the realm of Catholic truth because it was implied in Scripture and church teaching. The true doctrine on the matter had been defined by Nicholas III. Therefore, John was a heretic in denying it (pp. 845-846).

[2] *OND*, p. 844, "Sed forte dicet aliquis: Si illud, quod per clavem scientiae in fide ac moribus semel diffinierunt Romani pontifices etc., ergo quicquid iste (Ioannes) diffinit non licet in dubium revocare. Ad hoc isti dicunt quod quicquid iste diffinivit per clavem scientiae, dum erat summus pontifex, non licet in dubium revocare. Sed quicquid diffinivit contra diffinitiones Romanorum pontificum, non diffinivit per clavem scientiae, sed diffinivit per haereticam pravitatem ..."

theologians and canonists had taught that a pope did not incur the guilt of heresy merely by making an erroneous pronouncement. He became a heretic only if he obdurately persisted in maintaining a false doctrine after his error had been pointed out to him. Ockham brushed this argument aside. His own position was based on a distinction between implicit and explicit faith. Every Christian was bound to believe implicitly in all revealed truth: he was bound to believe explicitly those doctrines that came within the range of his understanding. A Christian who erred through simple ignorance or misunderstanding of a truth that he was required to believe in only implicitly did not incur the guilt of heresy unless he persisted in his error after due admonition. But a Christian who rejected a doctrine that he was bound to believe in explicitly became at once, ipso facto, a heretic.[1] A simple, uneducated Christian was required to know explicitly only the articles of the Creed and other basic doctrines that were commonly taught throughout the whole church—for instance, Ockham suggested, such cardinal principles of the Christian religion as "Hell exists" or "There are demons."[2] A bishop or master of theology was bound to believe explicitly much more than this. In the case of a pope, he was required to know and believe explicitly the truth concerning any matter of faith upon which he made an official pronouncement. If, then, he made an error in any of his pronouncements he was erring against a truth that he was bound to believe explicitly. He became at once a heretic.[3] For Ockham there

---

[1] Ockham used the distinction in the *OND* only to argue that in rejecting the doctrine of absolute poverty John erred in a matter that had already been explicitly defined (pp. 846-850). He applied the argument to all public teachings of a pope in the *Contra Ioannem* with particular reference to John's doctrine on the Beatific Vision.

[2] *Contra Ioannem*, p. 47.

[3] *Op. cit.*, p. 79, "Quicumque enim errat contra veritatem catholicam, quam credere tenetur explicite, incidit in haereticam pravitatem; talis autem non est verus papa ..." p. 104, "Summus pontifex et qui (se) pro summo pontifice gerit, tenetur explicite credere veritatem quaestionis fidei, quam explicite et sollemniter determinat et definit ... et ita omnes errores contra fidem in suis quibuscumque constutionibus dogmatizati et asserti, sunt contrarii veritatibus catholicis, quas explicite credere, et non solum implicite, fuit astrictus." There follows a rather tortured argument to the effect that, precisely because papal decisions concerning the faith were immutable, the pope had the duty to make himself certain of the truth before he pronounced on it. If he failed to do so his decision was void and the pope was always culpable. See also *OND*, p. 850. Here Ockham argued that, in the very act of defining an error as truth after full deliberation a pope convicted himself of pertinacious heresy. "Qui gerens se pro papa aliquam haeresim solemp-

could be no middle way in evaluating papal decrees. They could not be simply erroneous They were either immutable or heretical. And if a decree was heretical the man who promulgated it ceased ipso facto to be pope.

Evidently, Ockham's argument has not so far provided us with an adequate response to the question we posed at the outset. "How can a Christian know with certitude the truths of faith?" The principle, "What the supreme pontiffs have once defined endures immutably" provides no real answer to our question. Authentic papal decrees established immutable truths, according to Ockham; but a Christian could not find certain truth in all the decisions that emanated from the papal throne because the man sitting on the throne might be a heretic. It was necessary therefore for theologians to examine each doctrinal pronouncement of the apostolic see with exquisite care to determine whether it had been promulgated authentically, in which case it was binding on all Catholics for all time, or whether it had been promulgated "through heretical depravity" in which case it was null and void from the beginning.[1]

What criteria was the theologian to use in carrying out this delicate task? When re-stating his argument concerning the Michaelist use of the term "key of knowledge" in the *Tractatus contra Ioannem* Ockham explained that irreformable definitions on faith and morals were constituted by "everything that has once been truly and catholicly defined by the Roman pontiffs to be true."[2] But this does not help

---

niter ex ultima deliberatione diffinit esse tenendam est pertinax, et per consequens haereticus reputandus."

[1] *Dialogus*, p. 625, "... contra crimen haeresis papae est vigilantissime occurendum ..." p. 687, "... literae papae, quae super aliqua difficultate fidei emanare noscuntur, diligentissime sunt videndae et examinandae, et de iis disputare licet." The whole content of the treatises *OND*, *Contra Ioannem* and *Contra Benedictum* was devoted to precisely this procedure—a critical, hostile scrutiny of the words of the popes. De Lagarde, *La naissance*, Vol. V, p. 157 observed that, for Ockham, to criticize papal pronouncements became almost the principal duty of a Catholic. Throughout Ockham's writings there is a very strong emphasis on the right and duty of private theologians to criticize the popes. See especially *Contra Ben.*, p. 247, "Sed expositores sacrarum scripturaram sufficienter in sacris litteris eruditi, in exponendis scripturis, et per consequens in traditione seu assertione credendorum sunt summo pontifici praeferendi, teste Gratiano ... di. XX, § 1." See also *Breviloquium de potestate papae*, ed. L. Baudry (Paris, 1937), p. 135, "Si eciam erraret (papa) contra illa que periti scire tenentur, haberent periti judicare ipsum."

[2] *Contra Ioannem*, p. 118, "Quia hoc est principium epud eos, quod omne illud quod vere et catholice semel est definitum per Romanos pontifices esse verum, et est tale verum quod spectat ad fidem vel bonos mores ... nulli successori licet scienter in dubium revocare vel contrarium affirmare." A similar passage of the *Contra*

in our enquiry. How was the theologian to decide when the supreme pontiff was pronouncing "truly" and "catholicly"? Ockham gave his most explicit answer in another section of the *Contra Ioannem* where he considered the problem that arose when one pope seemed to contradict the doctrine of another.

> This is the general rule. If different supreme pontiffs are shown to have contrary opinions on anything pertaining to orthodox faith, recourse is to be had to sacred Scripture and the doctrine or assertion of the universal church .... No pope is the rule of Christian faith for he can err and be stained with heresy .... But sacred Scripture and the doctrine of the universal church which cannot err, this is our rule of faith.[1]

Here we seem to have a straightforward answer to our initial question. The Christian will find certitude in Scripture and the doctrine of the unerring church.[2] As usual, however, Ockham's position was more nuanced than it appears to be at first glance. To follow his thought further we shall have to consider in what sense he considered Scripture and church teaching to be complementary sources of Christian faith.

3. Sources of Christian Doctrine

The words of Ockham that we have just quoted can be interpreted in at least two ways. They may mean that all divine truth is contained in Scripture and that the teaching of the universal church interprets the texts of Scripture with unfailing truth. But Ockham's words may also mean that God reveals through the church truths of faith not

---

Benedictum, pp. 187-188, declares, "... illa, quae per clavem scientiae ... sunt recte et catholice a summis pontificibus definita, non licet eorum successori contraria affirmare." In this passage Ockham deployed the string of Decretist references which had become a standard part of the Michaelist armory of arguments to prove that a pope was bound by the doctrinal decisions of a predecessor (C. 24 q. 1 gl. ad c. 1, C. 25 q. 1 gl. ad c. 3, c. 6, c. 7). Here again Ockham explained that the use of the terms "key of knowledge" and "key of power" by John's adversaries was intended to convey simply a distinction between doctrinal and disciplinary decrees.

[1] *Contra Ioannem*, p. 72, "Haec enim est regula generalis, quod, si umquam summi pontifices diversi monstrarentur circa aliquid ad fidem pertinens orthodoxam contrarias assertiones vel opiniones habere, ad sciendum quae est alteri praeferenda, ad sacram scripturam et doctrinam seu assertionem universalis ecclesiae oportet recurrere. ... Nullus enim summus pontifex est regula fidei Christianae, cum possit errare et haeretica infici pravitate, di. XL, c. *Si papa*, et di. XIX, c. *Anastasius*. Sed sacra scriptura et doctrina universalis ecclesiae, quae errare non potest, est regula fidei nostrae."

[2] *Contra Ioannem*, p. 49, "Hoc tamen potest dici, quod unusquisque illa credere tenetur explicite, de quibus debet esse certus quod in scriptura sacra aut doctrina universalis ecclesiae continentur."

contained in Scripture. We have traced in earlier chapters a whole
Franciscan tradition of theologizing on this point. But earlier masters
of the Order had touched on the problem of the sources of faith only
incidentally in the course of discussing other theological issues. (The
problem arose usually in discussions on Franciscan poverty, on the
Eucharist, or on the *Filioque* clause of the Creed.) Henry of Ghent
and Gerald of Bologna had teased their minds with the speculation
that a teaching of the church might conflict with the words of Scripture. But Ockham was the first theologian who posed the problem,
De locis theologicis—the subject of a standard tractate in many later
compendia of Christian doctrine—as a major issue requiring investigation in its own right. In his *Dialogus* he presented a classical formulation of the problem which influenced the whole course of late medieval
ecclesiology.

Two major points of view existed according to Ockham's *Magister*.
Some theologians held that all Catholic truths necessary to salvation
were asserted explicitly or implicitly in the Bible.[1] Others maintained
that there were many such truths which were not stated explicitly
in the Bible and which could not be inferred from its contents. Asked
by his *Discipulus* to enumerate the sources of Catholic faith according
to those who held the second point of view, the *Magister* replied:

> They hold that there are five sorts of truth from which a Christian is not
> permitted to dissent. First, those truths that are expressed in sacred
> Scripture or that can be inferred from it by necessary reasoning; sec-
> ond, those that have come to us from the apostles by word of mouth
> or the writings of the faithful, but which are not found in sacred Scrip-
> ture nor to be inferred from it; third, those found in chronicles and
> histories worthy of trust; fourth, those than can be manifestly con-
> cluded from truths of the first and second kind alone or from one or the
> other of them combined with truths of the third kind; fifth, those that,
> apart from the truths revealed to the apostles, God has revealed or even
> inspired to others, or may reveal or inspire, provided that the revelation
> or inspiration has come to the universal church without doubt[2]

---

[1] *Dialogus*, pp. 410-411, "Circa quaesitum sunt diversae et adversae sententiae.
Quarum una est: quod illae solae veritates sunt catholicae reputandae et de neces-
sitate salutis credendae, quae in canone Bibliae explicite vel implicite asseruntur ...
Sed alii isti sententiae nequaquam consentiunt, dicentes: quod multae sunt veritates catholicae et fidem sapientes catholicam, quae nec in divinis scripturis habentur explicite: nec ex solis contentis in eis possunt inferri."

[2] *Dialogus*, pp. 415-416, "Tenent isti, quod quinque sunt genera veritatum, quibus non licet Christianis aliter dissentire. Primum est earum, quae in Scriptura sacra
dicuntur, vel ex eis argumento necessario possunt inferri. Secundum est earum,
quae ab Apostolis ad nos per succedentium relationem vel Scripturas fidelium

In a strict sense, the *Magister* was here proposing only three sources of essential Christian truth—Scripture, apostolic tradition, and post-apostolic revelation—for he went on to explain that offenses against the third category of truth were not, strictly speaking heresies, though they were perverse and "smacked of heresy," while the fourth category consisted merely of deductions from the first two. If we bear in mind the original formulation of the problem by the *Magister* we could reduce the sources of faith enumerated above to two essential categories—Scriptural revelation and non-Scriptural revelation.

As always in the *Dialogus* Ockham had propounded two antithetical points of view without indicating which one he himself preferred. As usual in modern scholarship a controversy has arisen concerning Ockham's own personal point of view. An older group of historians— both Protestants and Catholics— regarded Ockham as a forerunner of Luther in that he stated and espoused the *sola scriptura* principle of divine revelation.[1] One can see how this interpretation arose. Luther appealed from the teaching of contemporary popes to the words of Holy Writ. Ockham often followed the same procedure. Luther associated his protests against the papacy with an assertion that the Bible was the sole source of revealed truth. This same assertion can be found stated by the *Magister* in Ockham's *Dialogus*. Scholars more interested in Luther than in late medieval ecclesiology leaped to the conclusion that the *sola scriptura* argument expressed Ockham's own personal opinion. This interpretation of Ockham's position was effectively criticized by Van Leeuwen nearly forty years ago. More recently Oberman has presented Ockham as a principal inspirer of the "two-sources theory" of divine revelation which was eventually defined at the Council of Trent.[2]

---

peruenerunt, licet in Scripturis sacris non inueniantur insertae, nec ex solis eis possunt necessario argumento concludi. Tertium est earum, quas in fide dignis cronicis et historiis, relationibus fidelium inuenimus. Quartum est earum, quae ex veritatibus primi generis et secundi tantummodo, vel que ex eis vel alterius earum una cum veritatibus tertii generis possunt manifeste concludi. Quintum est earum, quas Deus praeter veritates reuelatas Apostolis; aliis reuelauit, vel etiam inspirauit, ac nouiter reuelaret, vel etiam inspiraret; quae reuelatio vel inspiratio ad uniuersalem ecclesiam absque dubitatione peruenit, vel etiam perueniret."

[1] See e.g. F. Kropatschek, *Das Schriftprinzip der Lutherischen Kirche*, I (Leipzig, 1904), pp. 314-317; H. Denifle, *Luther und Luthertum*, II (Mainz, 1909), p. 382.

[2] A. van Leeuwen, *art. cit.* (supra p. 209 n. 1); H. A. Oberman, *The Harvest of Medieval Theology* (Cambridge, Mass., 1963), pp. 361-369, 375-382. Besides calling attention to Ockham's earlier theological writings Van Leeuwen suggested that the whole manner of presentation of the opposing arguments on this question in the

Oberman's point of view is certainly correct. Ockham's doctrine on the sources of faith was formulated in his earliest theological works before he ever became involved in the struggle against John XXII; in his later polemical writings he never abandoned his earlier opinions but rather developed and refined them. The problem first arose for Ockham in his discussions on the Eucharist, where he adopted a position essentially similar to that of Duns Scotus. According to Ockham, Scripture taught plainly that, in the Eucharist, the body of Christ was truly present under the appearance of bread; but Scripture did not teach the specific doctrine of transubstantiation. Nor could human reason demonstrate the truth of this doctrine. Indeed, it would have been much more reasonable to have maintained that the substance of the bread remained after the words of consecration. According to Ockham, this interpretation of the Eucharist would have avoided all philosophical difficulties and would not have contradicted the words of Scripture. But Ockham adhered to the doctrine of transubstantiation simply because the church had proclaimed it— "through some revelation, I suppose," he wrote.[1]

These views were expressed in Ockham's Commentary on the Sentences and again in his *Quodlibeta*. In the *De sacramento altaris*, written after his Eucharistic doctrine had been attacked, he modified them to the extent of suggesting that some of the Fathers had held to the doctrine of transubstantiation and that they might have arrived at it either by divine revelation or "from the authorities of the Bible by diligent and skilled investigation."[2] But this same work provides

---

Dialogus indicated a preference for the two-sources theory. Oberman further developed this point.

[1] A. van Leeuwen, *art. cit.*, pp. 263-264 nn. 40, 42 citing *Sent.* IV q. 6, D and *Quodl.* IV q. 35, "Tertia opinio esset multo rationabilis nisi esset determinatio Ecclesiae in contrarium ... Nec contrarium illius habetur in canone Bibliae nec includit aliquam contradictionem corpus Christi plus coexistere substantiae panis quam eius accidentibus, nec repugnat rationi ... Ad argumentum principale dico quod aliquando sunt ponenda plura miracula circa aliquod ubi posset fieri per pauciora, et hoc placet Deo et hoc constat Ecclesiae per aliquam revelationem ut suppono, et ideo sic determinavit."

[2] T. Bruce Birch (ed.), *The De Sacramento Altaris of William of Ockham*, p. 172, "... sed hoc Sanctis Patribus creditur divinitus revelatum vel ex auctoritatibus Bibliae diligenti et solerti inquisitione probatum ..." Van Leeuwen assumed that Ockham used the words *revelatio* and *revelatum* to indicate the divine guidance received by the church in the interpretation of Scripture. L. Baudry, *op. cit.* (p. 205 n. 1), p. 93 criticized this interpretation, insisting on the disjunctive force of Ockham's word, *vel*. See also *Sent.* I Dist. 2 q. 1, "... non debet poni nisi ubi evidenter sequitur ex traditis in scriptura sacra vel determinatione ecclesiae propter

further clear evidence of Ockham's belief that some of the truths of faith that Catholics were bound to believe were not to be found in Scripture. At the opening of the work he defended himself against the charge of unorthodoxy by declaring that he wished to profess no other faith than the faith of the Roman church. Then he added that, since such implicit faith excused from guilt one who erred from ignorance concerning doctrines expressed in Scripture, still more did it excuse one who erred concerning those not expressed in Scripture.[1]

Thus, long before he came to write the *Dialogus* Ockham had already formulated a "two-sources" theory of divine revelation. De Vooght regarded the discussion of this problem in the *Dialogus* as marking a "turning point in the history of the theology of the sources of Christian doctrine." Yet he thought that Ockham had not clearly opted for either of the two positions expressed by the *Magister* and he observed that it was hard to understand why Ockham had ever raised the question at all.[2] In fact, to understand why Ockham raised the question is to understand which position he adhered to. Ockham's purpose in raising the issue of the sources of faith in the *Dialogus* was the same as his purpose in writing the work as a whole— to expound in detail all the arguments that could be useful to the Michaelist Franciscans in their feud against the pope. Ever since the days of Bonaventure an emphasis on the church as a source of divine revelation had been associated with the defense of the "new tradition" of St. Francis against the enemies of the Franciscan Order; and Ockham's whole intention in breaking with John XXII was still to defend the authenticity of Francis' teaching—even though what he was actually defending was an over-intellectualized, scholastic definition of the doctrine of poverty that Francis himself would hardly have recognized. Moreover, the assertion that the church as well as Scripture provided a certain guide to the truths of faith had been of particular importance in the Michaelist case against Pope John XXII (who consistently affirmed that Scripture alone was the source of immutable articles of faith). The Michaelists wanted to prove that John was a

---

cuius auctoritatem debet omnis ratio captivari," cited by R. Guelluy, *Philosophie et théologie chez Guillaume d'Ockham* (Louvain-Paris, 1947), p. 324 n. 1.

[1] Birch, *op. cit.*, p. 164, "Si ergo tantae efficaciae sit fides implicita ut excuset ignoranter errantem circa illa quae in scriptura canonica sunt expressa, multo magis excusabit ignoranter opinantem aliquid quod nec in scriptura canonica nec in doctoribus approbatis ab ecclesia fuerit expressum."

[2] P. de Vooght, *Les sources de la doctrine chrétienne* (Bruges, 1954), pp. 161-167, 259.

heretic because he erred against the determinations of the church as well as against the words of Scripture. This was Ockham's purpose too. The intent of this whole section of the *Dialogus* was made clear in the words of the *Discipulus* that introduced it. "I wish to ask many things about heresies ... but since knowledge of a thing is sometimes conferred by knowledge of its contrary I ask first what truths are to be considered Catholic." It is perhaps an unhappy reflection on Ockham's temperament as a controversialist that he was interested in exploring the sources of Christian truth primarily in order to discover in how many different ways Pope John XXII could be accused of being a heretic.[1]

In his other polemical writings Ockham persistently accused John of heresy for erring against "the doctrine," "the determinations," "the assertions" of the church. As we saw, he declared in the *Contra Ioannem* that the Christian's rule of faith was constituted by "Scripture and the doctrine of the Universal church." Ockham often used such language.[2] He constantly referred to two sources of faith without ever arguing (outside the *Dialogus*) that the two sources could be reduced to one—Scripture alone—an explanation that would certainly have been needed if Ockham was really intending to advance a single-source theory of divine revelation. In the *Contra Ioannem* he based his whole case against John's teaching concerning the Beatific Vision on the assertion that—even though some texts of Scripture seemed to support John's point of view—the contrary doctrine had been accepted by the universal church. While pursuing this question Ockham even asserted that, in case of apparent conflict between Scripture and a clear teaching of the universal church, the teaching of the church had to be accepted. If any man, even a pope, came on a text of Scripture that seemed to him to assert something contrary to a doctrine held by the church he ought to say, with Augustine, that his codex was faulty or the translation incorrect or that he did not understand the passage correctly. But he was not to give up the doctrine commonly admitted by the church in order to adhere to the words of Scripture.[3]

---

[1] *Dialogus*, p. 410, "Volo enim de haeresibus multa inquirere, sed quia nonnunquam cognitio unius contrariorum ad cognitionem alterius conferre dignoscitur, quero primo, quae veritates sunt catholicae censendae."

[2] The phrase "contra scripturam divinam aut doctrinam universalis ecclesiae" was used over and over again with minor variations in *OND*, pp. 847-853. (In these examples Ockham used the conjunctions *aut, vel, seu, et* indifferently.) See also *Contra Ioannem*, pp. 49, 140, 152, *Contra Ben.*, pp. 253, 254, 256.

[3] *Contra Ioannem*, p. 73, "... Ioannes XXII, si aliquam invenit auctoritatem scrip-

Very evidently, Ockham was no prophet of Luther's *sola scriptura* doctrine.[1] We cannot assume that every intricate detail of the argument presented by the *Magister* in favor of the two-sources theory of revelation reflected Ockham's own personal point of view. But in principle he clearly professed this doctrine and rejected the alternative one.

There is one final aspect of Ockham's doctrine on the sources of Catholic truth to be considered which will lead us back to our central problem concerning the nature of the pope's authority in matters of faith. It may have been noted that Ockham did not include "the doctrine of the universal church" among the five sorts of truth from which a Christian was not permitted to dissent although he often insisted in other contexts that the universal church could not err in faith. The *Magister* explained however, that it was not necessary to include determinations of the church as a separate source of Christian truth because the church, "rightly proceeding," did not define anything not contained in the already listed sources.[2] That is to say any truth of faith defined by the church had to be derived either from Scriptural or some form of extra-Scriptural revelation. The church's knowledge of divine truth could develop in the course of

---

turae sacrae, quae videbatur contraria veritati, quam universalis ecclesia tenet, quod animae sanctae in caelo vident divinam essentiam: vel debuit reputare codicem suum esse mendosum et codicem requirere veriorem, vel debuit aestimare interpretem non recte interpretatum fuisse, vel debuit absque dubio tenere se non intelligere auctoritatem, quae videbatur contraria veritati praedictae universalis ecclesiae; et in isto ultimo, ut videtur, debuit se tenere."

[1] The passages where Ockham appeals to Scripture and reason without mention of the doctrine of the church occur typically in the later works concerning church and state, most strikingly in *De imperatorum et pontificum potestate*, ed. C. K. Brampton (Oxford, 1931), p. 3, "... plus me monebit una ratio evidens vel una auctoritas scripturae sacrae sane intelligenda quam assertio totius universitatis mortalium ..."; and *An princeps*, p. 254, "Sed quaeret aliquis ... ad quem pertinet explicare et determinare in quibus casibus papa habeat potestatem et in quibus non habeat potestatem. Huic respondetur quod prima regula et infallibilis in huiusmodi est scriptura sacra et ratio recta." Here the context explains Ockham's departure from his usual formula. In the one particular matter of the limits of papal power in temporal affairs his whole case did indeed rest on an appeal to Scripture rightly interpreted. (The texts of the *Decretales*, which Ockham commonly cited as expressing the authentic doctrine of the church on other matters, were of no help to him here.) But this did not imply that Scripture was the sole guide to all other truths of faith.

[2] *Dialogus*, p. 416, "... ecclesia rite procedens nullam veritatem determinat aut diffinit, nisi in Scriptura sacra aut traditionibus Apostolorum aut cronicis historiis vel revelationibus indubitabilibus fidelium, vel his quae sequuntur ex praedictis aut aliquo praedictorum, vel in revelatione seu inspiratione divina modo debito manifesta valeant se fundare."

time and new understandings could be the subject of binding definitions—as we have seen in the matter of transubstantiation. But truth
itself was immutable. The determinations of the church could provide
new definitions of existing truth, but could not create new truths.

Ockham succeeded in presenting this essentially conventional view
as an attack on John XXII. Certain *moderni*, the *Magister* reported,
were asserting that the pope could make new articles of faith and were
claiming to prove this from the use of the word *Deinceps* in John's
Bull, *Cum inter nonnullos*.[1] (The pope had written that *henceforward* it
would be heretical to assert the doctrine of Christ's absolute poverty.)
Since Ockham expressed elsewhere his detestation of the idea that the
pope could simply "dominate" the faith of the church, in the sense
of being able to change it at will,[2] we can be sure that the *Magister's*
counter-assertion reflects Ockham's own point of view.

> Neither the supreme pontiff, nor the whole church of God can make an
> assertion true that is not true nor make an assertion false that is not
> false; so too he cannot make an assertion Catholic that is not Catholic,
> nor make an assertion heretical that is not heretical; therefore he cannot
> make a new article of faith.[3]

After defending this view at some length the *Magister* explained that
it did not by any means deprive definitions of all real significance.
He pointed to the distinction (common enough at this time) between
the definitions of private masters and the "authentic" definitions of
popes and general councils. After a master had defined some point
pertaining to the faith his opinion could still be disputed. But when
the pope determined some disputed matter—even though he did not
create a new truth but only declared existing truth by doing so—
important consequences followed; for any bishop or inquisitor could
launch charges of heresy against a man who rejected what the pope
had "rightly defined" although they could not have done so before
the definition.[4]

---

[1] *Dialogus*, p. 418.

[2] *Contra Ben.*, p. 245, "Ex quo sequitur, quod summus pontifex sic dominatur
fidei Christianae, ut possit totam fidem mutare et aliam invenire ... Et ista haeresis
peior est omnibus haeresibus ..." p. 250, "Sed papa per nullum statutum suum potest reddere dubium illum, qui fuit certus ante (de) catholica veritate."

[3] *Dialogus*, p. 419, "... non potest de assertione non catholica facere catholicam:
nec de assertione non haeretica facere haereticam, et ideo non potest novum articulum fidei facere."

[4] *Dialogus*, p. 421, "... post definitionem rectam summi pontificis licet cuilibet
episcopo et inquisitori pravitatis haereticae contra tenentes contrarium ... procedere iuxta sanctiones canonicas." The argument occurs also in *OND*, p. 848, "Qui

It is surprising that Ockham could not see, or would not acknowledge, that the doctrine he asserted here was precisely the doctrine of John XXII and his curial canonists. The view Ockham condemned—that the pope could make a Catholic truth out of something that had not been true beforehand—was precisely the view that John XXII had had expunged from the gloss of Zenzellinus de Cassanis. Ockham was not ignorant of canon law. When he plunged into his polemics against John XXII he quickly acquired a wide knowledge of the texts of the Decretum and *Decretales* together with their Ordinary Glosses, and he quoted those texts whenever they suited his purpose. But perhaps he never achieved any deep understanding of the whole structure of canonistic ecclesiology as it had developed from the twelfth century to the fourteenth. And certainly he felt a deep hostility toward the canonists of his own day. At the beginning of the *Dialogus* he called them "unintelligent, presumptuous, rash, deceitful, quibbling, ignorant people."[1] Even when their views for once were in accordance with his own, Ockham apparently could not bring himself to admit the fact.

4. IMPLICATIONS OF INFALLIBILITY

Ockham did not differ from contemporary canonists in denying that the pope could invent new truths of faith—everyone was agreed on that point—but in affirming that the doctrinal decisions of a pope (a true pope of course) were so authoritative as to be binding on all his successors. We can now consider how Ockham's insistence on this principle of irreformability (with its implication of infallibility) affected his whole structure of ecclesiology. Van Leeuwen pointed out perceptively that medieval writers typically approached the problem of infallibility in a different way from modern ones. Medieval theologians asked whether it was possible for a given institution of church govern-

---

non habet auctoritatem nec potestatem terminandi quaestionem motam de fide, non po test pro tali quaestione aliquem tanquam haereticum condempnare ... Sed nullus inferior summo pontifice potest quaestionem motam de fide terminare ..." See also *Contra Ioannem*, p. 119 (the pope's "power" makes his decisions on matters of faith "obligatory"); *Contra Ben.*, p. 263 (Those who know the truth in a matter of faith cannot punish their adversaries as heretics until a papal sentence is announced). The Magister's discussion in the passage just quoted ended with the comment that, if the pope was suspected of defining erroneously, an appeal to a general council should be made. On this see below p. 231 n. 1

[1] *Dialogus*, p. 401. Ockham contrasted the canonists of his own time with the original framers of the canonical texts. They had been "viri acutissimi in scientia naturali, morali, et theologia."

ment to err; modern theologians ask how we can determine which particular pronouncements of the institutional church are infallible. Ockham certainly did not neglect the medieval question. What Van Leeuwen failed to see is that he also addressed himself precisely to the modern one—and that, indeed, he was the first major theologian to do so. For Ockham, authentic papal definitions established truths of faith immutably; but not all definitions were authentic. The problem was to discriminate between the two classes of pronouncement.

We have seen how, in his handling of this problem, Ockham showed that the concept of infallibility could be used to undermine the authority of a reigning pope. With disconcerting simplicity—or apparent simplicity—he suggested that, if a true pope's pronouncements established immutable Catholic truth, then a pontiff who made an erroneous pronouncement was evidently no true pope. There are two further points to be made about Ockham's approach to this question. In the first place he demonstrated that the idea of infallibility could be used to undermine, not only the authority of a reigning pope but also the legitimacy of all existing institutions of church government. Precisely because the true church was infallible a church that erred on some particular point of doctrine—let us say in distinguishing between "right of use" and "bare use of fact"—could not be the true church (just as a pontiff who so erred could not be the true pope). Our second point is a little more subtle. Ockham not only created difficulties for his adversaries by his appeals to the principle of infallibility. He created difficulties for himself too. It may be that any attempt to explore all the logical implications of the concept of infallibility in relation to the whole life and history of the Catholic church can lead only to a tangle of self-contradictions. This sometimes seems to be the case with modern theologians. It was certainly the case with Ockham. He was able to attack the contemporary papal publicists quite effectively on many detailed points of doctrine (especially in the sphere of church-state relations), but he did not succeed in building up a coherent counter-ecclesiology of his own. In pursuing his arguments, one constantly has the impression that he was on the brink of reaching conclusions that would have been, if not orthodox, at least sensible. But the expectation is always disappointed. Each new argument leads on only to another level of paradox. And the paradoxes always arise from Ockham's conviction that the true church had to be infallible while the existing, institutional church was in error.

We can illustrate this by turning back once again to our original question. How can a Christian know with certitude the truths of his faith? Ockham's argumentation on this question, as we have pursued it so far, was reasonably straightforward. Catholic truth existed immutably; to ascertain truth with certainty a Catholic could turn to the authentic pronouncements of the papacy; to determine which papal pronouncements were authentic he could have recourse to Scripture and to the doctrine of the universal church "which cannot err." It is when we try to pursue Ockham's thought beyond this point that the difficulties begin. After all, when a dispute arises as to whether a given papal pronouncement is or is not an orthodox statement of Catholic faith the reason will almost always be that the relevant texts of Scripture are ambiguous or that theologians disagree as to what the teaching of the universal church affirms. When we ask where the Christian is to find a guide to the true interpretation of Scripture or a sure definition of the doctrine of the church Ockham can give us no answer. From this point onward our search for objective criteria of faith in his work leads only to a morass of total subjectivity.

This subjectivity in Ockham's approach to problems of ecclesiology was apparent already in the first document announcing his position to the Franciscan Order, his letter to the general-chapter of 1333.

> Before I would believe that the aforesaid errors are compatible with the Catholic faith I would believe that the whole church of God and all the promises of Christ about the Church enduring down to the end of the world can be preserved in a few persons, or even in one man, and I would judge all other Christians to err against the Catholic faith.[1]

The implications of this attitude become plain as soon as we begin to examine Ockham's handling of the two supposedly objective criteria that he proposed as the "rule of faith"— Scripture and the doctrine of the church. Scripture, Ockham wrote, was to be interpreted primarily in its literal sense and, like Thomas Aquinas, he insisted that mystical interpretations were not to be used to settle disputed problems of theology.[2] It would be pleasant to suppose that Ockham—as a faithful follower of St. Francis—was inviting his readers to eschew theological subtleties and become simple Bible Christians, following the

---

[1] *Epistola*, p. 15, "Ante enim quam omnes praedictos errores compossibiles fidei reputarem, totam fidem Christianam omnesque promissiones Christi de fide catholica usque ad finem saeculi duratura ac totam ecclesiam Dei in paucis, immo in uno, posse salvari putarem, et omnes alios Christianos contra fidem errare catholicam arbitrarer."

[2] *Breviloquium*, p. 131.

plain words of Scripture and caring for nothing else. But of course, this is absurd. Ockham's appeal to the plain literal meaning of the Bible worked rather well in his discussions on problems of church and state, where his opponents' arguments had often been based on an abuse of mystical interpretations. But, where the problems of Franciscan poverty were concerned, the plain words of Scripture far more often favored John XXII than the dissident friars of Ockham's party. Scripture seemed to assert clearly enough that Christ and the apostles had had a purse and that the apostles and the early Christian community had owned all things in common. Like earlier Franciscan apologists Ockham had to use considerable ingenuity to explain away such texts.

Scripture taken by itself then, in the most obvious literal meaning of its texts, was not a sufficient guide to the truths of faith. Scripture, according to Ockham, needed to be interpreted by right reason. Truth could be arrived at "by irrefragable argument from the things contained in sacred Scripture."[1] This seems a promising approach. There is also, at first sight, a kind of sweet reasonableness in Ockham's reiterated assertion that he would be willing to abandon his position if only his adversaries would demonstrate to him "reasonably" where he was mistaken.[2] Ockham was an innovator in the sphere of formal logic. Since he constantly emphasized the role of reason in the interpretation of Scriptural texts we may be tempted to suppose that his own conclusions from Scripture were based on some refinement of logical argumentation which he knew to be irrefutable but which his adversaries were unable to follow. Once again, however, this was not the case at all. One cannot for instance, by any process of formal logic, demonstrate irrefutably that a distinction between use and right of use may exist even in consumables from a text like "if you will be perfect sell all you have and give it to the poor"[3]—or from any other Scriptural texts on holy poverty. But Ockham's whole case against John XXII turned on subtle points of interpretation like this. Through-

---

[1] *Contra Ben.*, p. 255, "... irrefragibili argumento ex his, quae in sacris scripturis habentur, elicitur ..."

[2] *Contra Ioannem*, p. 156, "Si autem contra veritatem catholicam ... quocumque modo erravi, iustae correctioni et rationabili me submitto." *Breviloquium*, p. 2, "... a quocumque qui michi manifestare potuerit veritatem, corrigi sum paratus ... ut velim, si falsum est, sapiencioris judicio reprobari." *De Imp.*, p. 3, "... si non valuero rationabiliter respondere, me errasse fatebor." *Epistola*, p. 16, "Si quis autem mihi patenter ostenderit. ..."

[3] Ockham stated that such an implication did exist, e.g., in *OND*, p. 845.

out all the discussions on Franciscan poverty Ockham's argument amounted to a series of assertions that certain interpretations of inherently ambiguous Scriptural texts that he preferred had to be accepted as immutable truths of faith—and this in spite of the fact that these interpretations had been rejected by the contemporary pope and by virtually all the theologians of the church. In Ockham's polemical works right reason meant simply his own reason. More strictly it meant simply his own prejudices. When he was pressed to justify the assertion that his opinions constituted articles of faith he turned, not to abstruse logic, but to an argument from authority. The interpretations of Scripture that Ockham defended were expressions of Catholic truth, he argued, because in the past they had been approved by the pope and accepted by the universal church which could not err in faith.

It seems that perhaps we have finally arrived at an answer to our initial question. An individual pope could fall from the faith and, in doing so, cease to be a true pope. But if the universal church was always unerring could not the Christian find final certitude in the firm, authoritative, pronouncements of some properly constituted body set up to represent the whole church? Certainly not! Ockham destroyed this possibility also. Perhaps the most famous of all the passages in his writings is the series of chapters in the *Dialogus* where he demonstrated that the only unerring *Romana ecclesia* was the universal church, the congregation of all the faithful. Here the *Magister* showed first that the pope could err. Then he argued that the same was true of the cardinals, the general council, all the clergy, all the men of the church—until he finally came to the conclusion that the true faith and the true church might live on in women or, in the last resort, in baptized infants.[1]

The argument that the unerring *Romana ecclesia* was not a local church but the whole *congregatio fidelium* was a common doctrine of the Decretists, probably borrowed by Ockham from Johannes Teutonicus whom he quoted or from Huguccio whom he seems also to have known.[2] But Ockham departed from canonical tradition in his treatment of the general council. Even here some of his arguments

---

[1] *Dialogus*, pp. 467-483, 489-506. It is clear that the Magister's argument (at least in the broad outline) reflects Ockham's own view from the numerous other places in his work where he insisted that a small group of dissenters might represent the true church at any given time. See below p. 232 n. 1

[2] See "Ockham, the Conciliar Theory and the Canonists" (Above p. 208 n. 2).

were conventional enough. Ockham maintained, for instance, that a council was superior to a pope and could judge a pope in matters of faith.[1] This was the generally accepted teaching of the canonists in the early fourteenth century. Ockham also maintained that an appeal to a council was not actually necessary in order to justify resistance to a pope accused of heresy.[2] This position could find support in the glosses of Huguccio. It was a minority opinion in the fourteenth century but by no means peculiar to Ockham. Where Ockham departed from the generally accepted opinion of his age was in his assertion that a general council could not adequately represent the universal church and that, accordingly, the council, like every other institution of church government, could err in faith.[3]

Ockham arrived at this conclusion by combining in a new and disconcerting fashion two doctrines that had been commonly taught in the past—the doctrine that the universal church could not stray from the true faith, and the doctrine that the church could not fail to survive even though it might be reduced to a few members. One can trace a

---

[1] *OND*, pp. 296, 851, 853; *Contra Ioannem*, pp. 63, 149; *Contra Ben.*, p. 248. Ockham usually based this view on the *glossa ordinaria* to *Dist*. 19 c. 9, "... ubi de fide agitur ... synodus maior est papa."

[2] Ockham argued that a pope accused of heresy could be judged by any Catholic bishop or prince in whose territory he resided, *Contra Ben.*, pp. 311-322; *Octo Quaestiones*, *Opera politica*, I, pp. 60-66; also that a pope who became a heretic automatically ceased to be pope *ipso iure absque omni nova sententia* (*Epistola*, p. 15). See also *OND*, pp. 296, 853-854; *Contra Ioannem*, pp. 81, 156; *Contra Ben.*, pp. 228, 303.

[3] The detailed demonstration of the council's proneness to error is presented only in the *Dialogus*, principally at pp. 494-498. But elsewhere Ockham called the general council less than the universal church or only a part of the church. See *Contra Ioannem*, p. 54, "... ecclesia universalis sit maior concilio generali, sicut totum est maius sua parte ...," p. 63, "... concilium generale est pars universalis ecclesiae; omnis pars est minor suo toto," p. 68, "Damnatio tamen universalis ecclesiae videtur esse maioris auctoritatis quam damnatio concilii generalis." In the *Epistola*, p. 10 Ockham quoted the maxim "Quod omnes tangit ab omnibus tractari debet." Johannes Teutonicus had used this text in his *glossa ordinaria* to emphasize the authority of a general council in matters of faith. Ockham quoted Johannes' words but gave a quite new meaning to them. Johannes treated the council as equivalent to the whole church. Ockham distinguished between the council and the totality of the faithful. "... quando certum est assertionem illam veritati fidei repugnare, *non solum ad* generale concilium aut praelatos vel etiam *clericos, verum etiam ad laicos et ad omnes omnino pertinet Christianos*, di, XCVI, c. *Ubinam* (ubi glossa accipit argumentum: *Quod omnes tangit, ab omnibus tractari debet*; ex quibus colligitur evidenter, quod quaestio fidei etiam ad mulieres spectat catholicas et fideles ...)." On Ockham's use of the *Quod omnes tangit* principle (with additional references) see Y. Congar, "Quod omnes tangit ab omnibus tractari et approbari debet," *Revue historique de droit français et étranger*, 4e sér., 36 (1958), pp. 210-259 at pp. 250-256.

clear development in this matter in preceding ecclesiology. Bonaventure presented the two doctrines—infallibility and indefectibility we might say—quite separately from one another. Olivi began to associate them together in his teaching that the *congregatio fidelium*, the universal church whose unerring judgments provided a certain guide to the truths of faith, might, at any given time, consist of a tiny group of the elect. From the episcopalist camp, Henry of Ghent (developing the canonistic teaching on indefectibility) argued that the true church of God could stand in one single individual, dissenting from the doctrine of the visible, organized church. William of Ockham adopted views similar to those of Olivi and Henry of Ghent but deduced from them the further conclusion that a truth of faith could be established with certainty only when no individual member of the church dissented from it.

Ockham expressed this view most clearly in the *Tractatus contra Joannem* where he sought to prove that John XXII's teaching on the Beatific Vision was heretical even though it had not been formally condemned by any earlier pope or general council. Ockham asked here how a truth of faith could be established with certainty when the universal church could not meet together to define it. He replied:

> This happens whenever catholic truths are asserted and preached through all Catholic lands and divulged to all Catholic peoples as Catholic, *and no Catholic is found who resists such an assertion.*[1]

The passage continued with the usual argument from indefectibility. The Lord had promised that his church would endure until the end of time. It followed, therefore, that if false doctrine were taught as Catholic truth there would always exist someone, "cleric or layman, prelate or subject" who would resist such false doctrine. What the argument really implied of course was that no dissent from the generally accepted faith could be answered by an appeal to the authority of the institutional church. In Ockham's ecclesiology, the individual dissenter might well constitute the one true church. Quite consistently Ockham maintained (in the *Breviloquium*) that every individual Catholic had

---

[1] *Contra Ioannem*, p. 67, "Hoc autem contingit quandocumque aliquae veritates catholicae per omnes regiones catholicorum publice asseruntur et praedicantur, et apud omnes populos catholicos tamquam catholicae divulgantur, et nullus invenitur catholicus, qui tali assertioni resistat." The assertions that only absolute unanimity established a teaching of the church as certainly true and that the true faith might survive in one single person recurred over and over in Ockham's works. See *Epistola*, p. 15; *Contra Ben.*, p. 261; *Breviloquium*, pp. 164-165; *De Imperatorum*, p. 4.

the right and duty of judging the orthodoxy of papal pronouncements
by the light of his own knowledge of the faith.[1]

The section of the *Tractatus contra Ioannem* that we have been considering also contains an interesting variation on Ockham's argument
concerning the "doctrine of the universal church" as a rule of faith.
The Christian church, he pointed out did not consist only of the people
alive at any given time but of all the Catholic prelates and peoples
who had succeeded one another down the course of the centuries.
The authority of this church-of-all-the-ages provided the highest
certitude in matters of faith; its authority was perhaps even greater
than that of the Gospels.[2] John Morrall has much emphasized this
teaching, arguing that Ockham was essentially a traditionally-minded
Catholic, "appealing to the universal church in time as against the
universal church in space." It is true that, in Ockham's view, the
church of his own day—or almost the whole church—had departed
from the sound doctrine of the past and he was willing enough to use
past authorities against present aberrations. But his appeal to the
"church in time" does not really provide us with any objective
criterion for determining the truths of faith. The point is that Ockham
did not conduct any kind of theological or historical enquiry designed
to establish which documents or which oral traditions provided unimpeachable witness to the faith of the Church in past ages. He simply
projected his own beliefs back into the past and asserted—with no real
pretense at proof—that they had always been held. Thus he asserted
that the doctrine of the Beatific Vision that John XXII opposed had
been consistently held from ancient times and that no single Catholic
had ever opposed it.[3] The last statement is obviously unprovable. It

---

[1] *Breviloquium*, pp. 135-136, "Unde si papa diffiniret aliquid ... contra illa que
quilibet christianus credere tenetur explicite, quilibet haberet judicare isto modo
papam errare ..."

[2] *Contra Ioannem*, p. 65, "Sed auctoritas ecclesiae universalis, quae etiam fideles
non solum in hac vita simul degentes, sed sibimet succedentes praelatos et populos
catholicos comprehendit, valet ad fidem et certitudinem catholicae veritatis," p. 66,
"Haec enim ecclesia, quae Apostolos, Evangelistas, omnes Romanos pontifices cete-
rosque episcopos ac praelatos, martyresque et doctores, omnesque catholicos populos usque ad haec tempora comprehendit, maioris auctoritatis esse videtur quam
quodcumque concilium generale vel ecclesia, quae nunc in hac peregrinatione consistit. Et ideo illa ecclesia maioris auctoritatis est quam aliquis Evangelistarum ..."
The appeal to the church of the past is found also in *Contra Ben.*, p. 261. Here he
wrote that the whole church, including the apostles and evangelists, was greater
than any one of the evangelists, "eo quod totum maius est sua parte."

[3] *Contra Ioannem*, p. 67, "... nec aliquis apparuerit catholicus, qui eidem resiste-
rit ..."

is, in fact, not even true. The doctrine that Ockham defended was generally held by theologians of the fourteenth century but it was of rather recent origin. John XXII's doctrine could have found support in the writings of St. Bernard and St. Thomas.[1]

In fact, Ockham's insistence on unanimity, his reiterated assertion that the faith of the true church might live on in some small dissident group, destroyed the possibility of an appeal to the consensus of the past as a sure guide to the truths of faith just as effectively as it destroyed the possibility of an appeal to the consensus of the present. It followed as a logical conclusion from Ockham's premises that the true faith in his own day might have been represented by the adherents of any of the historic heresies that had lingered on into the fourteenth century, by the Nestorians of Syria or Monophysites of Egypt or, coming closer to home, by the Cathars of Provence. Ockham's appeal "to the universal church in time" amounts to nothing but an assertion that the traditional faith of the church was to be presumed always to have been what Ockham happened to be believing in 1335. Once again we are in a realm of total subjectivity. To maintain that the Catholic faith is what Catholics have always believed is a mere tautology. The problem is—how are we to identify the Catholics? Ockham can give us no meaningful answer.

We have said that Ockham seems constantly on the brink of reaching sensible conclusions but never quite succeeds in doing so. There could be one rational conclusion to his whole involved chain of argument. To emphasize the subjective element in man's quest for truth is obviously not in itself reprehensible and may be admirable. No doubt we need to be reminded from time to time that truth is hard to win; that every man must set his own mind against the mystery of the Universe; that each of us must strive to live in accordance with the truth he discerns. But if such an approach is ultimately to make sense it surely requires that each man respect other men's quest for truth. If Ockham had pursued his own ideas further he might

---

[1] Ockham's failure to formulate any rigid criteria for discriminating between truth and error in documents of the past—the actual witnesses to the traditional teaching of the church—left him free to range through the whole field of canonical authorities, selecting and rejecting them at will and imposing his own interpretations on them. Thus Nicholas III's decretal *Exiit* was immutable and irreformable; Innocent III's decretal *Solitae* was false and heretical unless a sound meaning could be "wrenched as if by violence" from its words (*Breviloquium*, p. 45). Both decretals had the same canonical validity so far as any external criteria were concerned.

have emerged as a heroic (if anachronistic) apostle of religious liberty. After all, if the only truths of religion that we can know with final certitude are those that all Christians have always believed unanimously then we are left with the barest essentials of the faith—that there is a God, that he is revealed to men in the life and death of his son, Jesus Christ—not much more. It would seem to follow as a necessary corollary that a wide variety of opinions on all other theological issues could be tolerated within the Church. On this theory it would be proper for each man to shape his own religious beliefs, the unlettered peasant relying on his hearsay knowledge of Scripture, the learned theologian calling on all the subtleties of his art to arrive at his chosen positions. Sometimes, when Ockham discussed the implicit faith of the simple and the duty of the learned to defend the truth, he wrote as though this might conceivably have been his own opinion. Some modern scholars have also been misled by his references to "evangelical liberty" into supposing that Ockham was an upholder of individual rights in something like a modern sense. The judicious Yves Congar even permitted himself to indulge for a moment in the pleasing fantasy that Ockham's *réflexe d'Anglais* predisposed him to be a champion of individual liberty.[1]

But this is fantasy indeed. Ockham wanted to see all his enemies punished as heretics. For him the main point of having the true faith defined authentically by a true pope was to facilitate the crushing of dissent by the Inquisition. There was no grain of tolerance in him; he was filled with *odium theologicum;* he raged incessantly against his enemies. The abusive words "heresy," "heretics," "heretical depravity" are scattered over almost every page of his polemical treatises. As Tabacco rightly observed, if by some twist of fate Ockham himself had ever become pope his enemies would have trembled before the severity of his judgments.[2]

In the end Ockham's conclusions were simply perverse. He wanted the institutional church to crush error while denying that any church institution could certainly define the truth. He offers us only dogma

---

[1] Y. Congar, *L'Église de saint Augustin a l'époque moderne* (Paris, 1970), p. 294. Ockham used the phrase *libertas evangelicae legis* to argue that the pope did not possess supreme power in the temporal sphere and could not impose works of super-erogation in the spiritual sphere. Ockham's rhetoric about evangelica lliberty was perhaps new and is certainly interesting; but the actual doctrines he associated with the phrase were commonplaces of medieval thought.

[2] G. Tabacco, *Pluralità di papi ed unità di chiesa nel pensiero di Guglielmo di Occam* (Turin, 1949), p. 8.

without order, anarchy without freedom, subjectivism without tolerance. And in a real sense it was Ockham's obsession with the idea of infallibility that drove him to such conclusions. Although he developed the concept in such tortuous ways his obsession with it was genuine. After all, it is possible to develop theories of ecclesiology that do not describe the church or the pope as infallible; and in such structures of thought Ockham's paradoxes do not arise. A Christian can believe that his church may err in formulating some recondite theological doctrine or in judging some fine-spun point of morality and still remain a true church. He could call his church a true Christian church because it preserved the essential core of Christ's teaching; because it administered true sacraments; because it engaged in works of Christian charity. If Ockham could have adopted some such stance he might have remained within the Catholic church of the fourteenth century. He could even have continued to defend his own personal views on apostolic poverty within that church. (Franciscans like Alvarus Pelagius who continued to argue that the doctrine of absolute poverty remained tenable even after *Cum inter nonnullos*, but without actually defying the pope, were not molested by John XXII.) But for Ockham all this was impossible. For him the true pope was infallible when he pronounced on matters of faith and the true church was unerring. Since John had erred he was no true pope. And since his followers erred they constituted no true church. The true church was by definition constituted by those who adhered to the true faith; and Ockham was convinced of the rectitude of his own position. It followed as a logical implication of his arguments that, if everyone came to disagree with him then he, Ockham, would alone constitute the true church. Ockham was a logician; he did not shrink from the implication. In his first letter, announcing his break with the papacy of John XXII, he declared that, rather than accept the pope's false teachings, he "would believe that the whole Christian faith ... can be preserved in one man." In his last major political treatise he was still sounding the same note. "The multitude commonly errs and we read in divine Scripture that sometimes, 'one alone fled all the rest.'"[1]

Modern adversaries of the theology of infallibility have always assumed that, pursued to its logical conclusion, the doctrine necessarily leads to authoritarianism in church government and blind fideism among the Christian people. Ockham showed how a belief in the

---

[1] *Epistola*, p. 15; *De imperatorum*, p. 4.

infallibility of the pope and the church (the true pope and the true church of course) could just as logically lead to a position of radical dissent. Ockham began by insisting on the unity-in-faith of the church. He ended by justifying the most radical sectarianism. Papal infallibility was utterly destructive of ecclesiastical authority when every Catholic had the right and duty to decide for himself which papal pronouncements were infallible.

CHAPTER SEVEN

PRO-PAPAL INFALLIBILITY: GUIDO TERRENI

The Carmelite friar, Guido Terreni, a native of Perpignan, studied under Godfrey of Fontaines at Paris and by 1313 had become a master of theology. He also made himself an expert in canon law; his writings include an important commentary on Gratian's Decretum as well as a major work of Scriptural exegesis. In 1318 Guido was elected prior-general of the Carmelites; then he became successively bishop of Majorca (1321-1332) and of Elne (1332-1344). During these years of service as a bishop Guido wrote his major treatises—*De perfectione vite* (1323), *Concordia quatuor evangelistarum* (1328-1334), *Commentarium super Decretum Gratiani* (1336-1339), *Summa de haeresibus* (1340-1342). Included in these works was a *Quaestio* on papal infallibility which Guido incorporated into both the Gospel concordance and the commentary on Gratian.[1]

Ever since the modern Carmelite scholar, B.M. Xiberta, published Guido Terreni's *Quaestio de magisterio infallibili Romani pontificis* in 1926 historians have realized that Guido played an important role in the evolution of the doctrine of papal infallibility. What has been less realized is that the *Quaestio* was only the tip of an iceberg. Guido did not merely present an isolated argument concerning papal infallibility. He demonstrated through the whole corpus of his writings—both theological and canonical—how this doctrine could be used to defend and enhance the authority of the contemporary popes. Guido, so to speak, rescued the doctrine of infallibility from the dissident Franciscans who, up to this time, had been its principal exponents and domesticated it for the use of the papal curia. Even historians of dogma who feel little sympathy for the idea of infallibility in any form may admire the shrewdness and technical skill with which he approached his task.[2]

---

[1] The major studies on Guido Terreni's life and works are those by B. M. Xiberta, "De Mag. Guidone Terreni, priore generali ordinis nostri, episcopo Maioricensi et Elnensi," *Analecta ordinis Carmelitarum*, 5 (1923-1926), pp. 113-206; "De doctrinis theologicis Magistri Guidonis Terreni," *ibid.*, pp. 233-376; *Guiu Terrena Carmelita de Perpinyà* (Barcelona, 1932). Xiberta summarized his conclusions in *De scriptoribus scholasticis saeculi XIV ex ordine Carmelitarum* (Louvain, 1931), pp. 137-141.

[2] B. M. Xiberta, *Guidonis Terreni quaestio de magisterio infallibili Romani pontificis*

According to Xiberta, Guido wrote so "accurately" concerning papal infallibility, the sources of Catholic doctrine and the relation of Scripture to Tradition, that, if he could have read his work after Vatican Council I, he would have needed to change hardly a word of it.[1] There is an element of pardonable exaggeration in Xiberta's enthusiasm for his medieval confrere. In fact Guido insisted on the unique authority of Scripture as the one fount of all Christian faith in a fashion not easily reconcilable with some later Catholic doctrinal formulations. Yet Xiberta was right to point out that Guido also insisted very clearly and explicitly on the infallibility of the pope. It is the systematic combination of the two doctrines in his work that gives Guido's thought its special distinction.

1. The Infallibility of the Pope

Guido Terreni, we have said, was a staunch defender of papal power. He was a trusted counselor of Pope John XXII; as an inquisitor he was active in suppressing the Beghards and Fraticelli of Southern France; he was one of the judges who condemned the *Lectura* of Pietro Olivi; he wrote against the heresies of Marsilius of Padua; he attacked with equal vehemence the aberrations of the Spiritual Franciscans and the errors of the dissident Michaelist faction of the Order. Yet, in spite of all this, Guido was not an extremist by the standards of the early fourteenth century. He rejected with distaste the positions of the radical right-wing papalists whose arguments concerning the pope's temporal and spiritual power rested on the abuse of mystical interpretations of Scripture or on the almost willful distortion of Biblical texts relating to Peter and the apostles. Even Guido's theory of papal infallibility was tempered by his sober regard for the words of Scripture and for traditional interpretations of them. (He was a patristic scholar of unusual erudition).

The obstacles in the way of developing a theory of "pro-papal infallibility" in the years around 1330 should not be under-estimated.

(Münster in Westf., 1926). According to Antoninus of Florence, Guido's contemporary, the Dominican John of Naples (d. ca. 1336), also asserted a doctrine of papal infallibility. On his views see M. Schenk, *Die Unfehlbarkeit des Papstes in der Heiligsprechung* (Freiburg, 1965), pp. 14-16. John, however, seems to have offered only an isolated comment. The importance of Guido's work is that he built a whole structure of ecclesiology around the doctrine of papal infallibility.

[1] "De doctrinis," p. 325, "... si post Concilium Vaticanum sua opera dictasset, nullum fere verbum addere vel mutare debuisset."

John XXII had condemned the teaching that each pope possessed a key of knowledge which rendered his doctrinal decisions irreformable—or at least the Michaelist Franciscans' formulation of that teaching. After John's pronouncements no orthodox theologian, it would seem, could base a theory of papal infallibility on the ancient doctrine of the power of the keys (at any rate for the time being). Again, the whole theory of the irreformability of papally defined doctrine had been created for the sole purpose of demonstrating that Pope John XXII was a heretic. And the pope himself showed little sympathy for the idea that he could be bound by any decrees of his predecessors. Finally, the whole canonical and theological tradition of the church took it for granted that a pope could err in faith.

We can best approach Guido's doctrine of papal infallibility and its relationship to earlier doctrines of infallibility and irreformability by considering first his attitude to the Franciscan theory of the "key of knowledge"—the theory that formed the basis of the doctrine we have called "anti-papal infallibility." In his commentary on Luke 11.52 ("You have taken away the key of knowledge"), Guido performed the considerable intellectual feat of upholding the orthodoxy of the proposition that doctrines of faith and morals established with the key of knowledge were immutable, while simultaneously denouncing as heretics the Franciscans who had first formulated that doctrine and lauding Pope John XXII for condemning them. The "heretics," Guido began, declared that the pope had erred by calling into question the existence of a key of knowledge as one of the "keys of the church." But, in fact, Guido pointed out, Pope John had merely "recited" various opinions concerning the keys without committing himself to any of them. The theory that there was only one key was not indeed heretical for it was upheld by some Catholic doctors; and therefore the pope had been quite justified in pointing out that, according to this theory, the "heretics'" doctrine was false. Guido, however, devoted most of his argument to the second theory, the one he himself preferred, holding that the church possessed two keys, a key of knowledge and a key of power. Some Catholics, he wrote, held that,

> There is one key of knowledge namely the authority of judging and discerning between leper and leper, between the worthy and the unworthy; the other is the power of binding and loosing.

Theologians disagreed as to whether the two keys were both expressions of one essential underlying power or whether they were in essence distinct from one another. But they all agreed that, in every act of ecclesiastical jurisdiction, the use of both keys was required.[1]

This was the central argument that Guido used to confute the doctrine of the Sachsenhausen Appeal. The rebellious Franciscans declared that definitions on faith and morals made with the key of knowledge were immutable. But then they added "It is otherwise in things that are established with the key of power." Guido pounced on this distinction, read into it a meaning that the original author had probably never intended, and insisted that its inclusion in the Sachsenhausen Appeal justified the pope's action in condemning this whole theory of the power of the keys. John XXII's adversaries, Guido declared, had plainly implied that the church sometimes defined questions of faith by the key of power alone, without using the key of knowledge; and this in turn implied that the church could err in its definitions, which was manifestly heretical. A definition made without the key of knowledge would be made without any discernment between the just and the unjust, between the true and false.[2] Again, to define without the key of knowledge was to define without the counsel of the Holy Spirit through whose direction the church "discerned" between the worthy and the unworthy. But the church never defined in matters of faith and morals without the guidance of the Holy Spirit. Therefore it never defined in such matters without using the key of knowledge.[3] It is far from clear that John XXII had any such ideas in mind when he condemned the doctrine of the Michaelist Franciscans.

In the discussion on Luke 11.52 Guido referred only to the unerringness of the universal church. He applied the theory of the "key

---

[1] *Quatuor unum. Concordia evangelica in quatuor evangelistas* (Cologne, 1631) *ad* Luke 11.52, pp. 372-373. Guido asserted the existence of a key of knowledge and a key of power as his own doctrine in his commentary on Matt. 16.19, *op. cit.*, p. 561.

[2] *Op. cit.*, p. 373, "Nam si in fide et moribus Ecclesia statuit per clavem potestatis et non per clavem scientiae. ... Ecclesia universalis erret in fide et moribus contra illud Lucae 22.32, *Rogavi pro te Petre* ... quia qui statuit sine clavi scientiae in statuendo errat; quia facit hoc, non discernendi dignum ab indigno, nec iustum ab iniusto, nec verum a falso. Igitur in his quae circa fidem et mores Ecclesia statuit per clavem potestatis et non per clavem scientiae errat. Quod sentire de sancta Ecclesia est haereticum manifeste."

[3] *Loc. cit.*, "Illud non statuit Ecclesia sine clave scientiae quod non statuit, nisi directa consilio Spiritus S. per cuius directionem discernimus dignum ab indigno, quia Spiritus sanctus docet omnem veritatem. Sed Ecclesia in his quae ad fidem et ad mores pertinent, semper statuit directa consilio Spiritus S. Ergo Ecclesia nihil statuit in his quae ad fidem et mores attinent per clavem potestatis sine clave scientiae."

of knowledge" to specifically papal decisions (though without using it to prove their actual infallibility) in his commentary on *Dist.* 20 of the Decretum. Here Gratian had written that "in the exposition of Scripture" the interpretations of great theologians were to be preferred to those of the popes because the theologians excelled in "knowledge"; but, "in the decision of cases" the decretals of the popes were to be preferred because the popes enjoyed the gift of power. Guido developed further the view of the Decretists that the term "decision of cases" could extend to definitions of doctrine:

> ... In deciding cases the canons are preferred although in the exposition of sacred Scripture knowledge is preferred. But where in the canons both knowledge and power are found together the canons are preferred to the expositors. Hence if the pope decides any question concerning sacred Scripture and makes his decision into a canon or decretal, the determination of the pope is to be preferred to that of the expositors. Thus we should rather adhere to the decree of the lord pope John XXII stating that Christ had property singly or in common than to any expositor asserting the contrary; and I adhere to the decretal of the lord pope Benedict XII stating that the souls in heaven see the divine essence rather than to any expositor asserting the contrary.[1]

Guido here maintained that the pope's authority to promulgate binding definitions in matters of faith depended on both "knowledge" and "power." But he clearly understood that the term "key of knowledge," at any rate when applied to the Petrine keys, did not refer to a *habitus*, a natural or supernatural gift of wisdom. In commenting on Matt. 16.19 he wrote, "... There are two keys, a key of power for binding and loosing and a key of knowledge, which is not taken to be a *habitus* of knowledge but an authority to discern."[2] For Guido it was the pope's exercise of his two-fold power, the *potestas ligandi* and the *auctoritas discernendi*, that rendered his doctrinal decisions

---

[1] *Commentarium super Decretum Gratiani*, MS Vat. lat. 1453 *ad Dist.* 20 *ante* c. 1, fol. 15vb, "... in causis decidendis prefferuntur canones licet scientia prefferatur in expositione sacre Scripture. Ubi autem in canonibus utrumque concurrit, scilicet scientia et potestas, canones prefferuntur expositoribus. Unde si papa decidat aliquam questionem de scriptura sacra, et de eius determinatione faciat canonem vel decretalem, potius standum est determinationi pape quam expositorum, ut potius stare decretali domini pape Johannis XXII quod Christus habuit in proprio vel communi quam cuicumque expositori contrarium asserenti. Et potius sto decretali domini pape Benedicti XII quod anime in celo vident divinam essenciam quam cuicumque expositori contrarium dicenti."

[2] *Concordia ad* Matt. 16.19, p. 561, "... ponuntur duae claves, clavis potentiae ad ligandum et solvendum, clavisque scientiae quae non accipitur pro habitu scientiae, sed pro auctoritate discernendi."

authoritative. (In the text of Benedict XII to which he referred Pope Benedict—as pope—had corrected a theological opinion advanced by John XXII as a private doctor.)

Ockham had come to rather similar conclusions concerning the key of knowledge. Indeed, in this matter, there was a striking convergence between the thought of Guido Terreni and that of his principal adversary. In the decades before 1324, the authority conferred by the key of knowledge had been understood to be simply an authority to conduct a judicial inquiry before imposing a definitive sentence. No one doubted that the church could err in using the key of knowledge. Guido and William—the inquisitor and the heretic—both maintained, on the contrary, that decisions on faith and morals promulgated with the key of knowledge were unerring and immutable. They agreed further that every authentic papal definition required the use of both keys—the key of knowledge and the key of power. Ockham offered this argument as a mere clarification of the terminology used in the Franciscan excursus of the Sachsenhausen Appeal while Guido used it to condemn the teaching of that document. But the Carmelite and the Franciscan were fully agreed that decisions on faith and morals could not be validly promulgated with the key of power alone.

In this last assertion Guido came perilously close to rejecting the doctrine that John XXII had affirmed. (John wrote "In defining anything each key, namely the key of discerning and the key of defining, is necessarily required—or it belongs to the key of power alone to enact and define.")[1] John XXII's decrees had made the task of a pro-papal champion of infallibility very hard indeed, and Guido's uneasy maneuvering in his attempts to uphold the theory of an unerring key of knowledge without approving the condemned doctrine of the dissident Franciscans provides a good illustration of this. Indeed, if Guido Terreni, the champion of orthodoxy, ever experienced a temptation against the faith, it was surely a temptation to interpret the key of knowledge in a sense different from that of John XXII. (The heretics' interpretation could have fitted in so beautifully with his own doctrine of papal infallibility.) However, if Guido experienced any such temptation, he manfully resisted it. The doctrine he affirmed—that both keys were needed for a valid definition—had been

---

[1] *Extrav. Joannis XXII*, Tit. 14 c. 5, col. 1231, "Quare restat, quod ad convenienter statuendum, seu aliquid diffiniendum, utraque clavis, scilicet cognoscendi et diffiniendi necessario requiratur; vel quod soli clavi potentiae statuere competat, et etiam diffinire ..."

recognized by John XXII, even if grudgingly, as one that it was possible for a Catholic doctor to hold. And, when Guido came to formulate his own theories on papal infallibility and on the irreformability of papal definitions he avoided any appearance of conflict with John's decrees by turning aside from the doctrine of the keys presented at Matt. 16.19 and Luke 11.52 to base his whole teaching on another of the famous Petrine texts, Luke 22.32, "I have prayed for you Peter that your faith shall not fail."[1]

In his theological commentary on Luke 11.52 Guido insisted on the infallibility of the universal church without referring specifically to the power of individual popes. In his canonical discussion on Gratian's *Dist.* 20 he upheld the authority of papal definitions without referring specifically to the question of infallibility. In the *Quaestio de magisterio infallibili*, to which we can now turn, the two streams of argument flowed together and, appropriately, Guido included this *Quaestio* in both of the major treatises that we have so far considered. For Guido Terreni, as for Ockham, the problem of papal infallibility arose out of the allegation that John XXII had revoked a doctrinal definition of his predecessor, Nicholas III, (an allegation that Guido held to be false). This is clear from the form in which he first posed his *Quaestio*, "It is asked whether, what a supreme pontiff establishes with the counsel of the cardinals to be believed by faith ... can be revoked by a successor and the contrary established." When he repeated the *Quaestio* in his commentary on the Decretum (written several years after John XXII's death) Guido gave it a new title which describes its content more accurately, "It is asked whether what the Roman pontiff establishes with the counsel of his brothers to be believed by faith can contain an error against the faith."[2]

As for the phrase, "with the counsel of the cardinals," Xiberta maintained that this was merely a "curial locution" intended to distinguish between the pope's solemn official pronouncements as head of the church and the opinions that he held as a private individual. This seems to be the correct interpretation. At any rate, there is no trace in Guido's work of the "curial corporatism" which was already finding some sup-

---

[1] *Questio de magisterio infallibili*, ed. Xiberta, p. 10. In another context he associated the idea of infallibility with Matt. 14.28, *Concordia*, p. 441, "Ex hoc miraculo multa colligimus ... quod sic apprehendit Petrum et suos successores, quod in his, quae ad fidem pertinent per eos declaranda et determinanda, non permittat eos a fide cadere et in errorem submergi."

[2] *Quaestio*, p. 9. Both versions of the title are given here by Xiberta.

porters at this time—that is to say the doctrine that the power of the apostolic see did not inhere in the pope alone but was diffused through a corporate body of pope-and-cardinals.[1] On the contrary, Guido often insisted that the whole power of the church was epitomized in the pope. On the other hand, the distinction between a pope's public pronouncements and his private opinions was essential to Guido's argument. Indeed, one of his major contributions to the development of the doctrine of infallibility lay in his way of handling this distinction.

Guido's *Quaestio* began with certain standard arguments against the inerrancy and irreformability of papal decrees. Any mortal man could err, and errors against the faith were always to be corrected. Therefore a pope could revoke and correct what his predecessor had erroneously defined. Guido presented several arguments in favor of the proposition that a pope, like other men, could err in faith. Pope Anastasius had favored the heretic Acacius; canon law clearly presupposed that a pope could err when it decreed that a heretical pope could be deposed; Peter himself had erred against the faith when he denied Christ and when he imposed a judaizing policy on his gentile converts.[2]

To all this Guido replied with a single text of Scripture, "I have prayed for you Peter that your faith shall not fail." Guido did not deny—indeed he often affirmed—that the traditional interpretation which treated Christ's words as a prayer for the faith of the whole church was a sound one. But he insisted over and over again that the words could also be applied particularly to Peter and to Peter's successors in the papacy.[3] To prove that the text could properly be applied to Peter's successors he cited a single authority of the schools—Thomas Aquinas[4]—and this seems to be the starting point of a long, but

---

[1] On this development see most recently G. Alberigo, *Cardinalato e collegialità* (Florence, 1969).

[2] *Quaestio*, pp. 9-10.

[3] For Luke 22.32 applied to the whole Church see above p. 241 n. 2. Also *Concordia ad* Matt. 16.19, p. 563; *Commentarium super Decretum Gratiani*, MS Vat. Lat. 1453 *ad* C. 24 q. 1 c. 2, fol. 151vb. For application of the text specifically to Peter's successors see *Concordia ad* Luke 22.32, p. 895, "Christus rogavit pro fide vicarii Christi ut concernit fidem totius Ecclesiae"; *De perfectione vite*, MS British Museum, Addit. 16632, fol. 2v, "Et pro petro et in eo pro ceteris petri successoribus rogavit ne fides eius deficeret ..."; *Commentarium super Decretum ad Dist*. 11 c. 11, fol. 10ra, "Et rogans pro petro rogat pro eius successoribus," and *ad Dist*. 40 c. 1, fol. 31rb; *Summa de haeresibus* (Cologne, 1631), p. 136.

[4] *Quaestio*, p. 10, "In oppositum videtur: Quia Salvator ait Luc. XXII°: Symon, rogavi pro te, ut non deficiat fides tua. Tu autem aliquando conversus confirma frates tuos. Et istud dictum secundum beatum Thomam secunda secunde q. 1 at.

very dubiously-based tradition of citing Thomas as an authority in favor of papal infallibility. (It is not clear whether Guido Terreni was ever aware that Pietro Olivi—whom Guido regarded as an arch-heretic—had interpreted the text *Ego rogavi pro te* as an argument for the infallibility of Peter and his successors much more plainly than Thomas did.) The bulk of the ensuing discussion was devoted to a series of arguments that moved from the acknowledged inerrancy of the universal Church to the necessary infallibility of the pope. The authority of the church did not inhere in any private person, Guido wrote, but in the supreme pontiff.[1] The stability of the church's faith could be maintained, therefore, only if the church's head was divinely protected from error.

This argument was repeated in several different forms. All Christians were bound to believe what the church defined and established concerning the faith. This was implied by the article of faith, *unam sanctam catholicam ecclesiam*. If then the church promulgated a false definition, all would be obliged to believe it and the whole church would fall away from the faith. But this was impossible for Christ had said "I will be with you until the end of the world" and he had prayed that the faith of the church should never fail. If even the possibility were admitted that the church could err in defining truths of faith

---

X est intelligendum de summo pontifice, ad quem spectat causas maiores et pertinencia ad fidem sentencialiter determinare ..." Thomas here cited Luke 22.32 to support the conclusion "ad solam auctoritatem summi pontificis pertinet nova editio symboli." But the underlying argument was not that a pope by himself could define the faith infallibly. Rather Thomas was arguing that the pope had the "sole authority" to summon a general council which was competent to promulgate a new creed. His argument ran thus, "... editio symboli facta est in synodo generali. Sed hujusmodi synodus auctoritate solius summi pontificis potest congregari ... Ergo editio symboli ad auctoritatem summi pontificis pertinet." The precise degree of authority attributed to an individual pope is by no means clear. Indeed, at every point where Thomas discussed controversial aspects of papal power his usual clarity of expression deserted him. His texts on spiritual and temporal power, on the relationship between pope and bishops, and on the teaching authority of the pope are all so obscure that modern scholars have been able to reach no agreement as to his real meanings. E.g., on spiritual and temporal power see I. T. Eschmann, "St. Thomas Aquinas on the Two Powers," *Mediaeval Studies*, 20 (1958), pp. 177-205; and on the relationship of pope to bishops, Y. Congar, "Aspects ecclésiologiques ...," *AHDL*, 36 (1961), at pp. 93-95. For the debate at Vatican Council I on whether Thomas did or did not teach the infallibility of the pope see U. Betti, "L'assenza dell'autorità di S. Tommasso nel decreto vaticano sull'infallibilità pontificia," *Divinitas*, 6 (1962), pp. 407-422.

[1] *Quaestio*, p. 20, "Ex quibus patet immutabilis et invariabilis ecclesie catholice auctoritas, que post Christum in solo summo pontifice et non in aliqua privata persona noscitur universaliter contineri."

"not evident from Scripture" everything would be thrown into confusion. (Guido believed that many truths were implicit in Scripture that were not "evident.") The definitions of the church would then be seen to depend "on fallible human reason not on infallible truth." If a decision on the faith were revoked by a subsequent decision the second decision might in turn be revoked, "and so no firmness, no concord, no stability" would remain in doctrinal definitions. If the principle of juridical sovereignty—*par in parem non habet imperium*—were applied to the faith of the church it would render the whole faith derisory.[1] To be sure any man, considered simply as a man, could fall into error, but men guided by the Holy Spirit could not err. The prophets of the Old Testament had not erred when they were inspired by the Spirit to speak concerning the faith; and the pope and the Roman church enjoyed the same divine guidance:

> Therefore, by the same authority, the supreme pontiff and the Roman church, guided by the Holy Spirit, teaches and determines the truth in things pertaining to the faith without error. Nor would the Holy Spirit, who teaches all truth permit the supreme pontiff or the church to err.[2]

There was still some ambiguity here as to whether the quality of infallibility resided in the "supreme pontiff" or in the "Roman church," and we have seen how ambiguous the latter phrase could be in medieval discourse. In his next argument, however, Guido referred more clearly to the pope as an infallible exponent of the church's faith. It was through the authority of the church, he wrote, that the books of the Bible were known to present the truth infallibly. Hence Augustine had written "I would not believe the Gospel unless the authority of the Catholic church so moved me." The church was acknowledged

---

[1] *Quaestio*, pp. 13-14, "Quia in hiis que ecclesia determinat fide credenda, que evidenter ex scriptura sacra non habentur, si in hiis posset ecclesia errare, fluctuarent fideles, an ecclesia errasset vel non; et qua racione prima determinacio in talibus que evidenter ex scriptura non habentur iudicaretur falsa et revocaretur, eadem racione posset sequens determinacio ecclesie revocari, quia quod videtur uni verum in talibus, videtur alteri falsum et e converso... Et sic nulla firmitas, nulla concordia, nulla stabilitas in fide ecclesie remaneret, immo racionabiliter posset dubitari quod sicut prima determinacio revocatur ut falsa contra veritatem fidei per sequentem, sic sequens revocaretur per aliam sequentem, cum par in parem non habeat imperium; et per consequens sequerentur scismata inter fideles et derisio fidei apud infideles."

[2] *Quaestio*, pp. 15-16, "Ergo eadem auctoritate summus pontifex et ecclesia romana per Spiritum Sanctum directa absque errore docet et determinat veritatem in hiis que ad fidem pertinent, nec in hiis Spiritus Sanctus, qui docet omnem veritatem, permitteret summum pontificem aut ecclesiam errare."

to have been so directly inspired by the Holy Spirit in fixing the canon of sacred Scripture that no one, not even the pope, could change that canon or contradict its teachings. But the corollary of this was that the church, since it still enjoyed the guidance of the Spirit—and the pope as its head —could never err in defining the faith:

> So it is to be believed that the supreme pontiff, with whom the authority of the Catholic church resides, does not err in the determination of the faith, but is ruled by the Holy Spirit.[1]

The same argument could be applied to the church's acceptance of the Apostles' Creed. Only through the infallible authority of the church could Christians be sure that the articles of faith in the Creed had in fact been propounded by the apostles themselves. And, again, the authority of the church was "universally in the supreme pontiff."[2]

The most interesting arguments of Guido's *Quaestio* were presented in the closing sections where he responded to the objection that Peter and other popes had in fact erred in faith. Even if a pope became a heretic, Guido wrote, he did not think that God would permit him to err against the faith in his doctrinal definitions.[3] Later, to explain this more fully Guido wrote:

> It is to be said of the supreme pontiff that although in himself he can err as a single person, nevertheless the Holy Spirit does not permit him to define anything contrary to the faith of the church for the sake of the

---

[1] *Quaestio*, pp. 17-18, "Et praeterea constat quod auctoritate ecclesie libri canonis habent robur auctoritatis. Unde per ecclesiam libri biblie admissi sunt in auctoritatem ... quia ut Augustinus dicit in libro Contra epistolam fundamenti "evangelio non crederem, nisi auctoritas ecclesie catholice me commoveret" ... Igitur si ecclesia in eleccione scripture canonice, ut non erraret, creditur fuisse directa Spiritu Sancto, sic quod non liceret summo pontifici aliquid detrahere de libris canonicis aut contra eorum veritatem expressam determinare: sic credendum est quod non erret summus pontifex in determinacione fidei, apud quem residet auctoritas ecclesie catholice, sed in hiis regitur Spiritu Sancto."

[2] *Quaestio*, p. 18, "Et eciam si non stetur circa fidem infallibiliter auctoritati ecclesie, que non est nisi in summo pontifice universaliter, eadem facillitate dicetur quod erratum est in articulis fidei et quod articuli non fuerunt editi ab apostolis." This seems a good instance of the snares that lie in wait for theorists of infallibility. Guido gave as a self-evident example of the church's "infallible authority" the universally held doctrine that the apostles themselves composed the Apostles' Creed. This belief of the medieval church seems to satisfy even William of Ockham's demanding criterion for the establishment of infallible truth. No Catholic, so far as we know, dissented from it. But no informed Catholic any longer believes in it.

[3] *Quaestio*, p. 25, "... non videtur mihi quod papa hereticus permitteretur a Deo determinare aliquid contra fidem."

community of the faithful and the universal church, for whose faith the Lord prayed.[1]

Van Leeuwen maintained that earlier medieval writers had not seen the need to distinguish between the pope's personal opinions and his official teachings and that Guido Terreni was the first to introduce such a distinction into medieval theology.[2] This is, to say the least, an over-simplification. The twelfth century Decretists had grasped quite clearly the difference between a pope's pronouncements *ut magister* and *ut papa*.[3] Innocent IV (while pope) published his commentary on the *Decretales* as the work of a private master, without pontifical authority, and it was universally accepted in the schools as such. Pietro Olivi clearly saw the need for such a distinction in his *Quaestio* on papal infallibility and he had begun to discuss the matter at the point where the *Quaestio* breaks off. The whole issue had come into prominence again in the course of John XXII's disputes with the Franciscans.[4] We can say with confidence that every theologian in Guido Terreni's time grasped clearly the distinction between a pope's teachings as a private doctor and his official pronouncements as a pope. The point is that, before Guido, all orthodox theologians believed the pope could err in his official pronouncements concerning the faith. And this Guido denied. He put the point with considerable force and clarity :

> We are not asking whether a pope can be a heretic in himself but whether he can err in defining anything in the church and obliging the faithful to believe, so that his error does not concern the person of the pope alone but concerns all the faithful and the whole church of Christ. For an error concerning his person can inhere in the pope, but not an error concerning the whole church ....[5]

---

[1] *Quaestio*, p. 28, "... dicendum quod summus pontifex, etsi ut est persona singularis possit in se errare, tamen propter communitatem fidelium et universalitatem ecclesie, pro cuius fide rogavit Dominus, non permittet eum determinare aliquid contra fidem in ecclesia Spiritus Sanctus ..."

[2] *Art. cit.* (supra p. 209 n. 1), p. 279.

[3] See above p. 41 and *Foundations*, p. 39 n. 2.

[4] In *Quia quorundam* John XXII replied to the argument that his predecessor Innocent V had asserted a doctrine of poverty different from his own by declaring, "Dicimus quidem quod hoc dixerit non ut papa sed ut frater Petrus de Tarantasio ..." John himself proposed his doctrine on the Beatific Vision as his own personal opinion but not as officially defined papal doctrine.

[5] *Quaestio*, p. 30, "Non enim querimus, an papa possit esse in se hereticus, sed queritur, an papa determinando aliquid in ecclesia et obligando fideles ad fidem credendum possit errare, ut error eius non solum concernat personam pape, sed concernat omnes fideles et totam ecclesiam Christi. Quia error concernens personam potest inesse pape, non autem error concernens totam ecclesiam ..."

Guido seems to have believed in a kind of preventive grace that would impede even a heretical pope from officially promulgating error as Catholic truth. If such a pope formed the intention of defining a false doctrine, Guido was convinced that God would intervene to stop him from doing so.

> God would impede such a pope from his evil intention either by death or by the resistance of others or in other ways.[1]

This line of argument provided a very adequate refutation of the objections to infallibility based on the errors of past popes. Peter, for instance, had spoken falsely when he denied Christ out of fear, but he had not erred in his heart; and, even if he did err, he had not defined his error as a truth of faith. It was the same in the matter of Peter's judaizing policy.[2] Peter had sinned and Paul was right to rebuke him. But, Guido pointed out, Peter had not actually defined any false doctrine. On the contrary, when the issue was finally settled at the Council of Jerusalem, Peter decided correctly.[3] As to the more recent problem, the alleged conflict between the Bulls of Pope John XXII and of Pope Nicholas III on the poverty of Christ, Guido simply denied that any real conflict existed.[4]

Guido's position was closer to the nineteenth century doctrine of papal infallibility than any that had been developed earlier. Hervaeus Natalis and Augustinus Triumphus had argued that, in its intrinsic nature, the papal office was infallible, but both had conceded that the individual pontiff could betray his office and misuse its authority by promulgating incorrect definitions. This Guido would not admit. Olivi and Ockham had taught that the decisions of a true pope were infallible. But, for them, an official pronouncement from the papal throne was simply the starting point for a theological enquiry into the validity of the doctrine defined. If the doctrine were sound, the pope was indeed a true pope and his teaching was immutable; if the doc-

---

[1] *Quaestio*, p. 28, "... immo talem papam a suo malo proposito impediret Deus sive per mortem sive per aliorum resistenciam sive per alios modos ut dictum est."

[2] *Quaestio*, p. 29, "Tum quia esto quod Petrus errasset ... non tamen determinavit aut statuit predictum errorem in ecclesia ..."

[3] *Quaestio*, p. 30, "Quod autem dicitur quod Petrus summus pontifex erravit in observancia legalium: dicendum quod, ut patet Act. XV°, Petrus ut summus pontifex non erravit immo veritatem cum Iacobo et aliis determinavit ... Et sic, licet errasset postea facto aliter agendo et contra suam determinacionem, non tamen erravit contra fidem determinando ..."

[4] See below p. 267.

trine were false its originator was a heretic who automatically ceased to be pope. Guido excluded from the outset the possibility that an official teaching of a man who had been lawfully elected as pope could ever be in error. The very fact that the Holy Spirit had not intervened to prevent the pope's definition being promulgated showed that the definition was in accordance with the true faith.

2. THE PRIMACY OF SCRIPTURE

Guido Terreni, we have seen, held the church to be unerring when it defined truths of faith "not evident from Scripture" and he also observed that the content of Scripture itself had been determined by the authority of the church. In another interesting passage of the *Quaestio* on infallibility he juxtaposed Scripture, the church and the faith in this fashion:

> I plainly state and confess that everything said or decreed contrary to the truth of faith or determined contrary to the doctrine of sacred Scripture ... is to be rejected, refuted and revoked. But it is in no way to be believed that God permits the church to err in faith or to decree or determine anything contrary to the faith and the truth of divine Scripture.[1]

Such passages raise the question whether Guido Terreni was, like William of Ockham, an exponent of a "two-sources" theory of divine revelation. In fact, he held a very different point of view. Faithfully following the doctrine of Pope John XXII, Guido was an outstanding defender of the view that all the immutable truths of faith were contained in Scripture explicitly or implicitly and that, accordingly, all teachings of the church on matters of faith were derived from Scripture "expressly" or "remotely." De Vooght, who has studied medieval doctrine concerning the sources of faith most thoroughly, interpreted Guido's thought on the whole in this way.[2] Two subsequent works, however, by Xiberta and Tavard have sought to present Guido as a supporter of the "two-sources" theory. The whole question needs reconsidering on the basis of a more adequate selection of texts than has been presented so far.

---

[1] *Quaestio*, p. 27, "... dico et confiteor plane quod omne dictum vel statutum contra veritatem fidei et contra scripture sacre doctrinam determinatum ... est repudiandum, reffellendum et revocandum. Sed nullo modo est credendum quod Deus permittat ecclesiam errare in fide aut statuere seu determinare aliquid contra fidem et veritatem scripture divine."

[2] P. de Vooght, *Les sources de la doctrine chrétienne* (Bruges, 1954), pp. 132-137.

Let us briefly restate the problem. The question at issue was this: Were all the truths of faith held by the church based on Scripture and authoritative interpretations of Scripture? Or did the church hold some truths of faith that were known only by extra-scriptural revelation? We may note first that Guido Terreni's comments on the Scriptural passages most commonly used to support the "two-sources" theory of revelation were terse and devoid of any reference to that theory. On John 16.12-14 ("The Spirit ... will teach you all truth") Guido commented, referring to the Son and the Holy Spirit, "Although the persons are distinct there is one nature, one doctrine, one teaching (*magisterium*)."[1] At John 20.30 ("Many other signs Jesus worked ... which are not written") Guido enquired why the evangelists had not written more fully. One of his answers was, "Because through the things that are written anyone is sufficiently instructed in the faith."[2] He offered no significant comment on John 21.25 ("There are many other things that Jesus did ...").

These brief remarks are indicative of Guido's attitude, but for a detailed exposition of his doctrine we must turn to the opening chapters of the *Summa de haeresibus*. At the beginning of this work Guido declared that a heretic was one who held "a false and erroneous opinion contrary to the truth of faith and the definition of the church in things necessary for salvation."[3] Then, in the course of defining in more detail what constituted heresy, he explained, by implication, what were the sources of the true faith. In the first place, any belief that expressly and evidently contradicted the texts of the Old and New Testament was heretical. Likewise a belief that contradicted truth evidently deducible from Scripture was heretical, even though the truth in question was not expressly written down.[4] Then, going beyond these

---

[1] *Concordia ad* John 16.14, p. 940, "Quia etsi distinctae sint personae amborum, tamen est una natura, una doctrina, unum magisterium." Most of the gloss was devoted to problems of Trinitarian theology. Guido was particularly hostile to the Joachimite idea that a future revelation of the Holy Spirit might modify the teachings of the Gospel. This is discussed below.

[2] *Concordia ad* John 20.30, p. 1033, "Quia per ea quae scripta sunt sufficienter quis instruitur in fide et qui his credit non indiget aliis ad fidei rationem."

[3] *Summa de haeresibus*, p. 5, "... falsam et erroneam opinionem contra veritatem fidei, et ecclesiae determinationem, quoad ea quae ad fidem pertinent et bonos mores, et quoad ea quae necessaria sunt ad salutem ..."

[4] *Summa*, p. 7, "Secundo modo potest dici contra scripturam sacram in suo antecedente, vel suo consequente per evidentem deductionem cui rationabiliter non potest contradici, quamvis illud non sit expresse scriptum ... Et isto modo dicere contra scripturam est haereticum."

clear-cut cases, Guido explained that a belief could contradict a truth of faith that was derived from Scripture "not directly, not expressly, not by evident and immediate but by remote deduction." In this area the determinations of the church were all-important. Opinions on such matters were not to be considered heretical until the church had pronounced for one side or the other in a controversy and promulgated a definitive decision on the point of faith at issue.[1]

This exposition can help us to understand what Guido meant when he wrote in the *Quaestio* on infallibility that the church determined matters of faith that were "not evident from Scripture." After all, ecclesiastical determinations were hardly needed in matters that were "evident." It was precisely in the realm of truths that were implicit in Scripture but not self-evidently implicit that the authority of the church came into play. At no point did Guido suggest that the church could define truths of faith that were not derived from Scripture, at least remotely. His underlying point of view seems to have been that meditation on Scripture as a whole gave insights into divine truths that were not strictly deducible from any particular text. The clear parts of Scripture shed light on the obscure parts.[2] And, as we have seen, the church was unerring in the interpretations of Scripture that it officially adopted.

Guido's emphasis on Scripture as the necessary basis for the whole faith of the church was maintained all through the opening chapters of the *Summa de haeresibus*. To deny any of the articles of faith in the Creed was heresy, he wrote. But this did not imply that there could be an error against the faith that was not also an error against sacred Scripture for the articles of faith were derived from Scripture "expressly." Guido observed that it was useful and expedient to have such a formula of faith "extracted from sacred Scripture"[3] and he went on to

---

[1] *Summa*, p. 8, "Alio modo dicitur contra scripturam sanctam non directe non expresse, non evidenti et immediata deductione, sed multum remota ... Sic etiam circa sic deducta ex scriptura sancta, quae evidenter non patent esse contra scripturam, possunt viri sancti absque periculo haeresis contraria opinari, donec per ecclesiam contra unam partem pro alia determinetur ... tamdiu error sustineri potest donec accusetur, hoc est donec per scripturam sanctam et per ecclesiam expresse et evidenter reprehendetur et damnetur ..."

[2] *Concordia ad* Matt. 13.52, p. 399, "non ergo oportet ut Doctor Scripturae sacrae omnia norit resolvere ad evidentes probationes sed sufficit quod ... possit explicare et obscura exponere per ea quae in dicta Scriptura alibi clarius exponuntur."

[3] *Summa*, p. 8, "Ulterius opinio est haeretica si sit ... contra articulos fidei ... nec est error contra fidem, quin sit contra scripturam sanctam, eo quod articuli fidei descendunt ex scriptura sancta expresse ..." p. 10, "Nec tamen inutile fuit,

cite an array of Scriptural texts from which, he claimed, all the various articles of the Creed could be deduced.

The same argument applied to general councils approved by the apostolic see and especially to the four great councils of the early church. Any one who condemned them was a heretic, but this was because the teaching of the councils was "consonant with sound doctrine and sacred Scripture";[1] and, again, Guido demonstrated at considerable length how all the major heresies condemned by the four councils were opposed to specific texts of Scripture. Guido concluded his argument by referring to the writings of the church fathers. These were to be treated with reverence, but to argue against particular doctrines contained in them was not strictly heretical so long as the patristic teaching was not evidently and expressly confirmed by holy Scripture and authorized by the church.[2]

For Guido, then, the church was unerring in its interpretations of Scripture; but Scripture was the essential source of the church's teachings. His arguments concerning the unique authority of Scripture were coherent and explicit. It may seem surprising that any controversy about his views should have arisen in modern scholarship. Much confusion has been caused, however, by the misinterpretation of one ambiguous text in the *Summa*,

> The church holds some things as altogether necessary and to be believed by faith: such are the things in sacred Scripture or expressly and necessarily deduced from it, as are the articles of faith, and other things which the church determines and commands to be believed.[3]

---

imo multum expediens et utile fuit habere symbolum fidei extractum de scriptura sacra ..." He gave an even fuller account of the Scriptural basis of all the articles of the Creed in discussing the errors of the Waldensians at p. 149.

[1] *Summa*, p. 10, "Doctrinae quoque generalium conciliorum per sedem Apostolicam confirmatorum et praecipue quatuor scilicet Niceni, Constantinopolitani, Ephesini et Chalcedonensis sic doctrinae sanae et scripturae sacrae consonant, quod illa quae praedicta concilia damnant, haeretica ab omnibus fidelibus sunt tenenda ..."

[2] *Summa*, pp. 11-12, "... ubi per scripturam sanctam evidenter et expresse non probantur nec firmantur nec per Ecclesiam auctorizantur ac determinantur, firmam veritatem et indubiam continere ... Ubi non est infallibilis veritas, ibi non est fides certa et indubia ..."

[3] *Summa*, pp. 13-14, "Unde sciendum est, quod ecclesia continet aliqua omnino necessaria et fide credenda, ut sunt quae in scriptura canonica aut per eam expresse et necessario deducuntur, ut articuli fidei, et alia quae praecipit seu determinat fide credenda." De Vooght, Xiberta and Tavard were all misled by a faulty reading of this text in the Paris (1528) edition of the *Summa*, "... sunt quae in scriptura canonica aut per eam expresse et necessario deducuntur, *et* articuli fidei et alia ..." The

The text could mean that the things which the church determined were, like the articles of faith, expressly deduced from Scripture. Or it could mean that they constituted a third class of truths that were to be held by faith. In that case, if the argument is to make sense at all in the context in which it occurs, we would have to suppose that the determinations of the church affirmed truths that were only "remotely" deduced from Scripture. There is no reason to suppose that Guido was contradicting the whole substance of his argument in this one text by presenting the church as a source of revelation not dependent on Scripture at all.

Nevertheless, both Xiberta and Tavard have used this passage to prove that Guido was an advocate of the "two-sources" theory which made the church a fount of non-Biblical revelation. Xiberta added several other arguments. For instance, Guido held that the apostolic origin of the articles of faith in the Creed was known only through the authority of the church. Xiberta saw this as an authorization by the church of extra-Biblical teaching;[1] but in fact Guido insisted that the articles of the Creed were expressly deduced from sacred Scripture. Xiberta's argument proves only that, according to Guido, the church (in this case the church of the apostles) could infallibly transmit and interpret the truths of Scripture. This is true of course, but it is not the point that Xiberta was trying to make. Again, Xiberta called attention to a text of Guido asserting that it was heretical to deny the church's right to enact statutes going beyond what was contained in the Gospel and the Epistles.[2] Guido certainly held this view. It was an old platitude of the canonists. But the right to enact positive legislation has nothing to do with the right to reveal new truths of faith. Positive legislation was by its nature variable; the truths of faith were immutable.

Xiberta's strongest argument was contained in a text that he quoted from Guido's Commentary on the Decretum. This asserted that the church held certain traditions handed down by the apostles which were not found in Scripture.

---

reading *ut* is obviously preferable. Guido can not possibly have written *et* in a disjunctive sense since he plainly held that the articles of faith at least were expressly deduced from Scripture.

[1] B. M. Xiberta, "Scriptura, Traditio et magisterium iuxta antiquos auctores ordinis Carmelitarum" in C. Balić (ed.), *De Scriptura et Traditione* (Rome, 1963), pp. 253-273 at p. 265.

[2] *Art. cit.*, pp. 264, 273.

> The general customs of the church, although they are not written in
> the New or the Old Testament are to be observed and not abandoned
> for three reasons: first, because, although they were not written in the
> Canon, they were handed down by Christ or by the Apostles ... second-
> ly, out of reverence for the authority of the church ... thirdly, on ac-
> count of their utility.[1]

The point here is that, for Guido (as for the twelfth century Decretists), not everything handed down by the apostles and held by the
universal church belonged to the sphere of the divinely revealed,
immutable truths of faith. Guido's most detailed exposition of this
point was presented in the *Concordia* on Matt. 16.18.

> In things which the universal church has observed from the beginning
> concerning the sacraments without the authority of Scripture, it is sure-
> ly to be believed that the apostles received them from Christ and that
> the church received them through the apostles and through their tra-
> dition ... for they left to us many things that are not written.[2]

At first glance this reads like a striking confirmation of Xiberta's
thesis. But the whole argument was introduced to prove the proposition that not everything handed down from the apostles was immutable.
The church could and sometimes did depart from ancient forms af
administering the sacraments. When the church received such usages
from the apostles she received them with the authority to change
them.[3] Such considerations of course sharply separated these non-
Scriptural traditions of the church from the immutable truths of faith.
For Guido, apostolic traditions, however venerable, were essentially
matters of positive law.[4] They had the authority of ancient custom
or of ecclesiastical legislation. They were subject to change. But the
enduring truths of divine faith did not change. None of Guido's

---

[1] *Art. cit.*, p. 273 citing Guido's *Commentarium ad Dist.* 11 c. 5, MS Vat. lat.
1453, fol. 9r-v.

[2] *Concordia ad* Matt. 16.18, p. 563, "In his enim quae circa sacramenta ab initio
universalis observat ecclesia et auctoritas Scripturae non habetur omnino credendum est, quod a Christo acceperunt Apostoli et per eos et per eorum traditionem
suscepit Ecclesia ... Multa enim non scripta nobis reliquerunt ..."

[3] *Loc. cit.*, "... sicut circa ea operatur in restringendo et ampliando vel mutando
sic a Christo per Apostolos cum auctoritate Ecclesia suscepit." Guido referred to
the church's changing the prohibited degrees of matrimony and regulating the
administration of the sacrament of penance.

[4] In another context (on Matt. 26.26, p. 875) he wrote of the Eucharistic fast.
This usage, Guido held, was inspired by the Holy Spirit and handed down from
the apostles, but still it could be abandoned in case of extreme emergency. To prove
this he cited the jurist's maxim, "necessitas non habet legem." Again, this was not
the way one wrote of immutable truths of faith.

texts on apostolic tradition suggested that the truths of faith themselves could be derived from any source other than Scripture.

Most of Xiberta's argument was not inherently unreasonable. The points he made can be accepted as valid so long as we clearly understand that the references to extra-Scriptural traditions which he found in Guido Terreni's work did not allude to revealed truths of faith. Tavard, perhaps misled by his general distaste for late medieval thought, adopted a more extreme and less defensible position. According to Xiberta, Guido presented Scripture and church as co-equal sources of faith. According to Tavard, Guido totally subordinated Scripture to the authority of the church.[1] The basis for this assertion was provided by Guido's text affirming that the church throughout the ages continued to enjoy the guidance of the Holy Spirit which had enabled it to fix the canon of Scripture correctly in the first place. This need not necessarily imply that the authority of the church was greater than that of Scripture. Tavard, however, commented, "That equation between the choice of the canonical books and the subsequent decisions of Councils and Roman Pontiffs, is a token of that devaluation of Scripture which preceded the Reformation"; and, again, "In all cases the ultimate source of the right doctrine remains the authority of the church and, particularly, of the apostolic see ... the theological point of comparison, the measure of authority, is no longer Scripture. It is the church." Thus, in Tavard's view, Guido Terreni "devalued" Scripture by exaggerating the authority of the church, the general council, and the pope. In fact Guido commented explicitly on the relationship between the authority of each of these three and that of sacred Scripture in his commentary on the Decretum; and, in every case, his real point of view was the exact opposite of the one that Tavard attributed to him.

In the first place Guido explained very carefully that the church's original choice of the books of the canon did not imply that, subsequently, the church's authority was greater than that of Scripture. Just the opposite was true. (Guido was commenting here on Augustine's "I would not believe the Gospel unless the authority of the church moved me"):

---

[1] G. H. Tavard, *Holy Writ or Holy Church* (London, 1959), pp. 31-34. Tavard noted that his interpretation was "exactly opposite to the views of Dom de Vooght." De Vooght replied, without presenting significant new evidence, in the article, "L'évolution du rapport Église-Écriture du XIIIᵉ au XVᵉ siècle," *Ephemerides theologicae Lovanienses*, 38 (1962), pp. 71-85.

This has to be soundly understood. For in truth the church follows the Gospel and not the Gospel the church. Whence the authority of the Gospel is greater than that of the church in itself and directly, when any assertion is known to be contained in it .... But the church, directed and taught by the Holy Spirit, chose the true Gospel ... Augustine spoke of this true choice.[1]

Tavard maintained that Guido regarded the council and the pope as sources of faith separate from Scripture and equal to it. Commenting on an assertion that the councils were to be venerated "like the four gospels" Guido wrote:

Not that they are of equal authority, for Augustine says ... that among all the divine authorities found in sacred writings the Gospel rightly excells. But it says *quasi quatuor* because, just as evangelical doctrine is especially received in the four Gospels ... so these four councils are so plainly and clearly approved by sacred Scripture as regards the truth of faith, that anyone who contradicts them seems manifestly to contradict sacred Scripture and, consequently, seems manifestly to be a heretic.[2]

In another comment, Guido suggested that the councils were ancillary to Scripture in the most literal sense of the word—they were mere "handmaids," servants of Scripture.[3] On the relationship of Scripture to papal authority Guido expressed himself in the same vein and with equal clarity:

It is not permitted to the supreme pontiff to establish anything contrary to what the Lord has said in the Gospel, for he is inferior to the Lord. If indeed statutes were in any way contrary to evangelical doctrine they would contain heresy for no Catholic believes anything con-

---

[1] *Commentarium super Decretum ad Dist.* 11 c. 9, fol. 9vb, "Quod est sane intelligendum, quia in veritate ecclesia sequitur evangelium et non evangelium ecclesiam. Unde pocior est auctoritas evangelii quam ecclesie per se et directe, scilicet cum scitur dictum in evangelio contineri. ... Set ecclesia directa et docta spiritu sancto et evangelium verum eligit ... ad hanc evangelii sinceram electionem loquitur Augustinus."

[2] *Commentarium ad Dist.* 15 c. 1, fol. 11vb, "Non que sint paris auctoritatis cum augustinus ... dicat inter omnes divinas auctoritates que in sacris litteris continentur, evangelium merito excellit. Set dicit *quasi quatuor* quia sicut evangelica doctrina maxime in quatuor evangeliorum ... suscipitur, sic hec IIII^or concilia ... luculenter et clare testimoniis scripture sacre probantur in fidei veritate, quod qui eis contradicit manifeste scripture sacre contradicere et per consequens hereticus appareat manifeste."

[3] *Commentarium ad Dist.* 15 c. 3, fol. 12vb. He was commenting on a text stating that the church approved the councils "after" the Scriptures, "*Post illas.* Significanter dicit "post" quia scriptura novi et veteris testamenti omnibus preeminet omnesque antecellit ut in veritate et eccellente (?) omnibus anteponatur que sibi cetere ancillantur, prov. c. IX 'vocavit ancillas ad menia civitatis.'"

trary to sacred Scripture …. What the Gloss says here, that the supreme
pontiff dispenses against Scripture in interpreting it, is not valid, for an
interpretation defers and should defer to the Gospel. Otherwise it
would not be an interpretation but a corruption. To interpret the Gospel in a good and Catholic sense, not contradicting the truth of faith
and holy Scripture—that is what is permitted to the supreme pontiff.[1]

It will be evident from this last passage how essential it is to grasp
correctly Guido Terreni's teaching on Scripture as the unique foundation of the faith if we are to achieve any real understanding of his
doctrine of papal infallibility. The truths of Scripture set the bounds
within which the pope's power of judgment could be exercised. The
scope of infallibility, we might say, was defined by the interstices of
Scripture.

3. The Defense of Papal Power

We have noted that there were many difficulties in the way of a
theologian who sought to develop a doctrine of "pro-papal infallibility" in the reign of John XXII. And yet, if a doctrine of infallibility
could be presented in a viable form—in a form that would not too
severely limit the sovereignty of contemporary popes—it could be of
enormous value to the Roman church. Two kinds of attack had been
mounted against the papacy of John XXII. The Michaelist Franciscans
acknowledged the principle of papal headship but insisted that John
was no true pope because his dogmatic decree, *Cum inter nonnullos*, had
proclaimed a heresy as the true faith. If one could establish that, once
a man had become pope, the Holy Spirit would preserve him from all
error in his public teachings, the Franciscan argument collapsed. The
other main line of attack on the papacy was the conciliarist one which
held that the pope was, in the last resort, subject to the authority of a
general council. An indispensable support for the conciliarist position
was provided by the assertion of the *Glossa Ordinaria* to the Decretum,
"In matters of faith … a council is greater than a pope." Again, if the

---

[1] *Commentarium ad* C. 25 q. 1 c. 6, fol. 169ra, "Quia contra ea que dominus in
evangelio dixit non licet summo pontifici cum sit inferior domino aliquid statuere.
Statuta quoque si qua essent contra doctrinam evangelicam, heresim continerent,
quia contra scripturam sacram nemo catholicus senserit … Nec valet quod Glossa
hic inducit quod summus Pontifex dispensat in evangelio interpretando ipsum quia
interpretatio obsequitur et obsequi debet evangelio. Alias non esset interpretatio
sed corrunptio. Interpretari quippe evangelium ad sensum bonum et catholicum
non contradicendo veritati fidei et scripture sancte, hoc licet summo pontifici."
Guido went on to argue that the pope could dispense only against apostolic counsels that were not commands and not part of the "doctrine of faith."

pope's personal infallibility could be demonstrated, the conciliarist position would be seriously undermined. The argument from infallibility may have seemed all the more attractive to Guido Terreni since the only alternative anti-conciliar argument—the one presented in its most extreme form in the work of Hervaeus Natalis—involved an abandonment of traditional Scriptural exegesis and a radical reinterpretation of the relationship between Peter and the apostles that was unlikely ever to commend itself to the universal Catholic episcopate (and Guido was, after all, a bishop himself).

Guido's defense of papal power was based on a simple, strongly-held idea that gave coherence to all his scattered ecclesiological writings. This was a deep, abiding conviction that the church of Avignon—with its pope, bishops, prelates, palaces, laws, lands and revenues—was exactly the church that Jesus Christ had come among men to establish on earth. Guido was not unaware of the need for reforms on the local level. He summoned reforming synods as bishop of Elne, and he acknowledged that, in the church on earth , evil men were intermingled with the good.[1] But the church itself was still holy because it was founded on Christ. Its essential institutions had been established by Christ, described in holy Scripture, and handed down intact from the age of the apostles to the church of his own day.[2]

In defending the existing organization of the church and the supremacy of the pope within that organization, Guido relied partly on a return to traditional interpretations of Scripture, partly on his own more novel theory of papal infallibility. Since he believed that the structure of the church had been defined once and for all in the New Testament Guido was vehemently hostile to any suggestions that church institutions might be radically transformed in some coming new age of the Holy Spirit. He attributed this error especially to Abbot Joachim and Pietro Olivi and called it "fatuous, fantastic, audacious, blasphemous and heretical."[3] The heretics taught that the new age

---

[1] *Summa de haeresibus*, p. 173, "... quamvis habeat commixtos bonos et malos ... ipsa tamen sancta est."

[2] *Concordia ad* Matt. 10.5, p. 271, "*Hoc duodecim misit Jesus* ... Voluit tamen eos mittere ... ut ordinem Ecclesiasticum in Ecclesia se instituere ostenderet in qua quosdam posuit apostolos ... quosdam Doctores et sic de aliis ... quorum gradum et ordinem ac potestatem non per alium quam per se instituit in monte ... Ut firmitatem et perpetuitatem ordinis Ecclesiastici quamdiu hoc seculum erit ostenderet, et contra haereticos ordinem Ecclesiasticum usque ad finem seculi non destruendum, quam ipse fundavit supra se petram declareret."

[3] *Summa de haeresibus*, p. 161, "Isti duo Ioachim et Petrus Ioannis multa fatua, fabulosa, temeraria, blasphema et haeretica dixerunt ..."

would be an age of liberty; but this was to deny that the Gospel was already a law of liberty.[1] They taught that in the new age the spiritual meaning of the Gospel would be revealed for the first time; but the apostles had preached and taught the doctrine they received directly from Christ. Did not Christ teach the spiritual meaning of his own Gospel?[2] Christ had indeed promised that the Holy Spirit would descend on the church, but he had made this promise to the apostles and he had fulfilled his promise to them.[3] Guido detested most of all the Joachimite notion that, in the coming third age, leadership of the church would pass from the order of clergy to a new order of spiritual monks or friars. Christ himself had established the orders of clerics. They would endure for all time, harmoniously working together without confusion, walking in the light of faith until the end of the world, never to be replaced by any other kind of church as the heretics asserted.[4]

Guido did not limit his attack to Joachimite aberrations. His hostility to the idea that any new-founded Order could exemplify a way of life more perfect than that handed down by the apostles through the traditional institutions of the church led him to denounce the whole Franciscan position as it had been developed in the writings of St. Bonaventure and his successors. According to Guido, Christ did not prescribe for the apostles a more perfect life in their capacity as "professors of poverty" than in their capacity as prelates. On the contrary, all the counsels of perfection were addressed to them precisely as prelates.[5] Guido rejected the whole doctrine of condescension as formulated by Bonaventure. In his own life, Christ never performed any actions that were intended as a guide for the imperfect only. All his actions were perfect in themselves and were intended as examples

---

[1] *Summa*, p. 166.

[2] *Summa*, pp. 168-169.

[3] *Summa*, p. 163.

[4] *Summa*, p. 171, "Unde non deficiet ordo Clericorum in tertio vel alio statu huius vitae. Absit enim ut ordo Clericorum quem Christus in Apostolis confirmavit ... non maneat ..."; p. 173, "Quae ecclesia usque ad finem scculi ut aurora per lumen fidei ambulat donec seculum durat ... nec alia est ei successura ut isti heretici fabulantur ..."

[5] *De perfectione vite*, MS British Museum, Addit. 16632, fol. 33v, "Non enim invenitur in christi doctrina seu sanctorum doctorum quod dominus aliqua precepta eis dederit in quantum erant prelati et alia in quantum erant professores paupertatis vel monachi. Ymmo omnia precepta eis data respiciunt eos secundum quod ordinabantur et mittebantur ad predicandum et curandum ut prelati ..." Guido developed at considerable length the argument that the state of life of a prelate was more perfect than that of a friar.

for "perfect prelates."[1] This applied especially to the holding of property. Christ and the apostles had a purse and, in the primitive church, the faithful laid all that they had at the feet of the apostles and held all things in common. Thus they established the perfect form of life to be observed in the church for all time. This form was observed by popes and prelates in their administration of church property and by all monks and religious "except perchance the church of blessed Francis." To claim that there could be a more perfect way of life was to say that the church of the apostles was imperfect, and that all popes, prelates, monks and abbots through the course of time had been imperfect; which was absurd.[2]

In describing Christ's foundation of the hierarchical organization of the church Guido Terreni steered a careful middle course between the radicalism of Marsilius of Padua and the extreme anti-episcopal papalism of writers like Hervaeus Natalis. The fullest exposition of his views was given in a long comment on Matt. 16.16-18. Here he explicitly denounced "Marsilius and his accomplice John (of Jandun)" for denying the divine origin of papal power. Scripture had to be understood according to the determinations of the church. This itself was known from Scripture since, at Luke 22.32, Christ prayed for the faith of the church when he spoke to Peter. But, according to the determination of the church, the words *Tu es Petrus* clearly designated Peter as prince of the apostles and vicar of Christ.[3]

Although Guido did not mention by name such authors as Hervaeus Natalis (they were after all in the same pro-papal camp as himself) he rejected their opinions just as decisively as those of Marsilius. Guido

---

[1] *De perfectione vite*, fol. 10v, "Unde Christus in omnibus que egit est a perfectis imitandus et oppositum dicere est Christo detrahere et eius perfectioni quod est erroneum et blasphemum ..."

[2] *De perfectione vite*, fol. 24v, "... Dominus in habendo loculos formam ecclesiastice pecunie instituit. Et hec forma maxime viguit in primitiva ecclesia in qua conversi ex iudeis omnia que habebant vendebant et precia eorum ponebant ante pedes apostolorum qui erant prelati ecclesie et dispensatores bonorum ... Constat autem quod tota primitiva ecclesia ... non erat imperfecta ... Hanc formam servavit et servat ecclesia perfectissimorum monachorum in monasteriis, ymmo omnis religio nisi forsan ecclesia beati francisci. Et ita totam ecclesiam Christi, Summos pontifices omnes et ceteros prelatos qui unquam fuerunt dicemus absque perfectione et omnes monachos et abbates? Quod est absurdum ..." Guido repeated the argument in the *Concordia ad* Matt. 10.9, p. 275; *ad* John 13.29, p. 890; *ad* Luke 22.35, p. 900. Similarly *Summa*, p. 171.

[3] *Concordia ad* Matt. 16.18, p. 564, "Sanus igitur intellectus secundum determinationem ecclesie, est illius Verbi, *Tu es Petrus* ... quod Petrus est caput Ecclesiae, Princeps Apostolorum, Vicarius Christi."

maintained quite explicitly and consistently that the apostles and their successors, the bishops, derived their authority—both orders and jurisdiction—directly from Christ and not from Peter. According to Guido, when Christ spoke the words at Matt. 16.19 "I will give you the keys of the kingdom of Heaven" he simultaneously chose Peter as the future head of the apostles by addressing him alone and also promised to confer the power of the keys on all of them (for Peter had spoken on behalf of all). This was made clear at Matt. 18.18 where Christ repeated his promise, this time addressing the whole group of apostles. The promise was fulfilled at John 20.22 where Christ said (again addressing all together) "Receive the Holy Spirit ..." Finally, at John 21.15-17 Christ appointed Peter as universal pastor and head of the church with the words "Feed my sheep, Feed my lambs."[1] Guido insisted that this interpretation was entirely compatible with the doctrine of papal supremacy. Christ himself, not Peter, had given power to the apostles, but he had subordinated the apostles to Peter. So too all future bishops were subordinated to Peter's successors, the popes. The pope was not the source of episcopal authority but he could "restrain and amplify" that authority as the needs of the church required.[2]

There is a notable coherence in Guido's handling of the whole collection of Petrine texts. When Christ prayed for Peter's faith he prayed for the faith of the whole church but also designated Peter and his successors as infallible teachers of the true faith. So too, when Christ promised the keys to Peter, he promised the power of remitting sins to all the apostles but at the same time designated Peter and his successors as head of the church.

---

[1] *Concordia ad* Matt. 16.19, p. 561, "*Et tibi dabo claves.* Hic Petrum dignificat a pontificali officio; hic ei promittit Pontificium totius Ecclesiae ... Sed Ioann. 20.22 cum aliis apostolis hic promissam potestatem accepit ubi Episcopi Apostoli sunt ordinati ... Petrum pastorem omnium fidelium et Apostolorum principem ... praefecit cum ei dixit, *Pasce oves meas.*"; pp. 561-562, "Dicendum quod sicut pro omnibus Apostolis Petrus respondit, ita in eo omnibus Apostolis Dominus claves regni promisit ... quia Matt. 18.18 Dominus ... omnibus Apostolis pluraliter dicit *Quaecunque alligaveritis* ... status Apostolorum et per consequens Episcoporum qui eis succedunt, habeat immediate potestatem a Christo, et non a Petro."

[2] *Concordia*, p. 563, "Igitur quamvis potestas Episcopalis sit immediate a Christo, tam ordinis quam iurisdictionis ... tamen Dominus papa, authoritate Christi, qua est superior Praelatus potest restringere et ampliare quoad usum ..." Guido gave the same explanation of the relationship between Christ, Peter and the apostles in various other contexts. See e.g., *Concordia ad* John 20.22, p. 1029; *Commentarium super Decretum ad Dist.* 21 *ante* c. 1, fol. 16ra; *ad Dist.* 21 c. 2, fol. 16va; *ad Dist.* 80 c. 2, fol. 48ra; *ad* C. 9 q. 3 c. 14, fol. 92ra; *ad* C. 24 q. 1 c. 4, fol. 151vb.

In the discussion that we have just considered, Guido was essentially reiterating the arguments of the twelfth century Decretists and the thirteenth century episcopalists which in turn rested on earlier patristic exegesis (mainly on Augustine). Guido's own contribution was to show how such doctrines—which were certainly more easily defensible than those of the extreme papalists—could be sustained without making any concessions to the conciliarist ideas that were coming to be associated with them. This was a major theme of his impressive work on Gratian's Decretum.

We have noted that, in commenting on Matt. 16.18, Guido rejected Marsilius' thesis that the primacy of Peter rested on merely human authority. He does not seem to have presented in any of his major works an explicit treatise directed against conciliarism in its more moderate form, that is to say in the form which acknowledged the divine origin of papal primacy while still maintaining that, in the last resort, the whole church or the general council was greater than the pope. But, throughout his *Commentarium* on Gratian's Decretum, Guido provided an implicit refutation of that thesis by deploying his doctrines concerning the unique authority of Scripture and the infallibility of the popes. Guido had in front of him as he wrote the Ordinary Gloss of Johannes Teutonicus—he referred to it from time to time. And at every point where Johannes had set down a comment that had been or would be or could be useful to conciliarist thinkers, Guido passed over the point in silence or, more commonly, offered an alternative explanation of the text.

One can trace this procedure through the whole course of the Decretum. The first example occurs at *Dist.* 4 c. 3. Here Johannes Teutonicus raised the question (without deciding it) whether the whole episcopate was of greater authority than the pope in a dispute over church law. Guido commented merely that all subjects were to obey the law and that only the founder of the law was qualified to interpret it.[1]

Dist. 15 c. 2 was a text of central importance for all conciliarist thinkers. Here Gregory the Great wrote "I revere the four councils like the four gospels ... because they were established by universal consent." At this point Johannes Teutonicus raised the whole problem of whether popes were bound by the decrees of general councils and decided that they were, at least where matters of faith were involved.

---

[1] *Commentarium super Decretum ad Dist.* 4 c. 3, fol. 3ra. The various texts of Johannes Teutonicus referred to in the following discussion are all printed in my *Foundations*, pp. 250-254.

Later he explained that this was because, in matters of faith, the council was greater than the pope. Other Decretists alluded at this point to the problems of corporate representation and consent implied by the words *universali consensu*. Guido passed over these points and was content to reiterate his own view that the councils were by no means equal in authority to the Scriptures. According to Guido, when Gregory the Great drew a parallel between the four Gospels and the four councils he meant only to indicate that the councils conformed to the Gospels in doctrine or were equal in number.[1] Guido did believe of course that a pope was bound by the dogmatic definitions of general councils but he based this doctrine on his theory of papal infallibility, not on any supposed superiority of the council. A conciliar definition was simply another form of a papal definition; and all papal decisions in faith and morals were irrevocable.[2]

Guido made this clear at *Dist.* 17. Here again Johannes Teutonicus had explored various arguments that were of interest to later conciliarists. Guido insisted simply that the whole power of a council resided in the apostolic see since the pope, as successor of Peter, possessed a universal power of binding and loosing over the whole church.[3] At *Dist.* 19 we come to the notorious case of the "heretical" Pope Anastasius. This was the place where Johannes Teutonicus had inserted his crucial gloss, "Where matters of faith are concerned, then a council is greater than a pope." Guido Terreni took a very different line. It was not impossible, he conceded, that Anastasius might have fallen into heresy as a private person. But then Guido went on to cast doubts

---

[1] *Commentarium ad Dist.* 15 c. 2, fol. 12vb, "Non intendit gregorius IIIIor concilia equare auctoritati sancti evangelii ... set denotat similitudinem quia conformia sunt doctrine evangelice quo ad veritatem ... et quo ad quaternarium numerum quod imitant."

[2] See e.g., *Commentarium ad* c. 25 q. 1 c. 1, fol. 168vb. Gratian's text referred quite explicitly to the binding force of decrees of general councils. Guido commented, ... clarum est quod determinationem sedis apostolice que prima est debet sequi et quantum ad pertinacia ad fidem a successore non potest revocari ut supra XXIIII q. 1 *hec est.*" The concluding reference was to Guido's *Quaestio* on papal infallibility. Again at C. 25 q. 1 c. 3, fol. 168vb, he dismissed the question of whether a pope was bound by the decisions of general councils in matters of faith with a reference to the *Quaestio* on papal infallibility.

[3] *Commentarium ad Dist.* 17 *ante* c. 1 fol. 13va, "Apud sedem apostolicam residet potestas generalia concilia congregandi. Et hoc rationabiliter ut penes eum resideat potestas conciliorum que omnes et universaliter ligant apud quem est universalis potestas ligandi et solvendi que residet in successoribus petri." Guido further discussed whether a council that met without papal authority could subsequently be ratified by papal approval. He concluded, "Credo quod sic. Quia licet de se esset nullum ex ratificatione tamen pape incipit habere vigorem et auctoritatem."

(with rather heavy-handed irony) on the veracity of the whole account as presented by Gratian. Guido did not know, he acknowledged, whether Anastasius was a heretic or not. But, if he was, it was very odd that his successor, Pope Hormisdas, had not condemned him; and it was very odd that Anastasius had written a letter rebuking the heretic Acacius; and very odd that Anastasius was still included in the catalogue of the popes; and very odd that he was revered at Rome among the holy pontiffs of the past.[1] There seems to be no precedent, in all the earlier Decretist literature, for this kind of attack on the text of the *Liber Pontificalis* as presented by Gratian.

At *Dist.* 40 c. 6, where the Ordinary Gloss argued that a pope could be deposed for any notorious crime, Guido limited the grounds of accusation strictly to obdurate heresy.[2] So it went on throughout the whole of the Decretum. At no single point did Guido admit the possibility that a general council might possess an authority greater than the pope's. Finally, toward the end of the work, he came to C. 24 q. 1. Here Johannes Teutonicus (like many other Decretists) discussed the meaning of the phrase "The Roman church cannot err" and came to the conclusion that the only unerring "Roman church" was the whole *congregatio fidelium*, since it was for the faith of the universal church that Christ had prayed when he said "I have prayed for you Peter that your faith shall not fail." Guido Terreni chose this place to present his *Quaestio* on papal infallibility with its alternative explanation that the words *Ego rogavi pro te* referred specifically to Peter and to his

---

[1] *Commentarium ad Dist.* 19 c. 9, fol. 15va, "Hic papa si fuerit hereticus favens accatio in errore nescio ... possibile est enim papa in fide errare prout est persona singularis. Set mirum est quod si anastasius papa favit accatio in errore cur orismada papa qui post anastasium fuit, dampnando accatium mortuum, anastasium non dampnavit. Et si favit accatio anastasius quod ipse accatium repprobat quod sacramenta offerebat ... Set magis mirandum quod si hereticus fuerit mortuus quod hereticus inter summos pontifices numeretur et non fuerit deletus de cathologo summorum pontifficum. Set est mirabilis quod Romana (ecclesia) Anastasius II ut sanctus festive veneretur. Nec apparet verum quod alius secundus Anasthasius sanctus dicatur, quia nullus nisi iste vocatus est inter summos pontifices anastasius secundus."

[2] *Commentarium ad Dist.* 40 c. 6, fol. 31vb. Guido did not deal fully with the problem of a heretical pope. He wrote here, "*A fide devius* ... quia tunc inferior potest et debet superiorem increpare et ei resistere," referring to Paul's rebuke of Peter. (He referred to the case of Paul and Peter also at *Dist.* 12 c. 2, fol. 10rb; *Dist.* 21 c. 4, fol. 16vb; *C.* 2 q. 7 c. 33, fol. 79va.) At C. 24 q. 1 c. 1, fol. 151va he declared that a pope who persisted in heresy was automatically excommunicated, "... non opporteret de novo contra eum procedere quantum ad sententiam excommunicationis quia iam excommunicatus est hereticus omnis ..."

successors in the papacy.[1] The whole commentary on the Decretum was a considerable tour de force. If Guido's interpretations had found general acceptance, fifteenth century conciliarism could never have developed in the way it did.

For a defender of "pro-papal infallibility" there remains the difficulty that Michael of Cesena and his followers had posed. To affirm papal infallibility was to limit the pope's freedom of action by binding him to all the doctrinal decisions of his predecessors. Guido was well aware of the difficulty. For him the problem of infallibility arose precisely out of the problem of irreformability. But in many ways he succeeded in minimizing it. He insisted that papal infallibility was limited strictly to the determination of questions of faith;[2] in all other matters a pope was free to change the rulings of his predecessors. (In this connection Guido several times quoted the principle of juridical sovereignty, *par in parem non habet imperium*.)[3] Also Guido's insistence that all truths of faith had to be derived from Scripture tended to limit the number of past papal decrees that could qualify as infallible. Finally, Guido showed considerable ingenuity in re-interpreting past decrees when it seemed expedient to do so. One of the most striking earlier exercises of papal power in the field of sacred doctrine had been Alexander III's decree *Cum Christus* which solemnly condemned the proposition, *Christus non esse aliquid secundum quod homo*. At C. 24 q. 1 c. 14 of the Decretum, immediately before launching into his exposition of papal infallibility, Guido explained that the phrase the pope had rejected could be given a perfectly orthodox explanation.[4] Apparently even propositions that had been infallibly condemned remained open to theological re-interpretation.

Guido's attitude was made very plain in his discussion on the conflict between the decrees of Nicholas III and of John XXII concerning apostolic poverty. He simply refused to admit that the earlier decree could have intended to affirm anything that the later one denied. John

---

[1] *Commentarium ad* C. 24 q. 1 c. 14, fol. 152ra.

[2] In the *Quaestio* on infallibility he did not even use the term "in faith and morals" but limited the scope of infallibility strictly to matters that were *de fide*. Similarly in the *Concordia ad* Matt. 14.28, p. 441. In his comment on *Dist.* 19 *post* c. 7, however, he wrote, "Numquid papa potest revocare decretales predecessorum. Credo quod sic illas que non tangunt doctrinam novi et veteris Testamenti nec fidem nec generaliter bonos mores." (fol. 15ra)

[3] *Quaestio*, p. 24; *Commentarium ad Dist.* 23 c. 1, fol. 17va; *ad* C. 25 q. 1 *ante* c. 1, fol. 168vb.

[4] *Commentarium ad* C. 24 q. 1 c. 4, fol. 152ra.

XXII had declared that Nicholas meant to affirm the Franciscans' dominion over consumables and their right of use over non-consumables. Therefore that was what Nicholas must have meant. The fact that Nicholas actually had asserted just the opposite opinions does not seem to have embarrassed Guido unduly. If the sayings of the Lord in the Gospels needed interpretation, he wrote, how much more the sayings of Pope Nicholas III![1]

Guido's real interest was to demonstrate the infallibility of the popes of his own day—of "the lord pope John" and "the lord pope Benedict" as he wrote. He wanted to prove that these pontiffs were infallible in order to defend them against the attacks of their adversaries. He was perceptive enough to see that this committed him to accepting the infallibility of earlier papal decrees also. But, for Guido, past decrees were infallible in a very malleable sort of way. Here he was a true prophet of the modern theory of papal infallibility or, at least, of one form of that theory.

Guido anticipated modern doctrine in various other ways. His assertion that the pope was infallible in his official definitions but not in his private opinions was all-important for the future. Also Guido distinguished very clearly between impeccability and infallibility in discussing the failings of Peter. And, very much in the manner of modern theologians, he presented the divine power that guaranteed papal infallibility, not as a positive inspiration, enabling a pope constantly to discern the truth, but rather as a kind of negative providence that impeded him from promulgating false doctrine even when he fell into personal error.

In one important respect, however, Guido's thought differed from that of more recent theologians. There is no trace in his work of the modern distinction between the "ordinary" fallible pronouncements of a supreme pontiff and the "extraordinary" infallible ones. In this matter Guido Terreni, William of Ockham and Pietro Olivi all adopted essentially the same point of view. Each of the three, to be sure, developed his thought in a different way. Olivi devised his theory

---

[1] *Quaestio*, pp. 22-23, "Cum enim dominus papa Nicolaus dixit quod in rebus. oblatis fratribus Minoribus nichil iuris et dominii habent fratres ipsi nisi solum simplicem usum facti ... papa Johannes non revocavit sed declaravit hoc debere intelligi in rebus in quibus potest separari usus a dominio et proprietate ... et declarat quod dominus Nicolaus intelligit quod fratres Minores in rebus, quibus utuntur, habent ius utendi ... si dictum Salvatoris ... recipit exposicionem et declaracionem, longe magis dictum domini Nicolai." Guido added that a decision on how the Franciscans should hold property was in any case not a matter of faith. But this ignored the doctrinal content of both Nicholas' decree and of John's.

of papal infallibility in order to protect the established teachings of
the Roman see against the assault of a coming pseudo-pope; Ockham
sought to prove that the reigning pontiff had ceased to be a true pope
because he had erred in defining the faith; Guido Terreni defended
the contemporary popes by arguing that all their official teachings on
faith and morals had to be accepted as infallible. But all three thinkers
shared a common conviction that every official doctrinal definition of a
true pope was necessarily unerring. The whole logic of their argumentation led to such a position. Guido Terreni maintained that, if a
possibility of error were admitted in any single definition, the whole
faith of the church would be rendered unstable. For Ockham, what the
pope had once defined remained immutable (providing that the "pope"
was a true pope of course). Olivi expressed a similar point of view with
vigor and clarity. It would be impossible for Catholics to be obliged
by God to follow the teachings of the pope, he wrote, if the pope
could err in his decisions. This is perhaps the best case that can be
advanced for papal infallibility. Olivi's argument is simple, strong
and persuasive. To quote one of the Decretists out of context, "It
would be beautiful if it were true." But of course modern theologians
know that it is not true. Seven centuries of official papal decrees
touching points of faith and morals have accumulated since the days of
Pietro Olivi and few serious scholars nowadays would seek to maintain
that they have all been infallible. Usually, therefore, modern Catholic
theologians teach a doctrine different from that of Olivi or Guido
Terreni—namely that Catholics can indeed be obliged by papal decisions on faith and morals which may well be erroneous .Their equivocations concerning "ordinary magisterium" and "extraordinary magisterium" have to be brought into play precisely in order to distinguish
the very rare infallible pronouncements from the mass of fallible
ones in which they are embedded. This particular development of
modern theology seems to have no precise antecedents in medieval
thought.[1]

---

[1] Yet medieval writers made a similar distinction in considering the problem of
sovereignty when they distinguished between a ruler's "ordinary power" and his
"absolute power." This in turn was derived from a distinction between the *potestas
ordinata* and *potestas absoluta* of God. For examples of such usages in medieval law
see F. Oakley, "Jacobean Political Theology: The Absolute and Ordinary Powers
of the King," *Journal of the History of Ideas*, 29 (1968), pp. 323-346. Guido Terreni
insisted that a pope could not decide a question of faith unless he was certain his
decision was "infallibly true." (*Quaestio*, p. 21).

4. THE AFTERMATH

Catholic theologians were very reluctant to adopt the doctrine of papal infallibility even after Guido Terreni had shown how it could be presented in such a serviceable form; but when they did come to embrace it they typically accepted a less cautious, more far-ranging theory than Guido had propounded. Although the Carmelite master anticipated so much of the later doctrine of infallibility we can hardly understand the subsequent development of that doctrine unless we realize that William of Ockham contributed as much to it as Guido Terreni. If Guido defined most accurately (according to later ideas) the subject of papal infallibility it was Ockham who indicated more correctly the object of infallibility—that is to say, not Scriptural teaching alone, but Scripture and an indefinable mass of unwritten tradition. In the course of the fifteenth and sixteenth centuries, Ockham's "two-sources theory" of revelation came to be accepted as Catholic doctrine principally in order to refute the *sola scriptura* principle as it was presented by Wyclif and later by Luther. The line of development flows from Ockham through Henry Totting of Oyta, Pierre d'Ailly, Jean Gerson, William of Waterford and Gabriel Biel to the theologians of Trent.[1]

Papal infallibility came to be accepted by Roman theologians in the end mainly because it seemed to provide the most effective refutation of conciliarist ideas (particularly as expressed in their post-medieval form in Gallican theology). At first though the doctrine made slow progress.[2] Herman of Schildesche (d. 1357) repeated the argument that God would not permit an erring pope to impose his false doctrines on the church; but otherwise Guido's teaching on infallibility seems to have found few echoes in fourteenth century theology. At the beginning of the fifteenth century the anti-Hussite, Czech master, John of Holešov, restated the essence of Guido's doctrine: The pope was infallible in his official pronouncements and, if he erred in his private opinions, God would prevent him from imposing his errors on the

---

[1] H. A. Oberman, *The Harvest of Medieval Theology* (Cambridge, Mass., 1963), pp. 361-412.

[2] Useful indications concerning the development of the doctrine of papal infallibility in the late medieval and early modern periods are given by P. de Vooght, "Esquisse ..." in *L'infaillibilité de l'église* (Chevetogne, 1962), pp. 99-146; Y. Congar, *L'église de saint Augustin a l'époque moderne* (Paris, 1970), pp. 340-389; S. Harent in *Dictionnaire apologétique de la foi catholique*, III (Paris, 1926), s.v. Papauté, col. 1436-1520.

church as formal definitions. But other Czech papalists seem to have written only of the infallibility of the corporate Roman church which they distinguished from the person of the pope.

The problem of papal infallibility came to the fore again in the later stages of the conciliarist movement. Perhaps the most effective way of refuting conciliarist theology would have been to distinguish clearly, once and for all, between the power to sustain the faith indefectibly and the power to govern the church as a sovereign ruler. Johannes Turrecremata made a heroic effort to formulate this distinction in 1439. He wrote that the Virgin Mary was the mother of God, queen of the world, full of grace, always steadfast in the faith—and yet it was to Peter that Christ gave the power of the keys.[1] But this argument does not seem to have convinced anyone, perhaps not even Johannes himself, for in his later writings he fell back on a theory—though a somewhat muddled theory—of papal infallibility. At about the same time St. Antoninus revived the formula of Hervaeus Natalis which asserted that papal decisions were unerring when they were supported by the universal church.

Only in the sixteenth century did the doctrine of the pope's personal infallibility begin to find considerable acceptance in Catholic theology. Albert Pigge (d. 1534) taught that the pope could never fall into heresy; but for this he was promptly rebuked by Adrian of Utrecht, the future Pope Adrian VI. Cajetanus (d. 1534), Cano (d. 1560) and Bannez (d. 1604) all defended papal infallibility in some form though with various qualifications and different shades of meaning and emphasis. Robert Bellarmine (d. 1621) held that the pope certainly could not err in his official pronouncements and probably not in his private opinions. Suarez (d. 1618) emphasized once again the key of knowledge. "The key of knowledge is in the Pontiff for defining truths of faith, the key of power for ruling the church."[2] The seventeenth century saw a great revival of theological Gallicanism. In reaction against it, papalist theologians came more and more to insist that the pope was personally infallible. By the end of the century Pope Innocent XI had conceived the idea of defining his own infallibility. And from this time onward, the doctrine of papal infallibility came to be commonly taught by Ultramontane theologians.

---

[1] E. Candal (ed.), *Oratio synodalis de primatu* (Rome, 1954), p. 55.

[2] "Clavis scientiae in Pontifice est ad definiendas veritates fidei; potentiae ad regendam Ecclesiam," cited in A. Villalpando, *De clavium potestatis existentia atque natura* (Washington, D.C., 1921), p. 40.

The advantages of adhering to a doctrine of papal infallibility, preferably expressed in an extreme form, have always seemed obvious to Ultramontanes. We must still ask how they overcame the disadvantage that would seem to be equally obvious from their point of view—the binding of the pope to an indefinite array of past decisions, the acceptance of an ever-present possibility that a whole edifice of current papal doctrine could be overturned by confronting it with some "infallible" decretal of the past. The answer is fairly straightforward. The simplest way of reconciling papal sovereignty with papal infallibility is to forget the past, to pretend that doctrine has no history. Gallican theologians appealed to history with some success; Ultramontanes came to prefer an appeal to the living voice of the church. "I do not like catechisms overloaded with proof-texts ..." wrote the eighteenth century Jesuit, Isaac Berruyer. "If I must base my belief on these historical facts, I shall often be reduced to distinctions and subtleties and definitions so that I may reconcile them all with the faith, the far surer faith of the Church of Rome who teaches and guides me."[1] Manning struck the same note amid the controversies of 1870, "It is not therefore by criticism on past history, but by acts of faith in the living voice of the church at this hour, that we can know the faith."[2] The theory of papal infallibility was accepted into the armory of papal apologetics in an era of a-historical dogmatic theology. The final irony in the history of the doctrine is that it was given a formal, dogmatic definition at just the point in time when new forms of historical study were beginning to re-shape the whole consciousness of Western man, including his religious consciousness. This is perhaps the underlying source of all the paradoxes that have marked the development of the doctrine during the last hundred years.

---

[1] O. Chadwick, *From Bossuet to Newman* (Cambridge, 1957), pp. 72-73.

[2] H. E. Manning, *The Oecumenical Council and the Infallibility of the Roman Pontiff* (London, 1869), p. 126. He added, "It is time that the pretensions of 'historical science' and 'scientific historians' be reduced to their proper sphere and limits. And this the Council will do, not by contention or anathema, but by the words, 'it hath seemed good to the Holy Ghost and to us.'"

CONCLUSION

HISTORY AND THEOLOGY

We have said that a historian cannot do the theologians' work for them and we shall not attempt the task in this brief conclusion. Theologians must bear in mind, however, that there is a whole historical dimension to the problem of infallibility. Vatican Council I did not simply decree that the pope was infallible. It declared that the dogma of infallibility belonged to "the ancient and constant faith of the church" and that, in promulgating it, the council was "adhering to the tradition received from the beginning of the Christian faith." Some theologians, moreover, are willing to acknowledge that theology itself is likely to "wither away in blind isolation" unless its conclusions can be endowed with some degree of historical credibility.[1] So far as the doctrine of papal infallibility is concerned, this desirable state of affairs has not yet been achieved.

All the standard Catholic discussions of infallibility emphasize continuity rather than change in the church's teaching on this matter; at most the authors acknowledge that the doctrine is one that has "ripened" in the course of the ages. But it is very hard for a historian to see the emergence of the doctrine of papal infallibility as the slow unfolding of a truth that the church has always held. He sees instead the rather sudden creation—for reasons that are complex but historically intelligible—of a novel doctrine at the end of the thirteenth century. The slow process of growth that followed was a growth in the understanding of the papacy that, given the circumstances of the times, the advantages of the doctrine for polemical purposes on the whole slightly outweighed the disadvantages.

For a typical treatment of the problem of historicity by an eminent modern theologian we can turn to the work of Charles Journet. In *The Church of the Word Incarnate* he took as his starting point a presupposition that the doctrine of papal infallibility had always formed an intrinsic part of the faith of the church. Then he enquired how the doctrine had been taught by the church before the solemn

---

[1] H. Riedlinger, "Hermeneutische Ueberlegungen zu den konstanzer Dekreten" in *Das Konzil von Konstanz*, ed. A. Franzen and W. Müller (Freiburg-Basle-Vienna, 1964), pp. 214-238 at p. 222.

definition of Vatican Council I. Journet suggested that Catholics could always have known this truth of their faith either from the universal consensus of theological opinion concerning it or from the teaching of the "ordinary magisterium." Evidently neither suggestion has any relevance for the historical period we have considered. Between 1150 and 1350 the doctrine of papal infallibility was not taught by any considerable number of theologians; nor was it proclaimed by pope and bishops in the discharge of their ordinary teaching office. Journet, however, suggested a third possibility. "However it be, it is certain that the Church has always believed, with divine faith, in the pontifical infallibility, at least in an indirect and radical manner, by explicitly believing other truths in which this infallibility was implicitly contained." Belief in papal infallibility, Journet explained, could be "unconscious" without losing its efficacy.

At this point again the historian must raise a question. He can see that the first protagonists of infallibility made use of earlier elements of Christian thought in constructing their thesis. The principal doctrines they relied on were the old ones regarding the primacy of the Roman see and the indefectibility of the universal church, both of which Journet naturally emphasized. To these old beliefs the thirteenth century theologians added a new concern with the authentication of "living Tradition," a concern with "development of doctrine" we might say. What is not clear is that the doctrine of papal infallibility was in fact implicitly contained in any of these ideas, taken separately or in combination. Journet's argument requires us to acknowledge that any believer would be led ineluctably to acknowledge the necessity of papal infallibility provided that he, could understand all the implications of earlier generally accepted doctrines concerning the pope and the church. But the point that must strike a historian of papal infallibility most forcibly is the disconcerting absence of ineluctability in the whole historical process that led to the creation of the doctrine. The idea of infallibility did not emerge inevitably because it had always been pre-supposed. It was invented almost fortuitously because an unusual concatenation of historical circumstances arose that made such a doctrine useful to a particular group of controversialists—circumstances involving Joachimite radicalism, Franciscan spirituality and the whole peculiar, ambivalent relationship between the Franciscan Order and the papacy.

Once the doctrine had been propounded, its defenders naturally tried to find support for it in earlier teachings. But the truth is that papal infallibility does not follow as a necessary logical or theological corollary of any previously accepted tenets of Catholic ecclesiology. Let us consider briefly the three most relevant doctrines—primacy, indefectibility and development of doctrine. Papal primacy does not necessarily imply papal infallibility. Indeed a sharp tension has always existed between the canonical conception of the pope as a sovereign ruler and the theological doctrine of the pope as an infallible teacher. Sovereignty frees the pope to innovate; infallibility, if it were taken seriously, would bind him to the decisions of the past. We have emphasized often enough that, in principle, to ascribe the quality of infallibility to all of a pope's predecessors does not enhance the authority of a reigning pontiff. Let us finally add that, in actual day-to-day practice, the attribution of infallibility to the pope has had exactly the opposite effect to that intended by the nineteenth century sponsors of the doctrine. After a hundred years of papal infallibility the main practical result of the definition of Vatican Council I has been to weaken the authority of the pope's "ordinary" pronouncements on faith and morals. Most theologians would not recognize as infallible any papal pronouncement that sought to settle a keenly disputed issue. (Infallibility, they commonly maintain, can come into play only when a doctrine has become so well-established that a consensus already exists). But the ordinary Catholic is left with a vague feeling that, if the pope were really certain of the truth of his own teaching, he would "make it infallible." He also feels that, if the pope is not really certain of his own teaching, there is no need to take his views too seriously. Such an attitude is no doubt unsophisticated but it is not unintelligible.

Papal primacy then does not imply papal infallibility. Nor does the indefectibility of the church imply infallibility. The two conceptions are quite different from one another and they should be separated more sharply than has been usual in modern Catholic theology. (This point has recently been much emphasized by Hans Küng.) The doctrine of indefectibility assures Christians that, as long as the human race endures, a Christian community will exist, holding fast to the truths that Christ taught to his first followers. The doctrine does not state or imply that the church or its head is endowed with the gift of pronouncing infallibly on the divers moral and theological conundrums—most of them undreamed of in the days of Christ—which are posed by human ingenuity when men seek to build doctrinal edifices on Christian foundations. The message of the Gospels was surely a message about charity—about divine and human charity and the revelation of charity in the life and death of Jesus. A Christian can reasonably claim that his church shows itself to be indefectible so long as it proclaims this message.

In every age, of course, the church teaches far more than this and properly so. Christian doctrine does not exist in a vacuum. It lives only in the life of the church. Always the church has to embody its perception of Christian truth in the life-styles of changing human cultures—in liturgies, literature, art, philosophies, institutions, folk-ways, popular cults. All this is not to be deplored. It is not only inevitable; it is desirable. Human culture has been enormously enrich-ed—morally, aesthetically, intellectually—by the influence of the church. But, inevitably, in this mingling of the divine and the human, possi-bilities of error arise. Above all there is a persistent tendency for theologians to confuse the moral or philosophical prejudices of their own particular civilization with the perennial truths of Christian revela-tion.

There are problems of language involved here too. Language is a human artefact. It reflects cultural pre-suppositions that change from age to age. The word trans-"substantiation" can have no precise connotation except for a person accustomed to thinking in the catego-ries of scholastic philosophy. The medieval (and modern) definitions of papal sovereignty will yield their full meaning only to those familiar with the juridical categories of Roman law. The same verbal formulas may well convey different meanings at different times. And it may be that no human formulation can adequately express a truth of divine faith. Such considerations are interesting and important. But it is no part of our purpose here to add to the burgeoning literature on the semantics of religious propositions. We would suggest rather that too narrow a concentration on questions of language may lead to neglect of other, equally important problems. In discussing the past pronouncements of the church on matters of faith and morals a modern scholar is not concerned merely with conflicts of words. Conflicts of meaning are involved too. The most serious problem for a Catholic theologian is not that the church has always had to express divine truth in inadequate human language. The problem is rather that the church has sometimes embraced error and taught it as truth.

The church can err because it is, at least in part, a human institution, always immersed in human history. That the church has erred must seem self-evident if we acknowledge that self-contradiction is an indication of error. One example will suffice. Let us consider the morality of religious persecution. The Fourth Lateran Council enacted the following decree in 1215:

> We excommunicate and anathematize every heresy that raises itself against the holy, orthodox and Catholic faith .... Secular authorities, whatever office they may hold shall be admonished and induced and if necessary compelled by ecclesiastical censure, that as they wish to be esteemed and numbered among the faithful, so for the defense of the faith they ought publicly to take an oath that they will strive in good faith and to the best of their ability to exterminate in the territories subject to their jurisdiction all heretics pointed out by the church.[1]

The Second Vatican Council declared in 1965:

> This Vatican Synod declares that the human person has a right to religious freedom. This freedom means that all men are to be immune from coercion ... in such wise that in matters religious no one is to be forced to act in a manner contrary to his own beliefs. Nor is anyone to be restrained from acting in accordance with his own beliefs.[2]

Of course, both conciliar statements can be dismissed as "not infallible". But the point we are making here is that, whatever divine guidance the church may have enjoyed through the course of the centuries, that guidance has not been such as to prevent the church as a whole from falling into grievous errors. To present the second statement as a "development" of a single unchanging Catholic truth that was implicit in the first one is surely to strain human credulity too far. A man who believes that will believe anything. If the morality of the Fourth Lateran Council is true the morality of the Second Vatican Council is false; and vice-versa. There is, to be sure, no great difficulty in explaining on historical grounds how the church came to adopt such sharply opposed attitudes in two such widely separated epochs. But some scholars seem to imagine that to explain by historical analysis why the church has contradicted itself is to demonstrate that the contradictions are non-existent. And this is nonsense of course. The church can err; but this same erring church has never ceased to preserve and proclaim the Gospel of Christ. It has always been indefectible. It has never been infallible. Indefectibility does not imply infallibility.

If the church can err—and if it is nevertheless to persist as a true

---

[1] H. J. Schroeder, *The Disciplinary Decrees of the General Councils* (St. Louis, 1937), p. 242.

[2] W. M. Abbott, *The Documents of Vatican II* (New York, 1966), p. 678.

church—it must retain a capacity to correct its errors before they eat away the heart of the Christian message itself. This consideration leads to the third strand of thought that influenced the emergence of the doctrine of papal infallibility in the years around 1300—the idea of "living Tradition" or "development of doctrine." Papal primacy, we have seen, does not imply papal infallibility; the indefectibility of the church does not imply the infallibility of the church; and, most clearly of all, the concept of doctrinal development does not imply the infallibility of either pope or church. Even if, in the last resort, the two concepts—development and infallibility—are not formally incompatible with one another, it is certainly easier to discern a persistent tension between them than to present them as logically interdependent. The process of development calls for an attitude that is not only willing to abandon error but that looks forward to the achievement of new, better, understandings of Christian truth in the future. The doctrine of infallibility tends to consecrate for all time the understandings (or misunderstandings) of the past.

Any consideration of development in the church involves the area of thought where the theologian's discipline and the historian's most obviously overlap. The problem here is to understand the relationship between the whole past life and teaching of the church and its mode of existence in the present. The concept of development in some form seems indispensable for any fruitful approach to this problem. (Every man must know that our knowledge of divine truth is imperfect; every Christian may hope that it will grow more perfect.) Development implies change; but, if we are to acknowledge the existence of "one holy Catholic church" in time as well as in space, there must also be something that endures, a core of truth that has persisted from the beginning through all the ages. The theologian's task is surely to ascertain this truth, to strive to understand its implications more deeply, and to express it in language meaningful to his own generation. It is a great task and a hard one. The theologian needs all the help he can obtain from other disciplines. And there is one sense in which history can properly be called a handmaid of theology.

All definitions of Christian faith are expressions of the life of the church as it existed at some particular time and place. (We do not detract from the unique authority of Scripture when we acknowledge that this is true also of the Gospels.) The expression of Christian truth through the necessary medium of the changing human cultures that have succeeded one another in time gives rise to possibilities of error, as we have observed. But it is precisely this historical process—if the theologian will make himself aware of it—that also makes possible a deepening understanding of the truth. Every Christian civilization will make its own errors; but also, characteristically, its particular emphases will illuminate new facets of divine truth. Each fresh generation succeeds to a richer heritage of Christian insights, perceptions, intuitions, which it can use—if it so chooses—to inform its own understanding of the faith. It also acquires a new perspective from which to judge what is ephemeral in the church's attempts to explicate its faith and what is enduring. (To many contemporary Catholics it seems that the various nineteenth century papal pronouncements condemning the principle of religious toleration can be dismissed as ephemeral products of a particular historical situation; at the time of their promulgation they were widely accepted as enduring statements of Catholic truth.) It is good then for a scholar who would expound the faith of the church to know something of the church's history. Any meaningful theory of development of doctrine must be based on a consideration of the whole experience of the church in time. This is most especially true when a theologian turns to ecclesiology, when he seeks to theologize about the intrinsic nature of the church itself. He cannot know the whole truth unless he knows the whole church.

The modern doctrine of infallibilty is singularly unhelpful in the incessant, never-ending struggle to deepen our understanding of Christian truth that is, or should be, at the heart of the theological enterprise. It encourages Catholic scholars to suppose that their proper task is to reconcile all the more solemn past pronouncements of the church with one another by ever more ingenious displays of hermeneutical dexterity; whereas the real task is to distinguish between the unfailing faith of the church—the heritage of truth it has preserved— and the human errors which, in every age, the church has associated and does associate with the proclamation of that truth. This applies not least to the dogma of papal infallibility itself. Recently, several scholars have pointed out that it is very hard to reconcile the decrees of Vatican Council I with those of the Council of Constance and that the decrees of Constance cannot be lightly dismissed as lacking in authority. So too, we have observed, it is hardly possible to reconcile the decrees of Vatican Coucil II with those of the Fourth Lateran Council. But it is surely a misconceived enterprise to attempt any sophistical reconciliation of such starkly opposed texts. The task for Catholic scholars and pastors is rather to distinguish between what was

true and what was false in the pronouncements of Vatican Council I
concerning papal authority, guided by the experience of a further
century of the life of the church in the world. (So too we need to
distinguish between what was true—if anything—and what was false
in the Fourth Lateran Council's pronouncements on religious persecution, with here the experience of seven and a half centuries to
guide us.) The purpose of such enquiries is not to undermine all the
doctrines of the past. The purpose is just the opposite—to seek out
and cherish all that is true and life-giving in the teachings of the church.
Theologians need to persist in such work if the term "development
of doctrine" is to mean anything other than mere license to indulge
in subjective fantasy.

The conservative defender of infallibility imagines that, in insisting
on the irreformability of the definitions of the past, he is providing
rocks of certainty to stand against an all-engulfing flood of relativism.
But in fact, his doctrine—principally because it engenders corrupt
principles of hermeneutics—makes it almost impossible for a Catholic
theologian to carry out his work convincingly. If the modern Catholic
church is to claim, with any appearance of credibility, to be the church
that Christ founded, the most urgent problems that face its theologians
are problems of historicity—the problem of distinguishing what is
permanent from what is transitory in the expressions of the church's
faith; the problem of explaining more sensitively the nature of a church
that, down the centuries, has always been prone to error and always
"unfailing in faith"; the problem of identity in change. The deepest
objection that a Catholic can offer to the doctrine of papal infallibility
is, not that it exalts unduly the power of the pope, but that it grievously
distorts the thinking of the most able Catholic scholars who have
addressed themselves to these problems in modern times.

Nowadays, ecumenically-minded Catholics often seem to assume
that the doctrine of papal infallibility defined in 1870 can be qualified
almost out of existence and then conveniently forgotten. But this is
only another way of falsifying history. The doctrine of 1870 exists.
It ought not to be forgotten. Conceivably, however, it ought to be
reconsidered. Of course the ultimate value of a doctrinal proposition
cannot be established purely and simply by historical analysis of the
kind that has been presented in this book. In principle we cannot determine whether a doctrine is true or false merely by explaining how it
first came to be formulated. But, in a rather unusual fashion, our particular doctrine of papal infallibility raises specifically historical problems

that not all theologians have been content to ignore. This is so for two reasons. In the first place, the dogma of Vatican Council I does not simply affirm an eternal truth about a transcendent godhead; it ascribes a particular characteristic to a succession of historical personages who, in our temporal world, have occupied the chair of St Peter for more than nineteen hundred years. In the second place, as we have already observed, a theologian who seeks seriously to uphold the doctrine of 1870 needs to argue, not only that the pope is infallible (and infallible in some meaningful sense of the word), but also that a belief in papal infallibility has inhered in "the ancient and constant faith of the church" throughout the whole history of the Christian era, "from the beginning of the Christian faith." Hence, although this book is addressed primarily to historians, its conclusions may possibly be of interest to other scholars who are interested in the problems of infallibility. The main points can be summarized very briefly. There is no convincing evidence that papal infallibility formed any part of the theological or canonical tradition of the church before the thirteenth century; the doctrine was invented in the first place by a few dissident Franciscans because it suited their convenience to invent it; eventually, but only after much initial reluctance, it was accepted by the papacy because it suited the convenience of the popes to accept it.

The doctrine of papal infallibility no longer serves anyone's convenience—least of all the pope's. The papacy adopted the doctrine out of weakness. Perhaps one day the church will feel strong enough to renounce it.

BIBLIOGRAPHY

I. SOURCES

(a) *Manuscripts*

Alanus, *Apparatus Ius naturale*; MS 3909, Bibliothèque Nationale, Paris.
—, *Gloss ad Compilatio I*; MS Aug. XL, Landesbibliothek, Karlsruhe.
Apparatus Glossarum ad Decretum; MS 676, Caius College, Cambridge.
Guido Terreni, *Commentarium super Decretum Gratiani*; MS Vat. lat. 1453, Biblioteca Vaticana.
—, *De perfectione vite*; MS Addit. 16632, British Museum.
Huguccio, *Summa ad Decretum*; MS 72, Pembroke College, Cambridge; MS Vat. lat. 2280, Biblioteca Vaticana.
John Baconthorpe, *Postill on Matthew*; MS B. 15. 12, Trinity College, Cambridge.
Peter de la Palu, *Quodlibeta*; MS 744, Bibliothèque de la Ville, Toulouse.
Pietro Olivi, *Lectura super Lucam*; MS Ottob. lat. 3302, Biblioteca Vaticana.
—, *Lectura super Matthaeum*; MS 49, New College, Oxford.
—, *Quaestiones de perfectione evangelica*; MS Vat. Lat. 4986, Biblioteca Vaticana.
Summa Cantabrigiensis; MS 0. 5. 17, Trinity College, Cambridge.
Tancred, *Gloss ad Compilatio III*; MS 17, Caius College, Cambridge.

(b) *Printed Editions*

Abbott, W. M. (ed.), *The Documents of Vatican II* (New York, 1966).
Accursius, *Glossa ordinaria* to the *Corpus iuris civilis* in *Corpus iuris civilis* (Lyons, 1627).
Acta Apostolicae Sedis (Vatican City, 1909-   ).
Alexander de Sancto Elpidio, *De ecclesiastica potestate* in J. T. Rocaberti, *Bibliotheca maxima pontificia*, II (Rome, 1698).
Alvarus Pelagius, *De planctu ecclesiae* (Ulm, 1474).
Augustine, *Contra epistolam Manichaei quam vocant Fundamenti* in J.-P. Migne, *Patrologia Latina*, 42 (Paris, 1841).
Augustinus Triumphus, *Summa de potestate ecclesiastica* (Rome, 1584).
Baluze, E. and Mansi, J. D., *Miscellanea*, 4 vols. (Lucca, 1761-1764).
Bede, *In Matthaei evangelium expositio* in J.-P. Migne, *Patrologia Latina*, 92 (Paris, 1850).
—, *Homilia in festo SS Petri et Pauli* in J.-P. Migne, *Patrologia Latina*, 94 (Paris, 1850).
Bernardus Parmensis, *Glossa ordinaria* to the *Decretales* in *Decretales D. Gregorii IX cum glossis* (Lyons, 1624).
Biblia sacra cum glossis (Venice, 1588).
Bonagratia of Bergamo, *De paupertate*, ed. L. Oliger in "Fr. Bonagratia de Bergamo et eius Tractatus de Christi et apostolorum paupertate," *AFH*, 22 (1929), pp. 292-335, 487-511.
Bonaventure, *Collationes in Hexaemeron*, ed. F. Delorme (Bibliotheca Franciscana scholastica medii aevi, VIII) (Quaracchi, 1934).
—, *Doctoris Seraphici S. Bonaventurae S.R.E. cardinalis opera omnia*, 10 vols. (Quaracchi, 1882-1902).
Bullarium Romanum, III (Turin, 1858).
Corpus iuris canonici, ed. E. Friedberg, 2 vols. (Leipzig, 1879-1881).

Corpus iuris civilis, ed. T. Mommsen and P. Krüger, 3 vols. (Berlin, 1908-1915).
De perfectione statuum in *Johannis Duns Scoti ... opera omnia*, ed. L. Vivès, XXV (Paris, 1895).
Francis of Assisi, *Opuscula sancti patris Francisci Assisiensis* (Quaracchi, 1904).
Gerard of Abbeville, *Exceptiones contra ... Manus quae omnipotentem*, ed. M. Bierbaum in *Bettelorden und Weltgeistlichkeit* (Münster-in-Westf., 1920).
Guido de Baysio, *Rosarium Decretorum* (Strasbourg, 1473).
Guido Terreni, *Summa de haeresibus* (Cologne, 1631).
—, *Quatuor unum. Concordia evangelica in quatuor evangelistas* (Cologne, 1631).
—, *Quaestio de magisterio infallibili Romani pontificis*, ed. B.-M. Xiberta (Münster-in-Westf., 1926).
Gulielmus Durandus, *Tractatus de modo generalis concilii celebrandi* (Paris, 1545).
Gulielmus Petrus de Godin, *De causa immediate ecclesiastice potestatis* (Paris, 1506).
Hrabanus Maurus, *Commentariorum in Matthaeum libri octo* in J.-P. Migne, *Patrologia Latina*, 107 (Paris, 1851).
Henry of Ghent, *Quodlibeta Magistri Henrici Goethals a Gandavo*, 2 vols. (Paris, 1518).
—, *Summa quaestionum ordinarium*, 2 vols. (Paris, 1520).
Hervaeus Natalis, *De iurisdictione*, ed. L. Hödl in *De iurisdictione. Ein unveröffentlichter Traktat des Hervaeus Natalis O.P. (+1323) über die Kirchengewalt* (Munich, 1959).
—, *De potestate papae* (Paris, 1647).
Hostiensis, *Lectura in quinque Decretalium Gregorianarum libros* (Paris, 1512).
Innocent III, *Sermones* in J.-P. Migne, *Patrologia Latina*, 217 (Paris, 1855).
Johannes de Turrecremata, *Oratio synodalis de primatu*, ed. E. Candal (Rome, 1954).
Johannes Teutonicus, *Glossa ordinaria* to the Decretum in *Decretum Gratiani* (Venice, 1600).
John Baconthorpe, *Quodlibeta Joannis Bachonis Anglici* (Venice, 1527).
John Duns Scotus, *Joannis Duns Scoti ... opera omnia*, ed. L. Vivès, 13 vols. (Paris, 1891-1895).
—, *Ioannis Duns Scoti ... opera omnia*, ed. C. Balić (Vatican City, 1950-   ).
John of Paris, *De confessionibus audiendis quaestio disputata*, ed. L. Hödl (Munich, 1962).
—, *De potestate regia et papali*, ed. F. Bleienstein, *Johannes Quidort von Paris. Über königliche und päpstliche Gewalt. Textkritische Edition mit deutscher Übersetzung* (Stuttgart, 1969).
Lewis the Bavarian, *Die Appellation Königs Ludwigs des Bayern von 1324*, ed. J. Schwalm (Weimar, 1906).
Mansi, J. D., *Sacrorum conciliorum nova et amplissima collectio* (Venice, 1778-1798).
Marsilius of Padua, *Defensor pacis*, ed. C. W. Previté-Orton, *The Defensor Pacis of Marsilius of Padua* (Cambridge, 1928).
Peter de la Palu, *Articulis de audientia confessionum* (Paris, 1506).
—, *Tractatus de potestate papae*, ed. P. T. Stella (Zürich, 1966).
Peter Lombard, *Sententiarum libri quatuor* in J.-P. Migne, *Patrologia Latina*, 192 (Paris, 1855).
Pietro Olivi, *De renuntiatione*, ed. L. Oliger in "Petri Iohannis Olivi de renuntiatione papae Coelestini V quaestio et epistola," *AFH* ,11 (1918), pp. 309-373.
—, *Epistola ad Conrad de Offida*, ed. L. Oliger, *ibid*.
—, *Quaestio de infallibilitate Romani pontificis*, ed. M. Maccarone in "Una questione inedita dell'Olivi sull' infallibilità del papa," *Rivista di storia della chiesa in Italia*, 3 (1949), pp. 309-343.
—, *Quodlibeta Petri Ioannis Provinzialis* (Venice, 1509).
Richard of Middletown, *Quaestio disputata de privilegio Martini papae IV*, ed. F. Delorme (Quaracchi, 1925).
—, *Super quatuor libros Sentententiarum* (Brescia, 1591).

Rufinus, *Die Summa Decretorum des Magister Rufinus*, ed. H. Singer (Paderborn, 1902).

Schroeder, J. H. (ed.), *The Disciplinary Decrees of the General Councils* (St. Louis, 1937).

Summa 'Elegantius in iure divino' seu Coloniensis, ed. G. Fransen and S. Kuttner (New York, 1969).

Thomas Aquinas, *Doctoris Angelici Divi Thomae Aquinatis ... opera omnia*, ed. L. Vivès, 34 vols. (Paris, 1874-1889).

Thomas of Celano, *Vita prima S. Francisci Assisiensis* (Quaracchi, 1926).

William of Ockham, *Breviloquium de potestate papae*, ed. L. Baudry (Paris, 1937).

—, *De imperatorum et pontificum potestate*, ed. C. K. Brampton (Oxford, 1931).

—, *Dialogus* in M. Goldast, *Monarchia S. Romani imperii*, II (Frankfurt, 1614), pp. 392-957.

—, *Guillelmi de Ockham opera politica*, ed. J. G. Sikes et al., 3 vols. (Manchester, 1940-1956).

—, *De sacramento altaris*, ed. T. Bruce Birch, *The De Sacramento Altaris of William of Ockham* (Burlington, Iowa, 1930).

William of St. Amour, *Magistri Guillelmi de S. Amore opera omnia* (Constance, 1632).

Zenzellinus de Cassanis, *Glossa ordinaria* to the *Extravagantes Joannis XXII* in *Extravagantes Ioannis XXII* (Antwerp, 1573).

II. SECONDARY WORKS

Alberigo, G., *Cardinalato e collegialità* (Florence, 1969).

Anciaux, P., *La théologie du sacrement de pénitence au XIIe siècle* (Louvain-Gembloux, 1949).

Arquillière, H.-X., "L'appel au concile sous Philippe le Bel," *Revue des questions historiques*, 45 (1911), pp. 23-55.

Balić, C., et al., *De Scriptura et Traditione* (Rome, 1963).

Balthasar, K., *Geschichte des Armutsstreites im Franziskanerorden bis zum Konzil von Vienne* (Münster-in-Westf., 1911).

Baudry, L., *Guillaume d'Occam, sa vie, ses oeuvres, ses idées sociales et politiques*, I (Paris, 1950).

Bayley, C. C., "Pivotal Concepts in the Political Philosophy of William of Ockham," *Journal of the History of Ideas*, 10 (1949), pp. 199-218.

Benson, R. L., *The Bishop-Elect* (Princeton, 1968).

Benz, E., *Ecclesia Spiritualis* (Stuttgart, 1934).

Betti, U., "L'assenza dell' autorità di S. Tommasso nel decreto vaticano sull' infallibilità pontificia," *Divinitas*, 6 (1962), pp. 407-422.

Beumer, J., "Heilige Schrift und kirchliche Lehrautorität," *Scholastik*, 25 (1950), pp. 40-72.

Bianchi, R., *De constitutione monarchica ecclesiae et de infallibilitate Romani pontificis iuxta S. Thomam* (Rome, 1870).

Bierbaum, M., *Bettelorden und Weltgeistlichkeit an der Universität Paris* (Münster-in-Westf., 1920).

Bihel, S., "S. Franciscus fuitne angelus sexti sigilli? (Apoc. 7.2)," *Antonianum*, 2 (1927), pp. 59-90.

Bilaniuk, P. B., *De magisterio ordinario summi pontificis* (Toronto, 1966).

Blasucci, A., "La costituzione gerarchica della chiesa in S. Bonaventura," *Miscellanea Francescana*, 68 (1968), pp. 81-101.

Bloomfield, M. W., "Joachim of Flora: A Critical Survey of His Canon, Teaching, Sources, Bibliography, and Influence," *Traditio*, 13 (1957), pp. 249-311.

Bloomfield, M. W., and Reeves, M., "The Penetration of Joachism into Northern Europe," *Speculum*, 29 (1954), pp. 772-793.

Boase, T. S. R., *Boniface VIII* (London, 1933).

Boehner, P., *Collected Articles on Ockham*, ed. E. M. Buytaert (St. Bonaventure, N.Y., 1958).

Bondatti, G., *Gioacchinismo e Francescanismo nel dugento* (Assisi, 1924).

Brooke, R. B., *Early Franciscan Government* (Cambridge, 1959).

Buisson, L., *Potestas und Caritas* (Cologne-Graz, 1958).

Buonaiuti, E., *Gioacchino da Fiore* (Rome, 1931).

Butler, C., *The Vatican Council*, 2 vols. (London, 1930).

Callaey, F., "Olieu" in *Dictionnaire de théologie catholique*, XI (Paris, 1931), cols. 982-991.

Chadwick, O., *From Bossuet to Newman. The Idea of Doctrinal Development* (Cambridge, 1957).

Clasen, S., *Der hl. Bonaventura und das Mendikantum* (Werl-in-Westf., 1940).

—, *Franziskus, Engel des sechsten Siegels* (Werl-in-Westf., 1962).

Congar, Y. M.-J., "Aspects ecclésiologiques de la querelle entre mendiants et séculiers dans la seconde moitié du XIIIe siècle et le début du XIVe," *AHDL*, 36 (1961), pp. 35-151.

—, *L'ecclésiologie du haut moyen âge* (Paris, 1968).

—, "Incidence ecclésiologique d'un thème de dévotion mariale," *Mélanges de science religieuse*, 8 (1951), pp. 277-292.

—, "Quod omnes tangit, ab omnibus tractari et approbari debet," *Revue historique de droit français et étranger*, 36 (1958), pp. 210-259.

—, *Tradition and Traditions*, transl. M. Naseby and T. Rainborough (New York, 1967).

Delorme, F. M., "Fr. Petri Joannis Olivi tractatus 'De perlegendis philosophorum libris,'" *Antonianum*, 16 (1941), pp. 30-44.

—, "Fr. P. J. Olivi Quaestio de voto regulam aliquam profitentis," *Antonianum*, 16 (1941), pp. 131-164.

Deneffe, A., *Der Traditionsbegriffe* (Münster-in-Westf., 1931).

Denifle, H., "Das Evangelium aeternum und die Commission zu Anagni," *ALKG*, 1 (1885), pp. 49-124.

—, *Luther und Luthertum*, 2 vols. (Mainz, 1904-1909).

Dietershagen, A., "Kirche und theologisches Denken nach Duns Scotus," *Wissenschaft und Weisheit*, 1 (1934), pp. 273-288.

Döllinger, J. J. I. von, *A Letter Addressed to the Archbishop of Munich* (London, 1871).

—, *Beiträge zur Sektengeschichte des Mittelalters*, 2 vols. (Munich, 1890).

—, *Fables Respecting the Popes of the Middle Ages*, transl. A. Plummer (London, 1871). *See also* Janus, Quirinus.

Doucet, V., "De operibus manuscriptis Fr. Petri Ioannis Olivi in biblioteca Universitatis Patavinae asservatis," *AFH*, 28 (1935), pp. 156-197, 408-442.

Douie, D., *The Conflict between the Seculars and the Mendicants at the University of Paris in the Thirteenth Century* (London, 1954).

—, *The Nature and Effect of the Heresy of the Fraticelli* (Manchester, 1932).

Dublanchy, E., "Infaillibilité du pape" in *Dictionnaire de théologie catholique*, VII (Paris, 1923), cols. 1638-1717.

Dupuy, B.-D., "Le magistère de l'église, service de la parole" in O. Rousseau et al., *L'infaillibilité de l'église* (Chevetogne, 1962).

Ehrle, F., "Die 'historia septem tribulationum ordinis minorum' des fr. Angelus de Clarino," *ALKG*, 2 (1886), pp. 249-336.

—, "Petrus Johannis Olivi, sein Leben und seine Schriften," *ALKG*, 3 (1887), pp. 409-552.

—, "Die Spiritualen, ihr Verhältniss zum Franciscanerorden und zu den Fraticellen," *ALKG*, 1 (1885), pp. 509-569; 2 (1886), pp. 106-164, 249-336; 3 (1887), pp. 553-623; 4 (1888), pp. 1-90.

—, "Zur Vorgeschichte des Concils von Vienne," *ALKG*, 2 (1886), pp. 353-416; 3 (1887), pp. 1-195.

Elizondo, F., "Bullae 'Quo elongati' Gregorii IX et 'Ordinem vestri' Innocentii IV," *Laurentianum*, 3 (1962), pp. 349-394.

Elter, P. E., "Un ouvrage inconnu de Hervé Nédellec," *Gregorianum*, 4 (1923), pp. 211-240.

Emmen, A., and Simoncioli, F., "La dottrina dell' Olivi sulla contemplazione, la vita attiva e mista," *Studi Francescani*, 60 (1963), pp. 382-445.

Englebert, O., *Saint Francis of Assisi*, 2nd English edition (Chicago, 1965).

Eschmann, I. T., "St. Thomas Aquinas on the Two Powers," *Mediaeval Studies*, 20 (1958), pp. 177-205.

Esser, K., *Das Testament des heiligen Franziskus von Assisi* (Münster-in-Westf., 1949).

Faral, E., "Les 'Responsiones' de Guillaume de Saint-Amour," *AHDL*, 25-26 (1950-1951), pp. 337-394.

Fasso, G., "Dio e la natura presso i Decretisti ed i Glossatori," *Il diritto ecclesiastico*, 67 (1956), pp. 3-10.

Feine, H. E., *Die katholische Kirche. Kirchliche Rechtsgeschichte*, I (Weimar, 1955).

Fernández Ríos, M., "El primado del Romano pontifice nel pensamiento de Huguccio de Pisa decretista," *Compostellanum*, 6 (1961), pp. 47-97; 7 (1962), pp. 97-149; 8 (1963), pp. 65-99; 11 (1966), pp. 29-67.

Fidelis a Fanna, *Seraphici Doctoris D. Bonaventurae doctrina de Romani pontificis primatu et infallibilitate* (Turin, 1870).

Finkenzeller, J., *Offenbarung und Theologie nach der Lehre des Johannes Duns Skotus* (Münster-in-Westf., 1961).

Fleming, J. V., "The 'Collations' of William of S. Amour against S. Thomas," *RTAM*, 32 (1965), pp. 132-138.

Fournier, P., "Jesselin de Cassagnes canoniste," *Histoire littéraire de la France*, 35 (1921), pp. 348-360.

Fusseneger, G., "Relatio commissionis in concilio Viennensi institutae ad decretalem *Exivi de paradiso* praeparandum," *AFH*, 50 (1957), pp. 145-177.

Geiselmann, J. R., *Die heilige Schrift und die Tradition* (Freiburg-Basel-Vienna, 1962).

Gewirth, A., *Marsilius of Padua*, 2 vols. (New York, 1951-1956).

Giacchio, O., "La Regola 'Quod omnes tangit' nel diritto canonico," *Jus. Rivista di scienze giuridiche*, New Series, 3 (1952), pp. 77-100.

Gieben, S., "Bibliographia Oliviana (1885-1967)," *Collectanea Franciscana*, 38 (1968), pp. 167-195.

Gilchrist, J., "Gregory VII and the Primacy of the Roman Church," *Tijdschrift voor Rechtsgeschiedenis*, 36 (1968), pp. 123-135.

Gillmann, F., "Clave non errante?" *Archiv für katholisches Kirchenrecht*, 110 (1930), pp. 451-465.

—, "Zur scholastischen Auslegung von Mt. 16.18," *Archiv für katholisches Kirchenrecht*, 104 (1924), pp. 41-53.

Gladstone, W. E., *The Vatican Decrees in Their Bearing on Civil Allegiance* (New York, 1875).

Glorieux, P., "Le conflit de 1252-57 à la lumière du Mémoire de Guillaume de Saint-Amour," *RTAM*, 24 (1957), pp. 364-372.

—, *La littérature quodlibétique de 1260 à 1320* (Kain, 1925).

—, "Prélats français contre religieux mendiants (1281-1290)," *Revue d'histoire de l'église de France*, 11 (1925), pp. 309-331.

Gratien, P., *Histoire de la fondation et de l'évolution de l'ordre des Frères Mineurs au XIIIe siècle* (Paris, 1928).

Grundmann, H., *Studien über Joachim von Floris* (Leipzig, 1927).

—, *Neue Forschungen über Joachim von Fiore* (Marburg, 1950).

Guelluy, R., *Philosophie et théologie chez Guillaume d'Ockham* (Louvain-Paris, 1947).

Haag, A., "Syllabus" in *The Catholic Encyclopedia*, XIV (New York, 1912), pp. 368-370.

Hackett, J. H., "State of the Church: A Concept of the Medieval Canonists," *The Jurist*, 23 (1963), pp. 259-290.

Harent, S., "Papauté" in *Dictionnaire apologétique de la foi catholique*, III (Paris, 1926), cols. 1436-1520.

Hefele, C.-J., and Le Clercq, H., *Histoire des Conciles*, 11 vols. (Paris, 1907-1952).

Hergenröther, J., *Anti-Janus* (Dublin, 1870).

Hödl, L., *Die Geschichte der scholastischen Literatur und der Theologie der Schlüsselgewalt*, I (Münster-in-Westf., 1960).

—, *Die Lehre des Petrus Johannis Olivi O.F.M. von der Universalgewalt des Papstes* (Munich, 1958).

Hofer, J., "Der Verfasser und die Entstehungszeit der 'Responsiones ad oppositiones'," *Franziskanische Studien*, 4 (1917), pp. 93-98.

Hofmann, F., *Der Anteil der Minoriten am Kampf Ludwigs des Bayern* (Münster-in-Westf., 1959).

Hogan, W. F., "Syllabus of Errors" in *The New Catholic Encyclopedia*, XIII (New York, 1967), pp. 854-856.

Holzapfel, H., *The History of the Franciscan Order*, transl. A. Tibesar and G. Brinkmann (Teutopolis, Ill., 1948).

Huber, R., *A Documented History of the Franciscan Order* (Milwaukee, 1944).

Huizing, P., "The Earliest Development of Excommunication *latae sententiae* by Gratian and the Earliest Decretists," *Studia Gratiana*, 3 (1955), pp. 278-320.

Janus, *The Pope and the Council* (Boston, 1870).

Junghans, H., *Ockham im Lichte der neueren Forschung* (Berlin, 1968).

Kaeppelli, T., *Le procès contre Thomas Waleys O.P.* (Rome, 1936).

Kantorowicz, E., *The King's Two Bodies* (Princeton, 1957).

Kirby, G. J., "The Authenticity of the *De perfectione statuum* of Duns Scotus," *The New Scholasticism*, 7 (1933), pp. 134-152.

Knoth, E., *Ubertino de Casale* (Marburg, 1903).

Knowles, D., *The Religious Orders in England*, 3 vols. (Cambridge, 1948-1959).

Koch, J., "Der Prozess gegen den Magister Johannes de Polliaco und seine Vorgeschichte," *RTAM*, 5 (1933), pp. 391-422.

—, "Der Prozess gegen die Postille Olivis zur Apokalypse," *RTAM*, 5 (1933), pp. 302-315.

—, "Die Verurteilung Olivis auf dem Konzil von Vienne und ihre Vorgeschichte," *Scholastik*, 5 (1930), pp. 489-522.

Kölmel, W., *Wilhelm Ockham und seine kirchenpolitischen Schriften* (Essen, 1962).

Kropatschek, F., *Das Schriftprinzip der Lutherischen Kirche*, I (Leipzig, 1904).

Küng, H., *Unfehlbar? Eine Anfrage* (Zurich, 1970).

Kuttner, S., *Harmony from Dissonance* (Latrobe, Penn., 1960).

—, "Pope Lucius III and the Bigamous Archbishop of Palermo" in *Medieval Studies Presented to Aubrey Gwynn S.J.*, ed. J. A. Watt, J. B. Morrall, and F. X. Martin (Dublin, 1961).

—, *Repertorium der Kanonistik, 1140-1234* (Vatican City, 1937).

Laberge, D., "Fr. Petri Ioannis Olivi, O.F.M. tria scripta sui ipsius apologetica," *AFH*, 28 (1935), pp. 115-155, 374-407.

Lagarde, G. de, *La naissance de l'esprit laïque au déclin du moyen âge*, revised ed., 5 vols. (Louvain-Paris, 1956-1970).

Lambert, M. D., *Franciscan Poverty* (London, 1961).

Landgraf, A. M., *Dogmengeschichte der Frühscholastik*, 8 vols. (Regensburg, 1952-1956).

—, "Scattered Remarks on the Development of Dogma and on Papal Infallibility in Early Scholastic Writings," *Theological Studies*, 7 (1946), pp. 577-582.

Langen, J., *Das Vatikanische Dogma von dem Universal-Episcopat und der Unfehlbarkeit des Papstes*, 4 vols. (Bonn, 1871-1874).

Le Bras, G., *L'âge classique, 1140-1378. Histoire du droit et des institutions de l'église en Occident*, VII (Paris, 1965).

Lecler, J., *Vienne* (Paris, 1964).

Leclercq, J., *Jean de Paris et l'ecclésiologie du XIIIe siècle* (Paris, 1942).

Leff, G., *Heresy in the Later Middle Ages*, 2 vols. (Manchester, 1967).

Lennerz, H., "Scriptura sola," *Gregorianum*, 40 (1959), pp. 38-53.

Longpré, E., "Le B. Jean Duns Scot. Pour le Saint Siège et contre le gallicanisme," *La France franciscaine*, 11 (1928), pp. 137-162.

—, *La philosophie du B. Duns Scot* (Paris, 1924).

Maccarrone, M., "Una questione inedita dell'Olivi sull' infallibilità del papa," *Rivista di storia della chiesa in Italia*, 3 (1949), pp. 309-343.

—, *Vicarius Christi* (Rome, 1962).

Mackey, J. P., *The Modern Theology of Tradition* (New York, 1962).

McKeon, P. R., "The University of Paris as *Parens Scientiarum*," *Speculum*, 39 (1964), pp. 651-675.

Maggiani, V., "De relatione scriptorum quorundam S. Bonaventurae ad Bullam 'Exiit' Nicolai III (1279)," *AFH*, 5 (1912), pp. 3-21.

Maier, A., "Per la storia del processo contro l'Olivi," *Rivista di storia della chiesa in Italia*, 5 (1951), pp. 326-339.

Manning, H. E., *The Oecumenical Council and the Infallibility of the Roman Pontiff: A Pastoral Letter to the Clergy* (London, 1869).

Manselli, R., *La 'Lectura super Apocalipsim' di Pietro di Giovanni Olivi* (Rome, 1955).

—, *Spirituali e Beghini in Provenza* (Rome, 1958).

Martin, V., *Les origines du gallicanisme* (Paris, 1939).

May, W. H., "The Confession of Prous Boneta" in *Essays in Medieval Life and Thought Presented in Honor of A. P. Evans*, ed. J. H. Mundy, R. W. Emery, and B. N. Nelson (New York, 1955).

Ménard, E., *La tradition, révélation, écriture, église selon Saint Thomas d'Aquin* (Paris, 1964).

Meulenberg, L. F. J., *Der Primat der römischen Kirche im Denken und Handeln Gregors VII* ('s Gravenhage, 1965).

Meyjes, G. H. M. P., *De Controverse tussen Petrus en Paulus: Galaten 2:11 in de Historie* ('s Gravenhage, 1967).

Miethke, J., *Ockhams Weg zur Sozialphilosophie* (Berlin, 1969).

Mochi Onory, S., *Fonti canonistiche dell' idea moderna dello stato* (Milan, 1951).

Moorman, J. R. H., *A History of the Franciscan Order* (Oxford, 1968).

Morrall, J. B., "Ockham and Ecclesiology" in *Medieval Studies Presented to Aubrey Gwynn S.J.*, ed. J. A. Watt, J. B. Morrall, and F. X. Martin (Dublin, 1961).

—, "Some Notes on a Recent Interpretation of William of Ockham's Political Philosophy," *Franciscan Studies*, N.S. 9 (1949), pp. 335-369.

Morrison, K. F., *Tradition and Authority in the Western Church, 300-1140* (Princeton, 1969).

Müller, C., *Der Kampf Ludwigs des Baiern mit der Römischen Curie*, 2 vols. (Tübingen, 1879-1880).

Müller, H., *Das Konzil von Vienne, 1311-1312* (Münster-in-Westf., 1934).

Munier, C., *Les sources patristiques du droit de l'église* (Mulhouse, 1957).

Oakley, F., *Council over Pope?* (New York, 1969).

—, "Jacobean Political Theology: The Absolute and Ordinary Powers of the King," *Journal of the History of Ideas*, 29 (1968), pp. 323-346.

Oberman, H. A., *The Harvest of Medieval Theology* (Cambridge, Mass., 1963).

Oliger, L., "Petri Iohannis Olivi de renuntiatione papae Coelestini V quaestio et epistola," *AFH*, 11 (1918), pp. 309-373.

Pacetti, D., *Petrus Ioannis Olivi O.F.M. Quaestiones quatuor de domina* (Quaracchi, 1954).

Partee, C., "Peter John Olivi: Historical and Doctrinal Study," *Franciscan Studies*, 20 (1960), pp. 215-260.

Paulus, J., *Henri de Gand. Essai sur les tendances de sa métaphysique* (Paris, 1938).

Peuchmaurd, M., "Mission canonique et prédication," *RTAM*, 30 (1963), pp. 122-144, 251-276.

Post, G., "Copyists' Errors and the Problem of Papal Dispensation *contra statutum generale ecclesiae* or *contra statum generalem ecclesiae*," *Studia Gratiana*, 9 (1966), pp. 359-405.

—, *Studies in Medieval Legal Thought* (Princeton, 1964).

Quillet, J., *Le défenseur de la paix* (Paris, 1968).

Quirinus, *Letters from Rome on the Council* (London, 1870).

Ratzinger, J., "Der Einfluss des Bettelordensstreites auf die Entwicklung der Lehre vom päpstlichen Universalprimat" in *Theologie in Geschichte und Gegenwart*, ed. J. Auer and H. Volk (Munich, 1957).

—, *Die Geschichtstheologie des hl. Bonaventura* (Munich, 1959).

—, "Offenbarung, Schrift, Überlieferung. Ein Text des hl. Bonaventura," *Trierer theologische Zeitschrift*, 67 (1958), pp. 13-27.

Reeves, M., *The Influence of Prophecy in the Later Middle Ages. A Study in Joachimism* (Oxford, 1969).

Reeves, M., and Hirsh-Reich, B., "The Seven Seals in the Writings of Joachim of Fiore," *RTAM*, 21 (1954), pp. 211-247.

Riedlinger, J., "Hermeneutische Ueberlegungen zu den Konstanzer Dekreten" in *Das Konzil von Konstanz*, ed. A. Franzen and W. Müller (Freiburg, 1964).

Rivière, J., *Le problème de l'église et de l'état au temps de Philippe le Bel* (Louvain-Paris, 1926).

Roensch, F. J., *Early Thomistic School* (Dubuque, 1964).

Roggen, H., "Saint Bonaventure second fondateur de l'Ordre des Frères Mineurs?" *Études franciscaines*, 17 (1967), pp. 67-79.

Rosato, L., "Ioannis Duns Scoti doctrina de Scriptura et Traditione" in *De Scriptura et Traditione*, ed. C. Balić (Rome, 1963).

Schenk, M., *Die Unfehlbarkeit des Papstes in der Heiligsprechung* (Freiburg, 1965).

Schleyer, K., *Anfänge des Gallikanismus im 13. Jahrhundert* (Berlin, 1937).

—, "Disputes scolastiques sur les états de perfection," *RTAM*, 10 (1938), pp. 279-293.

Scholz, R., *Die Publizistik zur Zeit Philipps des Schönen und Bonifaz VIII* (Stuttgart, 1903).

—, *Unbekannte kirchenpolitischen Streitschriften aus der Zeit Ludwigs des Bayern*, 2 vols. (Rome, 1911-1914).

Schulte, J. F. von, *Die Stellung der Concilien, Päpste und Bischöffe* (Prague, 1871).

Sikes, J. G., "John de Pouilli and Peter de la Palu," *English Historical Review*, 49 (1934), pp. 219-240.

Simons, F., *Infallibility and the Evidence* (Springfield, Ill., 1968).

Smalley, B., "Gerard of Bologna and Henry of Ghent," *RTAM*, 23 (1956), pp. 61-87.

—, "John Baconthorpe's Postill on Matthew," *Medieval and Renaissance Studies*, 4 (1958), pp. 91-145.

Stadter, E., "Das Problem der Theologie bei Petrus Johannis Olivi," *Franziskanische Studien*, 43 (1961), pp. 113-170.

—, "Die spiritualische Geschichtstheologie als Voraussetzung für das Verständnis von fides et auctoritas bei Petrus Johannis Olivi," *Franziskanische Studien*, 48 (1966), pp. 243-253.

Stickler, A. M., *Historia iuris canonici Latini*, I (Turin, 1950).

Tabacco, G., *Pluralità di papi ed unità di chiesa nel pensiero di Guglielmo di Occam* (Turin, 1949).
Tavard, G. H., *Holy Writ or Holy Church* (London, 1959).
Thils, G., *L'infaillibilité pontificale* (Gembloux, 1969).
Tierney, B., "Collegiality in the Middle Ages," *Concilium*, 7 (1965), pp. 5-14.
—, *Foundations of the Conciliar Theory* (Cambridge, 1955).
—, "Grosseteste and the Theory of Papal Sovereignty," *Journal of Ecclesiastical History*, 6 (1955), pp. 1-17.
—, *"Natura id est Deus*; A Case of Juristic Pantheism?" *Journal of the History of Ideas*, 24 (1963), pp. 307-322.
—, "Ockham, the Conciliar Theory and the Canonists," *Journal of the History of Ideas*, 15 (1954), pp. 40-70.
—, "Pope and Council: Some New Decretist Texts," *Mediaeval Studies*, 19 (1957), pp. 197-218.
Tocco, F., *La quistione della povertà nel secolo XIV* (Naples, 1932).
Töpfer, B., "Eine Handschrift des Evangelium aeternum des Gerardino von Borgo San Donnino," *Zeitschrift für Geschichtswissenschaft*, 8 (1960), pp. 156-163.
Tondelli, L., *Il libro delle Figure dell' Abate Gioachino da Fiore*, 2nd ed. (Turin, 1935).
Torrell, J.-P., *La théologie de l'épiscopat au premier concile du Vatican* (Paris, 1961).
Uhlmann, J., "Die Vollgewalt des Papstes nach Bonaventura," *Franziskanische Studien*, 11 (1924), pp. 179-193.
Ullmann, W., *The Growth of the Papal Government in the Middle Ages* (London, 1955).
—, *Medieval Papalism* (London, 1949).
Valois, N., "Jacques Duèse, pape sous le nom de Jean XXII," *Histoire littéraire de la France*, 34 (1915), pp. 391-630.
Van Hove, A., *Prolegomena* (Commentarium Lovaniense in Codicem iuris canonici, I, i) (Malines-Rome, 1945).
Van de Kerckhove, M., "La notion de juridiction dans la doctrine des Décrétistes et des premiers Décrétalistes," *Études franciscaines*, 49 (1937), pp. 420-455.
Van Leeuwen, A., "L'église, règle de foi dans les écrits de Guillaume d'Occam," *Ephemerides theologicae Lovanienses*, 11 (1934), pp. 249-288.
Vasoli, C., *Guglielmo d'Occam* (Florence, 1953).
Vellico, A. M., "De regula fidei iuxta Joannis Duns Scoti doctrinam," *Antonianum*, 10 (1935), pp. 11-36.
Villalpando, A., *De clavium potestatis existentia et natura* (Washington, D.C., 1921).
Vooght, P. de, "Esquisse d'une enquête sur le mot 'infaillibilité' durant la période scolastique" in *L'infaillibilité de l'église*, ed. O. Rousseau et al. (Chevetogne, 1962).
—, "L'évolution du rapport Église-Écriture du XIIIe au XVe siècle," *Ephemerides theologicae Lovanienses*, 38 (1962), pp. 71-85.
—, "La méthodologie théologique d'après Henri de Gand et Gerard de Bologne," *RTAM*, 22 (1955), pp. 125-129.
—, *Les pouvoirs du concile et l'autorité du pape* (Paris, 1965).
—, *Les sources de la doctrine chrétienne* (Bruges, 1954).
Watt, J. A., "The Early Medieval Canonists and the Formation of Conciliar Theory," *Irish Theological Quarterly*, 24 (1957), pp. 13-31.
—, *The Theory of Papal Monarchy in the Thirteenth Century* (New York, 1965).
Wehrlé, R., *De la coutume dans le droit canonique* (Paris, 1928).
Weigand, R., *Die Naturrechtslehre der Legisten und Dekretisten* (Munich, 1967).
Wilks, M., "The Early Oxford Wyclif: Papalist or Nominalist," *Studies in Church History*, 5 (1969), pp. 69-98.
—, *The Problem of Sovereignty in the Later Middle Ages* (Cambridge, 1963).
Xiberta, B.-M., "De Mag. Guidone Terreni, priore generale ordinis nostri, episcopo Maioricensi et Elnensi," *Analecta ordinis Carmelitarum*, 5 (1923-1926), pp. 113-206.

—, "De doctrinis theologicis Magistri Guidonis Terreni," *ib'd.*, pp. 233-376.
—, *De scriptoribus scholasticis saeculi XIV ex ordine Carmelitarum* (Louvain, 1931).
—, *Guiu Terrena Carmelita de Perpinyà* (Barcelona, 1932).
—, "Scriptura, Traditio et magisterium iuxta antiquos auctores ordinis Carmelitarum" in *De Scriptura et Traditione*, ed. C. Balić (Rome, 1963).
Zimmermann, H., *Papstabsetzungen des Mittelalters* (Graz, 1968).

INDEX

Acacius, 33, 56, 245, 266
Accursius, 30 n. 1
Acton, Lord, 2
Adam, 61 n. 1, 74 n. 3, 80
Ad conditorem, 178-180
Ad fructus uberes, 65
Adrian I, Pope, 30 n. 2, 54, 77
Adrian VI, Pope, 271
Agatho, Pope, 9, 11
Alanus, 23-24, 37, 42 n. 2, 49-52, 55
  n. 2, 194
Alexander III, Pope, 23-25, 30 n. 2,
  56, 96 n. 1, 194, 267
Alexander IV, Pope, 65
Alexander de Sancto Elpidio, 162 n. 2
Alvarus Pelagius, 131, 178 n. 1, 184,
  199, 236
Ambrose, St, 135
Anastasius II, Pope, 33, 37-38, 42, 53,
  55-56, 115, 120, 138, 152, 245, 265-
  266
Anselm of Lucca, 10
Antichrist, 94, 104-109, 126, 173, 197
Antoninus, St, 238 n. 2, 271
Apostles, as bishops, 66, 83, 103, 139,
  155, 157, 162-164, 167, 175, 263; and
  Peter, 31-32, 66, 83-86, 115, 119, 154-
  155, 158, 160-164, 168, 239, 260, 262-
  263; and poverty, 67, 69-70, 81-82,
  104, 166-168, 171, 173-175, 179-181,
  192, 198-199, 261-262; and Tradition,
  7, 54, 72-73, 134-135, 141, 167, 219-
  220, 255-256, 261-262. See also *Creed*
Apparatus Ius naturale, 37 n. 5
Apparatus Ecce vicit leo, 29 n. 2, 35 n. 2,
  42 n. 2, 44
Aristotle, 158
Arles, 145
Arnold of Rochafolio, 101 n. 2
Arquillière, H.-X., 159
Articles of faith, 23-24, 46, 56, 102,
  157, 176, 178, 182, 192-194, 201, 204,
  216, 225, 230, 246, 248, 253-255
Augustine, St, 15-16, 40-41, 61, 135-
  136, 142-143, 176, 180, 202, 223, 247,
  257, 264
Augustinus Triumphus, 6, 131, 147 n.
  3, 161, 164, 184-185, 250

Avignon, 183, 197, 200-201, 215, 260

Babylon, 101, 107
Bannez, Domingo, 271
Basil, St, 17, 21
Beatific Vision, 190 n. 1, 223, 232-233
Bede, 40, 44
Bellarmine, St Robert, 271
Benedict XI, Pope, 65 n. 2, 150-151
Benedict XII, Pope, 243, 268
Benedict St., 60
Benedict Gaetani, 65, 109 n. 1. *See also*
  Boniface VIII.
Benz, E., 108
Berengar Talon, 174
Bernard, St, 234
Bernardus Parmensis, 23 n. 2, 26-27, 29
Berruyer, I., 272
Boehner, P., 207
Bonagratia of Bergamo, 177, 178 n. 1,
  180-181, 183, 199 n. 2, 201
Bonagrazia of Giovanni in Persiceto,
  100
Bonaventure, St, 45, 58-59, 93, 96, 103,
  109-112, 115, 124, 144, 232; on Fran-
  ciscan poverty, 69-72, 81-82, 86, 89,
  98, 127, 165, 198, 199 n. 1, 261; on
  infallibility, 82, 86-92, 95, 125, 184,
  208; Joachimism of, 73, 76-82, 106;
  on papal sovereignty, 82-86, 92, 125,
  127, 130, 154, 160; on Scripture and
  Tradition, 73-76, 87-88, 193, 222
Boniface VIII, Pope, 65, 100, 102-103,
  105, 108-109, 150, 154, 158, 169, 176
Burchard of Worms, 10

Cajetanus, 271
Callaey, F., 108
Cano, Melchior, 271
Canonists, on general councils, 21, 25,
  45-53, 88, 158, 230-231, 264-267;
  on indefectibility, 35-38, 49, 208; on
  infallibility, of church, 33-39, of
  general council, 47, of pope, 10, 12-13,
  18, 32-33, 39, 53, 57, 89, 95, 116, 130,
  149, 152, 204, 264-267; on primacy,
  17-18, 22-57 *passim*, 83, 114, 116-117,
  127, 130, 149, 193-196, 226, 264-267;